Daily Bible Readings

BY

JOHN HEADING

JUNE 1988
Published by
GOSPEL TRACT PUBLICATIONS
411 Hillington Road, Glasgow G52 4BL

ISBN 0 948417 30 7

Other books by the author:

First Epistle to the Corinthians (1965)
Second Epistle to the Corinthians (1966)
Church Doctrine and Practice (joint editor) (1970)
Acts, a Study in New Testament Christianity (1975)
Treasury of Bible Doctrine (joint editor) (1977)
From Now to Eternity—the Book of Revelation (1978)
Types and Shadows in the Epistle to the Hebrews (1979)
Day by Day through the New Testament (joint editor) (1979)
Understanding 1 & 2 Chronicles (1980)
Luke's Life of Christ (1981)
The Book of Daniel (1982)
Dictionary of New Testament Churches (1984)
Matthew's Gospel. Vol. 2, "What the Bible Teaches" (1984)
Day by Day in the Psalms (joint editor) (1986)
John's Gospel. Vol. 6, "What the Bible Teaches" (1988)

Printed by
GOSPEL TRACT PUBLICATIONS
411 Hillington Road, Glasgow G52 4BL

Preface

OVER THE PAST YEARS, the author has played a part in the production of the three "Precious Seed Publications" entitled *Day by Day through the New Testament*, *Day by Day through the Old Testament*, and *Day by Day in the Psalms*. These three books are structured, in the sense that either Scripture order is followed throughout, or else a definite list of subjects is explored throughout the year. Such an ordered study, whether through Scripture books or by subjects, is essential for a proper grasp of the Word of God. Yet most of the Lord's people are also used to another style of ministry, that of the unstructured approach. For ministry meetings, gospel meetings, and the usual word of ministry after the Breaking of Bread, take up themes and scriptures that are quite distinct week by week, ranging far and wide throughout the Scriptures. This approach is also necessary, providing background teaching absent in more systematic studies.

Listen to an expert teacher dealing with a chapter of the Scriptures. Note how he handles the verses. He seems to wrap around them so helpfully a vast collection of references to other parts of Scripture, a background knowledge that has come from years of diligent searching and comparing scripture with scripture. Clearly this knowledge is just as important as the ordered exposition of a passage, for it adds spiritual freshness, and yields incentive to further study.

The present *Daily Bible Readings* takes up the unstructured approach, providing a different subject for each day, and hence will help readers acquire a thousand-and-one facts that perhaps they have not noticed before. The author has sought to make each page a wholesome spiritual meal, concentrating on some theme, word or idea as space allows. These themes and words deal with gospel truth, church truth, Christian service, typology, prophecy, etc., the Lord Jesus being given the prominent position throughout. These themes can be expanded if readers wish to explore further. If quotations are taken from unusual contexts, readers should look these up, so that minds and hearts can be built up in the faith.

Many a busy servant of the Lord may find here and there a theme that he may find useful to expand in his own ministry amongst that Lord's people. For the author has used many of the themes throughout the 366 pages of this book in his own ministry and teaching.

It should be pointed out that the style adopted is factual, containing few actual exhortations. Each reader has different needs, and the author trusts that his treatment of many topics will enable readers to note the applications that are relevant to themselves.

The book is commended to the Lord, who can bring light and spiritual cheer to His people in a world of moral and spiritual darkness. May He feed His people with food from the Scriptures as found in this book throughout the year in which it is used.

A comprehensive list of Scripture Readings is provided at the beginning, together with a detailed index at the end.

The author thanks the *Precious Seed* Committee for allowing him to copy the style used in their three *Day by Day* books. If readers are already familiar with the page layout in these three books, then they will find the page layout in the present book immediately familiar.

JOHN HEADING

List of Contents

READING: **John 21. 24-25**

THE BOOKS THAT SHOULD BE WRITTEN

ALL FOUR evangelists make mention of books and writing, and there appears to be an order of progression in their thoughts from Matthew, to Mark, Luke and John.

In Matthew, we read of "The book of the generation of Jesus Christ, the son of David, the son of Abraham", 1. 1. By the "book" in the context, Matthew refers only to verses 2-17 of chapter 1, showing the genealogical and scriptural validity of the Lord to be King of the Jews. Nothing is hidden in this book; good kings and bad kings, sinful attachments and the seventy years captivity — nothing could adversely affect the Lord's divine right to Kingship and the throne.

In Mark, the Gospel commences with "as it is written in the prophets", 1. 2. Here two complete books are implied, namely Malachi where the reference to God's messenger as John the Baptist is quoted, Mal. 3. 1, and where John's voice is quoted as crying in the wilderness, Isa. 40. 3. The Lord Jesus is prominently found in the O.T., but a passing reference is also found to John the Baptist and to Judas the betrayer.

In Luke, many books are implied, 1. 1-4, for many men had "set forth in order a declaration of those things which are most surely believed among us". By this, Luke means that their historical records were true, but clearly they were not inspired. Luke, on the other hand, wrote one book that was inspired, and God has preserved this one book for believers throughout the ages, while the many other records were not preserved for His people, since non-inspiration has no place in the Holy Scriptures that we handle daily.

In John (not at the beginning, but at the end, 21. 25), an infinite number of books could have been written about the life and teaching of the Son of God. The vast libraries of the world, then and now, could never have contained all the information that could have been written. John, therefore, had been very selective; as an eyewitness, he had seen and heard the works and teaching of his Lord and Master, and clearly valued the memory of these things, 1 John 1. 1. Yet the selection, compressed into one book by John as the inspired author, would accomplish his objective — to lead to the formation and deepening of faith in the Son of God, John 20. 31.

1

READING: **Acts 20. 31-32**

THREE YEARS AWAY FROM HOME

FOR NEARLY all the Lord's people, there comes the time when they must leave the family home where they have been brought up. A new place to live, a new place to work or to study, and a new assembly to attend — all bring new responsibilities and new dangers. When David left home, there was the fight with Goliath, and the necessity of playing the harp before Saul, but he was blessed, for he was chosen and loved by God. Some years after his conversion, Timothy was "well reported of by the brethren", Acts 16. 2; he left home and accompanied Paul, and remained faithful, adhering to all that Paul stood for, and becoming an exponent of Paul's teaching. And the Lord came down from heaven to the darkest of environments, yet He was as consistent on earth as in heaven.

No one must go downhill spiritually when away from home; the path is still upwards in faithfulness and maturity. For example, a student with three years' study before him can learn much both academically and spiritually. The former must not have precedence over the latter. The writer has had the joy of seeing progress in many young people, as they availed themselves of assembly fellowship and gatherings, for that is what God expects, a stedfast continuation, Acts 2. 42.

Thus for three years, Paul sought to build up the believers in Ephesus; he taught and warned them with tears night and day, and finally commended them to the Lord and His Word. How dreadful it would have been if he had had to say, "Behold, these three years I come seeking fruit on this fig tree, and find none", Luke 13. 7. Only grace allowed a fourth year! But then there was Rehoboam; "for three years" he walked in the ways of David and Solomon, 2 Chron 11. 17, and then forsook the law of the Lord, 12. 1.

Rather, every three years Solomon's navy brought gold, silver, ivory and peacocks, 1 Kings 10. 22, thereby enhancing the work of God in Jerusalem. Here was a gathering of spiritual spoil for later years. Wealth for the Levites was brought at the end of three years, Deut 14. 28; hence the service of God was maintained in their hands. Thus may all who have to leave home grow in faithfulness, determined to prosper spiritually, and to bring much treasure to the local assembly.

January 3rd

READING: **1 John 1. 1-7**

THE WORD

AS THE SPOKEN utterances of God and as the written Scriptures of truth, the use of the "word" is familiar to us all. But in his writings, the apostle John uses the idea of the "Word" three times as a title of the Lord Jesus Christ. Moreover, the title is used in three ways. In just the same way as spoken or written words are an expression of the heart of the speaker or writer, so the fundamental idea behind the title "Word" is that of expression.

(1) In his Gospel, John uses the title "Word" with no other addition. "In the beginning was the Word, and the Word was with God, and the Word was God", John 1. 1. Here the Expression of God is seen with God. He is then seen as the Creator of all things, possessing life, and being the Revealer of God because He is the Light, v. 9. Additionally, "the Word was made flesh, and dwelt among us", v. 14. So the One who was with God is now found with men.

(2) In his first Epistle, John uses the augmented title "the Word of life", 1 John 1. 1. In this verse, there is stressed the true physical nature of His humanity; in other words, He was with men. The thought of life then continues in verse 2, "that eternal life, which was with the Father". In other words, once again the Lord is seen as with men and with the Father. In verses 3, 7, the subject of fellowship is introduced; this is seen as "with the Father, and with his Son Jesus Christ" on the one hand, and "one with another" on the other hand, implying joy in assembly fellowship. Peter spoke of "the words of eternal life" that the Lord possessed, by which he implied that the only place of fellowship was with Him, John 6. 67-69.

(3) In the book of Revelation, John uses the title "The Word of God", Rev. 19. 13. This is a future manifestation of the Lord coming forth from an opened heaven, in order to fulfil the purpose of God to cleanse the world through judgment of all unrighteousness. In this great event, the Lord's people are seen with Him. He has the additional titles "Faithful and True" and "King of kings, and Lord of lords", vv. 11, 16. There may be a cross reference to John 12. 48, where "the word . . . shall judge him in the last day".

3

READING: Acts 11. 19-26

THE LORDSHIP OF CHRIST

THE DESCRIPTION of the early days of the church in Antioch in Syria is full of spiritual instruction. It thrived in every aspect of service because the Lordship of Christ was fully recognized by the believers forming the church.

They preached the Lord Jesus, Acts 11. 20. No other preaching, no other name, can establish a local church in keeping with the will of God. This is the way in which Paul "planted", 1 Cor. 3. 6; he would know no other than Christ and "him crucified", 2. 2.

The hand of the Lord was with them, Acts 11. 21. That is to say, the Lord was working through the evangelists; only the Lord could build the house, Psa. 127. 1, and Paul knew that the grace of God was with him in his labours, 1 Cor. 15. 10.

They turned unto the Lord, Acts 11. 21. To turn elsewhere would merely create a human organization or society. Thus God "gave the increase", 1 Cor. 3. 6, and that is why a spiritual church was formed both in Antioch and in Corinth.

They cleaved unto the Lord, Acts 11. 23. This was because of their purpose of heart; no head-leader was recognized amongst men, no Paul, Apollos or Cephas, 1 Cor. 1. 12. They could not turn to another, since Christ only had the words of eternal life, John 6. 66-69.

Much people was added unto the Lord, Acts 11. 24. Those that were being converted were not adding themselves; this was a divine work, as "the Lord added to the church daily", Acts 2. 47. People either join themselves or are elected to human societies, but spiritually God gives the increase, 1 Cor. 3. 6; the building is by God and for God.

They ministered to the Lord, Acts 13. 2. Here we find the direction of the service of the teachers and prophets in Antioch. Service amongst the saints and for the saints is really service Godward. "Inasmuch as ye have done it unto one of the least of these my brethren, ye have done it unto me", Matt. 25. 40.

Teaching and preaching the Word of the Lord, Acts 15. 35. This verse shows the continuation of service in the church at Antioch after several years. In days of no open vision, the Word of the Lord should be "precious", 1 Sam. 3. 1.

January 5th

READING: Isaiah 55. 1-4

BUY WITHOUT MONEY

IN A WORLD of trade, commerce and shops, it may appear to be a strange concept, "he that hath no money; come ye, buy, and eat". A man with no money may steal, but God issues an invitation to purchase when no money is available. To enter a shop and find that all the food, clothes and furniture are free would appear to be an impossible daydream; we might think that something is seriously wrong if we found such a shop!

But God's gracious gifts cannot be purchased with money; Simon of Samaria thought that "the gift of God may be purchased with money", but his money would perish with him, Acts 8. 18, 20. The Scriptures are full of gifts available freely from God, and many men have benefited from this divine liberality.

We may quote a few of these from the Scriptures, asking ourselves to what extent we have been and still are partakers.

Wilderness food was provided by God, "I will rain bread from heaven for you", Exod 16. 4. This was to be collected every day except on the Sabbath. We may pick the wild fruit from the hedgerows, but never manna of this wilderness variety!

There were 5,000 who were fed miraculously from the original five loaves and two fishes, Luke 9. 14. The people took what the Lord provided freely, "and were all filled".

Again, there were 4,000 who were fed miraculously from the original seven loaves and a few fish, Matt. 15. 34. It is recorded that "they did all eat, and were filled".

Turning now to spiritual things, we recall that the Lord promised both water and bread. The woman at the well could draw natural water quite freely, but of infinite and eternal value was the "living water" that the Lord would give, John 4. 10, 14. Again, He claimed to be the "bread of life" come down from heaven, and those who eat of that bread would live for ever, John 6. 48. Later, as the Good Shepherd, He stated that He gave His sheep eternal life, 10. 28.

As we take of the salvation that He procured at such great cost, we recall that He said, "freely ye have received, freely give", Matt. 10. 8. Our salvation is the gift of God, not of works, Eph. 2. 9; Rom. 11. 6. Even up to his old age, Paul was adamant about this truth, "not according to our works, but according to his own purpose and grace", 2 Tim. 1. 9.

January 6th

READING: **Isaiah 57. 13-21**

THE ONE WHO INHABITS ETERNITY

THE FIRST part of chapter 57 does not make very pleasant reading. In Isaiah's time, some of the people of Judah were taken up with idolatry, and to describe this from God's point of view a great metaphorical parable is used. Idolaters are seen as an unfaithful wife, having unlawful religious experiences with another than God, v. 8. In verse 7, this activity is described as, "Upon a lofty and high mountain hast thou set thy bed: even thither wentest thou up to offer sacrifice". One hundred years later, Judah was behaving in the same way as a "treacherous sister", Jer. 3. 7.

How small and impotent are the idols of men! The "lofty and high mountain" of the idolaters stands in contrast with "the high and lofty One that inhabiteth eternity, whose name is Holy", Isa. 57. 15. The material devices of idolaters have but a finite existence at the most; the material of which they are made by men was created in the beginning and will be burnt up at the end. But the sphere of the true God is eternity, and there is His habitation, though He also dwells "with him also that is of a contrite and humble spirit". Paul knew the difference, "an idol is nothing in the world, and that there is none other God but one", 1 Cor. 8. 4. Yet men would eliminate the existence of God by substituting an adherence solely on material things. Even believers must keep themselves from idols in this sense, 1 John 5. 21.

Men have treated the Lord Jesus in the same way. He is the One who inhabits eternity. On the isle of Patmos, He revealed Himself to John with the words (and we give a literal translation), "I am the living one, and became dead, and, behold, I am living to the ages of ages", Rev. 1. 18. Thus He was the Living One in eternity past; He became dead between His decease on the cross and His resurrection, and He is now living throughout the future eternity. Men would deny this and substitute their own ideas; thus the Pharisees refused to accept the Lord as the "I am" before Abraham, John 8. 57-59, and refused the apostolic testimony of the resurrection after His rising again. Again, in Revelation 1. 4, He announces Himself as the One "which is (the present), and which was (the eternal past), and which is to come (the eternal future).

6

READING: **Ephesians 5. 1-2, 21-33**

THE GIVING OF HIMSELF

THE PHRASE that the Lord gave Himself occurs six times in Paul's Epistles. The contexts mostly contain the thoughts of love and separation. These six occasions are found twice in Galatians, twice in Ephesians and twice in Timothy/Titus.

Galatians. "I live by the faith of the Son of God, who loved me, and gave himself for me", Gal. 2. 20. The love of the Son for the sinner is seen as leading to His sacrifice, and in turn this leads to the divine power for living in Paul's life. The apostle was separated from the law, since he would not build again the things that he had destroyed, v. 18.

"Our Lord Jesus Christ, who gave himself for our sins, that he might deliver us from this present evil world (age)", Gal. 1. 4. The giving of Himself has also delivered believers from a dark religious and moral environment; the Galatians needed to be reminded of this glorious fact, since they had drifted back to the law that had enslaved them previously.

Ephesians. "Walk in love, as Christ also hath loved us, and hath given himself for us an offering and a sacrifice to God for a sweetsmelling savour", Eph. 5. 2. The love of Christ is again to the fore, and this Christian walk is seen as separated from the defilement around, 4. 31; 5. 3-7, "Be not ye therefore partakers with them".

"Christ also loved the church, and gave himself for it", Eph. 5. 25. Here again is love, but the effect of this giving of Himself is that the church is seen as sanctified, cleansed, glorious, with no spot, wrinkle or blemish.

Timothy/Titus. "The man Christ Jesus; who gave himself a ransom for all, to be testified in due time", 1 Tim. 2. 6. This is in the context of prayer for all men and for those in authority, with a view to their salvation. Paul was separated to God as a preacher, an apostle and a teacher, and exhorted that prayer be made with "holy hands" lifted up.

"Our Saviour Jesus Christ; who gave himself for us, that he might redeem us from all iniquity, and purify unto himself a peculiar people, zealous of good works", Titus 2. 14. Here again is the separating power of His sacrifice: negatively, a redemption from all iniquity, and positively a purification with good works that adorn the doctrine of God in all things.

January 8th

READING: **Isaiah 6**

GLORY AND THE THREEFOLD "THEN SAID I"

IN THIS chapter, there are several sets of threes. Thus the wings of the seraphim were described in terms of three pairs, being used for covering their face and feet, and for flying, v. 2; thus these were used for worship, walk and work. Again, there was the threefold cry, "Holy, holy, holy" ascribed to the Lord of hosts whose glory Isaiah was privileged to behold, v. 3, a description of Deity that is also found before the throne in Revelation 4. 8. We may also mention the fact that there are six woes in chapter 5, found in vv. 8, 11, 18, 20-22. But Isaiah was content to use the word "Woe" once in connection with himself, 6. 5. Moreover, three times Isaiah has recorded, "Then said I".

The "Then said I" of cleansing, v. 5. Uzziah, who had sought to usurp the priesthood, had to die before the Lord's glory would be revealed to Isaiah. Isaiah too had to be cleansed before he could embark upon his service of prophecy; to testify to a people of unclean lips, he himself had to be quite distinct. So his lips were touched, v. 7, and his iniquity was taken away. Today, likewise, the Lord's servants must live out the message that they proclaim.

The "Then said I" of calling, v. 8. Only after such cleansing was Isaiah available for God to call to service; he heard the questions, "Whom shall I send, and who will go for us?". Like Paul, he was not disobedient to the heavenly vision, Acts 26. 19. The supreme example is that of the Lord Jesus, who at the appointed time said, "I come to do thy will, O God", Heb. 10. 7. Thus Isaiah said, "Here am I; send me", and then he received his instructions, with the knowledge that many who heard would not hear, see or understand. Today, the Lord's servants must be prepared for apparent disappointments and lack of response amongst the many, while being able to rejoice in the few who respond and grow in grace.

The "Then said I" of commission, v. 11. How long would Isaiah have to serve, and with what results? For the many, there would be nothing but desolation, removal and forsaking; yet there would be a remnant consisting of the "holy seed" that would return, finding blessing in the prophetic message. The commission in Matthew 28. 19 had a similar outcome.

8

READING: **Revelation 2. 24-29**

HOLD FAST

THREE TIMES in these seven letters in Revelation 2-3 the exhortation to "hold fast" appears, these being the direct words of the Lord Himself. They appear in the letters to the churches in Thyatira, 2. 25; Sardis, 3. 3, and Philadelphia, 3. 11. The exhortation occurs several other times in the N.T., such as "Let us hold fast the profession of our faith . . . as ye see the day approaching", Heb. 10. 23-25. There are also similar exhortations, such as "that ye stand fast in one spirit, with one mind", Phil. 1. 27; "Stand fast therefore in the liberty wherewith Christ hath made us free", Gal. 5. 1. All believers need such exhortations today. The interesting fact is that, in Revelation 2-3, the three occasions where "hold fast" occurs also contain a reference to the Lord's coming.

The "hold fast" to Thyatira, Rev. 2. 25. Here it is a question of doctrine, for there was a prophetess who was teaching the believers to engage in idolatrous practices, v. 20. We may be glad that there were some in the church who had not embraced this doctrine, v. 24. The Lord would have such faithful saints to continue in their rejection of what was false and to adhere to what was true; hence "hold fast" until He come, when there would be rewards for those who are overcomers. As Paul exhorted Timothy, "Take heed unto thyself, and unto the doctrine", 1 Tim. 4. 16.

The "hold fast" to Sardis, Rev. 3. 3. Here it is a question of works, referring no doubt to the service that the local church engaged in. They had "received" these things, but were elevated with "a name". By contrast, Paul had received many things, but remained humble. Those in Sardis had to repent, watch and hold fast, else their expectation for the coming of the Lord would diminish and He would come unawares "as a thief". As Paul exhorted Archippus, "Take heed to the ministry which thou hast received in the Lord", Col. 4. 17.

The "hold fast" to Philadelphia, Rev. 3. 11. Here it is a question of the Lord's word in verses 8, 10, something that is more than doctrine. Here is the whole pathway of life, the word being profitable for instruction in righteousness, 2 Tim. 3. 16; see Psa. 119. 9. The Lord promises to come quickly, with a crown for those who hold fast that which they have.

January 10th

READING: Matthew 6. 6-15; John 20. 14-17

THE FATHER

WE READ of the Father many times in the N.T. The truth had been made known even in the O.T., in such verses as "his name shall be called, the everlasting Father", Isa. 9. 6; "I am a father to Israel", Jer. 31. 9; "Have we not all one father? hath not one God created us?", Mal. 2. 10. But the full development of the subject of the Fatherhood of God is made in the N.T., in the teaching of the Lord Jesus and of His apostles. Yet there is more than one aspect to the subject, and any differences must be appreciated by the Lord's people.

The Lord's teaching in the Synoptic Gospels appears to be rather different from the presentation in John's Gospel. In the sermon on the mount, the Lord addresses His disciples, and speaks of "your Father which is in heaven", Matt. 5. 16; "the children of your Father", 5. 45; "thy Father", 6. 4; "your Father", 6. 8; "Our Father", 6. 9; "your heavenly Father", 6. 14, and so on. An examination of such verses will show that the Fatherhood of God relates to His providential care for His own. A deeper spiritual relationship is not implied. But it is certainly implied when the Son addresses the Father in Matthew 11. 25-27, where we read, "O Father, Father, my Father, the Father". Similarly we find this intimate relationship when the Son prayed in the garden of Gethsemane, "O my Father", 26. 39.

In John's Gospel, this providential relationship to the disciples is absent. Throughout the first 19 chapters, every mention of the Father is either "my Father" in relation to the Lord Jesus, as "My Father worketh hitherto", John 5. 17; "my Father giveth you the true bread", 6. 32, or "the Father", as "The Father loveth the Son", 3. 35; "true worshippers shall worship the Father", 4. 23. In His prayer in John 17, the Son used the titles "Father, O Father, Holy Father, O righteous Father". But throughout these chapters, "your Father" never appears, until after His resurrection. Then the Lord introduced "your Father" for the first time to Mary Magdalene, "I ascend unto my Father, and your Father", 20. 17. This spiritual relationship, as distinct from providential Fatherhood, is based on His resurrection. This is perpetuated throughout the Epistles; the Spirit makes this relationship real and precious whereby we can cry "Abba, Father", Rom. 8. 15; Gal. 4. 6.

January 11th

READING: **Exodus 26. 31-35**

PREPOSITIONS AND THE VAIL

IN THE Scriptures there are three vails associated with material structures: Moses' tabernacle, Solomon's temple and Herod's temple. Here we concentrate on that within Moses' tabernacle, used in Hebrews 10. 20 as a type speaking of the Lord Jesus Christ, "a new and living way". This vail can briefly be considered in connection with the prepositions that are used with it in the Scriptures.

With the vail; "thou shalt . . . cover the ark with the vail", Exod. 40. 3, 21. The throne of God was absolutely holy, so the ark was vailed from the sight of the priests, and also when the ark was moved through the wilderness, Num. 4. 5. But in the antitype, "we beheld his glory" as the Word tabernacled amongst men, John 1. 14.

Without the vail; "In the tabernacle . . . without the vail" would Aaron order the lampstand, Exod 27. 21; Lev. 24. 3; see also Exod. 40. 22 for the table. Thus in the holy place Christ is the Light and Food for His priestly people.

Before the vail; the incense altar had to be placed before the vail, Exod. 30. 6; see also 40. 26; Lev. 4, 17. Here is the place of worship for the Lord's people, an appreciation of the fragrance of Christ, and the value of His shed blood.

Unto the vail; any priest with a blemish "shall not go in unto the vail", Lev. 21. 23. God was very particular as to those who were permitted to approach Him in service. Sin that is unconfessed is a hindrance and a barrier; thus David could bring the "sacrifices of God" only after he had confessed his sin and repented of his deed, Psa. 51. 15-17.

Within the vail; the ark had to be brought in "within the vail", Exod 26. 33, a place absolutely holy for the throne of God. Thus Aaron could not come "within the vail" at all times, Lev. 16. 2, though once a year he could enter within the vail, vv. 12, 15. This is the place within the vail where the Lord Jesus our Forerunner has entered, Heb. 6. 19-20.

Through the vail; this is the privilege of believers today, "to enter . . . by a new and living way . . . through the vail, that is to say, his flesh", Heb. 10. 19-20. The new has displaced the old; the reality of grace goes far beyond what was ever visualized under the OT typical ceremony.

January 12th

READING: **Galatians 6. 14-18**

THE WORLD AND PAUL CRUCIFIED

THE GALATIANS had once run well; they had begun in the Spirit, but then they wanted to be "made perfect by the flesh", Gal. 3. 3. The joy of their salvation had been discarded, and the O.T. law had been reintroduced. Paul's correction involved showing that the Lord had died to deliver believers from this present evil age, 1. 4; that he, Paul, was dead to the law, refusing to build again his past religious legal experiences, 2. 18-19; that he had been crucified with Christ, yet Christ was living in him, 2. 20. He also used many O.T. analogies to prove his point, and was still pressing the truth as he came to the end of the Epistle.

Thus he wrote, "God forbid that I should glory, save in the cross of our Lord Jesus Christ, by whom the world is crucified unto me, and I unto the world", 6. 14. In other words, the crucifixion of the Lord in a physical sense at Calvary, leading to His death and resurrection, brought with it further acts of crucifixion in a moral and spiritual sense. (i) Paul could see the world crucified as far as his assessment of the world was concerned; others who loved the world would not notice that it had suffered death. (ii) Paul had been crucified as far as the world assessed his new kind of separated life.

The world crucified. The organized systems of men, whether political, religious or moral, had no place in Paul's spiritual experience. The world was dead, in the sense that the life of Christ was absent from it. Things that had been a gain for Paul were now counted loss for Christ; he had no confidence in his Pharisaical upbringing and its advantages, Phil. 3. 4-8.

Paul crucified. The world has no time for a devoted person whose life and interests are consecrated to Christ. The world has its own life, and if this is seen to be absent in a believer then the world effectively treats him as dead. Some kind of friendship with the world shows that a believer is not crucified to it, James 4. 4. A spiritual life prospers when a believer knows that he is crucified to the world, since he then has a fuller experience of Christ dwelling within. Sometimes, the world may treat a man whom it considers as dead in a despicable way; thus Paul was appointed to death as a spectacle to the world, being made as the filth of the world, 1 Cor. 4. 9-13.

January 13th

READING: **Numbers 8. 5-26**

GOD'S POSSESSION OF THE LEVITES

GOD HAD placed the service of the tabernacle in the hands of the Levites, namely, men between the ages of twenty-five and fifty of the tribe of Levi. It is interesting to trace why this was so, and to note the position of believers today.

From the time that the firstborn died in Egypt, Exod. 12. 29, the firstborn amongst the Israelites and their animals had had a special status before God, 13. 15. The firstborn of animals had to be sacrificed to the Lord, but the firstborn males of God's people had to be redeemed. How this was to be done was not immediately stated. Later, the firstborn with their tribes fell into idolatry, and only the tribe of Levi stood faithfully on the Lord's side, 32. 26.

Then in Numbers 3 we find that the redemption of the firstborn was a replacement process, "thou shalt take the Levites for me (I am the Lord) instead of all the firstborn among the children of Israel", v. 41. There were 22,273 to be redeemed, v. 43, but only 22,000 Levites to replace them; see verse 39. The remaining 273 were redeemed by five shekels each, making a total of 1,365 shekels totally, vv. 46, 50. (Note that the arithmetic is exact and not approximate.)

Thus the Levites were wholly given to the Lord instead of the firstborn, Num. 8. 16. They were cleansed by sin and burnt offerings. Because of this, they were chosen to engage in the tabernacle service. God said, "I have taken them unto me", v. 16; "I sanctified them for myself", v. 17; "the Levites shall be mine", v. 14. Finally they were given to the priests "as a gift", v. 19, to assist in the tabernacle service.

There is a marked similarity between this typology and the calling of the people of God today. Like the firstborn, we were dead in trespasses and sins, and even idolaters, 1 Cor. 6. 9, but we have been redeemed "with the precious blood of Christ, as of a lamb without blemish and without spot", 1 Pet. 1. 19. Thus we belong to God; He claims us as His own, and Paul could write, "ye are not your own . . . ye are bought with a price", 1 Cor. 6. 19-20. We are washed, sanctified and justified, v. 11, and enabled to serve God according to gifts that have been bestowed upon us, 12. 7, 11, which go hand-in-hand with our priestly functions of offering spiritual sacrifices, 1 Pet. 2. 5.

January 14th

READING: **Romans 8. 35-39**

THE LOVE OF CHRIST

DIVINE LOVE is a very precious asset appreciated by every believer. Direct statements of this love appear so often, particularly in the N.T.; for example, the love of God is found in John 3. 16: "For God so loved the world"; the love of the Father is found in John 16. 27, "the Father himself loveth you"; the love of the Son is found in John 15. 9, "so have I loved you", and Galatians 2. 20, "the Son of God, who loved me, and gave himself for me". Yet the actual phrase "the love of Christ" appears only three times, all in Paul's Epistles.

"The love of Christ constraineth us", 2 Cor. 5. 14, that is, this divine love of the Saviour compelled Paul to serve Christ faithfully. He knew "the terror of the Lord", v. 11, and that all must be judged, when men would receive according to what they have done in their lifetimes, whether good or bad. He knew that all men were dead in sins. Yet as a believer, he knew that Christ had died for us, so that we may live for Him— that He has been made sin for us, v. 21. Such divine love therefore constrained Paul, as an ambassador for Christ, to preach the glorious gospel of the grace of God.

"Who shall separate us from the love of Christ? . . . from the love of God, which is in Christ Jesus our Lord", Rom. 8. 35, 39. Once we are saved, we are always saved; the Lord was delivered up for us all, v. 32, and we are justified, so that all the troubles of life cannot separate us from the love of Christ. We are therefore more than conquerors through Him that loved us, so here is our certainty and security both now, and in the future. May we say with John, "what manner of love the Father hath bestowed upon us", 1 John 3. 1.

"To know the love of Christ, which passeth knowledge", Eph. 3. 19. This love is so great, that it appears to be almost unknowable in its fulness. Yet Paul was praying that the Ephesians might know this love. He had confidence that his prayer would be answered, because God can "do exceedingly abundantly above all that we ask or think", v. 20. And we may learn that love also—both initially through the gospel, and increasingly throughout our Christian life. Moreover, this love is permanent, and leads us to greater faithfulness. Alas, it is easy to talk about it, but more difficult to grow into it.

January 15th

READING: **Matthew 27. 15-26**

COMMON AND SIMPLE QUESTIONS

WE ARE always asking questions; others may answer them or we may have to look the answers up in a book. To a young child the details of his environment are absolutely mysterious, and he therefore tends to ask questions all the time. Some of our own questions may be simple, such as, What is the time?. Others may need a detailed answer, as when a student asks a teacher. Again, other questions may be spoken in anxiety, fear or desperation, of which there are several in the N.T.

A bad question. The Lord stood before Pilate, accused by the Jews. The governor could find nothing wrong, and to justify himself he sought to release Him at the feast. But the Jews wanted a murderer, Barabbas. Hence Pilate asked the question, "What shall I do?", Matt. 27. 22. As with so many today, Pilate gave way to the forces of evil, and the Lord was unjustly crucified. Believers, on the other hand, cast out evil, and receive the Lord into their hearts.

A good question. Peter's first sermon in Acts 2 was cutting and convicting; he preached the resurrection of the One whom his listeners had crucified, v. 36. Hence they asked, "what shall we do?", v. 37. Since salvation is not of works, the answer was that they should repent for the remission of sins, when they would receive the gift of the Holy Spirit.

A good question. Here was no longer a crowd, but one man in Philippi, Acts 16. 30. The jailor had experienced the earthquake, and thought that the prisoners had escaped. Fearing Roman judgment, he cried, "what must I do to be saved?". This was a natural question, but Paul turned it to spiritual advantage, and exhorted faith in the Lord Jesus for salvation.

A misinformed question. The rich young ruler desired salvation by works, so asked the Lord, "what good thing shall I do?", Matt. 19. 16. But no good thing could remove the barrier caused by lack of treasure in heaven. "Come and follow me", said the Lord, but his possessions caused him to turn away.

A practical question. Everything had gone wrong in the servant's life, and when called to account, he asked, "What shall I do?", Luke 16. 3. He answered his own question — be more careful in daily life. Truly, one who is faithful in what is least, is also faithful in much, v. 10.

READING: **Song of Solomon 2. 14-17**

MY BELOVED IN MINE, AND I AM HIS

THE BRIDE and the bridegroom share the mutual possession of each other. This is a truth that Paul brings out in 1 Corinthians 7. 2-4. It is also a truth that applies to Christ and the church, Eph. 5. 32. It also applies to the relationship between the Jews and Jehovah, "thou becamest mine", Ezek. 16. 8. This concept is found throughout the Song of Songs; in particular, there are three references that carry very important lessons for believers today.

(1) "I am my beloved's, and my beloved is mine: he feedeth among the lilies", Song 6. 3; the bride is speaking. The daughters of Jerusalem had asked her a question: where had her beloved gone? If there was a temporary separation, the truth of mutual possession remained. She knew that he had gone into his garden, to feed there among the lilies. There can be fellowship and service in the garden. Typically this speaks of service in the local church; Paul wrote to the church at Corinth as "God's husbandry", tillage, or cultivated plot. At its best, this would be a garden of pleasures; the Lord's servants would be planting and watering, but God would be there in the work, and He would be giving the increase, 1 Cor. 3. 6-9. In His garden, "we are workers together with God", v. 9; this is a permanent position and occupation.

(2) "I am my beloved's, and his desire is toward me", Song 7. 10, said the bride. She knew that his desire was towards her, and her desire was that both together they should go into the field and the villages to see what fruit there was. We may see this as partnership in the gospel, for the field is the world; the Lord has sent His servants into the world, but He Himself still continues to work with them, Mark 16. 20. There can be no fruit if a servant works alone, but when the Lord is also present, much fruit can be brought forth.

(3) "My beloved is mine, and I am his: he feedeth among the lilies", Song 2. 16, said the bride. Here is mutual pleasure in each other — "the fellowship of his Son", 1 Cor. 1. 9. The bridegroom saw her voice as "sweet" — she had been enriched "in all utterance", 1 Cor. 1. 5; the bride was waiting "Until the day dawn" — believers are "waiting for the coming of our Lord Jesus Christ", 1 Cor. 1. 7.

January 17th

READING: **Psalm 68. 15-18, 25-32**

THE LORD ON HIGH AND PRAISE

THE CONTEXT of Psalm 68 is very interesting. It speaks of a movement of the ark of the covenant in David's time, and can only refer to the occasion when the ark was taken up mount Zion for the first time, to be placed in the tent that David had prepared, 1 Chron. 15. 1-3, 28; 16. 1. Psalm 68 was sung by the singers at the ascent of mount Zion, while the further psalm recorded in 1 Chron. 16. 8-36 was sung by the singers once the ark had been placed in the tent on Zion. It was, in fact, a time of great rejoicing.

Psalm 68. 16 shows that there was opposition; other "high hills" were leaping, but mount Zion was unique, "this is the hill which God desireth to dwell in . . . for ever". The exalted position of this throne of God is seen in verse 18, "Thou hast ascended on high". During the ascent, the ark was in the midst of the singers and the instrument players, v. 25, while all the kingdoms of the earth were called upon to "Sing unto God", to the One who was riding on high in the heavens of heavens, vv. 32-33.

The meaning of this is not far to find, for the apostle Paul quotes the statement "When he ascended up on high" in Ephesians 4. 8. To Paul, the spiritual meaning of the ascent of the ark up mount Zion was the ascension of the Lord Jesus "far above all heavens, that he might fill all things". He was preeminent and unique in His ascension; men may erect their tower of Babel to reach to the heavens, Gen. 11. 4, but the Lord Jesus has been exalted to sit at God's right hand, Acts 2. 33-35. As He ascended, the apostles who witnessed the event "worshipped him", Luke 24. 52, corresponding to the singers in Psalm 68. 25. We cannot do that today, since the ascension was unique and cannot be repeated. But we join the ranks of the singers on mount Zion after the ark had been established there. For the Epistle to the Ephesians contains many references to praise and worship. "Blessed be the God and Father of our Lord Jesus Christ", 1. 3; "that we should be to the praise of his glory", 1. 12; "unto him be glory in the church by Christ Jesus", 3. 21; "speaking to yourselves in psalms and hymns and spiritual songs, singing and making melody in your hearts to the Lord; giving thanks", 5. 19-20.

READING: **2 Thessalonians 2. 1-2, 15-17; 3. 14-18**

OUR EPISTLE

THE WORD Epistle means "letter"; the word is not in common usage today, except in scriptural vocabulary. When Paul was writing his Epistles by inspiration, he was very conscious of the fact that they were letters, written to churches and to individuals. Even Peter could write, "our beloved brother Paul . . . in all his epistles", 2 Pet. 3. 15-16. Paul used the word "epistle (or letter)" 17 times, four of which occur in his second Epistle to the Thessalonians.

(1) "*By letter* as from us", 2 Thess. 2. 2. The apostle's teaching about the second coming of the Lord Jesus had been quite clear, both when he had been among them, and in his first Epistle. Yet there had been some men ready to contradict him, and to serve their end they wrote a forged letter as from Paul. The believers had been deceived into thinking that the persecution that they endured was the result of the day of the Lord having come. So in chapter 2, he explains that the day of the Lord would not come while the church was still on earth.

(2) "Hold the traditions which ye have been taught, whether by word, or *our epistle*", 2. 15. The Thessalonians had to have only one *source* of doctrine, namely, either Paul when he had been with them, or his Epistle (no doubt referring to the first Epistle). He knew that the time would come when some men would not endure sound doctrine, so he wanted faithful men like Timothy who would pass on the exact doctrine that he had proclaimed, 2 Tim. 4. 3; 1 Cor. 4. 17.

(3) "If any man obey not our word by *this epistle*", 2 Thess. 3. 14. Correcting doctrine is one thing, but wrong doctrine leads to bad behaviour, 1 Cor. 15. 33. Hence Paul would also correct the behaviour of some in Thessalonica who would not work, leading to disorderly conduct. Rather they should work so as to provide their own food; fellowship was to be temporarily withdrawn so that restoration might be effected.

(4) "The token in *every epistle*: so I write", 2 Thess. 3. 17; this was Paul's decision, to sign each Epistle to prevent any future forgery. Others may actually write an Epistle, such as Tertius, who wrote Romans, Rom. 16. 22. This would never detract from the true authorship, and this is an important point, for the truth of apostolic inspiration must be held fast.

READING: **Romans 12. 1-10**

SACRIFICE AND THE GOOD SAMARITAN

THE DOCTRINAL chapters of the Epistle to the Romans give way to practical chapters in 12. 1, "therefore". And even the practical paragraphs may appear to be doctrinal unless we can illustrate the principles involved, using both the Lord's parables and the historical events in the Acts.

In Romans 12 Paul could see that faithful and devoted service would arise only when a believer presented his body "a living sacrifice, holy, acceptable unto God", v. 1; when he was not conformed to the world, but transformed by the renewing of his mind, v. 2; when he realized the measure of faith that had been granted him, v. 4; and when he was kindly affectioned to others with brotherly love, v. 10. To live and serve like that is costly, perhaps financially, perhaps as far as natural promotional prospects are concerned, perhaps implying the giving up of many things and occupations that would be perfectly legitimate for other believers. This is where the illustration of the good Samaritan is of great use.

In Luke 10. 29, the lawyer wanted to know who his neighbour was, since he had to love him even as he loved himself. The Lord's answer showed that the Samaritan was the neighbour of him who had fallen among thieves, with the exhortation, "Go, and do thou likewise", v. 37. In other words, the lawyer had to act like the good Samaritan, like the neighbour himself! We can love our neighbour (the one who helps us) by acting as a neighbour ourselves to others in need. The service of the good Samaritan brings out the principles behind sacrificial service.

He was completely different from the priest and the Levite who passed by on the other side; in other words, he was not conformed to the religious world of the Jews. He was transformed, since he cast aside the tradition that Samaritans and Jews could not mix socially, John 4. 9; Luke 17. 16. Again, his service was sacrificial, since time had to be expended, oil and wine had to be used, money had to be given, with the promise of more if necessary. Brotherly love was shown when "he had compassion on him", when "he took care of him", and when his interest was such that he promised to come again to see how the man was faring. Our own sacrifice, like that of Epaphroditus, Phil 2. 25-30, must be similarly measured.

January 20th

READING: **Deuteronomy 34. 5-12**

FACE TO FACE

WHO IN the O.T. had been more in contact with God than Moses? And yet for believers today, their present experience and their future blessed hope are quite distinct, and certainly far more spiritually advanced. For Moses was the one "whom the Lord knew face to face", 34. 10. Yet there was the restriction that Moses could not bypass, "Thou canst not see my face: for there shall no man see me, and live", Exod. 33. 20. The reason is that God could see Moses' face, but he could not see God's face.

As far as Moses was concerned, it was what he heard rather than what he saw. In Exodus 33. 11, Moses went into the temporary tabernacle, and became charged with the glory of God. It was there that "the Lord spake unto Moses face to face, as a man speaketh unto his friend". It was the same in the actual tabernacle, where "he heard the voice of one speaking unto him from off the mercy seat", Num. 7. 89. Peter realized that it was more blessed to hear the word of prophecy than to see an open vision of the glory of Christ, 2 Pet. 1. 19.

When the Lord Jesus was here on earth, certainly His disciples were able to see Him face to face physically. Peter "beheld his glory", John 1. 14, and the Lord "looked upon Peter", Luke 22. 61. Yet now, we neither hear His voice nor do we see Him in a physical sense; faith overcomes this, and we can sing in wellknown hymns, "Gazing on Thee Lord in glory" and "We hear Thy welcome voice".

But as the Lord prepared His disciples for His absence, He prayed that they should be able to "behold my glory", John 17. 24. This is a future prospect for the people of God, in keeping with the hymn, "And I shall see Him face to face, And tell the story saved by grace". John no doubt had this promise before him when he wrote, "it doth not yet appear what we shall be: but we know that, when he shall appear, we shall be like him; for *we shall see him as he is*", 1 John 3. 2. So John uniquely sees the Lord under three distinct circumstances: first during His lifetime and in His resurrection when on earth; secondly when he saw Him on the isle of Patmos, Rev. 1. 12; and thirdly when he sees Him at His return. So John had a greater privilege than Moses. We shall only see Him at His return, but in the meantime the sight of faith is very real.

20

January 21st

READING: Luke 3. 1-2, 16-22

FROM POLITICS AND RELIGION TO THE SON OF GOD

THE PROPHETS in the O.T. had predicted that this would be the order of things. Man's great efforts in many spheres would prove to be useless and fleeting when God intervened. Thus in Daniel 2. 36-45, where Daniel interpreted Nebuchadnezzar's dream, the politics of the nations seeking territorial expansion, commencing with the king of Babylon and ending with the emperors of Rome, would lead to the Stone cut out without hands, and the establishment of God's kingdom that would never be destroyed, 2. 44-45. Again, in Daniel 7. 13-14, the kingdoms of the four beasts would give way to the revelation of the Son of man, with dominion, glory and a kingdom. Hence, in these days, are believers occupied with the kingdom of God or with the kingdoms and politics of men?

In the N.T., the beginning of the Lord's ministry is seen as a blessed replacement of all that men stood for. In Luke 3. 1-2, we find mention of Tiberias Caesar the emperor of Rome, of Pilate the Roman governor of Judaea, of the various leaders of named provinces, and of the Jewish religious leaders, the high priests Annas and Caiaphas (all was intrigue, for one had been deposed by the Romans and the other elected, yet the Jews still regarded both as high priests, though in God's eyes neither was high priest). Three years later, when the Lord was crucified, these men still held sway in high places.

How important to know that John the Baptist stood up to the evils of the day, at the same time introducing the Lord Jesus who ultimately would "purge his floor" of every evil, so that His kingdom may be established. God opened heaven, and said, "Thou art my beloved Son; in thee I am well pleased", Luke 3. 22. Only to the Son did God say this, stating elsewhere, "Yet have I set my king upon my holy hill of Zion" and "I shall give thee the heathen for thine inheritance", Psa. 2. 6, 8. Here is the great King and High Priest, who will ultimately have all authority over the nations, when the kings that remain will bring their glory and honour unto Him in the holy Jerusalem, Rev. 21. 24. All other authority claimed by men will disappear.

Leaders have responsibility today, even having been "ordained of God", Rom. 13. 1. But the basic character of those who love power for its own ends is clearly revealed in Scripture.

January 22nd

READING: Mark 10. 35-45

RANK — FIRST OR LAST

JAMES AND JOHN had already seen the preeminence of the Lord on the mount of transfiguration. The apostles did not appear in glory on the mount; only grace had allowed them to see the Lord transfigured before them. And yet, later, James and John wanted to sit in close proximity to the Lord in His glory, Mark 10. 37. They wanted an elevated place, implying an elevated status above that of the other apostles, who were "much displeased" when they heard what was being suggested.

James wrote, "these things ought not so to be", James 3. 10; the Lord said, "so shall it not be among you". Greatness is preceded by humility; the latter is self-imposed, while the former is God-imposed. The downward steps are (i) "shall be your minister", and (ii) "shall be servant of all". How good to see a servant of God who actually serves and does not expect to be served! The word "minister" is "deacon", a word in the N.T. that embraces many forms of service; the word "servant" means bondservant, the lowest possible position.

The Lord was correcting and exhorting the disciples, not in isolated elevation, but on account of His own experience, "not to be ministered unto, but to minister, and to give his life a ransom for many", Mark 10. 45. After this, He did not exalt Himself; rather "God hath highly exalted him, and given him a name which is above every name", Phil. 2. 9. He took upon Himself the form of a bondservant, knowing that He would be glorified, John 13. 31-32.

Alas that there should be those among the people of God who do not seem to know this truth. John the apostle had learnt the lesson from the Lord, and afterwards he could be a humble servant, able to recognize others who were not walking in the truth. For he claimed quite openly, without appearing to be hypocritical in any way, that Diotrephes "loveth to have the preeminence among them", 3 John 9. He would not receive the apostle John, nor the brethren, casting those out of the church who sought to do otherwise. Here was a man who wanted to be first, while in the event he was really last in the eyes of God, a man who was a church-dictator rather than a bondservant; he had his reward already. There can be no scope for men seeking lordship over God's heritage, 1 Pet. 5. 3.

January 23rd

READING: **Mark 15. 16-20; Luke 15. 21-24**

DRESS OF THE BEST AND OF THE WORST

THE BEST is dressed as the worst to be mocked, and the worst is dressed as the best for rejoicing.

Men can, of course, be dressed in their worst clothes or their best, depending on the occasion. Morally likewise they can be transformed. The filthy religious garments that the high priest Joshua had brought back from Bablyon were removed, and he was granted a "change of raiment", as his iniquity passed from him, enabling him to appreciate the Branch for the first time, Zech. 3. 1-5, 8.

The Lord could never pass that way, of course. His ordinary garments had been provided by the women who ministered unto Him; but on the mount of transfiguration "his raiment was white and glistering" as the light from His very Person burst through these garments, Luke 9. 29. But when He appeared before Pilate, in Mark 15 six times the title "King of the Jews" appears, vv. 2, 9, 12, 18, 26, 32, always in unbelief or mockery. To mimic kingship, the soldiers "clothed him with purple, and platted a crown of thorns", spitting on Him, bowing before Him, and worshipping, saluting Him with the words, "Hail, King of the Jews". Could anything be more blasphemous than this, since He really was the "King of kings" and will soon be manifested as such? The soldiers then put His own clothes on Him, Mark 15. 20, after which four soldiers divided these clothes amongst themselves, John 19. 23. But God will turn the tables upon men; John saw Him "clothed with a garment down to the foot", Rev. 1. 13, and later saw Him "clothed in a vesture dipped in blood" (of judgment), 19. 13.

What a contrast is presented by the prodigal son. He must have returned to his father dressed in rags — the result of his own desire to waste his substance with riotous living, Luke 15. 13. What love and mercy awaited him. "The best robe", a ring, and shoes were quickly given him, v. 22; the one who was dead and was then alive again caused this rejoicing over one sinner who repented. All sinners saved by grace pass that way; we are now clothed with garments of salvation, anticipating the time when, on high with the Lord, we shall have clothed ourselves with "fine linen, clean and white", to share in His triumph over all evil on earth, Rev. 19. 8, 14.

January 24th

READING: **Isaiah 2. 1-5**

JOURNEYS TO JERUSALEM

IN THE Old Testament, Isaiah had foretold that all nations would ultimately come to the Lord's house in Jerusalem — a place of divine blessing indeed. "Come ye, and let us go up to the mountain of the Lord, to the house of the God of Jacob . . . for out of Zion shall go forth the law, and the word of the Lord from Jerusalem", Isa. 2. 3. This was the place where God would seek to place His Name, and unto His habitation His people would come, Deut. 12. 5. But in New Testament times, this city had become a place of religious barrenness, with blessing often found on the outside. Three examples of this will help us to examine our own hearts before the Lord.

Ignorance of the Word of God. Wise men from the east, relying upon a divinely given star for guidance, came seeking the Lord Jesus as a Child, and as King of the Jews; see Matthew 2. 1-11. So they journeyed to Jerusalem, finding nothing except the priests, scribes and Herod the king. Quoting the Old Testament, the priests stated that it would be "In Bethlehem of Judaea" that the wise men would find the King, Mic. 5. 2. These leaders in Jerusalem did not believe the Word of God, but the wise men followed the prophetic word and the star outside to *Bethlehem*, and there they presented their gifts and worshipped the One born King of the Jews.

Ignorance of the Lord. Towards the end of His life, the Lord came to Jerusalem, riding on an ass and coming as King; the people did not know Him, asking, "Who is this?". The temple was full of ignorant religious leaders, and the priests were displeased at praise being offered to the Lord. So He departed from Jerusalem for *Bethany*, no doubt to the home of Mary, Martha and Lazarus, who loved Him, and knew His divine Person, Matt. 21. 1-7, 15, 17.

Ignorance of the Scriptures. In Acts 8. 26-39, a eunuch of authority came from Ethiopia to Jerusalem to worship. He must have left disillusioned; the temple ritual failed to deal with the problems of sin and salvation. But outside, in *Gaza*, Philip the evangelist met him, and showed the Lord Jesus as the One who died for sin, using Isaiah 53 as the basis.

For ourselves, to be outside man's religion is to be inside God's salvation, purpose and grace in Christ Jesus.

January 25th

READING: Revelation 4

THE THRONE

THE THRONE of God is the most awesome subject for a man to contemplate. The sovereign's throne in palace or parliament may seem distant, majestic, authoritative, and perhaps even irrelevant to ordinary people. But what of the universal and eternal throne of the Godhead, unseen, unheard and almost unknowable? Such an entity is revealed in a book of symbols, and even these convey a grandeur difficult to express in mere words. The subject is solemn, because the work of the throne manifests God's purpose and plan for men on earth.

In Revelation 3. 21, the Lord said, "even as I also overcame, and am set down with my Father in his throne". He sits at God's right hand, exalted because salvation for believers has been accomplished, and time is given to men to repent. This throne is a "throne of grace", Heb. 4. 16, where mercy and grace are given. It does not have that character for ever, but this is limited to the period of opportunity.

In Revelation 4, the throne in its character as prepared for judgment after the rapture is revealed. John saw a throne set in heaven, and "one sat on the throne", v. 2. Here is a throne prepared for judgment, a thing discounted by men who live as if the throne does not exist. The One who will exercise judgment upon the ungodly is the Lamb, seen in "the midst of the throne" in 5. 6. The Saviour is the Lamb of redemption to believers, but He is a Lamb of wrath for unbelievers, 6. 16. Concerning those who come out of the future great tribulation, we read, "the Lamb which is in the midst of the throne shall feed them, and shall lead them into living fountains of waters", 7. 17.

Then there is the millennial throne, for at that period there will be "a pure river of water of life, clear as crystal, proceeding out of the throne of God and of the Lamb", Rev. 22. 1. His servants will serve Him before the throne, v. 3. See Matthew 25. 31.

At the end, this throne becomes the "great white throne", Rev. 20. 11, from which the earth and the physical heavens will flee away, giving place to new heavens and a new earth.

Finally there is the eternal throne, with the One "that sat upon the throne" making all things new, 21. 5.

READING: Luke 2. 36-40

A MORE EXCELLENT WAY

IN THESE DAYS, it is to be regretted that some young believers are interested in, and engaged in, political matters in ways not healthy for their spiritual lives. Luke, in particular, draws attention to this matter, both in his Gospel and in the Acts. We may quote the following examples:

"*She . . . spake of him to all them that looked for redemption in Jerusalem*", Luke 2. 38. In her old age, through years of experience, she knew that the aspirations of the Jews were centred on redemption from the Roman yoke (as they had been redeemed out of Egypt). To them, the Romans were a cruel master. But the more excellent way was the Lord Jesus — a Babe recently born; so Anna spoke of Him.

"*When he was demanded of the Pharisees, when the kingdom of God should come*", Luke 17. 20. As leaders, the Pharisees objected to the presence of Roman leaders. To them, the kingdom of God meant a state in which they were the leaders. The Lord would not satisfy their political aspirations — the kingdom of God was moral, within their hearts, not with outward show.

"*They thought that the kingdom of God should immediately appear*", Luke 19. 11. The Lord was journeying up to Jerusalem, and the people sensed that something was afoot — their kingdom would be restored to them! The more excellent way was to know that the Lord was journeying to a far country, and men's responsibility was to be occupied until He come, v. 13, since His kingdom in glory was yet future.

"*We trusted that it had been he which should have redeemed Israel*", Luke 24. 21. The two on the Emmaus road were not ashamed to express their political aspirations to a "stranger in Jerusalem", as if the three days had something to do with it. They did not look for redemption from sin. The more excellent way was that their hearts were changed when the Lord opened their eyes so that they could know Him, vv. 31-32.

"*Lord, wilt thou at this time restore again the kingdom to Israel?*", Acts 1. 6. Having seen the Lord in resurrection many times, and having the promise of the Holy Spirit, their aspirations were still on the kingdom restored to Israel. This restoration rested in the Father's time and power, v. 7, with redemption granted when the Lord comes in glory, Luke 21. 28.

January 27th

READING: **Lamentations 2. 1-9**

THE LORD HATH CAST OFF HIS ALTAR

THE PATRIARCHS had their altars in Genesis, but God's instructions for the building of the permanent altar was given to Moses in Exodus 27. 1-8. It was constructed in 38. 1-7, and it was placed in position before the tabernacle in 40. 29. Its use degenerated over the years, when the priests kicked at the sacrifice and offering intended for God, 1 Sam. 2. 29. Shortly afterwards, the ark was removed from the tabernacle, and the altar remained before the forsaken tabernacle, Psa. 78. 60.

Later, Solomon built a larger altar, to stand before the temple in Jerusalem, 2 Chron. 4. 1; 1 Kings 8. 64. This altar remained throughout the period of the kings of Judah, until the Babylonians destroyed the temple and its contents, 2 Kings 25. 9-17. Even in Isaiah's day, the sacrifices offered on this altar ceased to mean anything to the Lord, Isa. 1. 11, so after the destruction of the temple, "The Lord hath cast off his altar, he hath abhorred his sanctuary", Lam. 2. 7. He had no interest in idolatry, pretence and hypocrisy.

After the return from Babylon, "the altar of the God of Israel" was rebuilt in sincerity, Ezra 3. 2-4. But when the Lord was here, the priestly ritual at the altar before Herod's temple had again degenerated, not to idolatry, but to the cold formality of unbelief characteristic of the lovers of ritual and ceremony. The Lord Jesus did not recognize this activity of the priests, and foretold the time when the temple would be destroyed, Matt. 24. 2, thereby putting an end in A.D.70 to Jewish ceremony at the altar. Once again, God had cast off the altar, this time so that there should be no Jewish rival to the Lord and His own sacrifice.

Since then, Christendom has erected its own altars in various guises, introducing over the centuries an idolatrous replacement of the sacrifice of Christ; effectively "they crucify to themselves the Son of God afresh", Heb. 6. 6. Believers may protest, but they have no power to eliminate present-day idolatry, which will remain until God casts the whole system off — not His altar, but the altars of men. For this is the blasphemy of Mystery Babylon the Great, with men "drunk with the wine of her fornication", Rev. 17. 1-6. Believers are separated from this, and can say, "We have an altar", Heb. 13. 10.

January 28th

READING: **Luke 1. 8-17**

"ACCORDING TO" IN LUKE'S GOSPEL

HAVE YOU noticed that the expression "according to" occurs eight times in Luke's Gospel — five times in chapter 2? These occurrences contain important lessons for the Lord's people, since the reasons for service or behaviour are spelt out.

(1) *Service.* Zacharias went into the temple "According to the custom of the priest's office", Luke 1. 9. He had to burn incense in the temple, not merely following traditional ritual, but because he was blameless in the Lord's commandments.

(2) *Submission.* Gabriel had promised Mary a son, who would be "the Son of God". This involved a miracle within her body, yet she submitted by saying, "Behold the handmaid of the Lord; be it unto me according to thy word", Luke 1. 38.

(3) *Sanctification.* After the Lord was born, His parents took Him into Jerusalem to the temple. The firstborn was "holy to the Lord", and Mary fulfilled "the days of her purification according to the law of Moses", Luke 2. 22; Lev. 12. 1-8.

(4) *Sacrifice.* Their obedience to the law on that occasion is stressed the second time; the sacrifice "A pair of turtledoves, or two young pigeons" was not their idea, but "according to that which is said in the law of Moses", Luke 2. 24.

(5) *Salvation.* During this visit to the temple, the old man Simeon knew by the Spirit that he would see "the Lord's Christ" before his death. He asked now to depart in peace, "according to thy word", having seen "thy salvation", Luke 2. 29.

(6) *Subjection.* During this visit to Jerusalem, the parents of the Lord displayed their knowledge of the law, and left nothing undone. They ultimately returned to Nazareth, having "performed all things according to the law of the Lord", Luke 2. 39. They knew why they were doing these things; it was the divine will revealed in the O.T. Scriptures.

(7) *Sabbath.* Other faithful men and women appeared in Luke's record after the Lord's crucifixion. Having placed the Lord's body in the sepulchre, they could do no more until the first day of the week. They "rested the sabbath day according to the commandment", Luke 23. 56.

(To conclude, we should point out that in Luke 12. 47 we find a different word. Here was disobedience not obedience; the servant did not do according to the lord's will.)

READING: **Psalm 69. 7-14**

SONG AND THE LORD'S DEATH

THE SUBJECT of song appears many times in the O.T., mainly in connection with the tabernacle and temple singers. In the N.T., the subject is not found many times, particularly in a physical sense. But when it appears in the context of the Lord's death, then evidently it assumes a greater importance.

Mostly, the service of song has a spiritual implication, but the reference in Psalm 69. 12 is exactly the opposite, "I was the song of the drunkards", or as others have translated it, "I was the song of the drinkers of strong drink". This is what the Lord observed when He hung upon the cross; wine was available for the soldiers, and some men may have been drunk, others may have been drinking such liquor, while others were behaving as if they had partaken of it, even if they had not actually done so. The Scriptures are full of the objectionable effects of wine, commencing with Noah's behaviour in Genesis 9. 20-21. They laughed, sang, mocked and made merry at the crucifixion of the Lord Jesus, and in this Psalm, the Lord was aware of this. Today likewise, drink removes inhibitions from men, and their mouths give rise to blasphemy against the Lord.

But there is a sweeter side to the subject of song. In resurrection, the Lord said, "I will praise the name of God with a song", Psa. 69. 30. The O.T. burnt offering shows up the perfection and acceptability of the Lord in His sacrifice, and in Hezekiah's time, "when the burnt offering began, the song of the Lord began also", 2 Chron. 29. 27.

In the N.T., when the Lord entered Jerusalem in order to die, the child temple-singers were saying, "Hosanna to the Son of David", Matt. 21. 15. The priests sought to stop this, but the Lord stated that the stones would cry out if such praise were to cease, Luke 19. 40. Nearer the time of His cross, we read that He and His disciples "sung an hymn" in the upper room, and went out to the mount of Olives, Matt. 26. 30.

Paul exhorted the Ephesians to draw a distinction between the song of those filled with wine, and those who spoke in "psalms and hymns and spiritual songs", Eph. 5. 18-19; this occurs in the context of Christ loving the church and giving Himself for it, vv. 2, 25. Finally, there is the new song to the Lamb; He is worthy as having been slain, Rev. 5. 9.

January 30th

READING: **John 14. 1-6, 26-30**

I WILL COME AGAIN

THE LORD had spoken before in more than one discourse of His coming again in power and glory: "they shall see the Son of man coming in the clouds of heaven with power and great glory", Matt 24. 30; "to receive for himself a kingdom, and to return", Luke 19. 12. This was in keeping with the prophecies already granted in the O.T. revelation. But in the upper room ministry, during the last night before He died, the Lord added something new, that would be a hope and a comfort to His disciples left behind after His return to the Father's presence.

"In my Father's house are many mansions . . . I go to prepare a place for you, I will come again, and receive you unto myself; that where I am, there ye may be also", John 14. 2-3. This is quite distinct from His coming in judgment to establish His kingdom; rather, the Lord promises that at His coming, believers will be introduced to the place where He is, into the Father's house on high. We call this "the rapture", and Paul through revelation describes it in greater detail in 1 Thessalonians 4. 13-18. By "mansions", or dwelling-places, no doubt the Lord is using typical language, referring to the various "chambers" built outside the walls of Solomon's temple for the use of the priests in their service, 1 Kings 6. 5. At His coming again, He will introduce us to a great variety of service in the Father's house on high throughout eternity.

The Lord refers to this again in verse 28, and this provokes love to the Lord since He has gone unto the Father.

But in verse 18, the Lord stated in His teaching, "I will not leave you comfortless (orphans): I will come to you". Here in the context He appears to be talking about His resurrection, for it relates to "the little while" when the world would see Him no more, but the disciples would see Him living again in resurrection. He amplifies this in John 16. 16, "a little while, and ye shall not see me: and again, a little while, and ye shall see me". Their weeping would refer to the period when His body would be in the tomb, v. 20, but their joy would refer to His resurrection. Thus He could say, "I will see you again", v. 22.

For us, His resurrection is a historical fact for faith, but we still have the future hope of His promised near return.

READING: **Hebrews 8**

THE OLD AND NEW COVENANTS

THE OLD COVENANT embraced both the law and ceremonial of tabernacle and temple. It originated through the commands of God to Moses, and ultimately became so formalized, that it was loved by priests, Levites and Pharisees, particularly when its precepts and ceremony were altered to suit the tastes of its adherents. Faith in Christ released men from its bondage, and it is sad to think that later some believers desired to return to the bondage of the first covenant. Galatians was written to correct those who wanted to return to the law; Hebrews was written to correct those who wanted to return to ceremony.

The difference between old and new is the same as the difference between works and grace. In those early days, it was difficult for men who had been brought up under a doctrine of works to change to the new doctrine of grace. It is the same in the present day; the doctrine of works is a basic tenet of Christendom, while the doctrine of grace is a basic tenet of evangelical believers. There were two parties to the old covenant — God who promised was on one side, and the people who had to obey His voice were on the other side; see Exodus 19. 5-8; 24. 3-8. But there was to be only one party to the new covenant — God Himself, Jer. 31. 31-34. This new covenant was made particularly with the houses of Israel and Judah, and it was "*not* according to the covenant that I made with their fathers". But when blessing comes from the work of God alone, how difficult it is for men to accept it!

The burden of the Epistle to the Hebrews is to show that the first covenant contained the seeds of its own dissolution. How can men be convinced that the Lord Jesus has a better ministry and is "the mediator of a better covenant"?, 8. 6. The writer shows that the first covenant was not faultless; the promise made in Jeremiah 31 shows where the fault lay — "because they continued not in my covenant", v. 9. In other words, sin was the fault. Hence why return to it? Again, the writer argues that the very existence of a new covenant is sufficient proof that the first covenant "which decayeth and waxeth old is ready to vanish away", v. 13. Hence why return to it? Thus abide in the blessings that derive from the new covenant, blessings that come through the blood of Christ, 9. 14-17.

February 1st

READING: **Mark 9. 14-29**

HELP THOU MINE UNBELIEF

The blindness of unbelief. The whole life of a man who lives in unbelief is a disaster. When preached to such men, the gospel message of the Lord Jesus "did not profit them, not being mixed with faith in them that heard it", Heb. 4. 2. God's standards are quite different from those of unbelievers. For example, "without faith it is impossible to please him", 11. 6; Paul called these "unreasonable and wicked men: for all men have not faith", 2 Thess. 3. 2; in all deeds and words, God's standard is "whatsoever is not of faith is sin", Rom. 14. 23.

And death is a disaster too. The Lord Jesus said, "he that believeth not is condemned already", John 3. 18, while John the Baptist added, "he that believeth not the Son shall not see life: but the wrath of God abideth on him", 3. 36. Again, the Lord said, "if ye believe not that I am he, ye shall die in your sins", 8. 24.

The beginning of faith. Faith in the Lord Jesus for salvation is not automatic; none is born with such faith. We are commanded to repent and to have faith, so it must have a beginning — and it is available for all. The man who desired the Lord to heal his child did not know whether he had faith or not! The Lord said to him, "If thou canst believe", and the man in desperation answered, "Lord I believe; help thou mine unbelief", Mark 9. 24. The child was healed, so the man had made a good start. On one occasion, the Lord said to Peter, "O thou of little faith, wherefore didst thou doubt?", Matt. 14. 31. No wonder the disciples asked, "Lord, increase our faith", Luke 17. 5. And the happy conclusion is the grand possibility held out to all, "your faith groweth exceedingly", 2 Thess. 1. 3.

The blessings of faith. All blessings come through the death and resurrection of the Lord Jesus. Ponder the following verses carefully: "whosoever believeth in him shall receive remission of sins", Acts 10. 43; "being justified by faith, we have peace with God", Rom. 5. 1; "whosoever believeth in him should not perish, but have eternal life", John 3. 16; "your work of faith", 1 Thess. 1. 3, showing that only those with faith can work for God; "that Christ may dwell in your hearts by faith", Eph. 3. 17. To gain this, "help thou mine unbelief".

READING: **Matthew 16. 13-23**

WHAT CHRISTIANS ARE AND ARE NOT

WE MUST admit that various Christian groups and denominations all appear to be different. The uncommitted man finds this very confusing, and when converted finds it difficult to decide the true church fellowship he should seek. These differences have arisen through men not adhering to the Bible, the only source-book of Christian doctrine. Tradition may sound authoritative, but should not be a guide. Old and modern heresies may stumble a young believer, but the Word of God enables the sincere seeker to steer clear of them. We can be thankful that there are still many devoted believers who find the Bible sufficient for their faith. We therefore give a few points to show what believers should stand for, and also those practices and doctrines that they should firmly reject.

The Person of Christ. Today, His historical Manhood is often denied; His Deity is rejected: His authority is questioned; and images supposedly in His likeness are idolatrously worshipped. But believers say with Peter, "Thou art the Christ, the Son of the living God", Matt. 16. 16, and with Thomas, "My Lord and my God", John 20. 28.

Salvation. Many reject the Lord Jesus as a Saviour, disregarding His cross, the value of His blood, and the truth of His resurrection. But believers say, "the blood of Jesus Christ his Son cleanseth us from all sin", 1 John 1. 7, and "the Son of God, who loved me, and gave himself for me", Gal. 2. 20.

The church and its service. Many think of the church as a denomination, or as an ornate building, with many strange ritualistic practices. But in Acts 2 the truth is that the church was formed when the Holy Spirit was sent to dwell in believers' hearts. The local churches formed by the apostle Paul are the only models for today. Consisting of believers only, each is a fellowship where men gifted as evangelists, teachers and elders can work for the development of the company, which continues "stedfastly in the apostles' doctrine and fellowship, and in breaking of bread, and in prayers", v. 42.

The future expectation. Most men fear death, and reject the promise of the Lord's coming, 2 Pet. 3. 3-4. But Christians believe in eternal life, and in the coming of the Lord", 1 Thess. 4. 13-18.

February 3rd

READING: **Hebrews 4. 14-16; 5. 1-6**

PRIESTS, OLD AND NEW

MEN EVERYWHERE think that they know what a priest is—he is recognized by his dress, career and service. Usually, however, they have no idea as to what the Scriptures have to say on the subject. The first named priest is remarkable, since he did not stem from Abraham, but was "king of Salem" and "priest of the most high God", Gen. 14. 18. Melchizedek was used to prefigure the priesthood of the Lord Jesus Christ, Psa. 110. 4; Heb. 5. 5-6. Later, priesthood in Israel was restricted to the sons of Aaron of the tribe of Levi; some were obedient to God's commands and others were disobedient.

However, the very existence of the promise of a priest after the order of Melchizedek in Psalm 110 showed that God intended to introduce such a priesthood in His own good time, thereby displacing the Levitical priesthood; this is the lengthy argument of Hebrews 7.

In the meantime, men gained control of the priesthood which would officiate in the temple in Jerusalem. The truth that "no man taketh this honour unto himself, but he that is called of God, as was Aaron", Heb. 5. 4, was entirely set on one side, and in the N.T. the Romans selected the Jewish high priests, quite independent of the mind of God. Thus Annas and Caiaphas were merely man-made high priests, in spite of their apparent great authority. The Lord Jesus did not recognize them (though one faithful priest stands out as an exception—Zacharias in Luke 1. 5, and strictly John the Baptist was a priest).

All the old system was swept aside by God, although men perpetuated it throughout the Acts, the high priests showing much opposition to the gospel. A form of priesthood (that is, involving status, career, service and ceremony) has been perpetuated throughout the centuries and throughout Christendom, so as to remain elevated over the so-called laity.

Of this, the Scriptures know nothing. Rather, "we have a great high priest, that is passed into the heavens", Heb. 4. 14; "We have such an high priest", 8. 1. Moreover, priesthood, far from belonging to the minority, is the portion of all believers, as Peter wrote, "ye also . . . are . . . an holy priesthood", 1 Pet. 2. 5, with the privilege to "offer up spiritual sacrifices". How different is the new from the old!

February 4th

READING: Acts 2. 22-36

RESURRECTION PROVED FROM THREE PSALMS

DURING THE LIFETIME of the Lord Jesus, the apostles displayed enormous ignorance of the O.T. Scriptures. As soon as the time was opportune, they had to learn the true meaning of these Scriptures. Thus He opened "their understanding, that they might understand the scriptures", Luke 24. 44-46. Peter was then a changed man, for in Acts 1 he was able to quote the O.T. in connection with the betrayal by Judas, verses 16 and 20 effectively referring to three Psalms, namely 41. 9; 69. 25; 109. 8. Surely believers today should likewise have their understanding richly formed by the Scriptures, being able to use them in the service of God. Moreover, when the Holy Spirit was given, Peter's knowledge of the Scriptures further expanded, since in Acts 2 he quoted from the Psalms three times to prove the resurrection of Christ to the Jews.

(1) *The Living One on the throne*, "thou wilt not leave my soul in hell (hades), neither wilt thou suffer thine Holy One to see corruption", Acts 2. 27; Psa. 16. 8-11. Paul also quoted this Psalm in Antioch, Acts 13. 35. David was not speaking of himself, since his body in death did see corruption; rather, he was a prophet, speaking of the miracle of the resurrection of Christ; the Psalm could refer to none other. Peter quoted this twice, in verses 27 and 31.

(2) *The King upon the throne*, "of the fruit of his loins, according to the flesh, he would raise up Christ to sit on his throne", Acts 2. 30; Psa. 132. 11. The Jews knew about the promised Messiah in the O.T.; the promise made to David in Psalm 132 was clear and definite. So if Messiah would enter into death, then the promise implied His resurrection so as to sit upon the throne. Hebrews 11. 19 uses a similar argument.

(3) *The Priest upon the throne*, "The Lord said unto my Lord, Sit thou on my right hand, until I make thy foes thy footstool", Acts 2. 34-35; Psa. 110. 1. Peter associated this with the Lord's ascension, and so resurrection was also implied. The Psalm leads on to the Melchizedek priesthood of the exalted Christ, ruling in the midst of His enemies.

Thus there was life on the throne, a right to the throne, and authority from the throne. No wonder when Peter concluded, the power of the Word brought about many conversions!

READING: **Psalm 90**

INDIFFERENCE, DESPAIR OR HOPE?

COMPARED WITH the lasting nature of the "everlasting hills" and of the sun and moon, our lives are short, described as "a vapour, that appeareth for a little time, and then vanisheth away". The Bible uses such pictures to show the brevity of life, which Moses describes as, "The days of our years are threescore years and ten; and if . . . they be fourscore years . . . it is soon cut off, and we fly away", Psa. 90. 10. After this brief life, the Lord taught that there will be for every man either a "resurrection of life" or a "resurrection of damnation". But how many, in the days of youth, health and prosperity, care for the future that seems so far away and almost irrelevant? To such men, the Lord says, "Thou fool, this night thy soul shall be required of thee", Luke 12. 20. Men consider the prospect of death and beyond from one of three points of view:

Indifference. The prosperous farmer was evidently only concerned with this present life. His outlook was described in his own words, "take thine ease, eat, drink, and be merry", Luke 12. 19. This was the attitude of those who, before the flood and in spite of warnings of disaster, "were eating and drinking, marrying and giving in marriage, and knew not until the flood came, and took them all away", Matt. 24. 38. But such indifference cannot put off the day of death, nor can it avoid the fact that God has appointed a day of judgment, Acts 17. 31.

Despair. On the other hand, many people adopt a hopeless attitude, knowing of the judgment day, and yet remain unable or unwilling to make provision for that day of fear and terror. A brave outward show may be displayed, but their inner soul senses deeply that they are on the losing side. "It is a fearful thing to fall into the hands of the living God", and "our God is a consuming fire", Heb. 10. 31; 12. 29.

Hope. Christian hope means absolute certainty of future blessing. Such hope by faith is like an anchor in heaven itself. Unbelievers are without hope, but believers already have the hope laid up in heaven, Col. 1. 5. Paul describes "Christ in you" as being the hope of glory, and that is why believers are so confident. Thus despair has gone, the future is bright and certain, and death has no fears, Heb. 2. 15.

February 6th

READING: **Matthew 6. 5-8; 7. 21-23**

THERE ARE TIMES WHEN ALL PRAY

Prayer that is no prayer. "There are times when all pray"; thus someone correctly described the anxious state of human hearts in moments of crisis during the last war. But during months and years with no crises in life, during peaceful times of family life and employment, most people today feel no need for prayer. Yet a crisis alters the state of mind of people, and in the face of the unknown they suddenly cry unto One higher then themselves. Sudden illness, bereavement, a family crisis, accidents, earthquakes, all bring to the heart of man his impotence when confronted with situations of fear, anxiety, pain, perplexity and death. Yet the sudden cry to God, rent from a heart that for years has lived without prayer as if God did not exist, is this cry really of any avail? Does the Eternal God, the Creator and Upholder of all things, the Reader of every thought and motive, have respect to a cry from a man who treats Him merely as an infrequent convenience? The Lord once told of men in a sudden crisis who cried, "Lord, Lord"; His response will be, "I never knew you; depart from me, ye that work iniquity", Matt. 7. 23. In other words, a prayer uttered to God who is normally depised and forgotten seldom can bring a positive response from Him who hears and knows all. Those who live in the coldness of unbelief should therefore take heed; crises arise unawares, and there may be no relief.

The prayer of a Christian, however, is heard immediately by the Lord, since He loves those whom He saved by dying for them on the cross. Their faith that accepts forgiveness of sins and eternal life is the same faith that approaches Him in prayer. Even one who is the weakest in faith is heard by the Lord in heaven, so we always have encouragement to pray at all times. "Pray without ceasing", exhorted the apostle Paul, 1 Thess. 5. 17, setting a good example himself by writing, "I do not cease to pray for you", Col. 1. 9. "Lord, save me" cried Peter, and he was saved, Matt. 14. 30. "Lord, help me" said the woman, and was immediately heard, 15. 25. The apostles prayed, "Lord, increase our faith", Luke 17. 5; Paul prayed "Lord, what wilt thou have me to do?", Acts 9. 6. May we be encouraged in prayer by these and many other examples.

READING: **1 Timothy 4. 6-16**

EXHORTATIONS TO YOUNG BELIEVERS

AS JOSHUA learnt from Moses throughout the forty years of wilderness wanderings, so Timothy learnt from Paul. They, with others, commenced when they were young, learning during the years of youth, in order to have a settled foundation for the later years of service. Not that Timothy was particularly young, both naturally and spiritually, when Paul wrote these exhortations to him; rather he wrote as a mature apostle to his son in the faith who could not possibly attain to apostolic maturity. (Twenty years had passed since Timothy's conversion.) We comment on a few aspects of Christian life and service for youth from these exhortations of Paul.

A good minister, 1 Tim. 4. 6. Paul had just described bad ministers, those who depart from the faith, and who issue strange commandments in their doctrine, vv. 1-4. There may also be neutral ministers, who fail to draw a distinction between bad and good doctrine. But God wants good ministers—strong ones who take a stand for the truth as expounded in the first three chapters; truth relating to behaviour in the local church, and concerning the Person of Christ, 3. 15-16.

What is profitable, 1 Tim. 4. 8. The usefulness of any deed or service must be assessed by the nature of its consequences as judged by the standard of God's Word. Living for the body only is of little profit, but living for Christ and as Christ lived is of value for the spiritual life, now and in the future. Thus godliness is profitable. Also, Paul wrote that "All scripture . . . is profitable for doctrine, for reproof, for correction, for instruction in righteousness", 2 Tim. 3. 16. Again, "good works . . . are profitable", but strivings about the law are unprofitable, Titus 3. 8-9.

An example, 1 Tim. 4. 12. A believer in his youth can be an example in many ways. Love, faith, purity, attendance to reading, exhortation and doctrine can be seen in young believers; also the employment of their gifts, and meditation upon the truth, so that all may see the profiting of faith. The fulltime occupation of a believer with the things of God is another manifestation of a good example; continuing in them shows sincerity witnessed by fellowbelievers, as does taking heed to oneself and to the doctrine professed and taught.

February 8th

READING: **Jeremiah 8. 13-22**

THE SUMMER IS ENDED; THE WINTER IS PAST

HOW TRUE it is that we always face the summer season with prospects of cheerfulness. Children anticipate it with the joy of holidays and visits away from home. Adults love it; the sun and weather are ideal, good things are available from garden and farm, while the long days present such a contrast to the cold and dark climate of winter. As Paul said, God "left not himself without witness, in that he did good, and gave us rain from heaven, and fruitful seasons, filling our hearts with food and gladness", Acts 14. 17. But the seasons change; after the flood, God promised, "seedtime and harvest, and cold and heat, and summer and winter, and day and night shall not cease", Gen. 8. 22. The summer is not permanent, neither its effects; as Jeremiah said, "The harvest is past, the summer is ended, and we are not saved", Jer. 8. 20.

The summer is ended. In that summer of which Jeremiah spoke, men had cried, "Peace, peace", but no peace came. There had been fruit, but afterwards, figs, grapes and leaves had disappeared; health had given way to trouble. Summer blessings gave place to winter barrenness because "we have sinned against the Lord"; see vv. 11-15. Today, the summer of the warmth of the love of God in Christ fails to attract men, because they refuse to confess their sins before Him. And when the opportunity is lost, they must confess, "we are not saved". The winter of eternal night, "the blackness of darkness for ever", Jude 13, awaits those who reject the Saviour.

The winter is past. It is remarkable that the O.T. also contains the opposite picture, "the winter is past", Song 2. 11. The barrenness of winter gives place to "the flowers appear on the earth; the time of the singing of birds is come; the fig tree putteth forth her green figs . . . Arise, my love, my fair one, and come away", vv. 12-13. The lesson is obvious. The Lord is calling those whom He loves unto Himself; if we listen to His voice by faith, we can follow Him who loved us even unto death. Morally, we are children of the day and not of the night or of darkness, 1 Thess. 5. 5. The winter night is past for believers, and the eternal summer of blessing cannot pass away. The fruit of the tree of life will always be there, but night shall exist no longer, Rev. 22. 2, 5.

February 9th

READING: **Galatians 1. 1-9**

THOSE OPPOSED TO THE LORD

THE MORE one knows the truth as it is in Christ Jesus, the more one can perceive those opposed to the Lord, and the ways in which this opposition is manifested. The apostle Paul could see these opponents, and he warned believers against them, their practices and doctrines. In particular, reference is made to them in all six chapters of the Galatian Epistle.

(1) In chapter 1, Paul warned of false evangelists; they perverted the gospel of Christ by preaching "another gospel" of a different kind, which could not possibly be "another" of the same kind, vv. 6-8. The apostle used strong language about such a man: "let him be accursed" (repeated twice).

(2) In chapter 2, Paul warned of "false brethren unawares brought in", v. 4. They wanted to spy out the differences that distinguished believers from Jewish religionists, in order to bring the believers back to the Jewish fold. Paul would have nothing to do with such men, "no, not for one hour", v. 5.

(3) In chapter 3, there were those who had "bewitched" the Galatians into thinking they could now be "made perfect by the flesh" instead of by the Spirit, vv. 1-3. This word "bewitched" means to be deluded by a spell. The reality of the Spirit is a fundamental Christian doctrine which is rejected by such men.

(4) In chapter 4, there were those who wanted to be "sheep stealers" from the local church. The R.V. of verse 17 reads more clearly, "They zealously seek you in no good way; nay, they desire to shut you out, that ye may seek them", that is, to turn the Galatians' minds after them and not after Christ.

(5) In chapter 5, men with false doctrine inevitably fall into a life lived after the flesh. Those "which trouble you", v. 12, were, in effect, introducing the works of the flesh, described in detail in verses 19-21. But the fruit of the Spirit stands in complete contrast; only that will satisfy God.

(6) In chapter 6, Paul warns of the Jewish legalizers, who wanted "to make a fair show in the flesh", v. 12. In other words, the rite of circumcision can lead only to the works of the flesh, and an abandonment of "the cross of Christ".

Paul knew where he stood—he would boast only in the cross, 6. 14, teaching only the gospel received from Christ, 1. 12, and refusing to build again his old Jewish practices, 2. 18.

40

READING: **1 Peter 2. 1-10**

ATTITUDES TO THE LOCAL CHURCH

TO THIS SUBJECT, men may be indifferent, living as if such a strange concept were completely irrelevant. They may accept tradition, that moulds attitudes according to the historical basis of the denomination in which they were brought up, perhaps with a superior smile at the divisions seen in present-day Christendom. Yet Christians believe that the Bible presents the church according to the purpose of God, that its pattern and service as given in the N.T. can be followed today in just the same way as when it was introduced in the apostolic age. Deviations have arisen over the centuries that give rise to the structure of Christendom today.

But happy are believers in the Lord Jesus who do not deviate from the truth, knowing that God desires and expects His people to meet together as local churches according to the pattern given in the N.T. Unfortunately the minds of men are so often blinded by bias, tradition and ignorance, with no attempt being made to search out the truth in the N.T. But its honest reading shows that God's plans are quite opposed to what is commonly found in the churches of Christendom today.

In God's local church, there are *no unbelievers*; all members are saved from their sins by the death of the Lord Jesus on the cross. Yet in men's churches, many reject the evangelical doctrine of salvation through divine grace.

God's local church is *not a material building*, although men's churches are usually equated to buildings in everyday language. A local church consists of baptized believers, named living stones, and "built up a spiritual house", 1 Pet. 2. 4-5.

In God's local church, there is *no ecclesiastical hierarchy*, that is so obvious in men's churches. Rather, God equips believers as "evangelists, pastors and teachers", Eph. 4. 11, and service is carried on by such gifted men.

In God's church, only the *holy doctrine* of the Bible is preached; unfortunately, in men's churches much of the Holy Scriptures is denied, miracles are rejected, the Deity of Christ is refused, while critical ideas replace the truth.

In God's church, *ritual is absent*. Worship is extempore in spirit from the heart. But in men's churches, ritual often reigns, repetition and formality pushing out spirituality.

February 11th

READING: Luke 23. 31-47

DIVINE NAMES USED AT THE CRUCIFIXION

IT IS always important to note the divine names used by Divine Persons, by believers and unbelievers. In the passage before us, a variety of names is used, showing the state and attitude of hearts of those using them.

"Jesus", v. 34, the name used by the Gospel writers in purely historical contexts. It was not a name used to the Lord face to face, except on very few occasions, Luke 18. 38.

"Father", said the Lord Jesus as the Roman soldiers nailed Him to the cross, v. 34. The relationship from the past eternity, during His lifetime, during His prayer in John 17, was still seen in His prayer for the soldiers.

"Christ, the chosen of God", v. 35. The Jewish leaders used this name as a contribution to their mockery and derision. In Psalms 2. 2; 132. 17, He is seen as the Lord's anointed, the promised Messiah. These leaders would not believe that this One now being crucified was this promised Messiah.

"The King of the Jews", v. 38, wrote Pilate in mockery, knowing that the Jews rejected this title, and that such a King would be contrary to the authority of Caesar in Rome.

"Christ" was used by one malefactor, v. 39, evidently copying the title used by the leaders in verse 35. If they used it in mockery, so would this malefactor, since copying of this nature was infectious in evil hearts.

"Lord" (though some Greek texts omit this title), v. 42. In some places it is translated as "Sir" where there is no spiritual recognition. But this second malefactor evidently recognized His authority, learning of His kingdom and Kingship from Pilate's inscription—what was mockery led to faith.

"Father", said the Lord at the end of the hours of darkness, v. 46. Here was the communion of the Son with the Father, when the sinbearing was complete, during which period of judgment He had used the name "God", Matt. 27. 46, and not "Father". Clearly the difference is very important.

"A righteous man", said the centurion, v. 47. It is remarkable that he should glorify God by making such a remark, yet he was constrained to confess this because of the great difference displayed by the Lord during His crucifixion. In Matthew 27. 54, the title was "the Son of God".

READING: **1 Kings 19. 1-18**

FORTY DAYS

HERE WAS Elijah, fleeing from Jezebel in a state of fear, desiring before God that he might die. There is an immediate contrast with the church at Thyatira, where the church allowed Jezebel a prophetess to work unhindered in their midst; she and her children would die, Rev. 2. 20, 23.

There are several periods of forty days in Scripture, and we can note several features of comparison and contrast:

The experience of Moses, Exod. 34. 28. God's servant had ascended Sinai the second time, to receive again the tables of stone. He was alone on the mountain top with God. Previously there was only one tribe, that of Levi, who took its stand with Moses, 32. 26, but now he was alone. Being with God, he was privileged to see His glory and to hear His voice speaking to him. Moreover, God provided the manna as food both before and after this ascent of Sinai, though he ate nothing during the forty days. This manna was "angels' food", Psa. 78. 25.

The experience of Elijah, 1 Kings 19. 5-8. God's servant had sat down in the wilderness as he fled from Jezebel. He was alone with God in the wilderness, but God informed him that He had 7,000 men who had not bowed the knee to Baal, v. 18. Being in the presence of God, he was privileged to hear His still small voice speaking to him, v. 12. Moreover, God provided food for His servant twice at the beginning of the forty days, an angel of the Lord being used to minister to him. In the strength of that food, Elijah was sustained through the days.

The experience of the Lord, Matt. 4. 2, 11. God's Servant had gone into the wilderness to be tempted of the devil. The Spirit was with Him, but Mark 1. 13 mentions also Satan and the wild beasts. As to His perfection before Satan, the Lord was absolutely unique. He used the spoken Word of God from the O.T., and this Word sounded out clearly in the wilderness through the divine lips of the Son. Moreover, God provided food for His perfect Servant only at the end of the forty days, when "angels came and ministered unto him", Matt. 4. 11; He certainly would not provide food for Himself by turning stones into bread.

We suggest that the reader notices all the similarities in these three events, from which spiritual lessons can be drawn.

February 13th

READING: **1 Samuel 3. 1-10**

NO OPEN VISION

SINCE THE TABERNACLE had been erected, there had been an "open vision", Exod. 40. 34-35. The glory of God had its abode between the cherubim above the mercy seat; sometimes it was seen openly in divine pleasure or in judgment, Lev. 9. 23; Num. 14. 10, and certainly the pillar of cloud or of fire could be seen above the tabernacle during the wilderness wanderings. But by Samuel's time, all this had ceased. Eli was not the correct high priest, while his sons committed evil before the tabernacle door. Certainly, Samuel grew in maturity; in 1 Sam. 2. 18, he ministered "before the Lord", and in 3. 1, he ministered "unto the Lord". But there was "no open vision"; the glory of the Lord was seen by none, and His direct voice was absent also. The few faithful ones had to be content with "the word of the Lord" which "was precious in those days", v. 1. The "word of the Lord" would embrace both the written word as available from Moses' time, and also the words of God through the prophet, 2. 27. Well may men of faith have said with the psalmist Asaph, "thou that dwellest between the cherubim, shine forth", Psa. 80. 1, with the face of the Lord shining upon His people, vv. 3, 7, 19. At least, God spoke openly to Samuel that night, 1 Sam. 3. 4, 6, 8, 10.

A similar, though distinct situation exists in the N.T. The apostles had beheld the Lord's glory on many occasions, openly, morally, and in miraculous power, Matt. 17. 2; John 1. 14; 2. 11; 11. 40. But after His resurrection and ascension He knew that His disciples would see Him no more; there would be "no open vision". Rather, the word of God was precious, and this is what was preached openly in powerful testimony; the O.T. Scriptures were also precious as believers used them so often in their preaching and testimony.

At the end of his life, Peter drew attention to the fact that he had been an eyewitness "of his majesty . . . from the excellent glory . . . in the holy mount", 2 Pet. 1. 16-18. The apostle could never forget this transfiguration of the Lord, but his converts had never witnessed that event. For them, there was no open vision. But "the more sure word of prophecy" was always available, v. 19. This is the light that shines now until the day dawn, and His glory is seen again.

February 14th

READING: **Acts 10. 33-48**

A GOSPEL MEETING

ANOTHER NAME for this meeting is an Evangelistic Meeting; both words mean "good news", preached by an evangelist (that is, a man who preaches the good news of salvation) seeking to evangelize his hearers who are not Christians. In daily life, we distinguish between good news and bad news, applying the word to most topics in life. But in the Bible, the word "gospel" has no such common meaning. Rather it refers to the good news that men can be converted through faith in Christ, that they can be turned from darkness to light, from Satan to God, Acts 26. 18, from death to life, from sinfulness to holiness, from hell to heaven, from selfishness to Christ-likeness, from worldliness to spirituality, from rejecting the Bible to accepting it by faith, from desiring to crucify Christ to accepting Him as the One "who loved me, and gave himself for me", Gal. 2. 20, from having eternal death and judgment as the ultimate destiny to having eternal life as the hope before the heart. What great differences! No wonder it is good news to those who desire relief from a life of living in sin, hopelessness and darkness.

Each Lord's Day evening, we have a meeting where this gospel is preached. In Acts 10, we read of the first Gospel Meeting at which Gentiles from Rome were present. The preacher was Peter, who "found many that were come together", v. 27. The speaker was introduced by Cornelius, and Peter started to preach straight away! He spoke of "peace by Jesus Christ", of His death and resurrection, and that "whosoever believeth in him shall receive remission of sins", v. 43. Then a miracle of grace occurred. All the unconverted Gentiles believed in the Lord, and were converted and baptized. Today, even one soul saved in a Gospel Meeting is well worth while.

Not all such meetings need to be as well attended as this one in Caesarea. In Ephesus, there was a meeting with only three present, the preacher, his wife and a man named Apollos who needed conversion. "The way of God more perfectly" was preached, Acts 18. 26, and Apollos was saved, becoming a great preacher of the truth himself. One's whole life can be changed through a Gospel Meeting, conversion leading to diligent service in the Lord's Name.

February 15th

READING: **Hosea 10. 1-15**

COVER US—FALL ON US

PEOPLE APPEAR to do ridiculous things at times, in particular, speaking to inanimate matter. Thus idolaters may speak to the sun in worship, Ezek. 8. 16; they may speak to Baal on Carmel, 1 Kings 18. 26. Of course, people still speak to material things today, but sensibly, into telephones and microphones. Enlightenment avoids the impossible, except in children's toys. But extreme despair in people who are even the most refined leads them to do what seems ridiculous. These will be kings, great men, the rich, chief captains, mighty men, freemen, and so on, Rev. 6. 15. Man is a creature designed to live on the earth's surface. Some explore caves for fun, but always expect a way out. It is a tragedy when a party is cut off, when there is loss of life in a mine accident, or when men are buried in an avalanche or rock fall. But there are times when men will think that it is an advantage to be buried alive under a mountain!

(1) Hosea 10 refers to the state of the inhabitants of the northern kingdom of Israel. Judgment had been prophesied, and the invasion and destruction would be so terrible with no human methods of escape, that men would "say to the mountains, Cover us; and to the hills, Fall on us", v. 8. This was impossible; none could escape from the judgments of God.

(2) In Luke 23. 27-31 we read the last words of the Lord Jesus before He was crucified. He would not have the faithful women weep for Himself, rather, for themselves and their children. If the "green tree" was crucified, what would happen to the "dry" tree—the Jews? This was a reference to the Roman destruction of Jerusalem in A.D.70, when again, men in their extremity would "begin to say to the mountains, Fall on us; and to the hills, Cover us", v. 30.

(3) In Revelation 6. 12-17, the sixth seal is opened, when there will be a great earthquake, with "every mountain and island moved out of their places". Men of every status will be terrified, seeking refuge in the dens and rocks of the mountains, saying "to the mountains and rocks, Fall on us, and hide us from the face of him that sitteth on the throne", v. 16. In the end times after the rapture men will know that there is no escape from "the wrath of the Lamb".

READING: **Exodus 33. 7-17**

NO VAIL

IN THE O.T. and N.T., there were physical structures designed for the service of God. Consider the following:

Moses' first tabernacle, Exod. 33. 7. This was a temporary one, intended, we believe, to receive the temporary ark with the tables of stone, Deut. 10. 1-5. But there was no vail; Moses and Joshua had free access into God's presence.

Moses' second tabernacle, Exod. 26. 31-33. Here was a vail, separating the holy place from the Holiest of all. It was a figure, showing that the way into the Holiest was not available for men, except for the high priest once a year, Heb. 10. 8-9.

David's tabernacle, 1 Chron. 16. 1. Here was the third tabernacle, made by David on mount Zion to receive the ark; in the record, it contained no vail. This tabernacle was essentially for the service of song, not for sacrifice, v. 4.

Solomon's temple, 2 Chron. 3. 14. This was a permanent structure built on mount Moriah. It had a vail, implying that there was no way of access into God's presence of glory.

Zerubbabel's temple, Ezra 3. 8; 4. 15. This house was built after the return from the captivity. and many difficulties were overcome. We presume that it contained a vail, since it was more or less a copy of Solomon's temple.

Herod's temple, John 2. 20; Matt. 27. 51. This was Herod's masterpiece, a gift to the Jews. Its service was but a cold sham, and the vail contained no ark. Its rending when the Lord died showed that the so-called holiest of all contained no ark, and that its service was not recognized by God.

The Lord's body, John 2. 21. This was the true divine Temple, for the Son tabernacled in this body of flesh. The remarkable thing is that His body is also called "the veil", Heb. 10. 20, as a new and living way that presents no barrier now to an approach to God by believers.

Believers now, a spiritual house, 1 Pet. 2. 5. What is merely physical is now defunct, and God recognizes only the spiritual house composed of true believers. There is no spiritual vail, since believers are not divided, and they form a living unity with the Lord Jesus in their hearts and midst.

The temple in heaven, Rev. 11. 19. This was open to John; he saw "the ark", with no vail as a barrier to his gaze.

February 17th

READING: **Luke 9. 27-36**

GLORY ON THE MOUNT

ON THE MOUNT of transfiguration, there was a display of glory, when the Lord was seen as coming in His kingdom.

Peter, who was present, later described the environment on high as "the excellent glory", 2 Pet. 1. 17. Matthew, Mark and Luke all describe this as a cloud that overshadowed them, out of which the voice from heaven said, "This is my beloved Son: hear him".

All attention fell upon the glory of the Lord Jesus; as Luke wrote of the apostles, "they saw his glory", 9. 32. He is described by Matthew, "his face did shine as the sun, and his raiment was white as the light", Matt. 17. 2. Mark 9. 3 adds, "exceeding white as snow", while Luke 9. 29 states, "the fashion of his countenance was altered, and his raiment was white and glistering". This was not artificial, as some would suggest, the sun shining on the snow and casting a white light upon Him. Rather, here was the intrinsic glory of His Person shining through His body and raiment. Truly, He shall come "in the clouds of heaven with great power and glory", Matt. 24. 30.

Moreover, Moses and Elijah also "appeared in glory", Luke 9. 31, their glory being only derived. They were not strangers to glory, as witnessed in the O.T.

The skin of Moses' face shone as God talked with him in the first tabernacle, and when he emerged to talk to the people, Exod. 34. 29-35. He covered his face with a vail, since the people were afraid, and since the fact that this glory was fading was to be hidden from them, 2 Cor. 3. 7, 13.

Elijah was a stranger to open glory during his lifetime on earth, but at the end (for he did not die) "there appeared a chariot of fire, and horses of fire", and Elijah was taken in this glory into heaven in a whirlwind, 2 Kings 2. 11.

What about Peter, James and John on the mount? There is no record that glory was manifested in them, and no wonder, for they fell asleep, and Peter's words were very unwise. James died before writing anything, but John wrote in his old age, "we beheld his glory", John 1. 14, while Peter wrote of being an eyewitness "of his majesty", 2 Pet. 1. 16. They both had the promise from the Son, "the glory which thou gavest me I have given them . . . that they may behold my glory", John 17. 22-24.

48

READING: 1 Corinthians 11. 17-34

LIGHT WITHIN, DARKNESS WITHOUT

PHYSICALLY THERE were "many lights in the upper chamber" in Troas, where the church was gathered together on the first day of the week, the apostle Paul being present prior to his departure. The church was gathered for the breaking of bread, and Paul used the occasion to preach until midnight. There was spiritual light too; this is shown by the objectives of the local assembly, by their zeal to remain for so long, and by the presence of Paul who would not have allowed anything unspiritual to take place. But everything else in Troas was in darkness—spiritual darkness in the hearts of the unsaved.

The same can be said for the upper room where the Lord Jesus and the apostles met during the evening before He was crucified. There, He instituted the breaking of bread and the drinking of the cup, Matt. 26. 26-28; there the Lord engaged in a long discourse prior to His decease the following day, John 13. 31 to 14. 31, after which they left the upper room on the way to Gethsesame. The light of the sanctuary was there, since the Lord Jesus as the Light was present, and all were engaged in spiritual activity. But it was necessary for Judas, who had just been identified by the Lord, to depart; he "went immediately out: and it was night", John 13. 30. In other words, the physical darkness without reflected on the nature of the hearts of men. For the leaders were ready for Judas to betray the Lord into their hands, and they knew that their object was the crucifixion of the Man Christ Jesus.

Would that we could see the same sharp difference in the assembly at Corinth. Certainly, there was darkness morally outside their gatherings, for the unsaved were "fornicators, idolaters . . . thieves, covetous, drunkards, revilers, extortioners", 1 Cor. 6. 9-10, and the believers had been like that before their conversion. But was there light in their gathering for the Lord's Supper? Alas, Paul had to write that "this is not to eat the Lord's supper", 11. 20. Rather, they were using the occasion to eat and drink to excess; some indeed were drunken, v. 21. Not discerning the Lord's body, some were being chastened by the Lord, and some were weak and sickly. How tragic that such an holy act demanding spiritual light within, should have degenerated to darkness within!

February 19th

READING: **Isaiah 55**

GOD'S THOUGHTS OR MEN'S THOUGHTS

THE DIFFERENCES in verses 8-9 are vital, "my thoughts are not your thoughts, neither are your ways my ways . . . as the heavens are higher than the earth, so are my ways higher than your ways, and my thoughts than your thoughts". In those days, man did not know of the astronomical distances extending out to the recesses of space, but God, the Creator of all things, knew far better than man does today. Hence the difference morally between God and created men is something beyond the understanding of men. We may consider various aspects of this.

Types. When God introduced the ceremonial types through Moses, He knew that they pointed to the Lord Jesus. But men in their lack of understanding, degenerated to the level of stealing the offerings, and cooking them according to their own taste, 1 Sam. 2. 12-17. Additionally, they also sunk to the level of offering only the worst animals, Mal. 1. 8.

The Person of Christ. When the true Antitype had come, the understanding of men was that of complete ignorance. They thought that He was John the Baptist, Elijah, Jeremiah, or one of the prophets, Matt. 16. 14. God's thoughts knew the eternal truth concerning His Son, "This is my beloved Son, in whom I am well pleased", 17. 5.

The Gospel. There will always be men who arise to take a contrary stand to any truth. Human understanding of the truth of pure grace rapidly sunk to the level of presenting "another gospel", Gal. 1. 6-8, which was one of legality and Jewish bondage. God knew the infinite truth of the value of the blood shed, so any false teacher was described as "accursed".

The Church. As Jeroboam copied the true ceremony carried on in Jerusalem, 1 Kings 12. 26-33, his thoughts being to prevent men from returning to God's centre, so the N.T. truth of the church has been falsely copied, so as to keep men in the grip of false thoughts. But God's thoughts are clearly shown in the N.T. for all believers to grasp and follow.

Prophecy. The near return of the Lord Jesus is clearly stated by the Spirit of inspiration. God's thoughts are that His Son should come for His own. But men have invented many strange doctrines, and confused many issues, so as to keep hopes set on earthly things instead of on heavenly things.

READING: 1 Thessalonians 5

PEACE AND SAFETY

PEACE IS a subject dear to most people, except perhaps those whose careers and promotion depend upon showing expertise in war. Men strive for peace—governments at international level, individuals at personal and family level. We are glad when peace reigns for many years, though the history of the nations has been essentially a history of warfare. It is easy to bring God into the matter. Pious religious people may consider it a proper subject for prayer, that "on earth peace, and good will toward men" should be the ultimate objective of permanent international relationships, Luke 2. 14.

But the Bible teaches something quite different. The Lord Jesus is often brought into pious statements about peace, but what did He really teach? On family relationships, He said, "Suppose ye that I am come to give peace on earth? I tell you, Nay; but rather division", Luke 12. 51. Again, "I came not to send peace, but a sword", Matt. 10. 34. These verses do not seem to suggest that the Lord was a pacifist, but then, He knew the hearts of men, and the only way for peace to be attained.

According to Paul, unbelievers will cry, "Peace and safety", 1 Thess. 5. 3, adding, "then sudden destruction cometh upon them . . . and they shall not escape". Hence a true Christian will never cry, "Peace and safety". In the O.T., we read, "There is no peace . . . unto the wicked", Isa. 48. 22, so there is no point in unbelievers trying to find it. False teachers said, "Peace, peace", but God added, "when there is no peace", Jer. 6. 14. Again, God said, "Destruction cometh; and they shall seek peace, and there shall be none", Ezek. 7. 25.

All this reflects upon our own time, with men thinking that they can soon beat swords into plowshares, and spears into pruninghooks, Isa. 2. 4. But for the present, the Lord asserts, "ye shall hear of wars and rumours of wars . . . nation shall rise against nation", Matt. 24. 7.

Now, peace is only for the Christian, "my peace I give unto you", John 14. 27; we have "peace through the blood of his cross", Col. 1. 20. *In the future*, God will introduce peace by removing from the world the root cause of enmity, namely evil men, with Satan bound for 1,000 years, Rev. 20. 1-3. Only then will peace exist throughout the world.

February 21st

READING: **Romans 1. 1-17**

CALLED TO BE SAINTS

TO PEOPLE in the world, titles such as Saint Peter, Saint John, Saint Andrew, are very familiar, ascribed to many church buildings and days in the so-called church calendar. Yet it is a fact that there is no verse in the Bible where any man is given the title "saint". We read of "son Timothy" and "brother Paul", but never "saint Peter" and so on. Clearly something has been added to the Bible, since the word "saint" occurs dozens of times. A dictionary gives the following meaning: "a holy person: one eminent for virtue: an Israelite, a Christian, or one of the blessed dead: one canonised: an angel: a member of various religious bodies: a sanctimonious person". But whatever does all this mean?

In the N.T., all Christians are called saints, not as a title, but as a name that characterizes all believers. Today, therefore, all Christians are saints. The usual word means "separated from the world", "not of this world". In N.T. days, when a person became a Christian, it was God Himself who made that person a saint. The world was full of sin, rebellion and unbelief; consequently, as soon as a person became a Christian, God marked him out as different—separated from the activity and aspirations of the world around: He made them saints.

It should be the same today. When a person is converted to Christ, he is different because of what God has done in him. The open sin, darkness, iniquity, rebellion, unbelief in the world is for him a thing of the past. He is separated from it; he is a saint. But not all Christians live as saints. They forget, if ever they knew, that God has separated them as saints, and are content to be contaminated with the pursuits of the world.

Many times Paul addresses his readers as "saints": "beloved of God, called saints", Rom. 1. 7; "called to be saints", 1 Cor. 1. 2; "to the saints at Ephesus", Eph. 1. 1; "to all the saints in Christ Jesus", Phil. 1. 1. Clearly this was a description of endearment to Paul, as he could see what God had done in and for these Christians. He also loved to refer to believers as saints: "I go to minister to the saints", Rom. 15. 25; "all the saints salute you", 2 Cor. 13. 13; "your love to all the saints", Eph. 1. 15. As saints through faith in Christ Jesus, may we enter into the spirit of this truth.

February 22nd

READING: **Psalm 2**

DIVINE TITLES—CHRIST, SON, KING

THIS PSALM is a prophetic psalm, speaking both of the Lord's rejection at His crucifixion and also of His coming triumph at His future kingdom in display. But the three titles "anointed", v. 2, "king", v. 6, and "Son", v. 7, also imply a divine possession, seen by the words "his" and "my". These three titles are also found in other connections.

(i) *Their occurrence in questions.*

"Art thou the Christ? tell us", asked the elders, chief priests and the scribes, Luke 22. 67; Matt. 26. 63.

"Art thou then the Son of God?", the same men asked Him, including Caiaphas the chief priest, Luke 22. 70; Matt. 26. 63.

"Art thou the King of the Jews", asked Pilate as the Lord stood before the governor, Matt. 27. 11; Luke 23. 3; John 18. 33.

(ii) *Their occurrence in suppositions.*

"If he be Christ, the chosen of God", said the rulers and one malefactor, Luke 23. 35, 39.

"If thou be the Son of God, come down from the cross", said the passers-by in mockery, Matt. 27. 40.

"If thou be the king of the Jews, save thyself", said the Roman soldiers, Luke 23. 37.

(iii) *Their occurrence in true confession.*

"Thou art the Christ", said Peter on at least two occasions, Matt. 16. 16; Luke 9. 20; John 6. 69.

"Of a truth thou art the Son of God", said the apostles in worship, Matt. 14. 33; 16. 16.

"Thou art the King of Israel", said Nathanael when the Lord first found him, John 1. 49.

(iv) *Their occurrence as a divine testimony.*

"I have ordained a lamp for mine anointed", said the Lord to Solomon, Psa. 132. 17, in response to the desire in verse 10, "turn not away the face of thine anointed". Literally, "mine anointed" means "my Christ".

"Thou art my Son", said the Lord in Psalm 2. 7, repeated in the N.T. at the Lord's baptism and on the mount of transfiguration, Matt. 3. 17; 17. 5.

"Yet have I set my king upon my holy hill of Zion", said the Lord in Psalm 2. 6.

Our faith can take up these three divine titles as well.

February 23rd

READING: **2 Thessalonians 1**

JUDGMENT TO COME

PEOPLE DO not like the word "judgment" in the Bible. If the law of the land is broken, various penalties are laid down when a defendant is proved guilty. On the other hand, many men think that a God of love cannot also be a God of judgment; the former is accepted but the latter rejected.

The author has not counted up the references, but he would assess that there may be more references to judgment and eternal punishment in the Bible than there are to God's love and salvation in Christ Jesus. For example, men in Noah's day perished by means of the flood; the Egyptians were judged at the Red Sea when they tried to pursue the escaping Israelites; priests were judged unto death for offering false incense, Lev. 10. 1-2; Korah died when he and other rebels went down "quick into the pit", Num. 16. 28-35.

It is no different in the N.T., even though the Lord Jesus came to die on the cross to remove the necessity of God's judgment upon those that believe. John the Baptist stated, "the axe is laid unto the root of the tree . . . and cast into the fire . . . he will burn up the chaff with unquenchable fire", Matt. 3, 10-12. In His parables, the Lord spoke of those that do iniquity being cast into a furnace of fire, Matt. 13. 43. He said, "cast ye the unprofitable servant into outer darkness", 25. 30. He told of the rich man being in hades, in torments in a flame, Luke 16. 23. In contrast to divine love, He said, "he that believeth not is condemned already", John 3. 18.

Paul wrote words of terror, "the Lord Jesus shall be revealed from heaven . . . in flaming fire taking vengeance on them that know not God, and that obey not the gospel . . . who shall be punished with everlasting destruction from the presence of the Lord", 2 Thess. 1. 7-9. The apostle who knew most of the love of God saw this terrible end of judgment, "I saw a great white throne . . . I saw the dead, small and great, stand before God . . . they were judged every man . . . (and) cast into the lake of fire", Rev. 20. 11-15.

How important to flee from this wrath to come, to know by faith that the Lord "delivered us from the wrath to come", 1 Thess. 1. 10, and from the blackness of darkness for ever.

54

READING: **John 19. 23-37**

THE WOMEN AT THE CROSS

THE CROSS of the Lord was a great attraction at the time for many onlookers, such as the priests, Pharisees, Pilate, the people and the Roman soldiers with their centurion. Today, the cross presents no attraction at all for unbelievers. But the apostle John and many women were watching the tragedy in quite a different state of heart and mind.

Luke 8. 2-3 gives us an ongoing background to the period of the Lord's ministry. There were women who had been healed by His power; their names with "many others" are given as Mary Magdalene, Joanna and Susanna. They "ministered unto him of their substance". In other words, they provided for the Lord's needs from their own funds, something perhaps that the apostles could not have done so easily, being men, although Judas kept the bag for the few funds that they possessed. Some of these women must have come from Galilee, accompaning the Lord to Jerusalem on His visits, and on His final visit. For Matthew 27. 56 names "Mary Magdalene, and Mary the mother of James and Joses, and the mother of Zebedee's children" as having "followed Jesus from Galilee, ministering unto him"; Mark 15. 41 explains that they ministered unto Him in Galilee, and that many other women came up to Jerusalem with Him.

When the Lord died, these women "were there beholding afar off", Matt. 27. 55; Mark 15. 40. In other words, their hearts were struck with pain, concern and reverence—unable to come nearer to the dying One whom they loved, and for whom they had sacrificed their private lives and their substance.

Luke 23. 27 informs us that "a great company of women" were weeping for Him; the Lord knew their future sorrows, and told them to weep for themselves and for their children on account of the judgment soon to fall upon Jerusalem. These women were amongst those who "smote their breasts, and returned", but those from Galilee "stood afar off, beholding these things".

In John 19. 25, the apostle mentions those who stood by the cross (evidently nearer than at the end when they stood afar off): the mother of Jesus, His mother's sister, Mary the wife of Cleophas, and Mary Magdalene. The Lord's few words caused John to lead the Lord's mother away from the scene, we suspect to the upper room, where they all gathered later, Acts 1. 14.

READING: **Matthew 13. 38-43**

ALONE WITH HIM

AS THOSE who are in the world, sharing in its rush, being fully occupied in daily work and in the Lord's service, it is very difficult to be alone with the Lord. This was so in Luke 9. 1-6; the disciples were rightly occupied in the world, preaching the gospel. Yet afterwards, the Lord "took them, and went aside into a desert place", v. 10. In Mark 6. 31, His words "rest a while" are added. It is good to examine some of these "private" occasions in Matthew's Gospel.

For private prayer, the Lord instructed the disciples to "enter into thy closet, and when thou hast shut thy door, pray to thy Father which is in secret", Matt. 6. 6. Note that He was giving this instruction to each individual separately.

In chapter 13, the parables of the sower, and of the wheat and tares, were spoken to great multitudes. But the meaning of these parables was not intended for the multitudes; this was reserved only for His disciples. So He went into the house, and there in the privacy of His presence, He explained the parable of the wheat and tares to them. In other words, there is teaching that is granted only when we are alone with Him.

We may mention the occasions when just three apostles were alone with the Lord—in the house at the time of the raising of Jairus' daughter, Luke 8. 51; on the mountain top at His transfiguration, Matt. 17. 1; in the garden when the Lord prayed in great agony, 26. 37. To know the Lord under these circumstances is a great blessing for the soul. "Here from the world we turn, Jesus to seek."

In a local church when there is private exercise before the Lord, He said "where two or three are gathered together in my name, there am I in the midst of them", 18. 20. Paul knew the truth of this when he wrote, "in the name of our Lord Jesus Christ, when ye are gathered together", 1 Cor. 5. 4.

For the great discourse on prophecy on the mount of Olives, His disciples "came unto him privately", Matt. 24. 3. The Lord did speak on prophecy to the multitudes, but the details and fulness of the message were for the disciples only.

In resurrection, only witnesses chosen beforehand were allowed to see Him privately, Acts 10. 41. Examples are found in Galilee and in Jerusalem, Matt. 28. 16; John 20. 19.

February 26th

READING: **Matthew 8. 5-13; Luke 7. 1-10**

THE CENTURION OR HIS FRIENDS—WHICH?

THE ACCOUNT by Matthew states that the centurion came to the Lord and confessed his unworthiness, but Luke's account states that he sent his friends to the Lord who spoke in the first person as if the centurion was speaking. Those who waver in the faith might suggest that there is a contradiction. But who did speak? Really, one man sent the others who spoke the words directly from the first man as if he were speaking. This is quite common in the Scriptures!

As far as Moses was concerned, God was the ultimate speaker, who was with Moses' mouth teaching him what to say, his mouth being to Aaron "instead of God", Exod. 4. 15-16; they were sent to the Israelites, speaking instead of God Himself. Thus in Leviticus 18. 1-2, the Lord spoke to Moses, instructing him to speak to the children of Israel. Moses commenced, "I am the Lord your God". Thus God was speaking, through Moses "my servant", Josh. 1. 2, who had been sent. See again Number 15. 1-2, where Moses spoke using the "I" of God.

Similarly with the prophets. David claimed, "The Spirit of the Lord spake by me", 2 Sam. 23. 2. God's words were placed in Jeremiah's mouth, who spoke these words using the "I" of God, Jer. 1. 7-9; 2. 1-2. Ezekiel received words from God, and was sent to speak as if God were speaking, Ezek. 2. 8; 16. 1, 6.

When Paul spoke, it was really Christ who spoke, for the apostle spoke "the word of the Lord", 1 Thess. 4. 15. In particular, he wrote, "since ye seek a proof of Christ speaking in me", 2 Cor. 13. 3. Thus Paul was sent, but Christ spoke.

The inspiration of the Scriptures proceeds along the same lines. The Spirit moved holy men to speak, 2 Pet. 1. 21, using all the details of their speaking and writing styles. Who speaks?—the Holy Spirit. Whom do men perceive speaking and writing?—the apostles. See Zechariah 7. 12.

It was the same with the Lord Jesus. Men heard Him speaking, but really He was the sent One speaking the Father's words; He said, "I have not spoken of (from) myself; but the Father which sent me, he gave me a commandment, what I should say, and what I should speak", John 12. 49. See Hebrews 1. 2. They saw and heard Him, but they saw and heard God, John 14. 9-10.

For the testimony of persecuted disciples, see Matt. 10. 20.

February 27th

READING: **1 John 4. 1-6**

YE—THEY—WE

THESE ARE the first words in the three verses 4-6, three personal pronouns, all in the plural, and evidently describing three different groups of people.

The context commences at verse 1, "believe not every spirit, but try the spirits whether they are of God: because many false prophets are gone out into the world". By "spirit", John refers to the inner motivation of a man that causes him to adhere to and propagate either truth or error.

They, v. 5. Here are the false prophets, those who at that time were denying that the Lord Jesus Christ had come in the flesh. It was the fashionable philosophy to deny this fundamental fact. John has asserted it in his Gospel, "the Word was made flesh", John 1. 14; he had recalled it in this Epistle, "our hands have handled, of the Word of life", 1 John 1. 1. Yet this "spirit of antichrist" denied with their theories that the Lord's body was not physically real. Such men were speaking of the world, and the world heard them gladly. Such antichrists certainly were not "of us", 2. 19, and were denying that "Jesus is the Christ", 2. 22.

We, v. 6. Clearly John does not refer to his readers, and he seems to refer to the band of faithful teachers who maintained in their doctrine the truth concerning the Word made flesh. The "spirit of truth"—truly the Holy Spirit Himself—maintained this doctrine in the hearts of these teachers. The readers would thereby recognize "the Spirit of God", v. 2, enabling them to distinguish between "the spirit of truth, and the spirit of error". Teachers today should by the substance of their ministry show forth the "Spirit of God" and "the spirit of error", for the Spirit of truth guides into all truth, John 16. 13.

Ye, v. 4. These were the readers of John's Epistle, who were recognized by John as "Beloved". They had overcome these false teachers and their doctrines by the Spirit of God who was "greater". They had heard that antichrist would come, so were forewarned about the spirit of antichrist in the many false teachers. Happy is the assembly that faithfully takes such warnings to heart, being determined to uphold the truth concerning the Person of Christ against all opposition.

February 28th

READING: **Song of Solomon 5. 9-16**

GOLD—TRUE OR COPIED

WE FIND a great contrast. In this passage we find in allegorical form how believers, by the Spirit of God, can view the Person of Christ with all His beauties. But in Daniel 2. 31-35, 37-45, we find how God views the great rulers of the kingdoms of men according to the flesh.

In the passage from Song of Solomon 5, we find the restoration of the testimony of the affection of the bride, ending with the confession, "he is altogether lovely". But in Daniel 2, we have the vision of the decay of the rule of man, ending in the image being broken in pieces and consumed. More generally, there will be the shaking and removal of all things made, so that which cannot be shaken will remain, Heb. 12. 27.

In Song of Solomon 5, the head is as fine *gold*; the hands as *gold* rings; the body as ivory; the legs as pillars of marble, and the feet of fine *gold*. Only the consistent best can figuratively describe the Lord as the Bridegroom. But in Daniel 2, the head is of fine *gold*; the arms of silver; the body of brass; the legs of iron, and the feet of a mixture of iron and clay.

The character of the Lord is eternally, uniformly and divinely glorious; gold describes His head, hands and feet. His authority, His deeds and His walk are divinely consistent. This is also seen in the tabernacle furniture made or overlaid with pure gold, speaking typically of the Lord Jesus in the sanctuary. This furniture was so distinct from the wilderness soil and was immune from its contaminating influence. The Lord was not of this world; He sanctified Himself, John 17. 14, 19, and believers should similarly be separated by the power of redemption. The Lord's preeminence is thereby extolled.

But in Daniel 2, the kingdoms of the world get more mixed up in baseness and decay with the elements of this world, becoming clay, unstable, ready for judgment as not being the work of God for eternity. Yet men do not like to see their influence and glory decaying. To counter this, Nebuchadnezzar replaced his vision-image by a physical image made all of gold so as to mimic Deity, Dan. 3. 1; all had to worship this, but God saved three faithful men in the burning fiery furnace.

"They shall perish; but thou remainest", Heb. 1. 11.

February 29th

READING: **2 John**

HERESY STALKS YOUR STREETS

THEY KNOCK at your door, often when only the lady is at home. There they stand, two by two, polite, with what looks like a Bible in their hands. The Bible warns, "If there come any unto you, and bring not this doctrine, receive him not into your house, neither bid him God speed: for he that biddeth him God speed is partaker of his evil deeds", 2 John 10-11. Writing on the same subject, elsewhere he wrote, "try the spirits whether they are of God: because many false prophets are gone out into the world", 1 John 4. 1. These hawkers of heresy may sound convincing, pointing out verses from their own special Bible translations, but they will not tell you the doctrines that they hold contrary to the common Christian faith. Many of these people hold a relatively new and heretical doctrine, but insist that they tell you in what way they diverge from evangelical Christians, so you can see whether they are purveyors of heresy. Ask why their books are not to be found in Christian bookshops, for example.

For example, the kinds of heresy and false doctrine that they bring are:

(i) Inevitably they deny the full Deity of the Lord Jesus Christ. They will call Him "a God" but not "the God"; their translations of the Bible are deliberately falsified to minimize His preeminence.

(ii) They will deny the value of His sacrifice on the cross, and the value of His blood shed by which our sins are put away, with complete and eternal forgiveness being granted to all those who believe on His Name.

(iii) They will deny the Personality of the Holy Spirit, claiming that this is merely an emanating influence from God, but not a powerful Personality sent down from heaven from the Risen Lord ascended to the throne on high.

Denials such as these cut at the very root of Christianity; hence, learn the truth in Christ, so as to be able to discern such false prophets at your doors. But if a true evangelist calls, telling of the true Christ and His salvation, receive him and his message, as one sent from God with this truth. But at the same time beware of any ecclesiastical bias, for even some evangelists fail to hold all the truth of Scripture.

March 1st

READING: **Exodus 35. 4-35**

A WILLING HEART

THE DETAILS of the design of the tabernacle, its furniture and the priestly garments had been given in Exodus 25-30. Now the time had come for the collection of all the materials for its construction; chapter 35 is occupied with this subject.

Today, before any believer can engage in any service that involves edification in a local assembly, spiritual material must be collected, else that service is dull and unedifying in the extreme. Service without spiritual material is like building a physical house without bricks, mortar and wood!

In verses 4-9, Moses gave the command relating to the actual materials; "whosoever is of a willing heart" were the people involved. Thus Paul built local assemblies on material that he had "received of the Lord", 1 Cor. 11. 23, and on what he called "the commandments of the Lord", 14. 37. Today, willing hearts must first collect in doctrine and life from the Scriptures what they later present to other believers.

In verses 10-19, those who were "wise hearted" had to come to make all the parts of the tabernacle from this material; they were given a list of every part. In other words, they did not work in a vacuum; they knew the objectives of their service. Today, there are objectives in service in a local assembly; these must be before every servant, just as school teachers have a syllabus before them throughout the year. In Paul's case, he preached, warned and taught, to "present every man perfect in Christ Jesus", Col. 1. 28.

In verses 20-24, we have the first record of the act of bringing by "every one whose heart stirred him up, and every one whom his spirit made willing"; men and women who were "willing hearted" brought their offerings. In verses 25-26, work was involved in the process by the women who were "wise hearted", and "whose heart stirred them up". Truly, we must first give ourselves to the Lord, 2 Cor. 8. 5.

Verses 27-29 is the second record of those "whose heart made them willing to bring for all manner of work".

Finally in verses 30-35, God had put it into the heart of special men whom he "filled with wisdom of heart" to teach and to work in the building process. Thus as servants of Christ, we are "doing the will of the Lord from the heart", Eph. 6. 6.

March 2nd

READING: **Psalm 137**

THE LORD'S SONG

IN THE DAYS of Moses' tabernacle, there was no organized service of song associated with the burnt offering. This was developed later by David, "the sweet psalmist of Israel", who recognized that the Lord's word was in his mouth, 2 Sam. 23. 1-2. This service of song was enacted before David's tent on mount Zion and in the courts of Solomon's temple. The principles involved are applicable today, as spiritual songs are made unto the Lord, Eph. 5. 19, and as we "offer the spiritual sacrifice of praise to God continually, that is, the fruit of our lips giving thanks", Heb. 13. 15; 1 Pet. 2. 5.

David prepared this service of song by choosing Asaph, Heman and Jeduthun with their sons as singers and instrument-players, 1 Chron. 25. 1-8. All were involved in this service, younger ones and older ones, the smaller and the greater, "the teacher and the scholar"; none was exempt because of age, experience or inadequacy. In verse 7, it states explicitly what their work was: "*the songs of the Lord*". Here was no entertainment of the flesh, but deep exercise before the Lord.

In Hezekiah's reformation, when the house was cleansed and its service reinstated, the commandment, instruments and words of David were revived, 2 Chron. 29. 25, 26, 30. In any revival, the Lord's people must go back to the beginnings of their faith and service, shunning all later innovations. The key verse in Hezekiah's revival is verse 27, "when the burnt offering began, *the song of the Lord* began also". The two went together, and so it is today—the "sacrifice of praise", the subject and the means, are both spiritual. Another Old Testament example is found in 2 Chronicles 20. 21-24; the singers went before the army, and after the victory they returned to the house of the Lord, v. 28.

Later, when the Jews were in captivity, their captives thought that the songs of Zion were of entertainment value, saying, "Sing us one of the songs of Zion", Psa. 137. 3. But the weeping captives thought only of Jerusalem as the place of worship, and answered, "How shall we sing *the Lord's song* in a strange land?". Today, our deepest exercise in praise is before the Lord in the sanctuary; no unbeliever can enter into worship expressed in spirit and in truth.

READING: **Colossians 2. 1-7**

STEDFASTNESS

THE TIME was approaching when the Lord should be received up; He therefore "stedfastly set his face to go to Jerusalem", Luke 9. 51. The Samaritans would not receive Him, since Jerusalem was His declared objective. He had put His hand to the plough, v. 62, showing true dedication to the Father's will, with a single divine eye that could not be deflected by the Samaritans through whose country He was passing.

Later, Stephen "looked up stedfastly into heaven", Acts 7. 55, enabled to do so since he was filled with the Holy Spirit. Faith indeed, but he was granted eyes on that special occasion to see heaven opened. The apostles too had "looked stedfastly toward heaven", Acts 1. 10, but this was questioned since they had work to do for the Risen Lord. Unlike Stephen's case, the ascending Lord vanished out of their sight.

Stedfastness in service. Because of the resurrection of Christ, Paul exhorted the Corinthians, "be ye stedfast, unmoveable, always abounding in the work of the Lord", 1 Cor. 15. 58. Because of the ascension of Christ, our hope as an anchor enters within the veil, and this hope is "both sure and stedfast", Heb. 6. 19. This raises our service to the highest level, attained by the early church in Jerusalem, when "they continued stedfastly in the apostles' doctrine and fellowship, and in breaking of bread, and in prayers", Acts 2. 42. The desire to engage in these assembly gatherings does not fluctuate when one is stedfast before the Lord.

Beware of dangers. Although Paul was in prison, and had never been to Colosse, the news that he received of them was counted as if he witnessed their behaviour, "joying and beholding your order, and the stedfastness of your faith in Christ", Col. 2. 5. But they had to beware of men and their philosophies, so as to remain "rooted and built up in him", vv. 7-8. Peter also could sense current dangers, so he wrote, "beware lest ye . . . fall from your own stedfastness", 2 Pet. 3. 17. Positively the believer must grow in grace, v. 18, and "stedfast in the faith" he must resist the devil, since he appears as a roaring lion, 1 Pet. 5. 8-9. By these means, we are enabled to "hold the beginning of our confidence stedfast unto the end", Heb. 3. 14.

March 4th

READING: **Amos 4. 6-13**

PREPARATION FOR THE FUTURE

THE TEXT "Prepare to meet thy God", Amos 4. 12, often used to be displayed before the public gaze. How many bothered to take heed? Perhaps they were too busy preparing for things in this life—for tomorrow's meals, for some school lessons, for an examination, for a driving test, or for a holiday. Some may be preparing for marriage, for the purchase of a house, or for retirement. This means that the unknown future is anticipated to the best possible advantage, though James wrote, "whereas ye know not what shall be on the morrow", James 4. 14. Again, men usually prepare for events after their decease by making a will, but this is no preparation for heaven. How wise, then, was Amos in saying, "Prepare to meet thy God".

For every one must meet God, whether we believe it or not; none can hide himself in that day yet to come. To the young, this day may seem remote, but when one is older, then this day is nearer. Christians are completely prepared to meet with God - there is no fear of judgment to come, for they are forgiven through the Lord Jesus and His sacrifice on the cross. But non-Christians have not prepared to meet God. If preparation is disregarded, then the day of meeting will occur when the dead, small and great, will stand before God seated on the "great white throne", Rev. 20. 11-12. Lack of preparation will mean that sinners stand before the Judge who will judge righteously, but there will be no eternal life.

Preparation starts here and now. In the Old Testament, one king named Jehoshaphat "prepared his heart to seek God", 2 Chron. 19. 3, while another king named Rehoboam "prepared not his heart to seek the Lord", 12. 14. What a difference, and what a warning these two opposite quotations imply!

The Lord promised that He was going away "to prepare a place", and He will come again for us in His own good time to take us to be eternally with Him there, John 14. 2-3. In order to achieve this, salvation is offered to all who exercise faith in Him; He prepared the way by dying on the cross for our redemption. At the same time, God has "prepared his throne for judgment", Psa. 9. 7, and this is for those who have not prepared themselves, in not accepting the salvation freely offered by the Lord Jesus.

March 5th

READING: **Judges 13. 1-11**

TRUSTEESHIP

AS IS WELL known, trustees are a group of people who hold and administer possessions not their own for the benefit of others. Absolute honesty and devotion are necessary for such a task. Thus trustees may be responsible for a gospel hall, or for charity funds. The buildings or funds trusted to them must be held tenaciously; such pearls must not be cast before swine.

Paul claimed to be a trustee: "according to the glorious gospel of the blessed God, which was committed to my trust. And I thank Christ Jesus our Lord, who hath enabled me, for that he counted me faithful, putting me into the ministry", 1 Tim. 1. 11-12. Thus the apostle was a trustee of the glorious gospel; every aspect of it had to be very carefully held both doctrinally and practically. As a responsible trustee, he delivered truth to the saints, 1 Cor. 11. 23. God chose him as a trustee, since He found Paul "faithful", 1 Tim. 1. 12. Our faithfulness commends us to God as suitable trustees in these days. Moreover, God "enabled" Paul in his work as a trustee, and so He also does for us. The apostle claimed that God was able to keep that which He had committed to him, 2 Tim. 1. 12 R.V. marg. (making better sense), and he urged Timothy to keep what had been committed to his trust, 1 Tim. 6. 20.

We see similar principles in Samson having been selected as a trustee. The trust committed to him is seen in Judges 13. 5; he would be a Nazarite and would begin to deliver Israel from the Philistines. He was enabled as the Spirit began to move him, v. 25; his service lasted for twenty years. Alas, he had faith, Heb. 11. 32, but he was hardly faithful, for he delivered the secret of his trusteeship into the hands of Delilah; he lost the Spirit, power, authority and his service.

In a certain sense, the blessed Lord was a divine Trustee when here on earth. He "was faithful to him that appointed him", Heb. 3. 2. Concerning His service, He said, "I have finished the work that thou gavest me to do", John 17. 4. As for being enabled, He had been anointed by the Spirit to preach the gospel to the poor, Luke 4. 18. He expressed the trust that had been given to Him in the words, "I have given unto them the words which thou gavest me", John 17. 8. We as trustees can be imitators of the divine Trustee.

March 6th

READING: **1 Corinthians 15. 11-28**

FALSE IDEAS ABOUT THE FUTURE

THE TRUTH concerning future events is quite clearly found on the pages of Holy Scripture. But in New Testament days, strange ideas were abroad in the churches and in the world; today, things are even worse. It is therefore good to see positive truth set against the errors of those early days.

There is no resurrection, 1 Cor. 15. 12. Resurrection has been a pillar stone of all evangelical teaching; this had been the main point stressed in Acts 2. To the rational mind, the concept of resurrection may appear to be overwhelming in its difficulties. How can it come about, when a body may have become corrupted over the centuries? Faith has no difficulty in believing what God has promised, but the Corinthians, who had these mental difficulties, adopted the easy way out—they merely denied the resurrection. Paul showed that this attitude asserts that Christ also is not risen, and that sins remain unforgiven, vv. 16-19. But the resurrection of Christ ensures the resurrection of all believers.

There is no hope for the future, 1 Thess. 4. 13. This can cause sorrow when believing loved ones pass away. This church knew about the day of the Lord, 5. 1-5, with its fear and destruction, and were allowing that to affect their hearts. But Paul presented the better way: the Lord would come again, and the dead in Christ would rise first, and all would rise to meet Him in the air to be for ever with Him.

The day of the Lord is present, 2 Thess. 2. 1-3. This would indeed cause fear if it were true! But it was not true; rather the Thessalonians had been deceived by a forged letter containing false doctrine. In fact, the antichrist (the man of sin and the son of perdition) had to be revealed first, and this certainly had not occurred. In other words, events after the rapture must not be confused with events before the rapture! The apostle had instructed them in this doctrine when he had been among them, v. 5.

There is no coming, 2 Pet. 3. 1-10. Here is the attitude of the world, conceited in its knowledge of the natural sciences. All things remain the same since the creation, they say. But God who created all thing will also terminate all things, and the Lord's coming in glory is part of that divine programme.

66

March 7th

READING: **Acts 16. 9-24**

IF YE HAVE JUDGED ME TO BE FAITHFUL

THE LORD is described as "the faithful witness" and "the faithful and true witness", Rev. 1. 5; 3. 14. Here we have His faithful testimony as on earth, declaring the will and purpose of the Father; moreover He was the faithful witness of the activity of every believer and local church.

It is good that believers can have the same description: God is faithful (that is, we can trust Him): "God is faithful, by whom ye were called unto the fellowship of his Son", 1 Cor. 1. 9. When we are faithful (that is, He can trust us), the Lord can speak of "a faithful and wise servant", Matt. 24. 45. Again, Paul knew that the Lord counted him faithful, thereby putting him into the ministry, 1 Tim. 1. 12.

Several believers are described as "faithful" in the N.T.

Lydia. She said to Paul, "If ye have judged me to be faithful to the Lord", Acts 16. 15. Paul discerned this since she worshipped God and her heart was opened, since she attended unto Paul's teaching and was baptized. By such means, older brethren can discern the faithfulness of young converts.

Timothy. In writing to the Corinthians, Paul described him as "my beloved son, and faithful in the Lord", because among other things he could speak of Paul's ways that were in Christ, as Paul taught in every church, 1 Cor. 4. 17. What a commendation to speak and live the apostle's doctrine!

Tychicus. He was the bearer of the Epistle to the Ephesians from Paul in Rome. He is described as "a beloved brother and faithful minister in the Lord", Eph. 6. 21, who would give a true report of Paul's affairs as a prisoner in Rome—with nothing added and nothing diminished. Paul wrote the same thing to the Colossians, Col. 4. 7.

Epaphras. Here was a messenger from Colosse to Paul in Rome; Paul recognized him as a "dear fellowservant" and "a faithful minister of Christ", Col. 1. 7. He declared to the apostle their love in the Spirit, and laboured fervently for them in his prayers, 4. 12.

Onesimus. Although recently converted, Paul could write of him as "a faithful and beloved brother", Col. 4. 9.

Silvanus. Peter described him as "a faithful brother" who had written the Epistle, 1 Pet. 5. 12.

March 8th

READING: **Romans 6. 1-11**

A BAPTISMAL SERVICE

IT IS a fact that Christians and non-Christians are divided as to how baptism is to be carried out, and what baptism means. Entrenched positions cause people to hold views to which they were introduced in childhood. Baptism is a Christian practice, so the only source book, the N.T., will provide us with all we need to know about the subject. In other words, we must read all the N.T. references to baptism.

Exhortations to baptism. Before His ascension, the Lord commanded that disciples should be baptized, Matt. 28. 19. But although He loved young children to come to Him, these were not the subject of His command. Later, in Acts 10. 48, the apostle Peter commanded that new believers in Cornelius' home "to be baptized in the name of the Lord". We cannot depart from this.

Examples of baptism. After Peter's first sermon in Acts 2. 41, there were 3,000 people that gladly received his word and were baptized. Later, Lydia's heart was opened; she was baptized, and was faithful to the Lord, 16. 14-15. Later still in Corinth, many "hearing believed, and were baptized", 18. 8, thereby forming the church in Corinth. In every example, there is faith in Christ for forgiveness and salvation, followed by baptism. We cannot depart from this.

Doctrine behind baptism. Why are believers baptized? By this act, the young Christian declares his intention before God and men to give up the old life of sin and waywardness, and live a new life suitable for Christ and His glory. As Romans 6. 6 puts it, "our old man (nature) is crucified with him, that the body of sin might be destroyed, that henceforth we should not serve sin". We cannot depart from this.

In the act of baptism, "we are buried with him by baptism into death . . . even so we also should walk in newness of life. For if we have been planted together in the likeness of his death, we shall be also in the likeness of his resurrection", Rom. 6. 4-5. No act other than complete immersion in water can fulfil this meaning. A river, the sea, or a heated baptistry may be used for complete immersion. But it is spiritually thrilling to see such obedience and intended loyalty to the Lord shown by young converts being baptized; its effects last throughout a life of Christian service.

March 9th

READING: **Matthew 11. 25-30**

THE LORD'S THANKS

THERE ARE four recorded events in which the Lord gave thanks. These are:

(i) Matthew 11. 25: "I thank thee, O Father, Lord of heaven and earth, because thou hast hid these things from the wise and prudent, and hast revealed them unto babes". This is the same as in Luke 10. 21. He said this after He was rejected by the unrepentant cities, but in Luke 10 it was after the return of the seventy whom He had sent forth to preach.

(ii) John 11. 41: after the stone was rolled away from Lazarus' grave, the Lord said, "Father, I thank thee that thou hast heard me". Here was a testimony for the Father; the Lord said this because of the people who were watching.

(iii) Matthew 15. 36: at the feeding of the 4,000, the Lord took the loaves and fish, "and gave thanks"; this is repeated in Mark 8. 6. But in John 6. 11, at the feeding of the 5,000, He distributed "when he had given thanks", and note that this is repeated in verse 23; to John, this was an important part of the miracle because he repeated this fact.

(iv) Luke 22. 19: He took bread "and gave thanks" in the upper room, repeated in 1 Cor. 11. 24. But in Matt. 26. 27; Mark 14. 23; Luke 22. 17, the Lord "gave thanks" after He had taken the cup. Both elements are thereby associated with the Lord's thanks.

Note, in (i) and (ii) the direct words of the Lord are given—He spoke to the Father. But in (iii) and (iv) the statement regarding thanks is indirect, and no name appears.

Likewise for the Lord's people. (i) Paul thanked God without ceasing, 1 Thess. 2. 13, since the Word of God had been received in truth, and not as the word of man.

(ii) "Prayer and supplication with thanksgiving" mingles prayer and thanksgiving, Phil. 4. 6. There seems to be thanksgiving before the answers to their prayers had been received from the Lord; this is the exercise of faith.

(iii) Food that has been given by God must be received "with thanksgiving" by those who know the truth; nothing is to be refused when it is received with thanksgiving, 1 Tim. 4. 3-4.

(iv) The sacrifice of praise is formed by "the fruit of our lips giving thanks to his name", Heb. 13. 15.

March 10th

READING: **1 Peter 1. 1-12**

THE OLD TESTAMENT FOR US

IN OUR DESIRE to dwell on the truth concerning our Lord Jesus, our salvation, assembly life and service, and future events, the New Testament proves to be our main source book of truth. The Old Testament savours of history, law, and the Jews (past and future), and yet it must not be discarded as if it has no value for believers today. Admittedly, the Lord and the writers of the New Testament books quoted profusely from the Old Testament, yet believers seem to be only indirectly concerned with its teaching, that is, until we find certain verses that place us in direct contact with the Old Testament.

(1) 1 Peter 1. 12: "that not unto themselves, *but unto us* they did minister the things". Here, Peter is writing about the prophets; they spoke of "the grace that should come unto you", and of "the sufferings of Christ, and the glory that should follow". These prophets were not only speaking to their own people in those days, but to all believers, "*unto us*", afterwards, even to ourselves. For the message of the prophets was repeated through the apostles by the Holy Spirit sent down from heaven. Thus the Old Testament speaks to us.

(2) Romans 4. 24: Genesis 15. 6 had recorded the fact that righteousness was imputed to Abraham on account of his faith; Paul adds, "it was not written for his sake alone . . . *but for us also*, to whom it shall be imputed". The book of Genesis is a book of beginnings, and cannot be disregarded on scientific and spiritual grounds. That vital statement about the imputation of righteousness was recorded for us.

(3) Acts 7. 38: Stephen spoke of Moses who was with the angel and the people; he received "the lively oracles to give *unto us*". We are not under the law, but we are not to regard the commandments as irrelevant. They were given "to us", and Stephen included himself. The law shows us what we are naturally; grace shows us what we are in Christ Jesus.

(4) Hebrews 10. 15: the Holy Spirit had inspired Jeremiah to speak the words of the Lord concerning the new covenant. These words in Jeremiah 31. 33 are quoted in Hebrews 10. 16. And although Jeremiah was speaking to the Jews, yet the Holy Spirit is "a witness *to us*", v. 15. Again, this shows that the divinely inspired Old Testament had us in view as readers.

March 11th

READING: **Psalm 27**

BEAUTY: SPIRITUAL NOT NATURAL

"TO BEHOLD the beauty of the Lord" is a wonderful exercise of soul, v. 4. To attain to this, David knew that he had to "dwell in the house of the Lord all the days of my life", for the world without was hardly conducive to such an objective.

When the Lord was here below, the apostles had gazed upon His glory, John 1. 14; three of them had seen His transfigured glory on the mountain top, Matt. 17. 2; John had seen Him in glory and beauty on the isle of Patmos, Rev. 1. 13-16. The bride had described His beauty in Song of Songs 5. 10-16. To what extent have we seen His beauty?

Moses' tabernacle itself was a structure of beauty in its hidden internal design; only few were allowed in, but Moses would know that this natural beauty spoke of God's beauty spiritually. But for David, things were different. In his day, Moses' tabernacle was situated at Gibeon, far from Jerusalem; but there was a second tabernacle on mount Zion that David had erected to receive the ark of the covenant as it was carried up mount Zion in triumph, 1 Chron. 16. 1. The material beauty of Moses' tabernacle and Solomon's temple are described in detail, but Scripture is silent about David's tabernacle, implying that there was no material beauty about it. It was but an ordinary tent, dedicated to God's presence. Thus when David desired to see "the beauty of the Lord", this was not through the natural beauty of the tent, but a spiritual aspiration from the heart, when his faith could behold His beauty, and David could enquire in this temple.

It is the same today. We are not attracted by the ornate decorations of certain ecclesiastical buildings, but faith sees the beauty of the Lord Jesus revealed in Scripture. The Man Christ Jesus displayed moral and spiritual beauty through His human form when on earth; if men could not see this beauty then they would not see anything special in His human form, for Isaiah 53. 2 says, "there is no beauty that we should desire him". God wants "the place of my sanctuary" to be beautified, Isa. 60. 13. This is achieved primarily through the beauty of the Lord Jesus, but His beauty is also seen in His people. Thus men "glorified God" in Paul, Gal. 1. 24, namely, the Lord was seen in him; see also 2 Cor. 4. 10.

March 12th

READING: John 3. 1-17

THOU, THEE, THY: YE, YOU, YOUR

IT IS well known that older translations such as the A.V., R.V. and that by J.N.D. use the former words in the title of this page, while the so-called modern translations never use these former words. The first three words are singular, while the last three are plural. The original languages made a difference between singular and plural, and so did the earlier translators. But the more recent translators draw no distinction between the singular and plural. If the context shows which is implied, no harm is done to the understanding of the text, but when no indication is given, then grave errors of understanding can exist in the minds of the readers.

Hence believers must beware greatly of modern translations, else completely false ideas may exist in their minds. As the writer reads passages in the Bible, and notices a "thou, you" in the same verse or passage, he makes a note of the verse in the back of his Bible. We draw readers' attention to a few of these, so that they can be forewarned.

John 3. 10-12. The Lord is speaking to Nicodemus alone, "Art *thou* a master of Israel?". Yet in the next verses, He said, "*ye* receive not our witness. If I have told *you* earthly things". In other words, this refers to the Lord's teaching to the Jews as a whole, not just to Nicodemus.

Matthew 23. 37-39. First the Lord addresses Jerusalem, "*thou* that killest the prophets" and then He speaks to all individuals in the city and Judaea, "*ye* would not" and "*your* house is left unto *you* desolate".

Luke 6. 30-31. Note the change from singular to plural in the Lord's teaching, "Give to every man that asketh of *thee* . . . as *ye* would that men should do to *you*".

Exodus 4. 15. What would this verse mean if no distinction is made? "I will be with *thy* mouth, and with his mouth, and will teach *you* what *ye* shall do".

2 Timothy 4. 22. "The Lord Jesus Christ be with *thy* spirit. Grace be with *you*". Thus others were implied beside Timothy in this final exercise of the apostle.

John 14. 9. "Have I been so long time with *you*, and yet hast *thou* not known me, Philip?". The Lord had been with all the disciples, but His question was directed to Philip.

March 13th

READING: **Numbers 25. 1-13**

THE ZEAL OF THE LORD

PSALM 69. 9, "the zeal of thine house hath eaten me up" is quoted in John 2. 17. John 2 took place at the beginning of the Lord's ministry; He was cleansing the temple courts, as had been done several times in the Old Testament. Psalm 69 refers to the end of the Lord's life; in His work of redemption, He anticipated the spiritual house to be built of living stones. Thus Peter first wrote of redemption and then of the spiritual house, 1 Pet. 1. 18-19; 2. 5. This divine work took place with the consuming passion of the Lord to do God's will for the building of this spiritual house.

Divine zeal is found elsewhere in the Scriptures. Thus in Hezekiah's time, deliverance from the Assyrians would enable the remnant from Jerusalem to be fruitful: "the zeal of the Lord of hosts shall do this", 2 Kings 19. 31. Isaiah gave the promise of a Child to be born who would occupy the throne of David: "The zeal of the Lord of hosts will perform this", Isa. 9. 7. God's anger would rest on Jerusalem: "they shall know that I the Lord have spoken it in my zeal, when I have accomplished my fury in them", Ezek. 5. 13.

God's people also should manifest zeal. The priest Phinehas turned away God's anger, and received His commendation: "he was zealous for my sake (with my zeal, Newberry marg.) . . . he was zealous for his God", Num. 25. 11, 13. As a result, the high priestly line passed through Phinehas. In the New Testament, the zeal of the Corinthians in financial matters provoked other churches, 2 Cor. 9. 2. Epaphras was concerned for the Colossian assembly, and as one of them, he laboured fervently for them in his prayers; Paul described this as, "he hath a great zeal for you", Col. 4. 12-13. Believers must also be "zealous of good works", Titus 2. 14. May the Lord's people manifest such zeal in their service and lives, in maintaining God's honour, and in helping His people at all times.

But zeal can also be misplaced, particularly in religious matters by the unsaved. Of his preconversion days, Paul wrote, "concerning zeal, persecuting the church", Phil. 3. 6. The elders in Jerusalem said to Paul that there were many thousands of Jews who believe, but who were "zealous of the law", Acts 21. 20; Rom. 10. 2. This is quite different from Christian zeal.

March 14th

READING: **Matthew 26. 30-46**

HE WENT A LITTLE FURTHER

THE CONTEXT of this quotation from verse 39 is as follows: the door of the upper room had opened, and the Lord had come out with His disciples. This was not the first time the door had opened, for previously it had opened to let Judas out, John 13. 30. Only then was the Son of man glorified; only then did He give the expanded discourses in John 13-16. Approaching the garden of Gethsemane at the foot of the mount of Olives, the Lord left eight apostles at the gate, and took three in with Him, while He would "go and pray yonder". The multitudes were outside, eight were at the gate, three were inside, while Christ was in the centre alone with His Father. We can see Christ absent, present, prominent and preeminent.

Matthew described the Lord as going "a little further", a "stone's cast" according to Luke 22. 41. It is the little further that costs, and a little further that counts. The cost for Christ was that He was in agony, when "his sweat was as it were great drops of blood falling down to the ground", v. 44, when an angel appeared strengthening Him. And His action counts, for had He not entered into these sufferings, there could be no saved believers today. We too must go a little further, for if this costs then it counts in God's service.

In Mark 1. 16, the Lord found Peter and Andrew, and He made them fishers of men. He then went "a little further", finding James and John, otherwise they would have been passed by.

After His resurrection, approaching Emmaus, "he would have gone further", Luke 24. 28, but the two men with Him delayed this, so He stayed with them and revealed Himself. Such a delay could not possibly have happened in the two events previously related.

In Paul's experience, all his service seems to have been a little further; he was so different even from the other apostles. This "little further" was accomplished "in weariness and painfulness, in watchings often, in hunger and thirst, in fastings often, in cold and nakedness", 2 Cor. 11. 27. This was beyond what the other apostles suffered; Paul never stopped and he never went back. The cost was great, but it counted in the results of his labours. In Caesarea, he was willing to take the furthest step, even to death, Acts 21. 13.

March 15th

READING: **John 18. 28-40**

IN AND OUT

THE LORD JESUS first appeared before the high priest Caiaphas, after which He was taken before the Roman governor Pilate, for only he could authorize crucifixion. These Jews were very zealous of the law, not to judge righteous judgment, but to avoid their own ideas of ceremonial defilement at the Passover, v. 28. Hence they would not enter the Gentile's house but remained on the outside. The Lord was taken inside, and Pilate had to enter in and out to speak to the Lord and then to the Jews respectively.

Pilate went out, v. 29. This was to ascertain from the Jews the nature of their accusation. In the other Gospels, this accusation was not religious but political, that the Lord was a King, in defiance of the authority of Caesar in Rome.

Pilate entered in, v. 33. Pilate questioned the Lord about this claim, to be informed that His kingdom was not of this world, and that His servants would not fight for a heavenly kingdom, v. 36.

Pilate went out, v. 38. Quite openly, he claimed that he found no fault in the Lord Jesus.

Pilate entered in, 19. 1. The Lord was scourged, not only that Pilate should ascertain the truth by this cruel means, but also to see if this infliction would satisfy the Jews.

Pilate went out, v. 4. Pilate brought the Lord out, in robes of mockery as a King. This did not satisfy the Jews either; they desired nothing else than crucifixion.

Pilate entered in, v. 9. The Lord made it plain that Pilate's authority derived "from above".

Pilate went out, v. 12. He heard the Jews' provocation, and hence brought the Lord out to be condemned to be crucified.

Pilate's activity may have been necessary from the Jews' point of view, but from Pilate's point of view he must have cut an embarrassing figure, moving in and out at the whim of the Jews.

How different in Acts 1. 21, where Peter recalled that the Lord "went in and out": "in" to be alone with the apostles, and "out" to minister to the crowds. Paul likewise in Jerusalem was with the church "coming in and going out", Acts 9. 28: "going out" to testify of the gospel to the Jews, and "coming in" as he sought the fellowship of the church in Jerusalem.

March 16th

READING: Psalm 106. 1-21, 43-48

SELECTION IN WORSHIP

IN 1 CHRONICLES 15-16, David had brought the ark home to mount Zion, an act that was typical of the Lord's ascension, Eph. 4. 8. Immediately, David instituted the service of song on mount Zion, and to this end, he gave a ready-made psalm into the hand of Asaph, 1 Chron. 16. 7. This psalm is found in verses 8-36, and it is a very remarkable composition. For a study of these verses shows what is suitable for worship and what is not. In fact, the psalm is divided into three sections, each of which is found in the book of Psalms.

Section 1, vv. 8-22, found in Psalm 105. 1-15. Here we have thoughts such as the giving of thanks, His wondrous works, to remember His covenant for ever, and the land as an inheritance. This is very suitable for worship, but the remainder of Psalm 105, namely verses 16-45, is not suitable for worship, for this second half concerns the hatred shown by Pharaoh in Egypt, the plagues, and the smiting of the firstborn in judgment. This distinction causes us to ask ourselves, what do we assess as suitable in our worship?

Section 2, vv. 23-33, being the whole of Psalm 96 in order. The present writer calls this "the ascension psalm", and the whole of its subject matter was suitable for worship on mount Zion. The subject matter deals with a new song, the declaration of His glory, the Lord who made the heavens, beauty in His sanctuary, the bringing of an offering into His courts, and the fact of the Lord reigning. The people are clothed in the "beauty of holiness", namely glorious garments; as such, can we be as discerning in worship?

Section 3, vv. 34-36, being the first verse and the last two verses of Psalm 106 dealing with thanks unto the Lord, with blessing from everlasting to everlasting. But the rest of the Psalm, verses 2-46, were not suitable for worship. Amongst many subjects, we find, "We have sinned", v. 6; men forgot His works, v. 13; God's judgments, vv. 17-18; the golden calf, v. 19; murmuring in their tents, v. 25, the subject getting worse and worse. Certainly this was not suitable for worship!

Such considerations should mould the worship of the Lord's people today, both silent and open, with the Lord Jesus and His work prominent, with no dwelling on sins of the past,

READING: **Ecclesiastes 3. 1-15**

TWENTY-EIGHT

THE SCRIPTURES present some surprises at times, and as one reads, comparing scripture with scripture, it is good to notice such surprises. It may be that no one else has ever noticed some particular feature that comes to our attention, though this can never be proved or disproved. The facts thus discovered may or may not be of relevance, but if they are of interest, then they are well worth reporting to others. Three lists each containing twenty-eight features form a surprise, and readers can examine these at their leisure.

(1) *The list in Ecclesiastes* 3. 2-8. Here are twenty-eight features that occupy the time of men in daily life, a few not necessarily being wholesome, since they are presented as fourteen contrasting pairs. There is a time to each activity, v. 1, but all such works of men contrast with the beautiful works of God that He has made in His time from the beginning, v. 11. What He does shall be for ever (that is, as long as creation lasts), v. 14, but the daily works of men cannot last, since they fade away without lasting profit, v. 9.

(2) *The list in 2 Corinthians* 6. 4-10. As a faithful servant of Christ, Paul knew the features that should characterize every servant, so that they may be approved "as the ministers of God", v. 4. Here we find physical sufferings sustained willingly in Christ's Name, vv. 4-5; here we find those Christian graces that derive from Christ Himself, vv. 6-7; and here we have a series of contrasts sustained by a suffering servant who also experiences a series of opposites granted as blessings from God, vv. 8-10. No doubt the totality of these twenty-eight features is out of the reach of most of the Lord's servants today, but this is the apostolic ideal for us all.

(3) *The list in Revelation* 18. 12-13. If the first two lists are carnal and spiritual, then this list is natural, for it gives details of the trade of the apostate church. Babylon will ultimately fall, together with its trade throughout the world. The list ends with "slaves (properly, bodies), and souls of men", for all false religion trades in these things, indoctrinating minds and using personnel for its abominable ends. So the saints are exhorted: "Come out of her, my people", v. 4. (Editors of the Greek text insert a twenty-ninth item.)

March 18th

READING: **Psalm 80**

SHINE FORTH

ONLY A FEW men were privileged to see the glory of the Lord; we may mention Moses, Solomon, Isaiah, Ezekiel, John and Paul. God's glory dwelt between the cherubim above the ark, but when Samuel was a child, "there was no open vision", so the Word of God was precious in those days, 1 Sam. 3. 1. In a spiritual sense, the holy temple was defiled, Psa. 79. 1, and God's glory was unknown; no doubt it was the same in Corinth when they failed to discern the Lord's body, 1 Cor. 3. 16-17.

But the singer Asaph, whose name means "one who gathers", desired better things. The ark of God dwelt under curtains, in the tent that David had erected on mount Zion. Certainly Asaph knew this when he cried to God, "thou that dwellest between the cherubim, shine forth", Psa. 80. 1. His knowledge was coupled with his desire. This recalls the Lord's desire for us, "that they may behold my glory", John 17. 24.

In this Psalm, three times one verse is repeated, "Turn us again, O God, and cause thy face to shine; and we shall be saved", vv. 3, 7, 19.

(1) The first occasion when this request is presented to God follows from verse 2, "come and save us". That is, from their enemies, as He had done during the wilderness journeys, when the pillar of cloud led them safely through the enemies' land.

(2) The second occasion stresses "thy face to shine", in evident contrast to the faces of men. For we read of "the bread of tears", v. 5; "tears to drink", v. 5; and the laughing of their enemies, v. 6. The shining of God's face in glory is so different from the weeping of His people, and the mockery of their enemies.

(3) The third occasion stresses "Turn us again", v. 19. For this thought appears in verses such as, "a vine out of Egypt" that was broken, plucked up, wasted, devoured, vv. 8-13. This leads to the plea, "Return . . . and visit this vine", v. 14, ending with the confession, "So will not we go back from thee", v. 18. Here is restoration to be brought about by the mercy of God shown to His own people.

Truly today, repentance leads to salvation, with weeping turned into joy, as the Saviour reveals Himself to the waiting hearts of His people, when His glory is known by faith.

March 19th

READING: **Acts 20. 1-12**

WHAT IS "SUNDAY"?

THE MEANING of the common word "Sunday" is, as with other names of the days of the week, rooted in ancient mythology. The fact that its name derives from "the day of the sun god" is irrelevant to people today. In fact, what was once a "holy day" has become a "holiday". Throughout the O.T., the last day (the seventh day) of the week was taken to be the Jewish Sabbath. In the Christian era, however, the characteristic day has always been the "first day of the week", also known as "the Lord's day", Rev. 1. 10. But the present trend is to regard the first day (the Sunday) as the last day. Men talk about a "long weekend" including a Sunday; many diaries place Sunday at the end of the week. So men use the day for their own pleasures, for homes, gardens, cars, outings, etc.

But God has chosen this day to be something special, so if men use the day merely for themselves, then they are neglecting the basic facts behind God's choice. For this was the resurrection day of the Lord Jesus Christ. Previously He had died on the cross, but, being divine, He could not remain in death, so God raised Him from among the dead in the triumph of resurrection on the first day of the week. Thus those who neglect the first day despise the death and resurrection of the Lord. Yet Christians who love the Lord, and who know that their salvation derives from His death and resurrection, properly treat this first day as the early Christians treated it in N.T. days. This is no joyless formality, but a great desire to honour the Lord by following His institutions. It was on the first day that Paul and the church came together to "break bread", that is, to partake of the Lord's supper; it was then that Paul taught them at length, Acts 20. 7. "Upon the first day of the week, when the disciples came together to break bread, Paul preached unto them".

In the expressions "the Lord's day", Rev. 1. 10, and "the Lord's supper", 1 Cor. 11. 20, a special Greek word is used for "Lord's", which occurs only twice in the N.T. It does *not* mean "the day of the Lord" and "the supper of the Lord". Rather it is a word that is related to "Lord" as "spiritual" is to "Spirit". It thus means, "having the character of what pertains to the Lord".

March 20th

READING: **Romans 16**

NUMERICAL NAMES

SOME MAY say, this is an uninteresting chapter, full of names that cannot easily be pronounced. But if the reader examines what is said about each name, then he can build up a picture of the church at Rome to whom the greetings were sent, and of the church at Corinth where the Epistle was written.

It is remarkable that, in the N.T., we find men with names meaning "second", "third" and "fourth". Not that ranking is involved with the second, third and fourth, since all are one in Christ, yet Paul does use the description "first, secondarily, thirdly" with respect to gifts, 1 Cor. 12. 28.

Secundus, Acts 20. 4, meaning "second". At the end of his third missionary journey, Paul returned from Corinth through Macedonia, though the others went by sea to Troas to await Paul and Luke. So they were altogether in Troas, meeting with the church there. In verse 4, men are named who came from churches formed on all of Paul's three missionary journeys. In particular, Secundus came from Thessalonica, a faithful man who travelled with Paul for a season.

Tertius, Rom. 16. 22, meaning "third". Here was a privileged man indeed, for he wrote the Epistle to the Romans, "I, Tertius, who wrote this epistle, salute you in the Lord", evidently Paul's amanuensis. Paul allowed him this little space to insert his name, work and greetings. He was clearly interested in the believers in Rome, and handled the Word of God carefully and exactly as he penned the Epistle.

Quartus, Rom. 16. 23, meaning "fourth". Here is a name just slipped into the text at the end. No doubt he entered the room, saw what was taking place, and as an act of fellowship with writer and readers, he requested that his name and personal greetings be inserted after Gaius and Erastus. Just an ordinary brother, yet his name appears in the Scriptures.

All these three were with Paul in Corinth. Paul was not the "first", since he claimed to be least, 1 Cor. 15. 9, though he wrote that he was "first" (*protos*) in sinnership, 1 Tim. 1. 15. But there was one who tried to be first, for Diotrephes "loveth to have the preeminence (i.e. to be first)", 3 John 9. But the One who is first is the Lord, "I am the first (*protos*)", Rev. 1. 11, 17; 2. 8; 22. 13; see Col. 1. 18.

March 21st

READING: **Mark 14. 12-26**

A LARGE UPPER ROOM FURNISHED

BOTH Mark and Luke describe this room as "a large upper room furnished", Mark 14. 15; Luke 22. 12. We normally associate this room with the Lord's introduction of the breaking of bread, but to the writer this room also had other uses. We believe that, just as the Lord prepared His disciples spiritually for His departure from them, so He also prepared for their physical welfare. In fact, we believe (because of (6) below) that He arranged for this room to be hired for many weeks for the use of the apostles and others. The following list is therefore of considerable interest.

(1) During this last evening, the breaking of bread was introduced by the Lord Jesus in this upper room, Mark 14. 22.

(2) Here the Lord washed the disciples' feet, and also taught them about His promised return and the giving of the Holy Spirit, John chs. 13-14.

(3) In Luke 22. 62, "Peter went out, and wept bitterly", to no other place in private than to the upper room.

(4) When the Lord on the cross said to John, "Behold thy mother!", he "took her unto his own home", John 19. 27. The word "home" does not appear in the Greek text; John did not have a home in Jerusalem, since his roots were in Galilee. We believe that he took her to this upper room, and then returned.

(5) After His resurrection, the Lord revealed Himself to the ten apostles where the doors were shut, John 20. 19. A week later He revealed Himself there again to the eleven, v. 26. This was the upper room, where the apostles were now living temporarily. In other words, the room that the Lord had left three nights before, John 14. 31, He now visited again as alive from the dead.

(6) They were not to depart from Jerusalem, Acts 1. 4, so the apostles and many others (about 120) dwelt in "an upper room", vv. 13-15. Strictly, the Greek text has "*the* upper room", referring to the one chosen by the Lord originally. Now we see why it was "large": whereas originally only the apostles had been there with Him, yet the Lord had provided abundantly for the 120 that He knew would be there later.

(7) The "one place" where they were gathered when the Spirit descended could be none other than this upper room, Acts 2. 1.

March 22nd

READING: **Acts 18. 18-28**

THE WILL OF GOD

ANY DISCUSSION of the will of God is not a subject that is merely open for exposition; it is something that is intensely practical.

The principle is found in James 4. 13-15. He visualises men who plan for the future, regardless of the shortness of life. The proper attitude of the Christian should be, "If the Lord will, we shall live, and do this, or that". We have to make plans for tomorrow, but there should be the sincere exercise to plan according to the divine will, a will that should be sought by various means, direct and indirect.

The example of the Lord Jesus is important to observe; as He came into the world, He said, "I come to do thy will, O God", Heb. 10. 9. In deep agony of soul in Gethsemane, just before the full outworking of this will at Calvary, He prayed, "not as I will, but as thou wilt", Matt. 26. 39. In His lifetime, He said, "I seek not my own will, but the will of the Father which hath sent me", John 5. 30.

The example of Paul. As he continued his second missionary journey, he and his fellowworkers tried this way and that way, but they were forbidden, Acts 16. 6-10, until the will of the Lord was manifested to Paul that they should pass over into Macedonia. Later on this journey, night and day he was praying that they might see the face of the Thessalonians, and that God should "direct our way unto you", 1 Thess. 3. 10-11. At the end of this journey in Acts 18. 21, Paul promised to return to Ephesus "if God will", and this happened at the beginning of the third missionary journey.

In Ephesus, Paul wrote the First Epistle to the Corinthians, and planned to visit the church there later. He wrote, "I will come to you shortly, if the Lord will", 1 Cor. 4. 19. He wrote the same thing at the end of the Epistle, "I trust to tarry a while with you, if the Lord permit", 16. 7. As we know, Paul did visit Corinth, showing that this plan was according to the will of God, Acts 20. 2-3. At that time, he planned to visit Rome. He therefore prayed for "a prosperous journey by the will of God", Rom. 1. 10, and that he could come with joy "by the will of God", 15. 32. But the will of God for Paul was shipwreck and imprisonment in Rome, Acts chs. 27-28.

82

March 23rd

READING: **2 Chronicles 9. 1-12**

THE QUEEN OF SHEBA

THE QUEEN OF Sheba came to Jerusalem, to see Solomon and the many remarkable aspects of his person, his royal glory, and the house of the Lord that he had built. Of these features, there are many that may be found in 1 Corinthians in a spiritual sense.

Wisdom, v. 3; this corresponds to 1 Corinthians 1-2. Paul discards the "wisdom of words", 1. 17, "the wisdom of the wise", v. 19, and the wisdom of the Greeks, v. 22. Rather, Paul would speak only of "the wisdom of God", 2. 7, a hidden wisdom, for Christ is made unto us wisdom, 1. 30.

The house, v. 3; this corresponds to 1 Corinthians 3. Paul calls it "the temple of God", v. 16, built upon the one foundation that Paul had laid, even the Lord Jesus, v. 10. Only precious things could characterize this spiritual building.

The table, v. 4, corresponding to 1 Corinthians 10. This contrasts with the table of demons, v. 21, that characterized the Corinthian religion. But the bread that is broken implies the unity of the saints who form the body of Christ.

The servants, v. 4, corresponding to 1 Corinthians 12; for here Paul dwells upon those who are called to serve in a local church. Each gift derives from the Holy Spirit, and each servant takes a differing part in the overall service of the church.

The attendance, v. 4, corresponding to 1 Corinthians 14; for in this chapter (although a corrective chapter) Paul deals with the activity of those who attend upon the Lord's service.

The apparel, v. 4, corresponding to 1 Corinthians 13. Paul wrote, "put on charity (love)", Col. 3. 14, regarding love as an outward spiritual garment. Thus the character of love is described in 1 Corinthians 13. 4-7, and when men see this they know that the love of Christ dwells within.

Cupbearers or butlers, v. 4, corresponding to 1 Corinthians 11, for here we see the Lord's people in their most solemn functioning—the breaking of bread and the drinking of the cup, in the way that pleases Him.

The ascent, v. 4, corresponding to 1 Corinthians 15. This ascent was a large viaduct connecting the west of Jerusalem to the temple courts on the east. The future resurrection of the body is the ascent for which believers wait today.

March 24th

READING: **Psalm 24**

THE KING OF GLORY

WE READ of the God of glory, the Father of glory, the Lord of glory, the King of glory, and the Spirit of glory. We must distinguish between "the God of glory" and "the glory of God"; the former relates to the Person of God that radiates glory, the fulness of His character, while the latter relates to the glory itself that God is radiating. "The glory of God" and "the glory of the Lord" appear far more frequently, particularly as associated with the tabernacle and the temple. For this glory filled the tabernacle, Exod. 40. 34, and also the temple at its dedication, 1 Kings 8. 11. It was seen by Ezekiel as it left the temple, Ezek. 10. 4, but it never dwelt in Herod's temple.

The God of glory, Acts 7. 2. Stephen commenced his last address with this title, speaking of the One who appeared to Abraham before he left his homeland. The One with this great title would deliver Abraham from the idolatrous city of Ur: "Get thee out . . . unto a land" was the revelation, this would form the basis of the new nation separated unto God.

The Father of glory, Eph. 1. 17. This title appears at the beginning of Paul's prayer for the Ephesians: the One who radiated glory was the One to grant wisdom and knowledge, the understanding of His power in resurrection.

The Lord of glory, 1 Cor. 2. 8. The Person who radiated moral glory when He was here was unknown to those who crucified Him, else they would not have sought His death. We read of this title also in James 2. 1, "have not the faith of our Lord Jesus Christ, the Lord of glory, with respect of persons". The appreciation of the unique One who radiates glory would be sufficient to dispel any attitude that distinguishes between rich and poor in a local church. His riches and His poverty, 2 Cor. 8. 9, turn all eyes to Himself in holy unity.

The King of glory, Psa. 24. 7. Appearing five times in this Psalm, this title shows the Lord radiating glory in the millennial environment of His kingdom.

The Spirit of glory, 1 Pet. 4. 14 R.V. This is preferable to "spirit" (with initial small letter "s", A.V.). Thus the three Persons of the Godhead are all described as radiating glory. For believers this is a very personal blessing, since all three Persons dwell in the believer, John 14. 17, 23.

March 25th

READING: John 8. 12-32

NOT OF THIS WORLD

ONE WORD for "holy" is *hagios*, composed of a negative and a root meaning world. A holy person, therefore, is one who is separated unto God. On three occasions in John's Gospel, the Lord used the explicit meaning "not of this world"

(1) *The Lord*, "I am not of this world", John 8. 23. The Lord was contrasting Himself with the Pharisees, who were engaged in their usual activity of opposition to His teaching (note their comments and questions in vv. 13, 19, 22). He spoke of the source of His journey to earth—it was "from above", while the Pharisees were "from beneath", v. 23. This descent from above therefore characterized His life, service and teaching. He personally was "not of this world", and He was "holy, harmless, undefiled, separate from sinners, and made higher than the heavens", Heb. 7. 26. He therefore had no contact with the dominating thoughts and activity of men.

In His prayer to the Father, He also divinely claimed, "I am not of the world", John 17. 16. He stated that He had been sent from the Father, with whom He had eternal glory; He sanctified Himself as living amongst men, and He was now about to return to the Father, completely undefiled and undeflected.

(2) *His kingdom*, "My kingdom is not of this world", John 18. 36. The character of this kingdom is from above, having no connection with the political philosophies so loved by men. Morally, His kingdom is righteousness, peace and joy in the Holy Spirit, Rom. 14. 17. Politically, it is so distinct from the kingdom of the fourth beast, Dan. 7. 7-8, for His kingdom shall not be destroyed, v. 14. Religiously, the people of the kingdom are called out of world religion, Rev. 18. 4.

(3) *His people*, "they are not of the world" repeated twice in John 17. 14, 16. They contrast with the Pharisees in John 8, "ye are of this world", v. 23; they would die in their sins, as being from beneath, and they could not come where the Lord was going. But the Lord's people are so distinct; both they and the Lord are not of this world. Hence both are sanctified, both are sent into the world, both are one, both have been given the word, both have glory, both are loved by the Father. We therefore must take a stand as being on the Lord's side; His character must be seen in our character.

March 26th

READING: **1 Kings 8. 10-21**

WELL IN THINE HEART

HERE IN this prayer of dedication of the temple, Solomon recalls the exercise of his father David (the full account of this is found in 2 Samuel 7 and 1 Chronicles 17). The ark had been placed in a tent on mount Zion, but this was not to be its permanent home during the period of the monarchy. As David recalled at the end of his life, "I had it in my heart to build an house of rest for the ark", 1 Chron. 28. 2. Previously, Nathan had said to David, "Do all that is in thine heart", 17. 2, but this was rather precipitous, for God would not allow David to build the temple. So Solomon recalls in 1 Kings 8. 18 that God had commended David for his exercise, "thou didst well that it was in thine heart" (this statement is not found in 2 Samuel 7 and 1 Chronicles 17). So David did all that he could, namely, he prepared with all his might for the house, and set his affection to the house, gathering all the material together, 1 Chron. 29. 2-5.

But in the Lord's case, His heart was set solely on what He would do according to the will of God. In His prayer to the Father, He said, "I have finished the work that thou gavest me to do", John 17. 4. There was no exercise that could not be fulfilled; what He said, He did.

In Paul's case, he laboured more abundantly than they all, 1 Cor. 15. 10, but there were some exercises of heart and mind that he could not fulfil. For example, "we would have come unto you . . . once and again", 1 Thess. 2. 18; "a prosperous journey . . . I long to see you . . . to the end ye may be established", Rom. 1. 10-11; "whensoever I take my journey into Spain, I will come to you . . . I will come by you into Spain", Rom. 15. 24, 28. Paul thus desired huge advances in the service of God in the gospel, but this was not possible; nevertheless, it was well that it had been in the apostle's heart, and that he was subject to the will of God.

What of believers today? If they live a full live before God and in His service, they cannot do more. But is it in our heart to serve God, or is He largely forgotten? There can be no excuse for doing nothing, Matt. 25. 25. In Mark 14. 8, the Lord commended the woman who had "done what she could"; perhaps she would have liked to have done more!

March 27th

READING: **Luke 9. 44-62**

JERUSALEM THE PLACE

THE GOSPEL by John is the gospel of the "hour"—when the Lord would die on the cross. But the Gospel by Luke is the gospel of the "place"—where the Lord would die. The Lord had the object of going to Jerusalem, and Luke in particular traces the stages of the Lord's journey there.

(1) Jerusalem is not mentioned in Luke 9. 22, though the name is found in Matthew 16. 21.

(2) Luke 9. 31. On the mountain top, with the Lord appearing in glory, the subject of conversation was "his decease which he should accomplish at Jerusalem". After the Lord had descended, Luke commences tracing His journey to Jerusalem.

(3) Luke 9. 51. Passing through Samaria southwards, "he stedfastly set his face to go to Jerusalem". Previously the Samaritans had received Him, John 4. 40-41, but now His destination offended them. The Lord's purpose remained undeflected, He was come to save men's lives, Luke 9. 56.

(4) Luke 13. 22. Luke had not forgotten that, in his narrative, he had left the Lord on the road to Jerusalem, so here He is seen still "teaching, and journeying to Jerusalem". The same day, v. 31, He spoke of "cures to day and to morrow", namely, His work on the cross. He implied that He could not die outside Jerusalem, v. 33.

(5) Luke 17. 11. Luke presents the Lord as going to Jerusalem, passing through Samaria and Galilee. In other words, the Lord's overall journey was not in a straight line—rather, it consisted of circles.

(6) Luke 18. 31. At this stage, the Lord was in Judaea beyond Jordan, Matt. 19. 1. He now told the apostles, "we go up to Jerusalem"; unfortunately, they did not know the implication of His words—this was "hid from them", v. 34.

(7) Luke 19. 11. At last, He was "nigh to Jerusalem", when, in the parable, He was going into a far country, v. 12. His servants had to "Occupy till I come".

(8) Luke 19. 28. On the eastern slopes of the mount of Olives, "he went before, ascending up to Jerusalem". At the top of the mount, He wept, as "he beheld the city", v. 41.

Luke 24. 31-36, after His resurrection, the Lord no doubt went with the two men, returning to Jerusalem to His apostles.

READING: **1 John 2. 18-29**

THE LORD ADDED

IN THE Gospels, the Lord chose the apostles one by one, and added them to the growing group who would form the twelve. It is important to note that they did not add themselves to the group—that was totally impossible.

In the Acts, this observation applies to all members of the church formed at Pentecost and throughout history. All the activity that took place in Jerusalem at Pentecost and afterwards concludes with, "the Lord added to the church daily", Acts 2. 47. Repentance, faith and baptism were the outward and inward signs that showed that addition had taken place. It was impossible for others to add themselves, for of the people, priests and Pharisees, "durst no man join himself to them", 5. 13. Membership of the church was not open to the will of man; yet, multitudes "were the more added to the Lord". Evangelists and the Word of God were used to this end.

Later in Antioch, "much people was added unto the Lord", Acts 11. 24. But this happy state of affairs did not last long. Certainly no man could add Himself to the church as the body of Christ, but to local churches it became easier to do so. In Acts 9. 26, the recently converted Paul sought to join himself to the Jerusalem church, but the disciples did not believe that Paul was a disciple, so they refused him until Barnabas convinced them that Paul was a new convert. But by way of contrast, Simon of Samaria continued with Philip, and they thought that he was a convert, until it was seen that he did not have the Spirit of God, Acts 8. 13, 18. This showed who he was, and according to Peter he would perish. After many more years, it became easier for men to join themselves to local churches, because of lack of watchfulness. Thus in Ephesus, Paul warned that "grievous wolves" would enter from the outside, and join even the eldership, Acts 20. 29. In Galatians 2. 4, Paul wrote that "false brethren" had been brought in unawares to spy out the believers' liberty in Christ; in other words, they had added themselves. In John's later years, he wrote of antichrists who "went out from us, but they were not of us", 1 John 2. 19. God had not added these men who denied the true humanity of Christ. Jezebel the prophetess in Thyatira had not been added by God, Rev. 2. 20.

READING: **Isaiah 42. 1-7**

BEHOLD MY SERVANT

THE GREEKS "would see Jesus", John 12. 21; John the Baptist was "looking upon Jesus", 1. 36, inviting men to "Behold the Lamb of God". After the Lord's resurrection, Mary "had seen the Lord", 20. 18, but concerning others it was said, "him they saw not", Luke 24. 24. Here, then, are various aspects of seeing and beholding, and the invitation was often given by men and by God in the Scriptures.

(1) *"Behold my servant"*, Isa. 42. 1. Here was the elect of God, the One in whom He delighted. This title corresponds to Mark's Gospel of the Servant. This verse is quoted in Matthew 12. 18, in the context of the Pharisees holding a council as to how they might destroy Him, v. 14.

(2) *"Behold the man"*, John 19. 5, a title that corresponds to Luke's Gospel, and the Manhood of Christ. It was Pilate who spoke these words, after he had scourged Jesus, and who brought the Lord forth wearing the robes of mockery. The immediate effect of this invitation was that the priests cried out, "Crucify him, crucify him". In Zechariah 6. 12, the invitation "Behold the man" was made to Joshua the high priest, and the immediate promise was that He would build the temple of the Lord.

(3) *"Behold your King"*, John 19. 14, a title that corresponds to Matthew's Gospel. Pilate said this to the people on the final occasion of his bringing Jesus forth, in readiness for pronouncing His crucifixion. Again, the Jews cried, "Away with him . . . crucify him". They claimed to have no king but Caesar, one whom they really detested, but he was to them better than the true King. In Zechariah 9. 9, the invitation is given, "behold, thy King cometh", a millennial promise, but this is quoted in Matthew 21. 5 referring to the Lord riding into Jerusalem prior to His crucifixion.

(4) *"Behold thy God"*, Isa. 40. 9, a title that corresponds to John's Gospel. Unlike the previous three titles, this one is not associated with cruelty and hatred. This is a millennial promise made to Zion and Jerusalem. For good tidings would come, and the Lord God would come with a strong hand, and His reward would be with Him, feeding His sheep and gathering His lambs.

March 30th

READING: **Mark 13. 14-23**

FALSE CHRISTS AND FALSE PROPHETS SHALL RISE

THERE WAS and is one true Christ, together with true brethren, true evangelists, true teachers, and true elders. But in any fair scene on earth, what was false quickly reared up its ugly head to mar the testimony of God in local churches.

False Christs, Matt. 24. 5, 23-24; Mark 13. 21-22. Men claiming to be Christ have risen in the past, including some Popes. It will be so in the future during the period of the great tribulation. Then there will be "the man of sin . . . the son of perdition" claiming to be God, 2 Thess. 2. 3-4, the antichrist, the beast deceiving men by great wonders and miracles, Rev. 13. 13-15. In Paul's day, "another Jesus, another spirit, another gospel" was available, 2 Cor. 11. 4.

False brethren, Gal. 2. 4. These were men who were "unawares brought in", to spy out the liberty that believers had in Christ, seeking to bring them back to the bondage of the law. Such men could infiltrate like a virus, but Paul took a stand for "the truth of the gospel", v. 5, although he had to suffer sometimes "among false brethren", 2 Cor. 11. 26.

False evangelists, Gal. 1. 6-9. These were men who openly preached "another gospel: which is not another", namely, "another gospel of a different kind, which is not another gospel of the same kind". Paul's gospel was unique as pertaining to Christ and His work; all else is spurious.

False teachers and prophets, 2 Pet. 2. 1. As in the O.T., so in the N.T. There are always men ready to expound false doctrine; John called them "antichrists", 1 John 2. 18, and also "false prophets" who deny that the Lord Jesus came in the flesh, 4. 1-3. The Lord warned of such men in the end times, Mark 13. 22.

False elders, Acts 20. 29-30. Some would rise from the outside, and others from the inside, being "grievous wolves", seeking to devour the flock. Paul was a prophet, and could see that such men would arise, as indeed they did. For the Lord commended the church at Ephesus: "thou hast tried them which say they are apostles, and are not, and hast found them liars", Rev. 2. 3. These men were "false apostles . . . transforming themselves into the apostles of Christ", 2 Cor. 11. 13. But the Lord's sheep "know not the voice of strangers", John 10. 5.

March 31st

READING: **Acts 1. 1-11**

JESUS BEGAN BOTH TO DO AND TEACH

WHAT GOD commences on earth continues until it is stopped or changed. Thus the creation commenced in Genesis 1. 1, and it continues until it will ultimately end, 2 Pet. 3. 7. The law commenced in Exodus, and continued until faith came, Gal. 3. 23-25. The same with God's work in His people, "he which hath begun a good work in you will perform (finish) it until the day of Jesus Christ", Phil. 1. 6.

Similarly the work that the Lord began, Acts 1. 1, continues now by His Spirit. Luke in his Gospel traced the beginning, while in the Acts he traces its continuation. Thus we find in the four Gospels: "From that time Jesus began to preach, and to say, Repent", Matt. 4. 17. "The beginning of the gospel of Jesus Christ", Mark 1. 1. "He began to say unto them, This day is this scripture fulfilled in your ears", Luke 4. 21. "This beginning of miracles did Jesus in Cana of Galilee", John 2. 11. The Lord's work was finished on earth, 17. 4; 19. 30, though He now continues His work by the Spirit, as Mark 16. 20 puts it, "the Lord working with them, and confirming the word with signs following".

Of all believers, it can be said that they have "begun in the Spirit", Gal. 3. 3. How all must ensure that they do not frustrate the continuing work of the Spirit, by being "made perfect by the flesh". This continuation of the divine work in His people can be seen in 1 Corinthians 3. 9, where believers are seen as "labourers together with God", accomplished through the grace of God which is given us. We labour "by the grace of God" which is with us, 15. 10. This is seen in the gifts that are given by the one Spirit, 12. 4, by the various ministries guided by the same Lord, v. 5, and by the results produced by the same God, v. 6. By these means, the work of the Lord that began when He was here below continues even to the present day through the sanctified service of His people.

This means that something of the character of His service should be seen now in His people as His work continues. He stated that He had given us an example, "that ye should do as I have done", John 13. 15; "do thou likewise", Luke 10. 37. We should also be those who emulate His zeal, His faithfulness, and His appreciation of the Father's will.

April 1st

READING: **Philippians 4**

THE INFLUENCE OF THE SCRIPTURES

WE ARE ALL influenced by what we listen to and by what we read, whether good or bad. An absorbing interest in a particular subject may arise by someone else's influence over us. Too much interest in reading and watching crime as entertainment has a detrimental influence on the mind. But if we follow Paul's advice, "whatsoever things are true, honest, just, pure, lovely, of good report . . . think on these things", Phil. 4. 8, then our lives are full of these virtues.

The most influential book is the Bible, the Holy Scriptures, the Word of God. Because it influences men towards the Lord Jesus Christ, towards forgiveness of sins through His sacrifice on the cross, towards eternal life and Christian living, men largely do not want its influence, and hence they avoid its teaching as far as possible. The best-seller is not read; the book that has come to us from the days of the apostles and prophets is rejected by rationalists, ridiculed by the ignorant, disbelieved by the worldly-minded, and criticized by theologians. Its message of divine love remains unknown; the broad path of unbelief leading downwards is desired instead of the narrow path of faith leading upwards, Matt. 7. 13-14.

But God's Word is very badly treated. In the O.T., in Isaiah 30. 10 there were many who said to God's preachers, "Prophesy not unto us right things, speak unto us smooth things, prophesy deceits". In the N.T. Peter claimed that the ignorant and unstable misinterpret Paul's Epistles and the other Scriptures to their own ruin. How good, then, to read about those who "received the word of God, not as the word of men, but as it is in truth, the word of God, which effectually worketh also in you that believe", 1 Thess. 2. 13. Here is power and life in the Word of God, moving men to repentance, faith and obedience, showing that His gift, freely given and lasting for eternity, can never be found in the mere fleeting books of men. Here is no academic approach to the Word of God; a new spiritual approach is necessary if its influence is to be real both to the unsaved and to the Lord's people. We need a childlike approach that believes because God has spoken, a desire to read and understand the Word of God daily, because in it are found divine love, mercy, guidance and eternal life.

April 2nd

READING: **Psalm 45**

THE ANOINTING

TO BE anointed implies that one is consecrated and set apart to a special position and for special work.

David anointed. Kings were anointed so as to demonstrate the peculiar position and authority that they held. Thus David was anointed three times before different groups of people. The first occasion occurred in private. Samuel came to Bethlehem, and the sons of Jesse appeared before him, and David came last. "Then Samuel took the horn of oil, and anointed him in the midst of his brethren", 1 Sam. 16. 13. From that day, David was God's man to replace Saul. The second occasion was after Saul's death: "the men of Judah came, and there they anointed David king over the house of Judah", 2 Sam. 2. 4; this took place before the tribe of Judah. The third occasion was seven years later, when before the elders of all Israel he was anointed king over Israel, 5. 3.

The Lord anointed. The first anointing was private, when the Spirit descended upon Him at His baptism; "he hath anointed me to preach the gospel to the poor", Luke 4. 18. The second occasion occurred in Bethany before His disciples, "Then took Mary a pound of ointment . . . and anointed the feet of Jesus", John 12. 3; see also Mark 14. 8. The third anointing is in heaven, "God, thy God, hath anointed thee with the oil of gladness above thy fellows", Psa. 45. 6-7. Here it is the exaltation of Christ before the hosts of heaven.

The Lord's people. Several N.T. verses refer to this. For example, "the anointing which ye have received of him abideth in you", 1 John 2. 27, referring to the Spirit who guides into all truth. Again, He which "hath anointed us, is God", 2 Cor. 1. 21; in the immediate verses, various aspects of the giving of the Spirit to a believer are set out, the anointing referring to equipment and calling in service. Who sees the effects of this anointing? Privately, God, who sees the inner motives and desires to please Him. Then the Lord's people see these effects, noting the zeal and the outworking of gift in a believer. And finally, heaven itself beholds the life and service of the anointed one. Paul was "a spectacle (or, theatre) . . . to angels" as pertaining to his sufferings, 1 Cor. 4. 9, and angels witness the godly obedience of women, 11. 10.

93

April 3rd

READING: **Numbers 22. 22-35**

I HAVE SINNED

IT IS GOOD to make such a profession, "I have sinned", but is it genuine? There are several examples of such a profession in the Scriptures, and these merit careful consideration.

The case of Balaam. The story of Balaam in Numbers 22-24 is well-known. He had been told by God, "Thou shalt not go with them", 22. 12, after which he adopted every excuse to get this commandment reversed. No wonder we read of "the way of Balaam", 2 Pet. 2. 15, "the error of Balaam", Jude 11, and "the doctrine of Balaam", Rev. 2. 14. Thus the angel announced that he had been ready to slay him, Num. 22. 33, after which Balaam had confessed, "I have sinned", v. 24. What hypocrisy, for afterwards in Numbers 25 the children of Israel committed trespass through "the counsel of Balaam", 31. 16. In other words, his hollow confession was not coupled with repentance, and he was slain shortly afterwards, 31. 8.

The case of Saul, 1 Sam. 15, 24, "I have sinned". This was hollow, and he was rejected by the Lord, v. 26.

The case of David. After David's sin in the matter of Bathsheba and Uriah, the message from Nathan, "Thou art the man", broke the king down completely, and he cried, "I have sinned against the Lord", 2 Sam. 12. 13; Psa. 51. 4. How sincere and repentant David was, with the result that his sin was put away, and again he was able to sing the praises of the Lord, Psa. 51. 15. Not that he was immune from sin afterwards, for later in another matter he cried, "I have sinned greatly", and he had to sustain chastisement from the Lord, 2 Sam. 24. 10.

The case of Peter, Luke 5. 8. "I am a sinful man, O Lord", he confessed. For he had drifted back to fishing after his first call by the Lord in John 1. 42. This second calling after the miraculous draught of fishes was permanent in Peter's experience; his repentance was complete, though he failed on many occasions afterwards. He was saved "with the precious blood of Christ", 1 Pet. 1. 19.

The case of the prodigal son, Luke 15. 18. The young man decided to return to his father, saying, "I have sinned against heaven, and before thee". He had sunk to the lowest position, before being raised to the highest; his confession was absolutely sincere, proved by what happened afterwards.

94

April 4th

READING: **Jeremiah 1. 1-10**

LIPS TOUCHED

THE TOUCHING of one's lips by the Lord must have been a marvellous experience, for power and ability were transferred from the divine reservoir to equip and sustain the feebleness of His servants. In the Lord's case, it is stated that "grace is poured into thy lips", Psa. 45. 2, though this act did not, of course, imply any weakness or need. During His early service of teaching, men "wondered at the gracious words which proceeded out of his mouth", Luke 4. 22, though later the chief priests sent spies "that they might take hold of his words", 20. 20, so as to seek to accuse Him.

Though the Lord needed no preparation for service, yet the four major prophets all needed divine help, and this help related very much to the subject of their lips. Perhaps we need to appreciate this more today, so that ministry may be more spiritual and effective.

The case of Isaiah. Before this prophet could embark on the major part of his ministry, cleansing was necessary. He knew that his lips were unclean, and that the nation was "a people of unclean lips", Isa. 6. 5, but one of the seraphim laid a live coal on his mouth, saying, "Lo, this hath touched thy lips", v. 7. Thus his mouth was cleansed and sanctified for the work to which he was called by God.

The case of Jeremiah. Even before his birth, Jeremiah was sanctified to be a prophet, Jer. 1. 5. But the prophet claimed weakness as a child, that he could not speak. So the Lord touched his mouth, v. 9, implying that God's words had been placed in his mouth. Note, not just a general message, but the *actual* words of the message, for theologians are very quick to insist that men of God (and the Gospel writers) formulated their writings with *their own* words.

The case of Ezekiel. The prophet ate the roll, and digested the writings of God, Ezek. 3. 1-4. God promised, "I will open thy mouth", 3. 27. All this implies inspiration.

The case of Daniel. In the third year of Cyrus, Daniel was an old man, displaying weakness by the river Hiddekel when he was granted a vision, Dan. 10. 1-9. Yet one touched his lips, enabling him to open his mouth to speak, v. 16.

But untouched lips support a far-off heart, Matt. 15. 8-9.

April 5th

READING: **2 Kings 20. 12-21**

CAST NOT YOUR PEARLS BEFORE SWINE

IN THE SERMON on the mount, amongst many other matters the Lord said, "Give not that which is holy unto the dogs, neither cast ye your pearls before swine, lest they trample them under their feet, and turn again and rend you", Matt. 7. 6. In other words, the Lord was instructing His disciples to be very careful as to those men who would hear their testimony of the most holy things. In the tabernacle, the most holy things were not for the ordinary people. And today, men in the world cannot appreciate the holy things of God; they often rend them by adverse criticism and mockery, using them for the purpose of entertainment. No wonder some of the parables in Matthew 13 were designed to hide their meanings from unbelievers; see verses 10-18, 34-36. And no wonder the holy ministry in John 13-16 was for the ears of the disciples only; here was material that could not be spoken to the multitudes in the temple courts and in the synagogues. Again, Paul declared "all the counsel of God" to the Ephesian believers, but not to the idolaters in Ephesus, Acts 20. 27.

What a contrast we find in the O.T. After Hezekiah had been miraculously healed, the king of Babylon (amongst the nations sunk in idolatry, and soon to destroy Jerusalem and its temple) sent letters and a present to Hezekiah, 2 Kings 20. 12. The result was that in verse 13 Hezekiah showed these messengers from Babylon "all that was found in his treasures: there was nothing in his house, nor in all his dominion, that Hezekiah showed them not". He was strongly rebuked by God through the prophet Isaiah, and the deportation into Babylon was prophesied, "nothing shall be left", v. 17. This story is completely repeated in Isaiah 39. 1-8.

Again, another example in the O.T. Instead of showing treasures to the enemy, Solomon showed his treasure to a queen of faith, 1 Kings 10. 1-13. For by faith she owned the work of the Lord, and the fact that He had placed Solomon on the throne, v. 9. She gave Solomon many treasures, v. 10, unlike the king of Babylon who would later take Hezekiah's treasures away. But the Lord Jesus was present as "a greater than Solomon", Matt. 12. 42. For ourselves, there are many things we can preach to the unsaved, but not the most holy treasures.

April 6th

READING: **Matthew 8. 18-34**

THE AMOUNT OF FAITH

ONCE WE ARE saved by faith, we can perceive the upward progress by which faith is deepened and strengthened. We may liken it to a ladder of faith, and all men stand somewhere in relation to it, the unsaved not having taken even the first step to the lowest rung.

No faith. In Moses' final song, he was rehearsing the idolatry into which the people would sink: "I will see what their end shall be . . . children in whom is no faith", Deut. 32. 20. In the N.T. after the calming of the storm, the Lord said, "how is it that ye have no faith?", Mark. 4. 40.

Little faith. Many times the Lord said this to His disciples. Regarding the obtaining of necessary things, He said, "O ye of little faith", if anxiety were to arise, Matt. 6. 30. After the storm, He also said, "O ye of little faith", 8. 26, When Peter was walking on the sea, and saw the waves boisterous, the Lord said to Peter, "O thou of little faith", 14. 31. When the disciples had forgotten the feeding of the 4,000 and the 5,000, He said to them, "O ye of little faith", 16. 8. At least they were on the bottom rung!

"Increase our faith". The apostles realized their weakness on occasions, and in particular their ability to forgive men who trespassed against them. Hence they asked, "Lord, Increase our faith", Luke 17. 5.

Great faith. It was not a Jew but a Roman centurion who said, "speak the word only". The Lord's commendation was, "I have not found so great faith, no, not in Israel", Matt. 8. 10.

Full of faith. In his service, Barnabas was described as a "good man, and full of the Holy Spirit and of faith", so he could help the believers and the church in Antioch, Acts 11. 24.

Strong in faith. God's purpose through Abraham was going to be accomplished by the physically impossible—he and Sarah would have a child in their old age. He staggered not at this divine promise, but was "strong in faith", Rom. 4. 20.

All faith. This "all faith" sounds very much like the ideal, particularly when it could remove mountains, yet Paul claimed that he was nothing if he did not have love. The motivation and character behind one's deeds is love, and this has precedence even over "all faith", 1 Cor. 13. 2.

April 7th

READING: **Mark 5. 21-43**

THE TWO TWELVES

IN THESE VERSES, we have two miracles, the first concerning the woman with the issue of blood being healed, and the second relating to the raising of Jairus' daughter. They are unusual in the sense that the two miracles are interlocked, the story of Jairus and his daughter being broken by the story of the woman who was healed. The number twelve appears in both: the daughter was twelve years old, v. 42, and the woman had been ill for twelve years, v. 25. Perhaps we should not ask why these events occurred, since they show up the gracious mercy of the Lord under all circumstances, but rather we should ask why these two miracles were recorded, evidently to show an aspect of truth not contained in the miracles themselves.

The answer evidently lies in the number twelve, for there were twelve tribes of Israel and twelve apostles; these did not cease to be relevant after O.T. and N.T. days, for in Revelation 21. 12-14 the twelve gates were associated with the twelve tribes and the twelve foundations of the wall with the twelve apostles of the Lamb.

The first miracle actually accomplished is inserted in a gap occurring in the story of the second.

The daughter being dead speaks of the valley of dry bones in Ezekiel 37. 1-2. A promise of restoration is made, vv. 5-6, and the context makes it clear that both Judah and Israel (all the twelve tribes) are included, vv. 16, 19. This promise corresponds to Mark 5. 24, the Lord going with Jairus.

Between the promise and its accomplishment, the church is now built upon the foundation laid by the prophets and apostles, Eph. 2. 20. The blessings of salvation do not come by works, vv. 8-9. This corresponds to the healing of the woman, who could not obtain healing by her works and the works of others, Mark 5. 26. Today, members of the church give testimony to the saving power of Christ, just as the woman "told him all the truth", v. 33, with the multitude hearing her words.

At the end of the church age, the promise of restoration to Israel will be fulfilled. The church will be with the Lord when this happens, as Peter, James and John went in with the Lord in Mark 5. 37. Truly the Redeemer shall come to Zion, and "they lived", Ezek. 37. 10; Isa. 26. 19; Dan. 12. 2.

April 8th

READING: **Genesis 6. 8-22**

MADE ACCORDING TO PATTERN

WE WISH to draw attention to three structures that had to be made in O.T. times according to God's patterns.

The ark. The details of this structure were given to Noah by God, and we read, "Thus did Noah; according to all that God commanded him, so did he", Gen. 6. 22. The only way to safety was by following God's instructions. This obedience of Noah is stressed again in 7. 5, 9, 16. Other men were "disobedient", 1 Pet. 3. 20; any attempt at seizing anything that could float met with failure (unlike Acts 27. 44).

The tabernacle. "See . . . thou make all things according to the pattern showed to thee in the mount", spoken to Moses in Exodus 25. 40, but quoted in Hebrews 8. 5. The conclusion of the matter was, "Thus did Moses: according to all that the Lord commanded him, so did he", Exod. 40. 16. To have done otherwise would have involved copying the tabernacle of the heathen, Acts 7. 43.

The temple. David had the pattern of the temple given to him "by the Spirit" J.N.D. (not "by the spirit" A.V.), indeed "in writing by his hand upon me, even all the works of this pattern", 1 Chron. 28. 12, 19. In 2 Chron. chs. 3-4, Solomon made all things according to this pattern; "do it" said David to Solomon, 1 Chron. 28. 20, and Solomon "made", repeated many times in 2 Chron. chs. 3-4. Anything else would have been copying the heathen, as did Jeroboam, 1 Kings 12. 31, and as Ahaz later copied the great altar that he had seen in Damascus, having sent its pattern to Urijah the priest, 2 Kings 16. 10.

These three acts of obedience should speak to the Lord's people today. As far as the obedience of the gospel is concerned, anything else is a false gospel, Gal. 1. 6-9. Paul used strong language when he asserted that men who preach such false gospels are accursed. Here were men who preached the law and claimed that it was necessary to keep it, Acts 15. 5.

The "true tabernacle" is found in Hebrews 8. 2, where Christ is the High Priest; anything else amounts to not holding the Head. And the true temple corresponds to the local church, 1 Cor 3. 16, concerning the service of which Paul issued the commandments of God, 14. 37. Else the church is defiled with the ritual of men, and this is far from the true pattern.

April 9th

READING: **John 15**

THE LORD'S OWN POSSESSIONS

IN JOHN 13. 1, we read about the Lord, "having loved *his own* which were in the world". We are not concerned here with the blessed reference to this divine love, but with the Lord's possessions, "his own". This is an important concept, for it removes selfishness, as Paul wrote, "ye are not your own . . . ye are bought with a price", 1 Cor. 6. 19-20. There are five particular references where the Lord states who are His.

My servants. This is in connection with the Lordship of Christ: "where I am, there shall also my servant be", John 12. 26; "if my kingdom were of this world, then would my servants fight", 18. 36; "a prophetess, to teach and to seduce my servants", Rev. 2. 20.

My disciples. This is in connection with the Lord as Master or Teacher: "Herein is my Father glorified, that ye bear much fruit; so shall ye be my disciples", John 15. 8; "Jesus showed himself to his disciples", 21. 14.

My sheep. This is in connection with the Lord as the Good Shepherd: "I am the good shepherd, and know my sheep, and am known of mine", John 10. 14; see verses 26, 27.

My friends. This is in connection with the Manhood of Christ: "Ye are my friends, if ye do whatsoever I command you", John 15. 14. Note that in verse 15 the Lord distinguishes servants from friends.

My brethren. This is in connection with the Sonship of Christ: "go to my brethren", John 20. 17; "go tell my brethren", Matt. 28. 10. See also Matthew 12. 48.

This is an impressive list, and we should appreciate that all these names apply to ourselves. It is interesting to note that most of these appear in John's Gospel, but not exclusively.

It is also interesting to note that we can claim the Lord as our own in these same five features. "My Lord", John 20. 27; "Rabboni (my great Teacher)", v. 16; "my shepherd", Psa. 23. 1; "my friend", Song 5. 16; "my God", John 20. 27. Truly, in keeping with a hymn. "I am His, and He is mine".

There is the same divine possession found in the O.T. We can but quote a few examples: "thou becamest mine", Ezek. 16. 8; "Thou art my people . . . Thou art my God", Hos. 2. 23; "in that day when I make up my jewels", Mal. 3. 17.

April 10th

READING: Matthew 20. 20-34

THE CUP, THE STORM AND THE SWORD

WE OFTEN sing the hymn commencing with the words, "O Christ, what burdens bowed Thy head". In verses 3-4, we find references to the cup, the storm and the sword, and these metaphorical pictures derive from various verses in the Bible.

The cup. The mother of James and John wanted special privileges for her sons James and John. The Lord replied, "Ye know not what ye ask. Are ye able to drink of the cup that I shall drink of? . . . They say unto him, We are able . . . Ye shall drink indeed of my cup", Matt. 20. 22-23. Here is a shared cup of sufferings: James was martyred, while John suffered imprisonment and exile. But the Lord's cup went far deeper, and was unique. In the garden of Gethsemane, His prayer concerned the cup that He would drink, Matt. 26. 39, while afterwards, He spoke of the cup that His Father had given Him, John 18. 11. Believers cannot partake of that.

The storm. Jonah 2 was a poetical discourse of Jonah when he was in the belly of the great fish. The prophet likened his predicament to: "all thy billows and thy waves passed over me", Jon. 2. 3. That is where Peter thought he was going to in the fear of the moment, Matt. 14. 30; Paul was in "perils of the sea", 2 Cor. 11. 26, and later suffered shipwreck, Acts 27. 39-44. But Jonah's words were prophetical of the unique sufferings of Christ, who was greater than Jonah. When He suffered the divine judgment that was our due, then the waves and billows of divine wrath fell upon Him during the hours of darkness. Believers cannot partake of that.

The sword. It is surprising that the apostles had some swords with them in the upper room when the Lord instituted the breaking of bread; they produced two swords, but the Lord said, "It is enough" (that is, the subject of conversation was at an end), Luke 22. 38. Peter used one sword shortly afterwards, vv. 49-50. John the Baptist and James suffered death by means of the sword, Matt. 14. 10; Acts 12. 2. But the Lord's case was unique, "Awake, O sword, against my shepherd . . . smite the shepherd", Zech. 13. 7; Matt. 26. 31. Here was the Good Shepherd, giving His life for the sheep, not seen as the work of the wolf, but as the work of God the righteous Judge. Believers cannot partake of that.

April 11th

READING: **Psalm 14**

THE NECESSITY OF ACCURACY

IN THESE DAYS, there is much slipshod quoting of the Scriptures, as if anything will do. Modern translations do not help in this matter. Yet printers of the Scriptures have very high standards to maintain, but even then unfortunate errors do creep into the printed word. However, in the old days, errors could creep in more easily.

Then, there were no type-setting machines, neither mechanical nor electronic; all the individual pieces of type had to be set individually in lines and pages. In the Authorized Version, there are 3,566,480 letters and spaces involved!

In 1630, in the reign of Charles I, one can imagine a man, tired, working under bad lighting conditions, perhaps with bad eyesight, laboriously putting the type of Psalm 14 together (not quite half way through the Bible) copying from another text. Accidentally he composes, "The fool hath said in his heart, There is a God", v. 1, instead of "There is no God". The proofreader did not notice the error, and this was not discovered until after the printing of the whole Bible, when it had been bound, and copies sold. The printers were fined £3,000, and all copies were destroyed, a vast amount and a tremendous sum to lose in those days. In other words, there is a need for complete accuracy, because it is the Word of God.

In 1702, Psalm 119. 161 appeared as "Printers have persecuted me without a cause", instead of "Princes have persecuted me without a cause". Perhaps a compositor had been blamed for something which was not his fault, and his mind was occupied with the injustice, and his work was then adversely affected!

In 1802, 1 Timothy 5. 21 appeared as "I discharge thee before God", instead of "I charge thee before God".

In 1711, Isaiah 57. 12 appeared as "thy works; for they shall profit thee", instead of "they shall not profit thee". The meaning was therefore reversed, introducing false doctrine.

In 1631, Exodus 20. 14 appeared as "Thou shalt commit adultery", instead of "Thou shalt not". It is difficult to see how something so fundamental could have been overlooked.

In 1810, Luke 14. 26 appeared as "If any man come to me, and hate not . . . his own wife also, he cannot be my disciple", instead of "life". (We shall provide more errors later.)

April 12th

READING: **Acts 16. 12-40**

THE FIRST CONVERTS IN PHILIPPI

IN EVERY city when a local church was established, there were initial converts. In this connection, Philippi is very special, since these initial converts are recorded in Acts 16.

Here was a large Roman city, where there was nothing for God; Roman heathenism was largely found there. But there were a few Jews possessing no synagogue, and so the women met on a river bank for prayer. Additionally, there was an evil spirit in a girl, bringing gain to her masters. There were also multitudes and magistrates quite ready falsely to accuse, leading to cruelty with beatings and imprisonment.

To such a city Paul and Silas came with the gospel, and we have the record of the power of God, for a woman and a man were saved under quite different circumstances.

Lydia was devout, one who worshipped God and who met for prayer. She was not saved, not knowing the Lord Jesus and His salvation. She was quite unlike the majority of the heathen, for her heart was ready to receive the gospel. Hence the Lord opened her heart (alas, men usually open their own hearts to the world), and she listened to the apostolic message, Acts 16. 14. She then asked Paul to assess her faithfulness to the Lord—dare we ask other Christians for their assessment of our faithfulness? So she received Paul and his teaching, being baptized, with her home worthy to be open to the gatherings of a local assembly which would then be formed, v. 40.

The jailor was quite different. Here was a man practised in Roman cruelty, following in the steps of the cruelty of the Roman beast described in Daniel 7. 7. He heard the midnight songs of praise from Paul and Silas, but remained unmoved until God acted in a spectacular way. All the doors were opened (contrast this with Lydia's heart being opened), and he thought that all the prisoners had escaped, for which he would pay with his life. Hence he cried in effect, What could he do to be saved from this Roman judgment? Paul changed the subject, that is, to salvation from God's judgment through the Lord Jesus Christ. So Paul spoke to him the Word of the Lord, and he was received into the jailor's house, and a baptism followed.

Later Paul recalled these events: "your fellowship in the gospel *from the first day* until now", Phil. 1. 5.

April 13th

READING: **John 21. 1-7, 15-25**

FOLLOW ME

EVERY DISCIPLE of the Lord Jesus should be learning of Him and following Him. Several times in the Gospels we find this exhortation, perhaps a commandment, given by the Lord, and it is important to trace this in Peter's experience.

It all begins with the testimony of John the Baptist; as a result, Andrew followed the Lord, John 1. 37. But he first found his brother Peter, and brought him to the Lord. However, the Lord did not say to him "Follow me", v. 42, and this might have been a test to see what Peter would actually do.

Clearly, Peter returned to his fishing, for in Matthew 4. 18 the Lord found Peter and Andrew working. This time, He said explicitly, "Follow me, and I will make you fishers of men"; as a result, they immediately followed Him, showing a desire after discipleship and after obedient service.

The story of the draught of fishes in Luke 5. 1-11 must be a distinct event; once again Peter had returned to his fishing, toiling all night and catching nothing. The miracle brought him to his senses, and because he had left the Lord twice, he confessed that he was a "sinful man". The result was that Peter forsook all, and followed the Lord, v. 11.

The night before He was crucified, the Lord stated to Peter, "thou canst not follow me now", John 13. 36, though he would follow afterwards, even to being crucified. Peter, as usual, was self-confident, and asserted boldly, "why cannot I follow thee now? I will lay down my life for thy sake". But he saw the waves of danger boisterous, and shortly afterwards he forsook the Lord and then denied Him. Clearly there was no following Him under those circumstances.

After the Lord's resurrection, and when the disciples had left Jerusalem for Galilee, several went fishing again, including Peter, John 21. 3. Again they caught nothing, and Peter did not realize that it was the Lord on the shore until John recognized Him. In the final conversation following this event, the Lord predicted that Peter would be crucified, John 21. 18-19, adding, "Follow me", in life, in service, in being persecuted, and in death. And so Peter did; no more returning to distracting occupations, until he wrote, "shortly I must put off this my tabernacle", 2 Pet. 1. 14.

READING: **Luke 2. 25-52**

THE WORD "TEMPLE"

THE WORD "temple" occurs a large number of times in the N.T., both physically and metaphorically, but it is not widely known that there are two quite distinct words translated "temple", and it is important to know the difference.

(i) *Naos* refers to the actual interior of the temple building, the inner shrine, the place where the priests served. The word is used of the temple in Jerusalem, of the Lord's body, of the church both locally and mystically, and it is used many times in the Book of Revelation.

(ii) *Hieron* signifies the totality of the temple buildings and the surrounding courts. Apart from the temple of Diana in Ephesus in Acts 19, the word is used about 70 times exclusively of the temple in Jerusalem.

The Lord Jesus never entered into (i); He was not a priest after the tribe of Levi. Inevitably, He was found in various ways in (ii), thus on the pinnacle of the temple, Luke 4. 9; teaching in the temple courts, 19. 47, and being shown the lavish construction of the temple, 21. 5. In some contexts, both words are used, presenting a sharp contrast.

Thus in John 2. 14, the Lord found "in the temple" those who were selling oxen; this word refers to the temple courts, where the public were allowed. But shortly afterwards, when He said "Destroy this temple . . . he spake of the temple of his body", vv. 19-21, He used the word for the inner shrine, a word far more suitable to describe the vessel of His holy body.

In Luke 1. 9, Zacharias was a priest, whose duty it was to enter the temple to burn incense; the word is that for the inner shrine. But in Luke 2. 27, 37, 46, the word for temple is the general word including the courts. For Simeon, Anna and the teachers of the law had access only to these courts, and it is only here where the Lord was brought after His birth and at the age of twelve.

In Acts 19. 24, the word for "silver shrines" made for Diana is the word (i). When Judas cast down the pieces of silver in the temple, it is remarkable that word (i) is used. Perhaps he asked a priest to take in the money of blood, Matt. 27. 5. And when the vail of the temple was rent at the Lord's death, it is word (i) that is used, v. 51.

April 15th

READING: **Jeremiah 7. 1-16**

FORSAKEN TEMPLES

IN THE O.T., the temple structures were physical, made with hands, but in the N.T. the temple structures are spiritual, not made with hands. Yet there is an important similarity in some respects which we must not overlook, and that concerns the forsaking of these structures.

Moses' tabernacle had been constructed so that God might dwell among His people, Exod. 25. 8. But the ark was taken out of this tabernacle during a battle with the Philistines, and it never returned, 1 Sam. 4. 4-5. Phinehas' wife said as she died, "The glory is departed from Israel: for the ark of God is taken", v. 22. Asaph later recalled this event, "he forsook the tabernacle of Shiloh", Psa. 78. 60.

Many years later, Solomon's temple suffered the same fate. In Jeremiah 7. 14, God said, "Therefore will I do unto this house . . . as I have done to Shiloh", vv. 12, 14. In other words, He would forsake it and would never return. The reason for this was "the wickedness of my people Israel", v. 12. And this act of forsaking is recorded by Ezekiel who witnessed it in vision form. "The glory of the Lord went up from the midst of the city, and stood upon the mountain which is on the east side of the city", that is, the mount of Olives, Ezek. 11. 23. Shortly afterwards, the temple was destroyed by Nebuchadnezzar.

Herod's temple was destroyed by the Romans in A.D.70, but the inner sanctuary had never been occupied by God's presence, so it was never forsaken by Him. The Lord left its courts for the last time in Matthew 23. 38; 24. 1, and never returned.

On a more solemn note, we consider the temple of the Lord's body, John 2. 21. Men would destroy it, in the sense that they would crucify Him. But in the depths of suffering, He cried, "My God, my God, why hast thou forsaken me?", Psa. 22. 1; Matt. 27. 46. That temple was intrinsically pure and holy, but it was our sin placed on Him that caused this forsaking. Prior to this, He had not been alone, John 14. 32, and afterwards in ascension glory, He had returned to the Father.

The lesson behind this is that we must recognize that the local assembly is a temple, 1 Cor. 3. 16, and if things become too seriously wrong, the lampstand may be removed, or Laodicea may be spued out of His mouth, and forsaken, Rev. 2. 5; 3. 16.

April 16th

READING: **Luke 19. 1-10**

THE LORD'S DWELLING PLACE

AT MANY stages in our lives, we have had relatives and friends come to stay with us; similarly, we went to stay with them. These perhaps invoque happy memories and happy future expectations. But there is something far better, for the Lord Jesus comes to stay with us, and we can dwell with Him. We must take care; He would not enter a home of darkness, sin and evil; He needs a dwelling place of light, purity and righteousness.

He dwells with us. In Luke 19. 1-10, we have the story of Zacchaeus and the sycomore tree. The Lord then issued the gracious self-invitation, "to day I must abide at thy house", v. 5. The people complained, but the Lord explained what was actually happening, "This day is salvation come to this house", v. 9. In other words, He personally was the Salvation. So the man received the Lord joyfully, with repentance.

There is another story in Luke 10. 38-42, where in Bethany Martha "received him into her house". Martha served and prepared the meal; Mary learned of His word. Had all been like Mary, nothing would have been prepared for the Lord! It was Martha and not Mary who made the great profession "I believe that thou art the Christ, the Son of God", John 11. 27.

For ourselves, we have the promise "That Christ may dwell in your hearts by faith", Eph. 3. 17. And there is also the future promise, "he . . . shall dwell among them", Rev. 7. 15.

We dwell with Him. After Andrew heard John the Baptist identify the Lord as the Lamb of God, he asked Him, "where dwellest thou?", John 1. 38. With the invitation "Come and see", he "abode with him that day", v. 39. In a spiritual sense, He invites us to His dwelling, and we can dwell in the house of the Lord for ever. For what is a present blessing extends to the eternal future. In His final teaching, the Lord promised that He would come again, "and receive you unto myself; that where I am, there ye may be also", John 14. 3. In other words, He will be the eternal dwelling place of His people. Paul taught this as well: "and so shall we ever be with the Lord", 1 Thess. 4. 17, the rapture being the beginning of this glorious experience. Yet this is not something that we must wait for until the rapture, for at his decease, Paul knew that he would go "to be with Christ" immediately, Phil. 1. 23.

April 17th

READING: **2 Kings 19. 8-19**

ENQUIRY IN THE HOUSE OF GOD

JERUSALEM was surrounded by the Assyrian armies, but because of fighting elsewhere they had to leave. Their general sent a letter to Hezekiah in Jerusalem, stating that they were not to believe that God had delivered them! Hezekiah did that which was right before God in face of such opposition.

The Right Procedure. He "went up into the house of the Lord", v. 14, and spread the letter before Him. As the highest authority in the city, there was no one Hezekiah could turn to, except to One higher in the heavens.

The Right Person. In verse 2, he had sent to Isaiah, but here he went to the Lord alone, and in humble worship the king described the Lord in verse 15.

The Right Place. He went into the house of the Lord, as David did in Psalm 27. 4 when he desired to dwell there all the days of his life, to behold the beauty of the Lord.

The Right Prayer. In verses 15-19, he first of all considered God Himself, then he explained the situation, and finally he made his request. Acts 4. 23-30 has the same form.

The Right Perspective. He had further perplexities in verse 17: the kings of Assyria had gained victories. Indeed the wicked seemed to prosper, Psa. 73. 3, 12, but the psalmist only understood when he entered the sanctuary of God, v. 17.

The Right Power. Hezekiah knew that only God in His power could effect deliverance, v. 19. Only He was the Lord God, as He said through Isaiah, "I will defend this city, to save it, for mine own sake", v. 34. This reminds us again of Acts 4. 29, the apostles' prayer for boldness, and this was manifested in verse 31 as they spake the Word of God.

The Right Presence. God was with Hezekiah, but not with the armies of Assyria, enabling the king to enquire of God. We think of the boyhood years of the Lord Jesus; He was enquiring in the temple in Luke 2. 46, while later men were enquiring of Him in the temple courts, 21. 37.

The Right Petition. Hezekiah was not selfish; he desired deliverance on account of its effects on the world: that all might know that the Lord is God through this deliverance. The act of being saved has value in testimony, as Rahab confessed to the spies in Joshua 2. 10-11.

April 18th

READING: **Philippians 2. 1-30**

LIKEMINDED, EVEN UNTO DEATH

THIS CHAPTER is very precious to the Lord's people; in particular, verses 5-11 speak of the descending and ascending of the Lord Jesus Christ, and they form a prominent part in the worship at the Lord's Supper. However, Paul was not writing these verses from the point of view of worship; rather, these verses about the Lord illustrate the principle in verse 4, "Look not every man on his own things". For it appears that in Philippi there were a few women who were looking at their own things, and this was causing a lack of unity in the church. They were to be "of one mind", v. 2.

Paul therefore illustrates this principle in relation to himself, to Timothy and to Epaphroditus.

The case of Paul, v. 17. The apostle regards himself as being poured out as a drink offering upon the sacrifice and service of their faith. Their faithful service in the gospel was fundamental, and Paul was poured out on account of his being a prisoner in Rome. Had Paul thought of himself, he would have ceased his testimony long ago; he could then have lived in safety. But he was always thinking of men needing salvation, hence he offered himself willingly to this end. At the end of his life, he was "ready to be offered", 2 Tim. 4. 6, when he would have fully kept the faith.

The case of Timothy, vv. 19-24. To Paul, Timothy was unique, since he explained, "I have no man likeminded, who will naturally care for your state", v. 20. He put himself out so as to serve the saints. Paul claimed that "all seek their own", v. 21, except Timothy, whom he could trust to give an account of the apostolic doctrine, 1 Cor. 4. 17.

The case of Epaphroditus, vv. 25-30. Paul called him "my brother, and companion in labour, and fellowsoldier, but your messenger", v. 25. He had come from Philippi, evidently to bring a gift to Paul, 4. 10, but during his stay in Rome, he had contracted an illness "nigh unto death", 2. 30. In other words, he thought not of himself, but of Paul, and also of the Philippians who were sorrowing on his behalf. Thus the giving of self in service is "for the work of Christ", v. 30.

These men of God knew what it meant to have that mind in them that was also in Christ Jesus, 2. 5.

April 19th

READING: **Isaiah 40. 1-11**

HE SHALL GENTLY LEAD

AT THIS time of the year, we can visualise the fields and the hillsides in spring. There will be thousands and thousands of sheep, together with their lambs, and these lambs will be engaged in feeding, playing, getting lost, and wandering loose on the country lanes and roads. Sometimes we can witness a large flock being moved from one field to another; there would be hundreds of sheep and their lambs hurrying along. Behind, there might be several men, and a number of sheep dogs running about to keep the sheep on the forward path; none is left behind, and none is allowed to stray into gardens or gates bounding the pathway.

The Lord Jesus is the Good Shepherd, the Great Shepherd and the Chief Shepherd. How differently He treats His sheep! He does not drive them with dogs, perhaps as sheep for the slaughter, seeking large profits in selling them for food. As Isaiah 40. 10 puts it, He feeds His flock; He picks the lambs up in His arms, and He gently leads those sheep which have lambs. This is a spiritual picture that we find many times in the Bible, as God took up everyday occupations and events, to use them for spiritual encouragement and lessons.

What constitutes His flock? David knew that the Lord was his Shepherd, Psa. 23. 1, the One who leads Joseph "like a flock", 80. 1, this flock being "his people", 77. 20. As the Lord Jesus looked around upon men, He knew that His disciples alone constituted the "little flock", Luke 12. 32; Peter and others were responsible to feed the Lord's lambs and sheep, John 21. 15-17. Elders, teachers and pastors have the same responsibility today.

The Lord Jesus was not a detached divine Observer in the heavens; He was here below to be the Good Shepherd who gave His life for the sheep, to deliver them out of the grasp of the wolf, John 10. 11-16, so that when He rose again there might be one flock and one Shepherd. Moreover, He now goes before them, v. 4, and His sheep recognize His divine voice, and will take no heed to the voice of strangers who bring false doctrine by leading into poisonous pastures. If one of His sheep goes astray, He seeks it, while at the end, the Chief Shepherd gives an unfading crown of glory, 1 Pet. 5. 4.

110

READING: **Mark 15. 1-15**

TWO SONS AND TWO FATHERS

JUDAS WOULD exchange the Lord Jesus for money, but the multitude would exchange Him for Barabbas. This story of Barabbas is well known; it appears in the records of all four Gospels, Matt. 27. 15-26; Mark 15. 6-15; Luke 23. 18-25; John 18. 39-40. No doubt the custom of Pilate to release to the Jews a prisoner at the feast of Passover carried with it the remembrance of the release of the nation from bondage in Egypt at the first Passover in Exodus 12. The Egyptians suffered, while the children of Israel went free. No doubt the Jews liked to think of the Lord Jesus as being on the level of the Egyptians as later men would think of Paul, Acts 21. 38. The multitudes before Pilate liked to contrast the Lord and Barabbas, seeking to discard the former and to retain the latter, seeking to blacken the character of the former, and to render as light the character of the latter.

Believers also like to contrast the Lord Jesus and Barabbas, but in exactly the opposite way. The Jews knew what believers should also know, but the implications of that knowledge are entirely different. The Jews knew that the Lord was "the Son of the Blessed . . . the Son of man", Mark 14. 61-62, and they knew that the name Barabbas meant "son of his father". (The word "bar" means "son"; see Matt. 16. 17; John 1. 42, where Peter is seen as the son of Jona; while "abba" means "father", as seen in Romans 8. 15.)

The Lord Jesus was, and is, the Son of His Father in a spiritual sense extending from eternity to eternity. God gave witness to this at the Lord's baptism, and on the mountain top, Matt. 3. 17; 17. 5. The Lord gave witness to this, both to His disciples, John 14. 13, and in prayer, 17. 1. He also expressed this truth to the Jews, "My Father worketh hitherto, and I work", 5. 17, and they knew that, as the Son, He was Deity manifest in the flesh, v. 18; 10. 33.

But Barabbas was not only the son of his immediate father, perhaps deriving his evil disposition from him by family influence, but he was also the son of his first father Adam, for "by one man sin entered into the world", Rom. 5. 12. *How unlike* the Son of God, for He also stemmed from Adam according to the flesh, but without sin being transferred, Luke 3. 38.

April 21st

READING: **Acts 18. 24-28**

RECEPTION INTO THE HOME

PRISCILLA AND AQUILA were a faithful married couple, having been expelled from Italy to Corinth, Acts 18. 2, and then moving to Ephesus, v. 18. They later returned to Rome, Rom. 16. 3, but had left Rome again when Paul wrote 2 Timothy, 2 Tim. 4. 19. This couple demonstrated the objectives that God expects from a Christian husband and wife. Their married life enhanced and did not diminish the opportunities to which they put their home in the Lord's service, for they were able to receive the apostle, Apollos and the assembly into their home. We shall consider these three aspects briefly.

The apostle received. Arriving in Corinth, Paul found this Christian couple, "and came unto them . . . he abode with them", Acts 18. 2-3. They lived together for more than one and a half years, having a common occupation as tentmakers, and they were "helpers in Christ Jesus" with Paul, Rom. 16. 3. All that Paul taught in Corinth, they learnt as well, such as the gospel and resurrection, 1 Cor. 15. 3, and the Lord's Supper, 11. 23. They would have held fast to every aspect of the apostolic teaching, being enabled to pass it all on later.

Apollos received. Remaining in Ephesus at the end of the second missionary journey, while Paul went to Jerusalem and Antioch, Priscilla and Aquilla were not public evangelists, but teachers in a quiet way. Hence, hearing Apollos as an eloquent teacher of the O.T. Scriptures, they received him into their home, where they "expounded unto him the way of God more perfectly", Acts 18. 26. They did not hide their light in their home, nor was their home so worldly that their testimony for the truth was lost. Rather, their testimony was one of correction and positive instruction, enabling Apollos to depart for Corinth as a teacher of Paul's doctrine.

The assembly received. In the previous two cases, doctrine had been preached and perfected; now it is practised. For there was a church that gathered in their house, 1 Cor. 16. 19; Rom. 16. 3, rather than in buildings devoted to that purpose, as today. What holy daily conduct was necessary if their home was to be a suitable meeting place for the Lord and for His people. Thus all churches of the Gentiles gave thanks for this godly couple, Rom. 16. 4.

April 22nd

READING: **John 7. 14-31**

EXAMINATIONS

IN MANY CASES, the results of examinations determine a student's future career. During the preparatory period of study, with lectures, written work, essays and projects, a student is either lazy and perhaps weak, or else diligent and producing good work. Sitting the examination can be an unpleasant experience, but marking the papers can also be a discouraging experience.

In a spiritual sense, God does the same for men now. Their lives prepare them for the future examination session, when believers must appear before the judgment seat of Christ, and unbelievers before the great white throne. One will either fail, as in Matthew 7. 21-23, or one will pass as in 25. 21.

But there is another aspect of the matter. By the Holy Spirit, we are being taught today and examined today. Many times in His teaching, the Lord asked questions; Paul did the same in his Epistles. These questions demand an answer. Below, we therefore present to the reader an examination paper with twelve questions: What will your answer be?

Answer all twelve questions.

1. "Why go ye about to kill me?", John 7. 19.
2. "Why persecutest thou me?", Acts 9. 4.
3. "Why are ye fearful, O ye of little faith?", Matt. 8. 26.
4. "O thou of little faith, wherefore didst thou doubt?", Matt. 14. 31.
5. "What doest thou here?", 1 Kings 19. 9.
6. "Why do thoughts arise in your hearts?", Luke 24. 38.
7. "What think ye of Christ? whose son is he?", Matt. 22. 42.
8. "Whom say ye that I am?", Matt. 16. 15.
9. "Dost thou believe on the Son of God?", John 9. 35.
10. "Did ye receive the Holy Spirit when ye believed?", Acts 19. 2 R.V.
11. "Could ye not watch with me one hour?", Matt. 26. 40.
12. "Did ye never read in the scriptures?", Matt. 21. 42.

May our correct answers receive the commendation, "Well done, thou good and faithful servant", Matt. 25. 21.

April 23rd

READING: **Luke 10. 38-42**

AT HIS FEET

THERE WERE quite a number of men and women in the N.T. who fell at the feet of the Lord Jesus, such as Jairus, Mark 5. 22, and the Syrophenician woman, 7. 25. Others were at His feet so as to show their humility and respect. In particular, Mary of Bethany is seen in this position on three distinct occasions.

(1) In Luke 10. 39, "Mary . . . sat at Jesus' feet, and heard his word". The Lord had come to Bethany, a village on the eastern slopes of the mount of Olives, and there He was welcomed into the house of Martha. Abraham had entertained angels unawares, Heb. 13. 2, but subsequent events show that Mary and Martha were not in ignorance of the One whom they would entertain in their home. Martha prepared a meal, but there were other things to be done. (As in John 4. 8, the disciples arranged for provision, but for the Lord there were other things to be done.) Mary chose the "good part" by sitting at His feet, and she listened to the gracious words from His mouth. Some are listeners and some are workers; if Martha had not served, there would have been no hospitality for the Lord in that home that day. Let not Mary speak against Martha and Martha against Mary; both are necessary in devoted service.

(2) In John 11. 32, outside their home, Mary "fell down at his feet, saying unto him, Lord, if thou hadst been here, my brother had not died". After Lazarus' death, Martha had first come to the Lord, saying the same words, v. 21. But she had also confessed Him as "the Christ, the Son of God", v. 27. Mary expressed intercession and trust, but with no confession of His Person. So in spite of Martha serving previously, her knowledge of Christ was in no way impaired.

(3) In John 12. 3, Mary "wiped his feet with her hair". Once again, the scene is in the Bethany home, with Lazarus present; the miracle was fresh in their minds, and now was the time for worship. Martha was still serving, but Mary anointed the Lord's feet, indicating her humble appreciation of the worthiness of His Person. Judas the thief might complain, but the Lord stated that this anointing was until the day of His burying, v. 7. In other words, this token of worship was with the Lord as He was crucified, and as His body was placed in a tomb. May our worship at His feet be as humble and effective.

April 24th

READING: **Psalm 52**

TREES IN THE HOUSE

ADMITTEDLY the wood that David prepared for the building of the temple, 1 Chron. 29. 2, and the timber that Solomon acquired, 2 Chron. 2. 8-9, was "dead" wood. Its spiritual meaning would enable "dead" wood to be used in a structure where the glory of God would dwell. But in a local church, the "wood, hay, stubble", 1 Cor. 3. 12, implied an attempt to introduce what was dead, and this could have no place in a spiritual temple where the Lord of life dwelt.

Thus David the psalmist knew that life was necessary in the house of God, "I am like a green olive tree in the house of God", Psa. 52. 8. The introduction to this psalm states that it concerns Doeg the Edomite, evidently an unpleasant character who was detained before the Lord at the tabernacle, 1 Sam. 21. 7. The high priest Ahimelech was also there, but he was not really God's chosen high priest. Moreover, Doeg slew all the priests at Nob where the tabernacle was, 22. 18-20. In other words, death reigned around the tabernacle, brought about by Doeg; David therefore composed Psalm 52, and contrasted life in himself as the green olive tree with all the scene of death that was around. Today, we can use the picture of the living vine, Christ Himself, John 15. 1, with His people being the living branches bringing forth fruit.

The psalmist returns to this theme in Psalm 92. 11-14, "The righteous shall flourish like the palm tree . . . Those that be planted in the house of the Lord shall flourish in the courts of our God. They shall still bring forth fruit in old age". Here, God is viewed as the One who planted the righteous one in the house; and with all spiritual nourishment from Himself, there will be growth and much fruit-bearing. But this fruit-bearing is seen as extending to old age, when maturity will have been attained in spiritual things. This is seen in Moses' old age before he died, in his song and in his blessing, Deut. 32-33; it is also seen in David in his final psalm of praise given in 1 Chronicles 29. 10-19. It is also seen in the bursts of praise in Paul's final prison and pastoral Epistles, when he described himself as "Paul the aged", Philem. 9.

As planted and rooted in His love in a local church, may all believers bring forth the fruits of praise, Eph. 3. 17.

115

April 25th

READING: Acts 12. 1-17

THE PRAYER MEETING

IMMEDIATELY after its formation, the church in Jerusalem continued steadfastly in "prayers", Acts 2. 42; namely, collective prayer was regarded as essential before God.

Not that this does away with individual personal prayer at home, something often abandoned these days. Paul was a man of personal prayer, praying that Christians might be filled with the knowledge of God's will, that they might walk worthy of the Lord, increasing in the knowledge of God, Col. 1. 9-10. Do we pray like that? We must ask in faith, nothing wavering, else nothing will be received from the Lord, James 1. 6-7.

Sometimes, a small group of believers may pray together. Thus in the large church in Jerusalem, just the twelve apostles were continually in prayer, Acts 6. 4; in Antioch, a few teachers engaged in prayer, 13. 2; in Miletus, Paul and the Ephesian elders were found in prayer, 20. 36-38.

But more generally, a local church is responsible before the Lord to come together regularly for prayer. It is a question of gathering in the Lord's Name, recognizing that He is in the midst, Matt. 18. 20. This is known by faith, so an unsaved person still in his sins would find a prayer meeting foreign, boring and wasteful of his time!

In a gathering of a local church for prayer, believers are said to "come boldly unto the throne of grace . . . to find grace to help in time of need", Heb. 4. 16. Here are no set prayers, but the spontaneous expressions of the desires of the hearts to lead the whole company in prayer to God. Only menfolk take part audibly, 1 Tim. 3. 8; there is no authority in the Bible for women to take part publicly in prayer.

A good example of a prayer meeting is found in Acts 12. Peter, in prison, awaited death from king Herod, and "prayer was made without ceasing of the church unto God for him", v. 5. This prayer was answered, and Peter was miraculously released. He came to the place where "many were gathered together praying", v. 12, showing that he knew where the meeting was held.

It is good therefore to pray for believers in need, for missionaries, for the preaching of the gospel to the unsaved, for the spiritual growth of God's people, for everyday aspects of life, and for those in authority, 1 Tim. 2. 1-2.

116

April 26th

READING: **Mark 1. 9-31**

IMMEDIATELY IN SERVICE

THE SERVICE of God is not something that is to be taken at leisure and at one's own convenience. Sometimes it means putting oneself out so that there is no delay. That is how the party with Paul behaved on the second missionary journey; when Paul had the vision, of the rest Luke wrote, "immediately we endeavoured to go into Macedonia", Acts 16. 10. This is seen in the initial ministry of the Lord Jesus: He was busy but never rushed. In His public ministry, nothing that had to be done was left undone until a more suitable occasion. The word "immediately" certainly characterized the Lord's work in Mark 1. We draw the reader's attention to many occurrences.

Verse 10. *Straightway* after His baptism in water, the Spirit descended for identification, commendation and anointing.

Verse 12. But the perfection of His character was demonstrated, particularly to Satan, prior to His taking up His ministry. So *"immediately* the Spirit driveth him into the wilderness". His service was thus accomplished in the light of this victory over Satan.

Verse 18. Seeing how the Lord was acting enabled Peter and Andrew *"straightway"* to forsake their nets, and to follow Him. No delaying excuses were made as in Luke 9. 57-62.

Verse 20. The Lord would gain other disciples without delay, so *"straightway* he called" James and John. They showed no hesitation in leaving all to follow Him.

Verse 21. There was no delay in Capernaum; the Sabbath day enabled Him *"straightway"* to enter into the synagogue to teach. The same may be seen in Paul when converted; *"straightway"* he preached in the synagogue in Damascus, Acts 9. 20.

Verse 23 R.V. *"Straightway"* there was a man in need in the synagogue, and the Lord healed Him, although later the performing of miracles on the Sabbath would bring trouble.

Verse 28. His fame *"immediately"* spread abroad. His power and authority were not hidden for a year or so!

Verse 29. *"Forthwith"* He entered Peter's house, having left the synagogue. The privacy of private fellowship was not left to a more suitable time. "Now is the day", 2 Cor. 6. 2.

See also *"anon"*, v. 30; *"immediately"*, vv. 31, 42; *"forthwith"*, v. 43. What an object lesson for us!

April 27th

READING: **Acts 21. 1-14**

THEY TARRIED SEVEN DAYS

THE REPETITION of a certain mode of behaviour demands investigation, for it would appear that there was a common objective in all three events. For in Acts 20. 6; 21. 4, and 28. 14, a period of seven days is mentioned, during which time Paul and those with him tarried or abode with the local church. We may not be reading too much into all three events, but it appears to the author that the reason why seven days is recorded explicitly is because a Lord's Day was involved. This was the important objective before Paul, and he would not move on until this Lord's Day had arrived when he would have fellowship with the local church.

(1) *Troas*, Acts 20. 6. A good number of the Lord's servants had left Corinth, those named in verse 4 travelling by sea to Troas, but Paul went over land to Macedonia and Philippi, from whence he crossed by sea to Troas. It is obvious from the record, that the "seven days" terminated on "the first day of the week", and that Paul was present with the local church. The previous time that Paul had been in Troas, he was ill-at-ease, and was unable to preach, 2 Cor. 2. 11-13. But now he had remained over the seven days, so as to partake in the breaking of bread with the local church, and to preach to them, even unto midnight.

(2) *Tyre*, Acts 21. 4. Paul and the party with him were now journeying to Jerusalem, and on the voyage they landed at Tyre. There they found disciples, evidently forming a local church in Tyre, so Paul tarried there seven days. We like to think that the apostle's motive was to ensure that they passed a Lord's Day with the church, no doubt at the end of the seven days. All that is recorded of this visit is that Paul was warned not to go up to Jerusalem (see also verse 11), and that the disciples and Paul engaged in prayer on the shore. Clearly, spiritual activity with spiritual believers.

(3) *Puteoli*, Acts 28. 13-14. As a prisoner, Paul was journeying northwards to Rome. They found brethren in Puteoli, and Paul and those with him "were desired to tarry with them seven days". Nothing is said about the purpose of the seven days, but reading between the lines we perceive that the blessing of fellowship on the Lord's Day was the objective.

April 28th

READING: **Revelation 14. 9-20**

CAN YOU REMEMBER AN AIR-RAID?

DURING A SERIES of nights in April 1942, there took place the so-called "Baedeker reprisal raids" against the cities of Exeter, Bath, Norwich and York. The number of people who can remember these raids diminishes annually, but the author, then unconverted, was living in Norwich during his later school days and can well remember the two raids that took place during the nights of April 27th-28th and 29th-30th. He can vividly remember these raids: the suddenness of the first attack when people had got used to the air-raid syren, tending not to bother. The rush to get to the shelters during the darkness of the beginning of the raids; the terrific sound of guns and bombs; the increasing crackling of fires in houses around; the smell of smoke; the knowledge that people were being killed and injured; that terrible damage was being done in the city. After perhaps an hour or more, silence would settle over the city; people would emerge from their shelters, finding what? A home damaged and in ruins, or on fire? Other damage with windows broken and tiles off? Friends no longer alive? Most people escaped, and later houses were repaired.

That is what man does to his fellows.

But what about God's judgment? The Bible sometimes calls this "wrath", the demonstration of His righteous anger against sinful man having lived a life of sin and utter indifference to His claims and to His offer of salvation.

Christians have been delivered "from the wrath to come", 1 Thess. 1. 10; "God hath not appointed us to wrath, but to obtain salvation by our Lord Jesus Christ", 5. 9.

But the position of unbelievers is quite different. The judgment will come suddenly, as in the case of an air-raid, but will be infinitely worse. There will be no shelter from the anger of God; none will escape, Heb. 2. 3; there will be no rebuilding of lives afterwards, Rev. 20. 15. "The wrath of the Lamb: for the great day of his wrath is come; who shall be able to stand?", 6. 16-17. "The angel thrust in his sickle into the earth, and cast it into the great winepress of the wrath of God", 14. 20. These pictures, and others, are dramatic, yet describe terrible scenes of future judgment. "Who hath warned you to flee from the wrath to come?", Matt. 3. 7.

119

April 29th

READING: **1 Chronicles 29. 1-19**

AFFECTION FOR THE HOUSE

THE AFFECTIONS of David were centered in a particular direction: towards the house that Solomon would build, but for which David would make extensive preparations. His exercise was not something that arose towards the end of his life, for he had contemplated the building of a house some 25 years before, 2 Sam. 7. 1-29. On that occasion, David "sat before the Lord", v. 18, and expressed a great psalm, vv. 18-29. After that followed David's great sin, but after his repentance he continued to make preparation for the house. Towards the end of his life, this house dominated his activity, as Paul was continually occupied with "the house of God, which is the church of the living God", 1 Tim. 3. 15, and his daily activity concerned "the care of all the churches", 2 Cor. 11. 28.

One of the chief characteristics of love is that it gives, and divine love is similarly manifested, John 3. 16. Thus David's affection for the house caused him to provide of his "own proper good", 1 Chron. 29. 3, above all that he had prepared for the holy house. The former relates to his personal possessions, while the latter to possessions as king, and to spoils gained in battle. Then follows a second great psalm on this subject, vv. 10-19. In this psalm, we find prayer, God's power, presence and provision, as well as David rehearsing his preparation.

In Psalm 26. 8, David confessed, "Lord, I have loved the habitation of thy house, and the place where thine honour dwelleth". The house is seen as a divine possession, the dwelling place of God's glory. Thus in a local church, the divine presence is found amongst three, Matt. 18. 20, and amongst the 3,000 in Acts 2. 41. In a mystical sense, divine love is fully seen, for "Christ also loved the church, and gave himself for it", Eph. 5. 25. Here, love gave, and acquired an eternal possession for the Lord.

Should we ask, which house? To David, there was only one house, and this was unique: "I was glad when they said unto me, Let us go into the house of the Lord", Psa. 122. 1. See also verse 9. There were other houses, such as the house of Dagon, 1 Sam. 5. 2, and Jeroboam's house, 1 Kings 12. 31. Can we ask, which company of Christians do we love and serve?

April 30th

READING: **Numbers 16. 1-11**

FURTHER EXAMPLES OF SINGULAR AND PLURAL

ON PAGE 72, we provided several examples showing that misunderstanding can arise in the interpretation of Scripture if the plural form "you" is always used, as in modern translations. The retention of "thou" permits the reader to see exactly what is implied in the sacred text. Here, we give some further examples of this.

Matthew 26. 64. First the Lord addressed the high priest. "Thou hast said" concerning the priest's question as to whether the Lord was "the Christ, the Son of God". Immediately the Lord added, "I say unto you, Hereafter shall ye see the Son of man sitting on the right hand of power, and coming in the clouds of heaven". This refers to the future, not to the high priest personally, but to the time when the Lord returns in glory and judgment to establish His kingdom in open display.

Numbers 16. 8-11. Moses was speaking to the rebel Korah, but also to his brethren and the company with him. Thus in verse 10, Moses' remarks are addressed to all of these men ("you" is used), but in verse 10, the remarks are made only to Korah ("thee" is used). Read these verses carefully.

Exodus 4. 15, when Moses was complaining that he could not speak properly: "thou shalt speak unto him . . . and I will be with thy mouth . . . and will teach you what ye shall do". If "you" were used throughout this context, if would not be clear that the teaching referred to both Moses and Aaron.

Luke 16. 25-26. Here is Abraham talking to the rich man in hades across the great gulf. "Remember that thou in thy lifetime receivedst thy good things . . . thou art tormented . . . between us and you there is a great gulf fixed". Verse 15 refers to the rich man only, but verse 16 refers to the whole population behind the great gulf.

Matthew 18. 9-10. "If thine eye offend thee, pluck it out, and cast it from thee . . . Take heed that ye despise not one of these little ones". The particular statements are made to individuals; the general statement is made to men in general.

John 1. 50-51. The Lord is answering Nathanael's confession, "Thou art the Son of God": "Because I said unto thee . . . I say unto you, Hereafter ye shall see heaven open". These last words are prophetic to the Jewish remnant in that coming day.

May 1st

READING: **Mark 14. 1-26**

THE TWO FEASTS

SOMETIMES WE sing, "Shut in with Thee, far, far above the restless world that wars below". Certainly this describes the two feasts that occur in Mark 14 just before the Lord was crucified. The war without is seen (i) in verses 1-2, where the chief priests and scribes were plotting the Lord's death, and (ii) in verses 10-11, where the chief priests were plotting with Judas to betray the Lord.

The first feast, vv. 3-9. Although the circumstances are similar, we believe that the feast described in John 12. 1-9 is distinct. Here was devoted worship, as the woman poured the "spikenard very precious" upon the Lord's head. Some present, not knowing the spiritual implication of this act, complained, and we believe that Judas was the chief complainer. He was the apostolic treasurer with "the bag", keeping what was placed in it, John 12. 5-6. The selling price of 300 pence seemed attractive to him. But the Lord reinterpreted the woman's action in a way that no one else realized was about to take place. She had anointed the Lord's body "to the burying", Mark 14. 8. It was no use pouring such ointment on His clothes, since these would be taken away when He was crucified. But on His head and feet — here the ointment would have remained, and would still have yielded its perfume when He was placed in the tomb. The Lord's commendation of the woman in verse 9 must be understood in the light of this act of faith.

The second feast, vv. 10-26. If Judas could not have the 300 pence, then he would adopt other tactics: 30 pieces of silver to betray the Lord, v. 11; Matt. 26. 15, apparently less in value that the price of the spikenard! The Lord's divine discernment of Judas in verse 21, "good were it for that man if he had never been born", stands in sharp contrast with His statement about the woman, v. 9. In this large upper room furnished, there was another session of worship after the Passover feast. The bread and the cup that He gave them, and the fact that this feast is perpetuated, shows that worship is an ongoing feature of the believer's exercise. We take what He offers, and we give what we can, as in the first feast. No doubt, the apostles, like the woman, did not know what they had done, but they learnt afterwards.

May 2nd

READING: **Matthew 21. 33-46**

COMPLETE SURVEY OF THE BIBLE

THE ADDRESS by Stephen in Acts 7 is a detailed survey of the O.T., but the Lord's parable of the vineyard, though briefer, is an even more comprehensive survey, extending to the N.T. and to the prophetic future. The principal items in this parable are:

The purpose of God in the nation: the fruitfulness of the Jews, vv. 33-34.

The Jewish treatment of the prophets, vv. 35-36.

The Jewish treatment of the Son of God, vv. 37-39.

Consequences: Jews removed, and Gentiles brought in, v. 41; the Lord raised, v. 42; Gentile fruitfulness, v. 43; judgment on Jews and Gentiles, v. 44.

God brought a vine out of Egypt, and planted it in the land, Psa. 80. 8-9. His presence in the pillars of cloud and fire was openly seen on the long journey, but then it was no longer manifested — He had gone "into a far country". The judges and later the kings were then responsible for the welfare of the vine. God sent His servants the prophets, Heb. 1. 1; "I have even sent unto you all my servants the prophets", Jer. 7. 25.

The usual Jewish treatment of these prophets was awful; the noble vine had turned into a degenerate plant, and their own sword had devoured the prophets like a destroying lion, Jer. 2. 21, 30. The Lord stated this in Matthew 23. 30-31, and Stephen said the same thing in Acts 7. 52. They were stoned, sawn asunder, and slain with the sword, Heb. 11. 36-37.

The Son of God came seeking worshippers and fruit, but the Jewish leaders sought to turn religion to their own advantage, so killed the Lord of glory, so that they might continue their rule unchallenged and unaltered.

Verse 41 is not part of the parable, but how true!, but they condemned themselves (like David did in 2 Samuel 12. 5). The Lord implied His resurrection in verse 42, quoted from Psalm 118. 22-23. Then in verse 43, the Lord announced a new testimony on earth, that of the church, to bring forth the fruit of the Spirit in the present time. In the church, it is God who gives the increase, 1 Cor. 3. 6. Finally, the Stone is seen as a Stone of judgment, falling on Jew and Gentile alike, those who ultimately refuse to accept His authority.

May 3rd

READING: **Genesis 8. 13-22**

FRUITFUL SEASONS

THE POET Keats once wrote, "Season of mists and mellow fruitfulness". Some years may be exceptionally good years for the production of summer and autumn fruit both in the garden and by the wild plants of the countryside. An abundance of gooseberries, strawberries, raspberries, with plums in clusters on the trees, and later brambles in the country hedges, with apples in plenty to be picked. There may be an exceptional corn harvest, even if there has been a drought.

Men may consider this merely as the course of nature, but believers can see that this is a witness of God, "he left not himself without witness, in that he did good, and gave us rain from heaven, and fruitful seasons, filling our hearts with food and gladness", Acts 14. 17. Paul said this to restrain the people of Lystra from offering sacrifice to himself and Barnabas. The people understood this, but it was quite impossible to use the gospel message to restrain idolatry!

In the past. The O.T. shows what God introduced in the beginning. The "tree yielding fruit", Gen. 1. 12, was perfect, not marred or subject to disease. Sin came in, the ground was cursed, and all was badly affected. Man does his best to overcome, yet the promise remains, "seedtime and harvest, and cold and heat, and summer and winter, and day and night shall not cease", 8. 22. There is a better harvest spiritually, lasting for eternity, for the Lord was the seed, John 12. 24; and all believers form the fruit that never dies nor fades.

In the present. In Matthew 13. 3, the Lord is the Sower, sowing the seed as the Word of God. That which falls on good ground brings forth abundant fruit, and this refers only to believers. Otherwise, fruitless trees are hewn down, 3. 10. For only the gospel brings forth fruit, so that believers are fruitful unto every good work, Col. 1. 6, 10.

In the future. Isaiah 53 has a prophetic bearing upon the results of the Lord's sacrifice on the cross. "He shall see his seed . . . He shall see of the travail of his soul, and shall be satisfied", vv. 10-11. The beginning of eternal days is described in Revelation 22. 2; there is the tree of life yielding her fruit, when there shall be no more curse, for light and the throne of God shall be there.

May 4th

READING: **1 Thessalonians 3**

PAUL'S PRAYER FOR THE THESSALONIANS

AT THE BEGINNING of this Epistle, Paul claimed to thank God "always" for them, remembering "without ceasing" their work of faith, 1. 3-4; 2. 13. Such continuity of thanksgiving and prayer is also found in many other Epistles. Moreover, this was not just an apostolic exercise; he exhorted *them also* to "Pray without ceasing", 5. 17. The exercise was therefore mutual; even today, prayer is not only the province of those who labour in the Word and doctrine, but also that of all the Lord's faithful people. Paul wrote similar words in the second Epistle: "We are bound to thank God always for you", 2 Thess. 1. 3.

When Paul had been with the Thessalonians during his second missionary journey, he recalled: "labouring *night and day* . . . we preached unto you the gospel of God", 1 Thess. 2. 9. Now that he was no longer with them, he could not preach, but he wrote, "*night and day* praying exceedingly that we might see your face, and might perfect that which is lacking in your faith", 3. 10. At the same time, he was rendering thanks to God for them, v. 9. Let us examine a few examples of the subject-matter of Paul's thanksgivings and prayers.

He thanked God for the joy that he had for them before God, v. 9. Many features can lead to thanksgiving; thus "faith in the Lord Jesus, and love unto all the saints", Eph. 1. 15-16, caused Paul to "cease not" to give thanks.

Paul never forgot his converts and the churches that he had established; here, his prayers were "night and day"; for the Philippians it was "always in every prayer", Phil. 1. 4.

His prayer was that he might see their face again, v. 10, for he had had to leave Thessalonica with a pledge not to return; he was concerned with their edification, to perfect what was lacking in their faith. He was concerned with the effectual working of the Word in those who believed, 2. 13. He was interested in their "work of faith, and labour of love, and patience of hope", 1. 4, a faith that was growing exceedingly, 2 Thess. 1. 3, and that had patience in persecutions, v. 4.

His prayer concerned the work of God, 1 Thess. 3. 11-13. He prayed that God would direct his way back to them; that their love might increase, and that there might be suitable practical conduct ready for display in the day of the Lord's return.

May 5th

READING: **Matthew 9. 1-13**

BE OF GOOD CHEER

FOUR OCCASIONS are recorded when the Lord Jesus gave these words of encouragement, "Be of good cheer".

(1) *The "Be of good cheer" because of forgiveness of sins*, Matt. 9. 2. The man had both a physical and a spiritual need of healing: he was sick of the palsy and he was a sinner. Both these adverse effects were incurable apart from the Lord Jesus Christ. It was the faith of four men who brought him to the Lord, Mark 2. 3. There was order in the Lord's dealing with this man. First, he expressed hope and comfort, "be of good cheer". The genuineness of this was seen in His second statement, "thy sins be forgiven thee", and thirdly physical healing was granted. There was a hostile reaction to the Lord forgiving sins, but today the reaction is usually to deny that sins need forgiving at all.

(2) *The "Be of good cheer" to calm fear on account of lack of faith*, Matt. 14. 27. The disciples were alone on the sea, while the Lord was alone on the mountain praying. But during the storm, He comes to them walking on the sea. A new experience usually brings fear, and hence the Lord's words of cheer, coupled with "it is I". After Peter had walked on the sea, and when the wind ceased, the disciples worshipped Him, owing Him as the Son of God. Today, the Lord grants us the cheer of His presence during the problems of life.

(3) *The "Be of good cheer" in times of tribulation*, John 16. 33. This was the last night before the Lord died, and the walk from the upper room to the mount of Olives was nearing its end. The Lord concluded His talk knowing that they would leave Him alone, and that they too would be alone after His departure by way of the cross. He knew that they would suffer tribulation in the world, but there was One greater; hence He offered His words of comfort, "be of good cheer; I have overcome the world", a comfort that remains for us today.

(4) *The "Be of good cheer" in times of loneliness*, Acts 23. 11. Paul was now in prison in Jerusalem, his missionary journeys concluded. All was uncertain, but the Lord stood by him one night, saying, "Be of good cheer . . . so must thou bear witness also at Rome". The divine purpose and presence was certain, and this is the promise for us also.

May 6th

READING: **Numbers 11. 1-10**

THE MIXED MULTITUDE

WE READ of "the mixed multitude" three times in the Old Testament. However, it was not a phenomenon that was restricted to the Old Testament; we find that it affected the local churches in the New Testament as well. As we extract information from these three occasions, we shall note that the principles behind them are found in John's three Epistles.

The first occasion, Exod. 12. 38. Right from the time when the children of Israel came out of Egypt, there was with them "a mixed multitude". But God would put a difference between those who were His, and those who merely tacked themselves on to His people. No strangers were to partake of the Passover unless they submitted themselves to the Jewish rites, vv. 43-45. In the New Testament, local churches were "holy temples", 1 Cor. 3. 16-17; alas that men infiltrated into these holy temples, such as the antichrists in 1 John 2. 19. Previously, Paul had described them as "false brethren unawares brought in", Gal. 2. 4.

The second occasion, Num. 11. 4. In the wilderness, "the mixt multitude" commenced to lust after their favourite meals in Egypt, and they adversely affected the children of Israel, who also wept for the good things of Egypt. Typically, this would speak of false doctrines, deriving from the religious teaching learnt in unconverted days. In 2 John 7, the apostle warned of many deceivers in the world, who did not abide in the doctrine of Christ. Believers were to have no contact with men who promulgated false doctrine, even in their own homes.

The third occasion, Neh. 13. 3. "The mixed multitude" lived amongst the Jews in Jerusalem after the temple and the wall of Jerusalem had been rebuilt. Nehemiah 13 describes the many false practices that this multitude engaged in, and God's people were adversely affected by them. Tobiah was one such man, who actually used one of the side rooms attached to the temple walls. In the New Testament, such men arose in the local churches. In 3 John 9-10, there was Diotrephes, who acted as a big dictator, casting believers out of the church; John would act as Nehemiah, restoring the situation. Paul warned the Ephesian elders that a mixed multitude would enter into their numbers, unless they took heed, Acts 20. 29.

May 7th

READING: **Psalm 134**

NIGHT IN THE HOUSE OF THE LORD

IN A LOCAL church, Paul may preach until midnight, Acts 20. 7, but this was, and is, exceptional. Otherwise, no doubt, most of the Lord's people would unintentionally fall asleep like Eutychus. In heaven there are those who "rest not day and night" in their expression of worship, Rev. 4. 8.

In the O.T. likewise, there was a continuity of praise in the courts of the house of God. There was no difficulty to maintain the service of song throughout day and night hours, since the 288 singers were grouped into twenty-four shifts, 1 Chron. 25. This service of song was first commenced when David brought the ark up to mount Zion, 1 Chron. 16. 7, 37. This work continued in the temple courts when Solomon's temple was built on mount Moriah, 2 Chron. 5. 12-13. God was entirely worthy to receive this ongoing expression of praise. Thus one of the Psalms of degrees embraced this thought of God's servants standing by night in the house so as to bless the Lord, lifting up holy hands in the sanctuary, Psa. 134. 1-2; at the same time, the Lord would reciprocate and bless each individual singer (note the change from "ye" to "thee").

In the N.T., the situation is spiritual rather than only physical. At the beginning, there was one faithful soul, Anna by name, who at the advanced age of 84, "departed not from the temple, but served God with fastings and prayers night and day. And . . . gave thanks likewise unto the Lord", Luke 2. 37-38. But the concept of "night" then evolved to a moral environment, rather than describing physical darkness. The change can be seen in John 13. 30, "it was night" when Judas went out, not only mere darkness at nighttime, but moral darkness, with Jerusalem full of men who were plotting the death of the Lord Jesus. This moral environment of darkness was perpetuated the next day, when the Lord said, "I cry in the daytime, and thou hearest not; and in the night season, and am not silent", Psa. 22. 2.

Today, the Lord's people should have such a sense of the sinfulness of sin, that they should realise that conditions of darkness reign around them. Yet we are children of the day and not of the night, 1 Thess 5. 5, although "in the night his song shall be with me, and my prayer", Psa. 42. 8.

May 8th

READING: **Mark 16**

DIFFICULTIES ABOUT THE RESURRECTION

IT IS SURPRISING that the Lord's disciples had doubts about His resurrection, though after the giving of the Holy Spirit, these doubts were removed, and they became faithful exponents of this resurrection of their Lord, Acts 4. 33. The doubts that many have today (including religious people) are nothing new, for they can be traced back to the New Testament itself.

Before the event. The Lord charged secrecy on the part of Peter, James and John "till the Son of man were risen from the dead", Mark 9. 9-10. The result was that they questioned "one with another what the rising from the dead should mean". In Luke 18. 34, "they understood none of these things".

On the day of the event. (i) Mary Magdalene "knew not that it was Jesus", John 20. 14. (ii) Then her words to the apostles "seemed to them as idle tales, and they believed them not", Luke 24. 11. (iii) The two on the Emmaus road went and told the fact to the rest in Jerusalem, "neither believed they them", Mark 16. 13. (iv) The Lord upbraided the apostles "with their unbelief and hardness of heart", Mark 16. 14. (v) Thomas said, "I will not believe", John 20. 25. (vi) The soldiers told lies that they knew were not true, "His disciples came by night, and stole him away while we slept", Matt. 28. 13.

After the event. (i) In spite of the clear-cut testimony of the disciples, the Sadducees always denied the resurrection, Matt. 22. 23; Acts 23. 6-8. (ii) Even when the Lord appeared in Galilee, we read, "but some doubted", Matt. 28. 17. (iii) The men of Athens, listening to Paul's testimony, thought that "Jesus" and "the resurrection" were the names of two gods, Acts 17. 18. As soon as the apostle reached "the resurrection" in his last address, men mocked, Acts 17. 31-32. (iv) In Corinth, they were having difficulty in understanding how resurrection could take place, "How are the dead raised up?", 1 Cor. 15. 35, and this led to a denial of the resurrection. Paul argued for the truth from every angle, that both Christ has been raised and that believers will be raised. (v) Later, such a denial became an organized body of doctrine, 2 Tim. 2. 18.

Believers should not allow themselves to be beset by so-called difficulties; faith should believe the Lord's words, "I will raise him up", John 6. 40.

May 9th

READING: **Ezra 7**

MAINTAINING REMNANT REVIVAL

SIXTY YEARS had passed since the house had been rebuilt in Jerusalem. When Ezra came on the scene, he found that much was lacking and that needed restoration. Many important features can be found in this chapter, both concerning Ezra the priest, and concerning the people who needed restoration. These features appear to have their counterparts in 1 & 2 Timothy.

Ezra could trace his genealogy back to Aaron, 7. 1-5, an important matter for a leader. We can trace God's purpose for us back to "before the world began", 2 Tim. 1. 9.

Ezra was a "ready scribe" in the law of Moses. For believers today, they must "give attendance to reading . . . to doctrine", 1 Tim. 4. 13, implying instruction in the Word of God.

Ezra "had prepared his heart to seek the law of the Lord", Ezra 7. 10. We should be vessels prepared unto every good work, 2 Tim. 2. 21.

Ezra was one of whom it could be said, "thou art sent", Ezra 7. 14. Similarly with the service in our hands; we are sent by God. Thus Timothy was instructed by Paul to remain in Ephesus, 1 Tim. 1. 4, while Paul himself was under the control of the Lord Jesus, who had put him into the ministry, v. 12.

Ezra had to offer sacrifice, Ezra 7. 17. Paul offered the spiritual sacrifice of praise as often as he could, for example, in the expressions of praise in 1 Tim. 1. 17; 6. 15.

The will of God was to be diligently adhered to, Ezra 7. 18; thus Paul was an apostle "by the will of God", 2 Tim. 1. 1.

God's command for the house was to be done diligently, Ezra 7. 18. Thus Timothy was to allow no other doctrine in the church at Ephesus, 1 Tim. 1. 3, and he was to continue in the things that he had learnt, 2 Tim. 3. 14. These represent the will of God for the spiritual house in which Timothy served.

Ezra was responsible "to beautify the house of the Lord", Ezra 7. 27. Nowadays, this corresponds to spiritual and moral behaviour in the house of God, the church of the living God, 1 Tim. 3. 15. In Christ, this corresponds to "the mystery of godliness", as set out in verse 16.

As strengthened, Ezra gathered together the chief men to be with him in Jerusalem, Ezra 7. 28. This answers to the elders in a local church, described in 1 Timothy 3. 1-7.

May 10th

READING: **Acts 18. 1-11**

BIBLE STUDY IN THE CHURCH

THE STUDY of the Bible is not something to be left to the theologians, but this is also the province of all Christians, whose study can be individual at home, and also collective in a local church. They study the Bible to obtain true doctrine, since everything else rests upon this foundation: doctrine concerning the Father, the Lord Jesus Christ and the Holy Spirit; concerning salvation and forgiveness through the sacrifice of Christ on the cross; doctrine concerning church matters, and God's future prophetical programme. Ignorance of these truths reduces a Christian to the level of unbelievers, not knowing how to walk and to please God.

The Lord Jesus often declared the importance of Bible study: "Search the scriptures . . . and they are they which testify of me", John 5. 39. He warned, "Ye do err, not knowing the scriptures", Matt. 22. 29. After His resurrection, in Luke 24. 27 "he expounded unto them in all the scriptures the things concerning himself".

Church meetings for Bible teaching started in the Acts. The church in Jerusalem was based on "the apostles' doctrine", Acts 2. 42, so the apostles gave themselves "continually . . . to the ministry of the word", 6. 4. The church at Antioch was desirous of scripture teaching, so Paul and Barnabas "a whole year assembled themselves with the church, and taught much people", 11. 26. On his first missionary journey, Paul "exhorted them to continue in the faith", 14. 22. On the second journey, he continued for a year and a half in Corinth "teaching the word of God among them", 18. 11. On the third journey, Paul spent three years in Ephesus publicly teaching the gospel of the grace of God, 20. 20, 24.

Every servant of God must be nourished up in the words of faith and good doctrine, 1 Tim. 4. 6. As a teacher, Timothy had to teach in the local churches, setting a good example to others to take in holy truth. Paul wrote, "These things command and teach. Be thou an example of the believers, in word, in faith. Give attendance to reading, to exhortation, to doctrine. Meditate upon these things", 1 Tim. 4. 11-16.

All meetings for Bible study should be profitable, so as to pass on truth for all Christians' hearts, minds and lives.

May 11th

READING: **Psalm 8**

A LITTLE LOWER THAN THE ANGELS

THIS PSALM is most remarkable, particularly when other translations are consulted. We refer to verse 5, which we shall quote from two translations:

"For thou hast made him a little lower than *the angels*, and hast crowned him with glory and honour", A.V.

"For thou hast made him but little lower than *God*, and crownest him with glory and honour", R.V.

The O.T. Greek translation known as the Septuagint is quoted in Hebrews 2. 7, "Thou madest him a little lower than the angels; thou crownedst him with glory and honour".

The point is that the word translated "angels" in Psalm 8. 5 is throughout the O.T. always translated "God", except in this one verse. For some reason unknown to the author, the Greek translators chose the word "angels" instead, and hence this appears in Hebrews 2. 7. Quite apart from the Septuagint, both the word "God" and the word "angels" are justified by divine inspiration, as appearing in the Hebrew O.T. and the Greek N.T. We must therefore accept both renderings, and since Psalm 8 is a Messianic Psalm, we must ask what its verse 5 means.

Nothing that is said must diminish the full force of the truth of the absolute Deity of the Lord Jesus, and that this was not relegated in any way when He took upon Himself human form. Otherwise we are on the brink of heresy.

The Lord Jesus took upon Himself a form "for the suffering of death", Heb. 2. 9. This was the form of man, the Word being made flesh, yet sin apart. He died in perfection, yet being made sin with our load of sin being placed upon Him. No angel could have done this, for they were spirit in nature, and had no incarnate form. Thus the Lord Jesus, during the days of His flesh, was made lower in *human form* than the angels (yet in Deity always being infinitely above them).

The same may be said about Psalm 8. 5. A "little lower than God"? Never, as far as absolute Deity is concerned. Yet God is Spirit in absolute nature, John 4. 24, but the Lord Jesus took upon Himself "the seed of Abraham", Heb. 2. 16, having partaken of flesh and blood. *In this form*, he was lower than His preincarnate form of Spirit, though retaining the blessed fact that He was *God* "manifest in the flesh", 1 Tim. 3. 16.

May 12th

READING: **Nehemiah 8. 1-12**

THE NECESSITY OF ACCURACY

ON PAGE 102, we gave some examples of extraordinary printing errors in various editions of the Bible in former years. By this, we sought to stress the necessity of accuracy in reading and understanding the Holy Scriptures. Here, we provide the readers with some more examples of printing errors.

In 1823, a Bible was printed containing "And Rebekah arose, and her camels", Gen. 4. 61. This should be "and her damsels".

In 1792, Luke 22. 34 was printed as, "I tell thee, Philip, the cock shall not crow this day, before that thou shalt thrice deny that thou knowest me". As every reader (and printer) will know, it was Peter who denied the Lord.

In 1807, a very solemn mistake was made in the printing of Hebrews 9. 14, "How much more shall the blood of Christ, who through the eternal Spirit offered himself without spot to God, purge your conscience from good works to serve the living God?"; this should, of course, read "dead works". This is not merely a factual error, but a doctrinal error of the first degree.

In 1638, Luke 7. 47 appeared as, "Her sins, which are many, are forgotten", instead of "forgiven". No doubt true according to Hebrews 10. 17, but one cannot alter the Lord's words!

In 1829, Isaiah 66. 9 was printed as, "Shall I bring to the birth, and not cease to bring forth?", instead of "cause to bring forth".

In 1804, a Bible was published containing many errors, such as "the murderer shall surely be put together", instead of "shall surely be put to death", Num. 36. 18; "the flesh lusteth after the Spirit", instead of "against the Spirit", Gal. 5. 17.

In 1641, Revelation 21. 1 was printed as "and there was more sea", instead of "no more sea".

In 1801, Jude 16 appeared as "These are murderers, complainers . . . " instead of "These are murmurers".

In 1562, an early Bible contained "Blessed are the place-makers", instead of "peacemakers", Matt. 5. 9.

In 1653, a disastrous error in 1 Corinthians 6. 9 occurred, "Know ye not that the unrighteous shall inherit the kingdom of God?"; this should, of course, be "shall not inherit".

Some of these errors may make us smile, but they should convince us of the necessity of accuracy in Bible study.

May 13th

READING: **2 Corinthians 6. 10**

THE APPROVED MINISTER

IN THESE VERSES, the apostle Paul shows the character expected of a minister of God. He provides 28 features that marked the apostolic service. Admittedly, these features refer more particularly to himself, though he would have liked to have seen some of these features in the Corinthians, for as things were they were too straitened instead of being enlarged, vv. 11-13. It is good to compare or contrast our own experience (i) so that the ministry should not be blamed, and (ii) so that God's servant should be approved. It goes without saying that if such features are desirable in the Lord's servants, then they had previously been manifested in the life and service of the Lord as He served here below amongst men, as they watched every word and deed carefully. In particular, in verses 8-10 we have six trials at the hands of men (though contrasted with God's provisions), and three trials in the wilderness (though contrasted with God's blessings). We may examine a few of these:

By honour and dishonour. "Ye do dishonour me", said the Lord, John 8. 49; but "he received from God the Father honour and glory", 2 Pet. 1. 17.

By evil report and good report. Two false witnesses were found to misquote His words about the destruction of the temple, Matt. 26. 60; the good report came through the words of the Father, "This is my beloved Son", 3. 17.

As deceivers, and yet true. In John 7. 12, some men claimed, "he deceiveth the people", while after His death the priests said to Pilate, "we remember that that deceiver said", Matt. 27. 63. By contrast, the One who was "the truth", by whom "grace and truth came", said of Himself, "a man that hath told you the truth", John 8. 40.

As unknown, and yet well known. Men thought that He was John the Baptist, Elijah or Jeremiah, Matt. 16. 14. Yet the Lord was well known, both by the Father, "no man knoweth the Son, but the Father", Matt. 11. 27, and by His own people, for He said of them, "I . . . know my sheep, and am known of mine", John 10. 14.

We shall continue these thoughts tomorrow, but we should ask ourselves, What relevance does His example have for us?

READING: **2 Corinthians 8. 1-16**

THROUGH HIS POVERTY

WE CONTINUE to examine the contrasts in 2 Corinthians 6. 9-10, as seen in the character and experience of the Lord Jesus when He was here below.

As dying, and, behold we live. Men sought to kill the Lord Jesus on many occasions. "The Jews sought the more to kill him", John 5. 18; "because the Jews sought to kill him", 7. 1; "Then took they up stones to cast at him", 8. 59; 10. 31. Yet during all this persecution, His life was preserved; it was impossible for men to kill Him before the appointed time. "We live" does not correspond to His life after His resurrection, rather to that eternal life lived on earth in spite of the many death threats and actions against Him.

As chastened, and not killed. The word "chasten" is the same as "chastise". The Lord suffered chastisement only at the hands of Pilate, Luke 23. 16, 22. Men could die under such affliction of body, but in the Lord's case, it was not possible for men to take His life. He lived through such sufferings, until He gave His life when hanging on the cross.

As sorrowful, yet alway rejoicing. On the one hand, the Lord wept over Jerusalem, Luke 19. 41, at the tomb of Lazarus, John 11. 35, and was very sorrowful in Gethsemane's garden, Matt. 26. 37. On the other hand there was the joy set before Him, Heb. 12. 2, and He could rejoice in spirit, Luke 10. 21.

As poor, yet making many rich. During the forty days and nights in the wilderness, the Lord possessed nothing from a natural point of view, and thus He hungered, Matt. 4. 2. In Matthew 15. 22, when the Lord had no bread personally, He accomplished the miracle so that the 4,000 were fed. Truly He became poor, that through His poverty many might be enriched, 2 Cor. 8. 9.

As having nothing, and yet possessing all things. The Lord said, "The foxes have holes, and the birds of the air have nests; but the Son of man hath not where to lay his head", Matt. 8. 20. Yet He really possessed all things: "the most high God, possessor of heaven and earth", Gen. 14. 19; "The heavens are thine, the earth also is thine: as for the world and the fulness thereof, thou hast founded them", Psa. 89. 11; "all that is in the heaven and in the earth is thine", 1 Chron. 29. 11.

May 15th

READING: **Exodus 40. 17-38**

WHAT IS FINISHED LEADS TO GLORY

GLORY IS a characteristic of God; it is the outshining of His Person, His perfection and His holiness, often seen in brilliant physical light in the Scriptures. When anything is finished according to His will, He is satisfied, and on many occasions His glory was associated with His satisfaction.

1. *The creation.* Some scientists have introduced the concept of "continuous creation", but the Scriptures inform us that "the heavens and the earth were finished, and all the host of them", Gen. 2. 1. The result was that He has set His glory above the heavens, Psa. 8. 1. Nothing of His creation could have a position above His personal glory.

2. *The tabernacle.* It took Moses and his helpers only five months to construct all the various intricate parts of the tabernacle. In Exodus 39. 32, all the parts were finished, and in 40. 33, the tabernacle was erected for the first time: "So Moses finished the work". As a result, "the glory of the Lord filled the tabernacle", vv. 34-35. He had said that the tabernacle would be sanctified by His glory, and so He took possession of a dwelling place amongst His people.

3. *Solomon's temple.* This temple took seven years to build, but this was time well-spent, for "all the work that Solomon made for the house of the Lord was finished", 2 Chron. 5. 1. As a result, God took possession of His house, and His glory filled the house of God, v. 14.

4. *The Lord Jesus.* In His prayer, He said, "I have finished the work that thou gavest me to do", John 17. 4, and when He died on the cross, He said, "It is finished", 19. 30, this being one word in the Greek text. After these things, He would "enter into his glory", Luke 24. 26. See also John 17. 5; Heb. 12. 2.

5. *The apostle Paul.* In Acts 20. 24, he anticipated being able to finish his course with joy, while in 2 Timothy 4. 7, he claimed to have finished his course. But he knew that there was to be a body of glory, Phil 3. 21; 2 Cor. 5. 1.

4. *Believers today.* We are exhorted, "Take heed to the ministry . . . that thou fulfil it", Col. 4. 17; 2 Tim. 4. 5; and the Lord gives us glory, John 17. 22, with a "Well done" as we enter into the joy of our Lord, Matt. 25. 21.

May 16th

READING: **Exodus 26. 15-30**

THE TABERNACLE BOARDS AS FRAMES

THE MAINTENANCE of the pre-eminence of Christ was necessary even in the types. The boards forming the three sides of the tabernacle are typical of the saints; (i) the wood implied humanity; (ii) the preparation showed how the Lord's people are prepared to be God's dwelling place; (iii) the sockets of silver speak of redemption; (iv) the gold speaks of imputed righteousness and glory granted; (v) they formed the dwelling of God, as do the saints today.

The ordinary description of these boards suggests that they were made of solid wood, but herein lies a difficulty. (i) Only four wagons and eight oxen were given for the transport of these boards, Num. 7. 8. (ii) The innermost tabernacle curtains (of coloured fine twined linen with woven cherubim) would have been largely hidden from the gaze of the priests, except by looking upwards; the boards would have hidden the rest. Such an arrangement would not be in keeping with its typical import, "that in all things he might have the preeminence", Col. 1. 18.

It is better to regard the boards as wooden frames, through which the curtains could be seen. Typically, the Lord's people look upwards, and see the beauty of the Lord on high. But they also look sideways, perceiving each other, and they should see Christ in their fellow-believers, rather than their oddities and weaknesses. This concept answers to several New Testament scriptures: "Christ in you, the hope of glory", Col. 1. 27; "they glorified God in me", Gal. 1. 24; "that the life of Jesus might be made manifest in our body", 2 Cor. 4. 10; when Christ is "admired in all them that believe", 2 Thess. 1. 10. If believers seek to reverse this, it must be resisted at all costs, as did Paul in Lystra, when men asserted that "The gods are come down in the likeness of men", Acts 14. 11.

By this means, the Lord's people form the body, of which the Head is seen; they form the building, of which the topmost Stone is seen. May nothing mar this view of Christ.

"Not I, but Christ", be honour'd, loved, exalted;
"Not I, but Christ", be seen, be known, be heard;
"Not I, but Christ", in ev'ry look and action;
"Not I, but Christ", in ev'ry thought and word.

May 17th

READING: **Psalm 106. 25-48**

SEPARATION

THE TRUTH of separation from what stands in opposition to God is most difficult to learn, particularly for some believers, whether in moral or religious issues. The matter is of importance, since a garden reverts to a wild type if it is neglected. The Lord Jesus showed the way (though He was never attached to opposition, and was only with it in a physical sense). Thus He was called out of Egypt, Matt. 2. 15; He went out of the temple courts, John 8. 59; He went out of the city, Luke 24. 50. In everything, He was holy, harmless, undefiled.

The case of Abraham. Abraham (as Abram) was called out of Ur of the Chaldees, Heb. 11. 8, "not knowing whither he went". Thus by faith he left his country, and by faith he resided in the land of promise. He would not go back, though had his faith been weak there would have been the opportunity, v. 15. Admittedly, his faith was weak when he went into Egypt, Gen. 12. 10, though he quickly returned to the altar. At the end of his life, Joshua exhorted the people to choose the land or to return to the idolatry of Ur, Josh. 24. 14-16.

Out of Egypt. In Exodus 13. 5-10, the Israelites were commanded to keep the feast of unleavened bread, because "the Lord brought thee out of Egypt". Believers are in the same position today; morally they have come out of Egypt, so they are exhorted to "keep the feast", 1 Cor. 5. 8. The life of the Christian imports nothing from the Egypt of preconversion days. Alas, in the wilderness there was rebellion; the people wept, "Why came we forth out of Egypt?", Num. 11. 20.

A wilderness example. Psalm 106. 28-31 refers to the story in Numbers 25; the people were joined to the heathen, Psa. 106. 35, 41. When deliverance came, the priest Phinehas was commended, and there was prayer and praise, "gather us from among the heathen", v. 47. Such praise can only come from hearts filled with heaven, not with the vanities of earth.

The Lord's people today. Paul knew the dangers of false attachments being made by his converts. Thus he wrote to the Corinthians, "Wherefore come out from among them, and be ye separate, saith the Lord, and touch not the unclean thing; and I will receive you", 2 Cor. 6. 17. Believers thus stand on the Lord's side, perfecting holiness in the fear of God.

May 18th

READING: **Deuteronomy 12. 13-32**

TAKE HEED

BOTH THE Old Testament and the New Testament contain this important injunction, "Take heed". The Lord through Moses was preparing the people for entry into the promised land; there would be many dangers caused by the idolatry around.

Thus in Deuteronomy 11. 16, "Take heed to yourselves, that your heart be not deceived, and ye turn aside, and serve other gods, and worship them". In 12. 13, the Lord's altar was to be the only altar for sacrifice, "Take heed to thyself that thou offer not thy burnt offerings in every place that thou seest"; in 12. 19, "Take heed to thyself that thou forsake not the Levite as long as thou livest upon the earth", for the Levites had to be supported in their service; and in 12. 30 another exhortation against idolatry through following the nations, "Take heed to thyself that thou be not snared by following them . . . saying . . . even so will I do likewise".

The Lord's people today are not immune from corresponding dangers, in their lives and spiritual service.

The dangers of religious ensnarement. "Take heed and beware of the leaven of the Pharisees and Sadducees", warned the Lord, Matt. 16. 6. "Take heed that no man deceive you. For many shall come in my name, saying, I am Christ; and shall deceive many", 24. 4-5. Many groups of men seek the ears and hearts of their fellows, but Christians are always on guard.

The dangers involved in leadership. Timothy was left in Ephesus to teach Paul's doctrine; "Take heed to thyself, and unto the doctrine", 1 Tim. 4. 16, else even an able teacher may go astray if he does not constantly watch his pathway and the contents of his teaching. Elders in local churches likewise have to be constantly on their guard, "Take heed therefore unto yourselves, and to all the flock", Acts 20. 28. They must feed the flock to avoid the danger of false elders entering to damage the flock with false doctrine and false practices.

The dangers involved in personal service. Paul had laid the foundation, but what happens next? "Let every man take heed how he buildeth thereupon", 1 Cor. 3. 10. Then only things of divine truth will be built. Archippus can represent us all: "Take heed to the ministry which thou hast received in the Lord, that thou fulfil it", Col. 4. 17.

139

May 19th

READING: **Mark 11. 1-19**

HE LOOKED ROUND ABOUT ON ALL THINGS

IN VERSE 11, not only did the Lord see things in the temple courts, but He saw men, their motives and their deeds; "he knew what was in man", John 2. 25. Let us list a few classes of men that the Lord could see, and assess to what extent He can see the same kinds of men today.

Priests. In the Old Testament, there were many faithful priests, such as Aaron, Ithamar, Phinehas, Zadok and Joshua, but when the Lord was here, no faithful priest is named except Zacharias, Luke 1. 5-6. The high priests Annas and Caiaphas, 3. 2, were men of opposite character, full of corruption and hatred towards the Lord Jesus. They maintained ceremony, but not towards God, loving ritual but not righteousness.

Publicans. These were the Jewish taxgatherers, being collaborators of the Romans. They were hated by the Jews, and sought to cream off part of their proceeds for themselves; Zacchaeus, having turned to the Lord, was willing to return these false gains fourfold, Luke 19. 8.

Pharisees. Here were members of a fanatical religious Jewish sect, adhering to the synagogue and their traditions of the law. They were always hostile and critical of the Lord, and were seeking His death. The Lord denounced them as being of their "father the devil", John 8. 44, and He called them a "generation of vipers", Matt. 23. 33, and hypocrites.

Prodigal. In His parables, the Lord took up common things and situations, so the people could understand. The prodigal son, Luke 15. 12-16, was therefore one of many. The far country described his moral state, wasting natural benefits that God had showered down upon all men for their wellbeing.

People. These constituted the majority of men. No doubt, some were sincere and devout, desiring the Lord's teaching, but of the rest He quoted Isaiah, "This people draweth nigh unto me with their mouth, and honoureth me with their lips; but their heart is far from me", Matt. 14. 6-7. It was the multitudes who cried out, "Crucify him" and "We have no king but Caesar".

Pilate. The Roman governor Pilate was active during the ministry of the Lord, Luke 3. 1. He moved between Caesarea and Jerusalem, and in spite of his better judgment, he misdirected justice so that the Lord should be crucified without cause.

May 20th

READING: **Matthew 12. 1-8, 38-42**

GREATER THAN

"HE SHALL be great", said Gabriel, Luke 1. 32. Five times in the Gospels, the expression "greater than" occurs, three times spoken by the Lord, and twice by others as questions.

Greater than the temple, Matt. 12. 6. The Pharisees made much of ceremony, but the Lord showed that Scripture transcends ceremony. In verse 4, David entered "the house of God", but strictly the tabernacle in David's time was not the house of God, since God had forsaken it never to return, Psa. 78. 60. In verse 5, the priests had certain duties to do daily, and were blameless if these were done on the Sabbath day. Nothing was wrong in what David and the priests did. Hence, neither in what the Lord did, for here was "one greater than the temple". The heart transcends the hands in all necessary deeds on the Sabbath, though the Pharisees refused to recognize this.

Greater than Jonah, Matt. 12. 41; Luke 11. 32. Jonah had no desire to preach repentance; he showed no interest when Nineveh repented, and he was not dead in the "whale". But the Lord preached and delighted in repentance, and the Lord truly died and rose afterwards in the power of resurrection. Hence in all things, the Lord was "greater than Jonah".

Greater than Solomon, Matt. 12. 42; Luke 11. 31. Solomon engaged in many indiscressions, and his wisdom did not overcome these. He went to the arkless tabernacle at Gibeon and not to Zion, 2 Chron. 1. 3-4; he built the house on Moriah and took the ark out of Zion, 1 Kings 8. 1; he married Pharaoh's daughter, 2 Chron. 8. 11; he had many strange wives at the end of his life, 1 Kings 11. 1. Even the visit of the queen of Sheba did not keep him on the narrow way. How different, how greater, was the Lord Jesus, and yet the Pharisees did not own Him.

Greater than Jacob, John 4. 12. At the well-side, the Lord announced to the woman that He could provide "living water"; hence the woman asked if He were "greater than our father Jacob?". The Lord answered by amplifying what He had to offer: "everlasting life", something that Jacob's well could not offer.

Greater than Abraham, John 8. 53. For Abraham passed into death, but the Lord promised that a man "shall never see death", v. 51. Indeed the Lord was greater, "Before Abraham was, I am", v. 58, at which the Pharisees sought to kill Him.

May 21st

READING: **Matthew 16. 13-28**

LACK OF UNDERSTANDING

THE DISCIPLES had but little difficulty in understanding the Lord's teaching on moral matters, though occasionally their questions showed otherwise, Matt. 18. 10. Parables were sometimes not understood, 13. 10, 36, neither was deep spiritual teaching, John 2. 22. But there was one important matter that always showed up ignorance, namely He had come to die and to rise on the third day. Consider the following:

Matthew 16. 21-23. After Peter's confession, and the Lord's announcement regarding His church, vv. 16-18, the Lord stated that He must suffer, "and be killed, and be raised again the third day", v. 21. Peter, content with the present situation, rebuked the Lord, "Be it far from thee, Lord: this shall not be unto thee". This was Satan working in Peter's mind prior to the giving of the Spirit that would remove all ignorance.

Matthew 17. 9-13. The Lord spoke of His rising from the dead, and of His sufferings, but the disciples were more interested in Elijah and John the Baptist.

Mark 9. 10. In the same context, the disciples questioned "what the rising from the dead should mean".

Matthew 17. 22-23. Again the Lord spoke of His betrayal, His death and rising again. The disciples' reaction was "they were exceeding sorry"; they did not want this event to happen.

Mark 9. 31-32. In the same context, "they understood not that saying, and were afraid to ask him". In other words, there was a certain lack of confidence in the Lord.

Luke 9. 44-45. In the same context, "they understood not this saying, and it was hid from them, that they perceived it not: and they feared to ask him of that saying". The hiding was the result of Satan's activity in their hearts.

Luke 9. 54. The Lord was going to be received up, and He set His face to go to Jerusalem. The result was that judgment of fire was in the apostles' minds, rather than the Son of man coming to save men's lives.

Luke 18. 31-34. Shortly before His decease, the Lord predicted the same things again. The result was, "this saying was hidden from them, neither knew they the things which were spoken". Satan snatched away the spoken word, but when the Spirit had come their hearts were then full of the truth.

May 22nd

READING: **2 Corinthians 12. 1-12**

THOUGHTS ON PRAYER

THE MORE a person becomes attached to the world and its pleasures, the less time that person has for engaging in prayer. It is a tragedy when the very thought of prayer is cast off, when such people go on through life completely adrift from their Creator God. An overwhelming crisis may suddenly hit a man when he is far from God; he may cry "O God" in despair, and find that the opportunity to seek God and speak to Him has vanished, and that he is alone and helpless in his crisis, with friends unable to offer relief.

Can a man really expect God to help when a life has been lived as if God does not exist? For the Bible shows that prayer is not something reserved for a crisis, but that it is a daily experience of Christians who love quietly and reverently to speak to God through the Lord Jesus Christ. Only those who have faith can approach God in prayer. For faith is what we call a saving faith; when we are forgiven nothing comes between us and God, and our sincere prayers reach up to heaven. He hears us daily as we speak to Him.

The Scriptures are full of records of men of prayer, and what their prayers were about. We are privileged to hear them speaking firstly of their praise and worship to God, and secondly of their deep needs that they felt in life and service.

The Gospels show that the Lord Jesus found that prayer to His Father God was so necessary. Thus in Luke 6. 12, "he went into a mountain to pray, and continued all night in prayer to God". The whole of John 17 is a prayer spoken the night before He died, a prayer for the disciples who would be left behind. The prayer in Luke 22. 44 is for us an unattainable divine example of prayer.

Paul was the greatest apostle, yet he engaged in constant prayer. He prayed for himself, "I besought the Lord three time", and the answer was, "My grace is sufficient for thee", 2 Cor. 12. 8-9. He prayed for individuals, for Timothy, "without ceasing I have remembrance of thee in my prayers night and day", 2 Tim. 1. 3. He prayed for churches, "we do not cease to pray for you", Col. 1. 9. He prayed for the nation of Israel, Rom. 10. 1, and "for kings, and for all that are in authority", 1 Tim. 2. 2. We would almost think that Paul had no time for anything else in his life and service!

143

May 23rd

READING: **Colossians 4. 1-18**

EPAPHRAS OUR DEAR FELLOWSERVANT

PAUL ATTRACTED around himself men of like spiritual outlook and character. This did not make Paul the centre, but Christ who should have the pre-eminence. Paul loved to write good words about such men, of whom Epaphras of Colosse was one.

Our dear fellowservant, Col. 1. 7. This means a beloved fellow-bondman, for Paul was in prison as a bondman for Christ. Both Paul and Epaphras could take the lowest position in the service of Christ.

A faithful minister of Christ, namely a faithful deacon in his service for the Colossians, 1. 7. Faith acquires salvation, and thus we trust God. Faithfulness should be a result, and God trusts us in His service. Several men are called "faithful" in the N.T., including Paul, for the Lord counted him faithful for the ministry, 1 Tim. 1. 12.

He declared their love in the Spirit, Col. 1. 8. This man informed Paul of the state of the Colossian church; this report contained no exaggeration, but a holy review of the saints. Here was no idle gossip, no coloration effects, but the truth. Compare this with the reports by Titus of the Corinthians, 2 Cor. 7. 7, and of Timothy, 1 Thess. 3. 6.

One of you, Col. 4. 12. Here was deliberate membership of a local assembly. Epaphras did not drift when he was away from Colosse, but was permanently recognized as a member of the Colossian church. Onesimus, v. 9, is similarly described.

A servant of Christ, Col. 4. 10. In 1. 7 Epaphras was a fellow-bondman with Paul; here he is a bondman of Christ, so deeply involved was he in Christ's service. In Philippians 1. 1 Paul and Timothy were bondmen of Christ.

Always labouring fervently for you in prayers, Col. 4. 12; in 1. 9 Paul did not cease to pray for them, and now Epaphras did likewise. Such an exercise in prayer should mark individual and assembly prayers for other saints and churches.

He had a great zeal for them, Col. 4. 13, and also for other churches, Laodicea and Hierapolis. Zeal for the house of God, John 2. 17, absorbs the whole personality and energy.

Epaphras, my fellowprisoner, Philem. 23. Poor Epaphras! In Rome with Paul, he now shared the apostle's imprisonment; yet he could send greetings to Philemon in Colosse.

May 24th

READING: **Numbers 32. 1-15**

AN INCREASE OF SINFUL MEN

WHATEVER THE rights or wrongs of this matter, Moses could see danger, "an increase of sinful men".

Perhaps most people would say that "sin" is a theological word, in which case they would disregard the subject. This is most unhelpful, since from the beginning to the end of the Bible God concerns Himself with the sin of man. The fact that Adam sinned in the garden of Eden is not something about which God would have us close our eyes, for the consequences were, and still are, too awful. Paul wrote, "as by one man sin entered into the world, and death by sin; and so death passed upon all men, for that all have sinned", Rom. 5. 12. This is God's assessment, so none should be self-satisfied.

Even believers sometimes need to be reminded of the Biblical teaching about sin. "The soul that sinneth, it shall die", said God through Ezekiel the prophet, Ezek. 18. 4; do we believe this? The apostle John wrote, "He that committeth sin is of the devil", 1 John 3. 8, a verse showing the relationship of men with Satan, this permanent contact bringing sin into the lives of those who are not Christians. And it is not possible "to get away with it", for "ye have sinned against the Lord: and be sure your sin will find you out", Deut. 32. 23. As a palliative, some men may still insist that the word "sin" cannot possibly describe their own lives. But God will not tolerate such self-righteousness, for "If we say that we have no sin . . . If we say we have not sinned, we make him a liar, and his word is not in us", 1 John 1. 8-10.

But believers know that there is better news than that! We are responsible before God to repent and confess our sins to Him. David said, "I will confess my transgressions unto the Lord; and thou forgavest the iniquity of my sin", Psa. 32. 5, and "Wash me throughly from mine iniquity, and cleanse me from my sin", 51. 2. Thus Nathan said to David, "The Lord hath put away thy sin", 2 Sam. 12. 13 (and his sin was a particularly horrendous one!). The reason is that "God commendeth his love toward us, in that, while we were yet sinners, Christ died for us", Rom. 5. 8; "he appeared to put away sin by the sacrifice of himself", Heb. 9. 20; "the blood of Jesus Christ his Son cleanseth us from all sin", 1 John 1. 7.

May 25th

READING: **Isaiah 40. 1-17**

THE ONE BRINGING GOOD TIDINGS

THIS PASSAGE is prophetical, for the Lord shall come to Zion with good tidings. He was the Apostle, the sent One from the Father, bringing news of salvation to men. There were also many of God's servants who brought good news. In the Old Testament, Abraham's servant went into Mesopotamia bringing good news to Laban, that Abraham was seeking a wife for his son Isaac, Gen. 24. 34-49. Of the spies sent by Moses to spy out the promised land, only two brought back a good report, Num. 14. 7-9. Where there is lack of faith, there will be an evil report, not bringing glory to God.

There are a number of examples in the New Testament, and we may consider three cases of messengers coming to Paul.

(1) During his second missionary journey, Paul had been forced to leave Thessalonica. Worried about the effects of persecution upon them, he sent Timothy to find out what was happening. "But now when Timotheus came from you to us, and brought us good tidings of your faith and charity, and that ye have good remembrance of us always, desiring greatly to see us, as we also to see you", 1 Thess. 3. 6. Here was comfort for the apostle through the news brought by a messenger, good news that caused rejoicing in Paul's heart.

(2) Towards the end of his third journey, Paul was journeying to Corinth through Macedonia. But he would not come to Corinth until he had news from Titus, informing him of the state of the Corinthians after they had received his first Epistle to them. He had waited for Titus in Troas in vain, 2 Cor. 2. 12-13, but in Macedonia Titus arrived at last: "he told us your earnest desire, your mourning, your fervent mind toward me; so that I rejoiced the more", 7. 7. Here was a message showing that the Corinthians had repented, once again accepting Paul's apostolic authority.

(3) Epaphras came from Colosse to Paul when he was a prisoner in Rome, and he declared "your love in the Spirit", Col. 1. 8. Verses 4-6 may also be understood as forming part of Ephaphras' message: their faith, love and hope, with the gospel bringing forth fruit. Restricted in prison, Paul must have thrilled in his soul to know that the grace of God was still taking root even though he could no longer work outside.

146

May 26th

READING: **Hebrews 13. 18-25**

GOOD WORK

AS EVERY believer knows, salvation does not come from works, "lest any man should boast", Eph. 2. 9. Paul wrote the same thing in 2 Timothy 1. 9 and Titus 3. 5. And yet once one is saved, the question of good works cannot be dismissed. Paul was able to recognize in his converts when their works were good or bad, and he warned that "every man's work shall be made manifest" in that coming day of divine discernment when there will be rewards from the Lord, 1 Cor. 3. 13-14.

Let us collect together various verses that speak of "good work" and note the use of the word "every" in this connection.

Hebrews 13. 20. "Now the God of peace . . . make you perfect in every good work to do his will, working in you that which is wellpleasing in his sight, through Jesus Christ". This shows the origin of "every good work", and the objective, "to adjust thoroughly". A similar thought occurs in Ephesians 2. 10, "we are his workmanship, created in Christ Jesus unto good works", so that we might walk in them.

Colossians 1. 10. Paul's prayer was that they should be "fruitful in every good work".

Titus 3. 1. In Crete, Titus had to exhort the believers "to be ready to every good work, to speak evil of no man".

1 Timothy 5. 10. Paul is dealing with the responsibility of the local church to widows; their character had to be such that they were "well reported of for good works . . . (having) diligently followed every good work".

2 Timothy 2. 21. Men who have purged themselves from false doctrines and false teachers are "meet for the master's use, and prepared unto every good work". In 3. 17, Paul writes about being "furnished unto all good works" ("good work" in the Greek text). Note: this thought comes in all three Pastoral Epistles.

2 Corinthians 9. 8. Paul is dealing with the necessity of Christian giving, "that ye . . . may abound to every good work".

2 Thessalonians 2. 17. Concluding the great prophetical chapter concerning the future man of sin, Paul writes that they may be established "in every good word and work".

It goes without saying that this idea appears in the Lord's service, "Many good works have I showed you", John 10. 32, and even the Jews recognized "a good work" though they hated Him.

147

May 27th

READING: **Ecclesiastes 12. 1-7**

SPIRITUAL WEAKNESS OR STRENGTH

THIS IS A METAPHORICAL description of life from youth to old age and death, for youth commences in verse 1, and the passage ends with death in verse 6, the breaking of the silver cord. There are three physical stages in life, (i) when there is accumulation of energy in the morning of life, (ii) when there is a balance between energy and its use in the afternoon of life, and (iii) when there is a decline in the evening of life. But this should not be so spiritually. When one is born again, one has a new life, eternal life, and one can go on increasing unto the perfect day. Unfortunately, some may "get used to having been saved", and thus the above stages may be manifested in their lives. If the means of grace, of partaking of the Word of God, and of prayer, are not neglected, then the last stage is better than the first; there is an increase from strength to strength. The physical stages through life can never undermine the spiritual stages.

Hosea 7. 9 tells of a fall: "Strangers have devoured his strength, and he knoweth it not: yea, gray hairs are here and there upon him, yet he knoweth not". It is bad to have thus slipped and not to know it; everyone can see this fact except himself. The verse strictly speaks of Ephraim as a nation, but the metaphor is equally applicable to individuals.

The reverse is found in Exodus 34. 29, "Moses wist not that the skin of his face shone while he talked with him (God)". It was impossible to know this when in the tabernacle, but when he came out, everyone else could see what had happened. It was reflected in his face that he had been in the presence of God. Moses was over eighty years old when this occurred, so he was going on from strength to strength. If spiritually a believer is firmly rooted, then he grows, perhaps unknowingly to himself, but others take notice that such a man has been with the Lord Jesus. Indeed, Isaiah 40. 31 says, "they that wait upon the Lord shall renew their strength". Alas, there are other examples of an unconscious decline. In Judges 16. 20, with his hair cut, Samson "wist not that the Lord was departed from him". But may we be like Paul who, as the end of his life, wrote, "I have fought a good fight, I have finished my course, I have kept the faith", 2 Tim. 4. 7.

May 28th

READING: **Luke 22. 7-23**

THE BREAKING OF BREAD

MEN MAY call it "communion", but the Bible calls it either "the breaking of bread" or "the Lord's supper". In the Old Testament, the nation of Israel had to observe the passover annually by means of the killing of a passover lamb, so as to commemorate their exodus from Egypt. This ceremony became more elaborate as the centuries passed. Today God does not want ceremony, so He brought the old passover remembrance to an end, the last one being observed by the Lord Jesus the night before He died on the cross. *He* is now called "our passover", 1 Cor. 5. 7, since it was as a Lamb that He died on the cross. So important was His sacrifice, that God wants Christians to remember the Lord Jesus in a special way. Thus immediately after the last passover in the upper room before He went forth to die, He instituted the breaking of bread.

We quote Matthew 26. 26-28, "as they were eating, Jesus took break, and blessed it, and break it, and gave it to the disciples, and said, Take, eat; this is my body. And he took the cup, and gave thanks, and gave it to them, saying, Drink ye all of it; for this is my blood of the new testament, which is shed for many for the remission of sins". Luke 22. 19 adds, "this do in remembrance of me".

In practice, this remembrance was carried out by the church on the "first day of the week", Acts 20. 7, otherwise called "the Lord's day", Rev. 1. 10. Here was no spasmodic attendance, as if Christians were free to be absent at the slightest whim or provocation. Rather they "continued stedfastly in . . . the breaking of bread", Acts 2. 42. To them this was no ritual, no formality; by eating the bread and drinking the cup, these believers showed "the Lord's death till he come", 1 Cor. 11. 26. By remembering the Lord, they were engaged in an act of worship, praise and adoration.

Today, alas, non-Christians often "take communion"; the service is reduced to cold formality. Some Christians think that there is now no need to follow the Lord's instructions to break bread. In some circles the body of Christ is even reckoned as being sacrified again! How far are these practices from the simple truth of remembrance and worship, having grown up over the centuries in opposition to the New Testament.

149

May 29th

READING: **Galatians 3. 1-14**

THE JUST SHALL LIVE BY FAITH

THE STATEMENT in Habakkuk 2. 4, "the just shall live by his faith", is quoted three times in the New Testament. The prophet could see the invading armies of the Chaldeans, 1. 6, a nation lifted up with pride and cruelty. But there was a contrast in a faithful remnant in Judah. These could be described as "the man that is more righteous", 1. 13, and a man who would live by his faith, 2. 4.

The quotation in Galatians 3. 11. The Galatians seemed to think that they knew better than God. They had commenced in the Spirit, but now had been perverted by false brethren who would trouble them, to turn them back to the law. But it was not possible for any law to give life and righteousness, 3. 21, so Paul was pressing the truth of the gospel that was based on a Person outside of self. This knowledge of the Person and the truth can only come by faith, otherwise Christ is dead in vain. Hence Paul quoted "The just shall live by faith", showing that the Old Testament supported the New Testament truth that Paul was expounding.

The quotation in Romans 1. 17. Romans is another one of the Epistles that presses the subject of faith, also seen in the Old Testament. The Epistle is not one of correction, but one of instruction. Verses 1-17 form the introduction, and at the end of this introduction Paul quotes "The just shall live by faith" to demonstrate the truth that the righteousness of God is revealed "from faith to faith", (i) from Paul's faith to the Romans' faith, (ii) from faith demonstrated in the Old Testament to faith acquired in the New Testament, and (iii) from initial saving faith to a continuous living by faith.

The quotation in Hebrews 10. 38. This is another corrective Epistle, using the Old Testament itself to correct believers who fell back to the ceremony of old. The quotation "the just shall live by faith" is introductory to chapter 11, where there appears a long list of Old Testament men who lived by faith, commencing with Abel and ending with David and the prophets, v. 32. Although the Hebrews were going back to ceremony, yet the writer had good thoughts of them, that they believed to the salvation of their souls, with "things that accompany salvation", 6. 9-11. These come only by faith.

May 30th

READING: **1 Kings 20. 28-43**

BUSY HERE AND THERE

THE LIVES of some believers are like this; the things that should have been done are not done, because other trivial matters have interfered with spiritial priorities.

"As thy servant was busy here and there, he was gone", or as the margin reads, "he was not", v. 40. The story is as follows: Ben-hadad, king of Syria, "was drinking himself drunk", v. 16, and Israel gained the victory. A second victory for Israel was gained in verses 28-30. The king of Syria then pleaded for mercy, so Ahab king of Israel granted this, and so failed to destroy him according to the command of God, v. 42. A prophet enacted a parable to get the message across to Ahab; apparently wounded in battle with a prisoner to keep, he lost the prisoner because he was "busy here and there", just as Ahab had lost Ben-hadad by making a covenant with him, v. 34.

People are like that today under different circumstances; they think about the little things and are occupied with them, and the large things of life and service are not accomplished.

Do men treat their lives like that? God has given men *one* life, which will be reviewed in the future, Rom. 2. 6. All men are responsible for the use they make of their lives; opportunities are given, but business here and there throughout the years may cause all to be lost, with nothing to be shown before God. Paul used his converted life to the full, 2 Tim. 4. 7-8; nothing was omitted in his service in the gospel through empty activity.

Do men treat their souls like that? The soul is like a jewel in a casket, but men spend so much time on their bodies, that sometimes the opportunities for salvation seem to have disappeared. Pharaoh falsely repented, playing with God, and then God hardened his heart. In Romans 1. 24-28, men were busy, but "God gave them up (over)" (three times). In Revelation 22. 11, opportunities had gone, and those that were unjust and filthy remained in that state until the Lord comes quickly.

Do men treat Christ like that? Time for business and time for pleasure, but no time for Christ crucified. God's Spirit will not always strive with men, Gen. 6. 3. In Mark 5. 17, the Lord departed out of the coasts of the Gadarenes at their request; there is no record that He returned again with salvation.

May 31st

READING: **Proverbs 29. 1-27**

WITHOUT A VISION THE PEOPLE PERISH

THE AUTHOR once heard a preacher say that he read one chapter in Proverbs every day, arranging his reading of the 31 chapters so as to cover the whole book each month. Certainly the word-pictures embrace a multitude of truth, and verse 18 is no exception, "Where there is no vision, the people perish". Paul was a man of vision, as he saw the men perishing without the gospel, and knew the call of God on many occasions during his years of service. We may not have direct visions today, yet a consideration of Paul's visions can be a help to us, as our service develops according to the will of God.

1. Acts 9. 3-6. Here was Paul's first vision of the Risen Living Christ, not in the tomb, but in glory. He was saved by grace, adding later that he "was not disobedient unto the heavenly vision", 26. 19, for here he received his commission to be sent unto the Gentiles to open their eyes.

2. Acts 9. 12. Being blind in Damascus, Paul was granted a vision, seeing a man who would come to him that he might receive his sight.

3. Acts 22. 17-21. In Jerusalem later, Paul knew that his testimony would not be accepted. He saw the Lord speaking to him while he prayed in the temple. The Lord urged him to depart quickly from Jerusalem, to be sent far hence to the Gentiles. This sending forth did not actually take place until about ten years later in Acts 13. 2-4.

4. 2 Corinthians 12. 1-4. It is usually understood that this vision, as caught up into the third heaven, took place during the first missionary journey, when he was stoned in Derbe and left as dead, Acts 14. 19. He was either killed or so near death that he was allowed to see into heaven, but he was not allowed to utter what wonderful words he had heard.

5. Acts 16. 9-10. Here was guidance granted to Paul during the second journey; the sinner's need was shown to him.

6. Acts 23. 11. When he was a prisoner, the Lord stood by Paul, stating that he would have to bear witness in Rome.

7. Acts 27. 21-25. During the storm on the voyage to Rome, the angel of God confirmed that he would arrive there safely.

8. 2 Timothy 4. 17. At the end of his life in Rome, the Lord stood with Paul and strengthened him.

June 1st

READING: **Luke 9. 18-36**

THE PRAYERS OF THE LORD IN LUKE

IT IS solemn to contemplate the words spoken by the Lord directly to His Father in prayer. The other Gospels contain other prayers, but in Luke's Gospel we find ten.

1. Luke 3. 21. Here the Lord was praying as He was baptized prior to His public ministry. The other Gospels do not record this fact; John must have heard what the Son said, and of course he heard the Father's words, "Thou art my beloved Son".

2. Luke 5. 16. At this early stage in His ministry, the Lord was popular, v. 15. In the midst of this, His reaction was to withdraw into the wilderness to pray.

3. Luke 6. 12. Here oppression by men was commencing, and the Lord was about to select twelve apostles from His many disciples. He therefore went into a mountain, "and continued all night in prayer to God".

4. Luke 9. 18. The Lord was alone praying, but the disciples interrupted Him. He then announced His death for the first time.

5. Luke 9. 29. Only Luke records the fact that He went up into a mountain to pray prior to, and at, His transfiguration.

6. Luke 10. 21-22. The Man of sorrows could rejoice in things in which men would find no cause for rejoicing. The Father hid "these things" from the wise, but revealed them to babes.

7. Luke 11. 1. The Lord was praying "in a certain place". He was not interrupted until He had finished, and then one asked Him, "Lord, teach us to pray". The thoughts in the model prayer were Godward (Thy) and manward (us).

8. Luke 22. 41-44. Here was His prayer of intense supplication as in an agony He contemplated in the Father's presence the sufferings through which He would pass on the following day, yet a prayer in which He was subject to the Father's will.

9. Luke 22. 31-32. Here was a prayer for Peter, "I have prayed for thee, that thy faith fail not". This was a prayer of intercession and sympathy, recorded only in Luke's Gospel.

10. Luke 23. 34. Only Luke records this brief prayer, spoken as the Lord was being crucified: "Father, forgive them; for they know not what they do". We feel that this referred to the Roman soldiers who were actually crucifying Him.

These prayers all entered the Father's heart, as He watched and heard His Son on earth. He hears our prayers too.

June 2nd

READING: 1 Kings 2. 12-46

PUT OFF BEFORE BUILDING THE HOUSE

SOLOMON CAME to the throne, but there were many sinful and unspiritual men around that had to be disposed of before the temple could be built. In fact, there had to be replacements, and four such pairs appear in this chapter.

Adonijah, Solomon. Where does true authority lie? God had chosen Solomon both to sit on the throne and to build the house, 1 Chron. 28. 5-6. Adonijah, Solomon's brother, knew that it was Solomon's "from the Lord", 1 Kings 2. 15, yet he exalted himself saying, "I will be king", 1. 5. As a result, the command was given that Adonijah should be killed, 2. 25.

Today, many high religious leaders claim authority, but Christians know that authority is vested in the exalted Lord, the One who is greater than Solomon.

Abiathar, Zadok. Where does true priesthood lie? During David's reign, there had been two high priests, Abiathar of Ithamar's line, and Zadok of Eleazar's line. But there could be no rivalry in the temple, so Abiathar was deposed, as not being in the true highpriestly line, 1 Kings 2. 27.

Today, all believers are priests, but we have only one High Priest, the exalted Christ. Others who claim to be priests are like Abiathar, but their claims are not substantiated by God.

Joab, Benaiah. Who is subject to military authority? Joab was a man of blood, who had trampled on more righteous men, 1 Kings 2. 31-32, but Benaiah was one of David's trusted men. Joab, therefore, was slain, v. 34.

Today, believers do not war after the flesh, as others may do, for this is making war after the flesh, 2 Cor. 10. 2-5, instead of with weapons "mighty through God". Each believer must be "a good soldier of Jesus Christ", 2 Tim. 2. 3, saying with Paul, "I have fought a good fight", 4. 7.

Shimei, Barzillai. Who is subject to moral authority? Shimei had cursed David, and cast stones at him, 2 Sam. 16. 5-6, but Barzillai an aged man had brought many provisions, 17. 28; thus Shimei had to die, 1 Kings 2. 46, while the sons of Barzillai were blessed with kindness, v. 7.

Today, the Spirit should be manifested in conduct in the house of God, the church of the living God. Alas, the Shimei spirit has sometimes split local churches, 2 Cor. 12. 20.

June 3rd

READING: **1 Thessalonians 2. 1-20**

NOT THIS BUT THAT

THIS IS no doubt the first Epistle that Paul wrote, written shortly after he had left Thessalonica during his second journey. It contains many examples of a special style adopted in the Epistle, namely "not . . . but . . . ": note these.

Paul's preaching in Thessalonica. (i) The cleanness of preaching: "our exhortation was not of deceit, nor of uncleanness, nor in guile, but as we were allowed of God to be put in trust with the gospel", 2. 3-4a. (ii) The motive of preaching: "not as pleasing men, but God, which trieth our hearts", v. 4b. (iii) The manner of preaching: "neither at any time used we flattering words . . . But we were gentle among you", vv. 5-7. (iv) The object of preaching: "we were willing to have imparted unto you, not the gospel of God only, but also our own souls", v. 8.

The results of Paul's preaching in Thessalonica. It is important to see what was accomplished when preaching was of this standard. (v) Something was accomplished: "our entrance in unto you, that it was not in vain: but . . . we were bold in our God to speak unto you the gospel of God", 2. 1-2. (vi) Spiritual work: "our gospel came not unto you in word only, but also in power, and in the Holy Spirit", 1. 5. (vii) The word worked effectually: "the word of God . . . ye received it not as the word of men, but as it is in truth, the word of God, which effectually worketh also in you that believe", 2. 13.

The results of believing. (viii) Faith was made known openly: "from you sounded out the word of the Lord not only in Macedonia and Achaia, but also in every place", 1. 8. (ix) Faith was made known by conduct: "God hath not called us unto uncleanness, but unto holiness", 4. 7. (x) Faith watches for Him: "Let us not sleep . . . but let us watch", 5. 6.

The results of not believing. (xi) "He therefore that despiseth, despiseth not men, but God, who hath also given unto us his holy Spirit", 4. 8.

Of course, we can think of other contrasts "not, but" in the New Testament; all demand our attention. "Lay not up for yourselves treasures on earth . . . but lay up for yourselves treasures in heaven", Matt. 6. 19-20. "Not as I will, but as thou wilt", 26. 39. See also John 6. 27.

June 4th

READING: **Luke 2. 8-20**

THE ANGELIC MESSAGE TO THE SHEPHERDS

Observation, v. 8. The shepherds were watching their flock by night. This was a humble occupation, something that David did, yet who was raised to kingship, Psa. 78. 70-71. God is interested in true shepherds, those who care for His new creation, and not like the hirelings.

Visitation, v. 9. The glory of God was revealed to the selected few. There was fear at the unexpected (as in Luke 24. 37; Rev. 1. 17), but comfort in the words "Fear not".

Evangelization, v. 10. Here was the announcement of the "good tidings". Normally we think of the apostles as the initial evangelists, but an angel was the first evangelist, with a message for "all people".

Salvation, v. 11, Christ the Lord being "a Saviour". In the O.T., God's interest centred in Him through prophecy and types; in the future, all interest is centred in the Lamb in Revelation 5. But now interest is centred in Him as Saviour, Lord and Christ, being born in order to die on the cross.

Humiliation, v. 12. He was "lying in a manger" at His birth, later rejected by Herod, and then by the leaders, and finally He humbled Himself even unto the death of the cross, Phil. 2. 8, thus accomplishing that work whereby He would be a Saviour.

Exaltation, vv. 13-14. All praise is offered to God for such a Person and such a plan. The angels did not praise as recipients of salvation, for these had never had part in the fall. Thus we exalt with *greater* joy and understanding.

Consultation, v. 15, "Let us go even unto Bethlehem"; they were willing to talk about this spiritual revelation, and they were willing to follow the divine exhortation. There was, in fact, a desire to come to the Saviour, and to see David's greater Son born in the flesh.

Manifestation, v. 16. Thus they found Mary, Joseph, and the Saviour-Babe. As Simeon said shortly afterwards, "mine eyes have seen thy salvation", v. 30, and as John at the cross, "he that saw it bare record", John 19. 35.

Proclamation, v. 17. In keeping with the angelic message, they announced the saying to others. Those who heard "wondered", but there is no record that they saw the Saviour.

June 5th

READING: Acts 3. 12-26

THE FOURFOLD MUST

IN THE GREAT divine programme for the Son of God, there was the necessity of His death, resurrection, ascension and His return. There is, alas, a danger of believers taking these things very much for granted, but as we know, an infinity of repercussions hinged and hinges upon these great facts. We therefore cannot afford to neglect or overlook them. In Acts 1, we find reference to these four great facts: "his passion", v. 3; "he showed himself alive", v. 3; "he was taken up", v. 2; He "shall so come", v. 11. Similarly in chapter 2 we find reference to these four great facts: He was "crucified and slain", v. 23; He was "raised up" and He could not see corruption, vv. 24, 27; He was "by the right hand of God exalted", v. 33; and ultimately at His return in glory God will make His enemies His footstool, v. 35. These facts have implications for salvation, for service, and for the future winding up of all things. Thus there was the absolute necessity of these things, as the Lord said, "all things must be fulfilled, which were written", Luke 24. 44. Let us consider the fourfold "must" relating to these events.

(1) John 3. 14. "As Moses lifted up the serpent in the wilderness, even so must the Son of man be lifted up". The roots of this great act thus go back to the days of Moses. The people quoted this later in John 12. 34, "how sayest thou, The Son of man must be lifted up?". They could not understand the significance of His death, nor of the "must" attached to it.

(2) John 20. 9. At first on the resurrection day, Peter and John "knew not the scripture, that he must rise again from the dead". The eternal Son of God could not remain in death; if He had to die, then He had to rise again afterwards.

(3) Acts 3. 21. "Jesus Christ . . . whom the heavens must receive until the times of restitution of all things". Heaven having received Him, there followed the giving of the Holy Spirit and the establishment of the church as the body of Christ.

(4) 1 Corinthians 15. 25. "He must reign, till he hath put all enemies under his feet". This reflects upon His future victory here on earth, prior to the eternal state. This reign refers to the millennial reign, for which He will return in glory to put down His enemies and to reign in triumph.

June 6th

READING: **Luke 15**

THE JOY OF THE LORD

THE LORD JESUS was a Man of Sorrows, and He was acquainted with grief; He knew what it meant to weep, and He was moved by the afflictions of men. His pathway was one of trial and oppression, and throughout His life He was anticipating the sufferings of the cross. Yet there were those occasions when there was joy and rejoicing in His heart. We may consider a few, to note the consequences.

1. *His rejoicing that truth was hidden or revealed*, Luke 10. 21-22. His disciples had returned with joy that demons were subject unto them; but the Lord would not have this to form a basis of their rejoicing, v. 20. It was then that He "rejoiced in spirit". Men's thoughts are not God's thoughts, for men would think it strange that the Lord could rejoice because the truth was hidden from the wise and prudent, but revealed unto babes. The religious leaders, boasting and self-satisfied with their religion, knew nothing of God, and wanted nothing from Him, so the truth was hidden from them, as in Matthew 13. 11-15. But the disciples received the truth, and this was "good" in the Father's sight.

2. *The joy of anticipating the throne*, Heb. 12. 2. As the Lord moved through His years of public ministry, and as the sufferings of the cross came upon Him at the appointed hour, what sustained His soul? It was the joy set before Him, that the right hand of the throne of God awaited Him as He returned to heaven. This was an eternal joy beyond the night of sufferings that He endured on the cross.

3. *The joy at repentance*, Luke 15. 10. When the piece of silver was found, when one sinner repents, "there is joy in the presence of the angels". This does not refer to the angels, but to One surrounded by the angels, namely the Lord Jesus on the throne in their presence. Consider also the joy in the father's house when the prodigal son returned.

4. *The shared joy*, John 15. 11. The Lord stated that His joy should remain in the disciples, "that your joy might be full". Their joy is not the joy and pleasure of the world, but rather the Lord's joy, inasfar as it can be shared by His people. Their joy is "full", meaning that nothing else of the fleeting joys of time and sense need be added.

READING: **Isaiah 49. 1-13**

LABOUR IN VAIN

SOMETIMES the service of the Lord's people can be almost in vain, with a bit of vanity and pride, a bit of entertainment that is fleeting with no lasting effects, and with nothing useful accomplished. Have we done even one thing in our service for the Lord that has not been in vain?

Isaiah 49. 4 shows the Lord's words in principle, "I have laboured in vain, I have spent my strength for nought, and in vain: yet surely my judgment is with the Lord, and my work with my God". Cities would not repent; many disciples went back and followed Him no longer; the truth of His Person was refused; men sought to kill Him for His conduct on the Sabbath day; they claimed that He worked miracles by Beelzebub; they mocked Him when He was on the cross; even His own apostles forsook Him and fled. Nevertheless, all work done according to the will of God, and using spiritual methods, is not in vain, however small outwardly the results may be. Read what is said in verses 6, 8, and 9: "I will also give thee for a light to the Gentiles, that thou mayest be my salvation unto the end of the earth". This is not in vain, rather it is of infinite spiritual value.

We may sometimes feel like the apostle Paul felt, as he surveyed his service in the Lord's name. How did he react when things were apparently going wrong?

1. The Galatians were going back to the law, observing "days, and months, and times, and years". Paul wrote, "I am afraid of you, lest I have bestowed upon you labour in vain". Yet he exhorted them, "be as I am"; Gal. 4. 10-12.

2. In the midst of a crooked and perverse nation, believers at Philippi were to shine as lights, holding forth the word of life, "that I have not run in vain, neither laboured in vain", Phil. 2. 15-16. Paul would be offered on their service of faith.

3. Paul feared that the Thessalonians might have been tempted by the tempter, "and our labour be in vain", 1 Thess. 3. 5. But he had desired to have imparted to them his own soul, 2. 8, so everything really would be alright if that were so.

4. The Corinthians were still in their sins if there was no resurrection. But Paul exhorted them, "be stedfast, unmoveable . . . your labour is not in vain in the Lord", 1 Cor. 15. 58. As for Paul, he laboured more abundantly than they all, v. 10.

159

June 8th

READING: **Isaiah 21. 1-12**

WATCHMAN, WHAT OF THE NIGHT?

THIS MAY BE a difficult passage to understand at a first reading, but it has its part in that section of Isaiah that is composed of the various burdens of the nations. In verse 6, a watchman is set, who stands upon his watchtower day and night, v. 8. In verse 11, twice the watchman is asked, "what of the night?". Spy satellites may be used in the present day, but the Lord's people, although heavenly-minded, must exercise their watchfulness while on the earth.

For we are watchmen in the night season; how much of the night has gone? Paul supplies the answer, "The night is far spent, the day is at hand", Rom. 13. 12. We can pictorially consider the time of testimony to be like the opportunities of a week, the end of which is the Saturday night, leading to the blessings of the following Lord's Day. We are now living in the Saturday night of the history of Christian testimony. This is Satan's night, a time of revelling for men in the world. The godless sin and celebrate as if the following day can still be used for their pursuits. Christians should be watchmen, observing these things, but detached from them.

For the coming of the Lord draws nigh. The beginning of the time of the end is not far away. As Paul wrote, "the mystery of iniquity doth already work", 2 Thess. 2. 7. For the world is in a state of increasing wickedness and rebellion. There will be a falling away first, v. 3; a denial of the power of godliness, 2 Tim. 3. 5, and false teachers bringing in damnable heresies, 2 Pet. 2. 1. In the last century, a prediction was given about the present century: there would be religion without the Holy Spirit, Christianity without Christ, salvation without regeneration, politics without God, and heaven without hell. The sins that brought about the flood, and the destruction of Sodom and Gomorrah are increasing today.

But are God's watchmen warning men to flee from the wrath to come? For believers, His coming should be one of joyful anticipation, but for the men of darkness, they will enter the terrors of the day of the Lord. For the Lord warned, "as the days of Noe were, so shall also the coming of the Son of man be", Matt. 24. 37. Consequently, as faithful and wise servants, we are exhorted to "Watch therefore", vv. 42-47.

June 9th

READING: 1 Timothy 3. 8-16

DEACONS AND THEIR SERVICE

THE WORD "deacon" is a direct transliteration from the corresponding Greek noun, and its cognate verb, to minister or to serve. The A.V. translators had to follow the ecclesiastical practices of the day, and hence we find "to use the office of a deacon" twice, when all this means is "to serve". The idea of a deacon is found in the hierarchy of the established church, but the scriptural idea has nothing to do with a set office that raises an ordained deacon above the congregation.

Definition. The verb is used in connection with the Lord's service, "the Son of man came . . . to minister, and to give his life", Matt. 20. 28. The noun and verb are used for almost every form of spiritual service by the Lord's people: "ministers by whom ye believed", 1 Cor. 3. 5; "the ministry of the word", Acts 6. 4. The words are also used of practical service: "serve tables", 6. 2; "I go to Jerusalem to minister unto the saints", Rom. 15. 25, that is, financially. Sisters are included: "Phebe our sister, which is a servant of the church", Rom. 16. 1; "many women . . . which followed Jesus from Galilee, ministering unto him", Matt. 27. 55.

Qualifications. Not all in a local assembly are necessarily deacons; they must first be proved before they can serve, 1 Tim. 3. 10. There must be a mark of maturity, and young believers (who can serve in their measure while they are growing in the faith) are later proved with a good report. The rest of the chapter lists many qualifications; a further very comprehensive list is found in 2 Corinthians 6. 3-10.

Selection. This has nothing to do with training in a theological college, nor with the so-called process of ordination. (i) For spiritual work, when spiritual gift is exercised, the selection is by the Risen Lord. Grace is given to every one, Eph. 4. 7-11, according to the divine will. Of course, a gifted brother may be requested to come and help, as in the cases of Peter and John, Acts 8. 14; Peter, 9. 38; Paul, 11. 26; and Timothy, 16. 3. (ii) In financial matters, etc., the selection may be made by a local assembly, as in Acts 6. 5, where seven already spiritually able brethren were chosen to "serve tables". The same may also be found in 1 Corinthians 16. 3, and 2 Corinthians 8. 19.

June 10th

READING: **Genesis 1. 1-31**

THE FAITH OF A MATHEMATICIAN

GOD CAN count; He did so before man was created, as in Genesis 1, where numbers up to seven occur. He also counts what He has made, "He counteth the number of the stars", Psa. 145. 4, something Abraham could not do, Gen. 15. 5. But men gradually invented almost everything else, either as a subject of pure thought, or as a means with which to explore the intricacies of the nature and outworking of the whole universe. The present writer is such an applied mathematician, no doubt perceiving the physical realities of nature through different eyes than most other people. He can see the why and the wherefore. But being a Christian at the same time enables him to believe that one explores the very methods by which God maintains His universe. Mathematics explores the orderly divine mind, by which God reveals Himself to men, "his eternal power and Godhead", Rom. 1. 20.

If that were all, a Christian would be poverty stricken indeed. For much of God's activity lies beyond His natural creation, and cannot be investigated mathematically. His love, grace and mercy in the Lord Jesus Christ are also revealed to those who have faith to understand. The writer's interest in mathematics at school and subsequently did not make him a Christian. It was on this present date in 1943, during his last year at school, that the Lord led him, a religious young man not seeking after God, unexpectedly to the home of a Christian schoolmaster lying ill in bed, a man who would only speak of the Lord. The result was that he was saved there and then! Truly, "I was found of them that sought me not", Rom. 10. 20. Since then, faith has grown, as has the knowledge of the Scriptures, with service extending in many directions.

Army and student life, and academic life afterwards, never diminished the desire for fellowship with the Lord's people in many places. Academic attainment is no drawback to faith, as some would suggest. Rather, faith assesses the values of things that no unbeliever could ever assess. Mathematics has remained the writer's interest over the decades, but never supplanting the priority of the Scriptures. Many academics seek to destroy the Scriptures, but faith sees the paucity of their arguments that are intended to trap the unwary.

162

June 11th

READING: **Genesis 18. 1-22**

HOSPITALITY

THIS WAS a solemn occasion, of which Hebrews 13. 2 states, "Be not forgetful to entertain strangers: for thereby some have entertained angels unawares". Some believers also have this opportunity to entertain the Lord's servants in their homes, "Use hospitality one to another without grudging", 1 Pet. 4. 9; "given to hospitality", 1 Tim. 3. 2.

After his first missionary journey, on the way to Jerusalem, Paul experienced the practical fellowship of the saints. The Lord's people provided the necessities of life for the apostle and Barnabas, "being brought on their way by the church", Acts 15. 3. Such hospitality was the outcome of Christian faith and love; Paul experienced it, and he expected it. Thus when outlining to the Romans his exercise to visit Spain with the gospel, he wrote, "I trust to see you in my journey, and to be brought on my way thitherward by you, if first I be somewhat filled with your company", Rom. 15. 24. The saints' homes formed Paul's home; instead of selling houses as in Acts 4. 34, this sharing of a home with God's servants appears to have taken the place of this practice.

On his second journey in Corinth, Paul shared the home of Priscilla and Aquila, Acts 18. 2-3. Anticipating his journey through Corinth later, he wrote, "it may be that I will abide, yea, and winter with you, that ye may bring me on my journey", 1 Cor. 16. 6. Many years afterwards, John wrote to Gaius of the hospitality he showed to full-time workers, "Beloved, thou doest faithfully whatsoever thou doest to the brethren, and to strangers; which have borne witness of thy charity before the church: whom if thou bring forward on their journey after a godly sort, thou shalt do well: because that for his name's sake they went forth, taking nothing of the Gentiles", 3 John 5-7. Such hospitality is stated to be the work of "fellowhelpers to the truth", v. 8.

This is "ministry", in just the same way as is "the ministry of the word" given by able teachers of the Scriptures. The Lord Jesus was shown the same loving hospitality in the home of Martha and Mary in Bethany, Luke 10. 38-42; John 12. 1-2. The work of Martha was just as necessary as that of the others, for the Lord's servants bring good tidings of the work of the Lord.

June 12th

READING: **Romans 1. 13-25**

AN EVANGELICAL THEME

A Saviour needed. On one occasion, the Lord Jesus stated that He had not come to destroy men's lives, but to save them, Luke 9. 56. In other words, the Lord came to meet a need; judgment needed to be replaced by salvation. So terrifying will judgment be, that Paul could write of a "day of wrath", Rom. 2. 5; while John the Baptist spoke of the "wrath of God" being on every unbeliever, John 3. 36. This wrath will be "against all ungodliness and unrighteousness of men", wrote Paul, Rom. 1. 18. Because this future eternal judgment appears to be a long way off, men disregard it, and deny that a God of love can ever intervene in judgment. But the truth of Scripture is better than denials of unbelieving men, so all should take heed: a Saviour is needed.

A Saviour provided. This is why the Lord Jesus came into the world long ago. He came into the world to save sinners, 1 Tim. 1. 15; God "sent the Son to be the Saviour of the world", 1 John 4. 14. When He came into the world, an angel stated, "he shall save his people from their sins", Matt. 1. 21. Yet it was not by His birth that God provided salvation, rather by His death. As Paul wrote, the preaching of the cross is the power of God to those who are saved, 1 Cor. 1. 18. This gospel is that by which we are saved, 15. 2; it is the power of God unto salvation, to all who believe, Rom. 1. 16. Moreover, when we are "justified by his blood, we shall be saved from wrath through him", 5. 9. God has declared that He has provided only one Name, that of Jesus, whereby "we must be saved", Acts 4. 12.

A Saviour accepted. Such divine love and mercy can be neglected until it is too late. By faith, Christians have accepted the gift of God unto salvation. "Thy faith hath saved thee", said the Lord, Luke 7. 50; "By grace are ye saved through faith", Eph. 2. 8; if we believe, we shall be saved, Rom. 10. 9; Mark 16. 16. "Believe on the Lord Jesus Christ, and thou shalt be saved", Acts 16. 31. Hence to receive salvation, we must call on the Name of the Lord, 2. 21. Then we become Christians, and looking back we can say like Simeon that our eyes have seen "thy salvation", the Lord Himself, Luke 2. 30, and that God, according to His great mercy, has saved us, Titus 3. 5. But beware, unbelievers "neglect so great salvation", Heb. 2. 3.

June 13th

READING: **Philippians 4. 1-23**

THOSE THINGS SEEN IN ME, DO

IN THE EARLY stages of one's physical life, development comes by imitating. A child's capabilities, speech, habits, likes and interests, are largely copied from his parents. The process of learning by heart, of learning a language or a trade, all come by copying. Children's toys are a copy of the underlying reality. One's garments or house are a copy from a pattern or architect's plans. Even the act of singing hymns is a copy of existing words and music. Later in the growth process, one may become more independent. It is good to develop skills and initiatives that demand independence, but spiritually, independence can be full of dangers. This is seen in verses where men seek to be independent of God:

"We have turned every one to his own way", Isa. 53. 6; "they are greedy dogs . . . they all look to their own way", 56. 11; "There is a way that seemeth right to a man", Prov. 14. 12.

But God has provided a Pattern! We all love to think that Christ is the One to imitate, since He was the Perfect Man doing God's will. The expression "Follow me" occurs dozens of times: "he that followeth me shall not walk in darkness", John 8. 12; "I have given you an example", 13. 15. But the Lord started His life in perfection, whereas we started in sin. We therefore also have another pattern to copy, one involving conversion, but one that does not detract from Christ, and that is Paul who wrote, "I obtained mercy . . . for a pattern to them which should hereafter believe on him", 1 Tim. 1. 16.

There are quite a number of verses that show Paul as a pattern to be imitated. "Be ye followers (imitators) of me, even as I also am of Christ", 1 Cor. 11. 1; "be followers together of me, and mark them which walk so as ye have us for an ensample", Phil. 3. 17. Having given a list of spiritual and moral features that should mark a believer, Paul adds, "Those things, which ye have both learned, and received, and heard, and seen in me, do", 4. 9. "Ye know what manner of men we were among you for your sake. Ye became followers of us, and of the Lord", 1 Thess. 1. 6; "to make ourselves an ensample unto you to follow us", 2 Thess. 3. 9. Finally, Paul spoke to king Agrippa, "(that thou) were both almost, and altogether such as I am, except these bonds", Acts 26. 29.

June 14th

READING: **Psalm 37. 1-24**

THE EXPLOITS OF THE WICKED

DAVID MUST have lived amongst some objectionable men, since this Psalm shows how a believer should view the wicked activity of men. Verses 1-2 summarize what David had to say: "Fret not thyself because of evildoers, neither be thou envious against the workers of iniquity", since their ultimate portion would be to be cut off, having nothing. These men prosper with their wicked devices, v. 7, but the Lord's people must "Rest in the Lord, and wait patiently for him". They may possess but little as compared with the wicked and their gains, but "A little that a righteous man hath is better than the riches of many wicked", v. 16. See Proverbs 24. 19-20.

Asaph, one of the contemporaries of David, viewed things through the same kind of eyes, though he needed instruction that David seemed to have possessed already. "I was envious at the foolish, when I saw the prosperity of the wicked", and "these are the ungodly, who prosper in the world; they increase in riches", Psa. 73. 3, 12. It was only when he went into the sanctuary of God that he understood their end, v. 17.

In the New Testament, we find such men described in James 5. 1-6. Here were the rich employers who refused to pay their employees, v. 4. Yet in the sight of God, their riches were corrupted, and their gold was debased in value. Theirs would be heaped treasures of judgment in the last days. But believers who suffered under them had to be patient, since the coming of the Lord was nigh, and He would rectify all things, and it is only as in the sanctuary that we can understand the end of such men and their ungodly riches of corruption. Alas, that there is so much corruption in business circles, but the Lord's people should remain separated from such policies.

We find various examples of this. (i) In Luke 16. 19-31, the Lord told the story of the rich man. He "fared sumptuously every day", v. 19, yet provided nothing for Lazarus. Both had their respective rewards; Lazarus would only understand the situation when safely in Abraham's bosom. (ii) The future Mystery Babylon the Great will be full of religious corruption, enhanced by commercial enterprises, Rev. 17. 4; yet all her riches will come to nought, and the rich merchants will be weeping, 18. 15. But heaven will rejoice, v. 20.

166

June 15th

READING: **Luke 6. 20-49**

THREE-FOLD GOOD

IT IS OBVIOUS that most of this section appears to be a repetition of parts of the Sermon on the Mount in Matthew chs. 5-7. We believe that this was spoken on a different occasion, since good truth is worth repeating in different places to different people. In verse 35, there is the exhortation to "do good", regardless of circumstances. In verse 38, there is the thought of reciprocation; a disciple gives, and "good measure" is returned to him; the end of the verse implies that he has given what is good in the first place. In verse 43, there is implied that a good tree brings forth good fruit. The vital principles are laid out in verse 45; we find there (i) a person who is good, (ii) a good heart, and (iii) good deeds being brought forth. A good man, good treasure from a heart, and good fruit. We expect such principles to be found first in the Lord Jesus, and then in His people, for the disciple shall be as his Master, v. 40.

Applied to the Lord. (i) As to His Person, one called Him "Good Master", Luke 18. 18. Since there is One only who is good, the Lord in an oblique way claimed Deity. Others in John 7. 12 owned Him as good. (ii) In the good treasure of His heart, there were hid "all the treasures of wisdom and knowledge", Col. 2. 3. (iii) Deity brings forth "Every good gift", James 1.17, and we are recipients of such grace.

Applied to believers. (i) As to the person of a believer, we have the description of Barnabas, that he was "a good man, and full of the Holy Spirit and of faith", Acts 11. 24. Joseph of Arimathaea was also "a good man, and a just", Luke 23. 50. In the two parables of the talents and of the pounds, servants are called "good", Matt. 25. 21; Luke 19. 17. (ii) As to the heart and its treasure, it is God who fills the hungry spiritually "with good things", 1. 53. This is quite unlike the rich man who in his lifetime received "thy good things", 16. 25. (iii) As to deeds and gifts, the Lord spoke of "good fruit" (and its opposite) in Matthew 7. 17-20, while in a practical sense believers are supposed to "communicate . . . all good things", Gal. 6. 6.

Readers may like to know that there are two words for "good" in Greek, though a dictionary and a concordance must be used.

167

June 16th

READING: **1 Corinthians 14. 29-40**

THE COMMANDMENTS OF THE LORD

THE WORD "commandments" is not a word relegated to the Old Testament, as if it had nothing to do with the Lord's people today. We are not under the law, and the "ten commandments", though mostly restated in the New Testament, must be understood in the light of the believers' position of grace.

But there are commandments today. The Lord said, "A new commandment I give unto you, That ye love one another", John 13. 34. When properly understood, this embraces everything else. Many years later, John amplified this new commandment in 1 John 2. 3-11, calling it now "an old commandment", the keeping of which shows that we know the Lord. Moreover, he gave an apostolic "new commandment", an echo of the Lord's words in John 13. 34 that believers should love one another.

The apostle Paul used the expression "the commandments of the Lord", 1 Cor. 14. 37, in relation to the use of spiritual gifts in meetings of the local church. Only a man who is "spiritual" can acknowledge that Paul's writings are the commandments of the Lord. An unspiritual man will seek to deviate, introducing ideas of his own, and inventing reasons why Paul's instructions should be understood in the opposite sense to what the relevant verses really mean. Only then can "things be done decently and in order".

In the Old Testament there are commandments that are not really "legal" commandments. We refer to the instructions given to Moses for the building of the tabernacle. When the day for its erection had arrived, final instructions were given, Exod. 40. 1-16, ending with the overall statement, "according to all that the Lord commanded him, so did he". But in verses 17-32, we read a detailed expansion of Moses' work, the expression "as the Lord commanded Moses" occurring seven times, vv. 19, 21, 23, 25, 27, 29, 32, dealing with the erection of the tabernacle, the placing of the ark, the table, the lampstand, the golden altar, the altar of burnt offering, and the laver. Moses was exact in all he did! Much of this reflects typically on the service of the Lord's people in a local assembly, so may their obedience be as complete and effective as was that of Moses. Only then will the glory of the presence of the Living Christ be known in the gathering.

June 17th

READING: Psalm 63. 1-11

THIRSTING AFTER GOD

THERE ARE some believers in great spiritual weakness, who are searching for greater satisfaction, but not finding it in the pursuits of the world to which they have sunk, whether in holidays, homes, work, sport, pleasure, television, politics, study or philanthropy. They may not speak openly about their state, but they grope, and God knows too. Others may seek help in meetings, seeking quietly, yet with no one aware of any conflict, fear and doubt within the heart. But God knows. The psalmist also was in spiritual need, and he expressed this need openly; no doubt the record is for our help. It is a remarkable fact that there are three Psalms that present the deep longing of a soul after God: these Psalms are 42, 63, 84, evidently forming a pattern (with 21 added each time), and all three open with deep longings of soul.

Psalm 42. "As the hart panteth after the water brooks, so panteth my soul after thee, O God. My soul thirsteth for God, for the living God: when shall I come and appear before God?", vv. 1-2. The psalmist was cast down for several reasons; he had been a man of weeping while mocked by his enemies; he remembered the past joy of going into the house of God; God's waves and billows had gone over him. Yet God was his rock who would command His lovingkindness.

Psalm 63. "Thou art my God; early will I seek thee: my soul thirsteth for thee, my flesh longeth for thee in a dry and thirsty land, where no water is", v. 1. David longed to see God's power and glory, as he had once seen in the sanctuary. The psalmist had essential hope and satisfaction, rejoicing in the shadow of the eternal wings. He did not dwell upon his thirsty state, but quickly found the Living God.

Psalm 84. "How amiable are thy tabernacles, O Lord of hosts! My soul longeth, yea, even fainteth for the courts of the Lord: my heart and my flesh crieth out for the living God", vv. 1-2. This seems to be the cry of an exile far from the house of God, and far outside Jerusalem. Yet he trusted that God would be a sun and shield, enabling Him to be found when he gained a doorkeeper's position in the house of God.

In all three cases, there is the past experience of the house of God; that is where the praise of restoration is made.

June 18th

READING: **Romans 12. 1-17**

THE GIVER, THE GIFTS AND THE GIFTED

NOT ALL evangelical believers know that there is a divine distribution of gifts given to every Christian; some seem to think and act as if the reception of gift is restricted only to a certain class of men. However, the Scriptures know nothing of such a restriction, and wherever the subject of gift occurs in the Epistles, there also occurs the statement that everyone is embraced. In the parable of the talents, it is implied that the Lord gave the talents to His servants who were responsible for their use and increase, Matt. 25. 15. The following passages should be carefully noted.

(1) Romans 12. 3-15. Every man must "think soberly, according as God hath dealt to every man the measure of faith", v. 3. Paul then goes on to show that members, forming one body in Christ, are nevertheless distinct the one from the other. He then gives a list of gifts, some being "speaking" gifts, but many others certainly not having this public character. The totality of these gifts forms true ministry.

(2) 1 Corinthians 12. 7-13. "But the manifestation of the Spirit is given to every man to profit withal . . . all these worketh that one and the selfsame Spirit, dividing to every man severally as he will", vv. 7, 11. Here the Spirit divides the gifts, and again "every man" is stressed. The variety of members is also stressed, but none is excluded. The Spirit here is the One who enables a man to confess Jesus as Lord, v. 3. Hence unbelievers are excluded from the free distribution; any one who refuses to confess the absolute Lordship of Christ has no divinely given gift, whatever may be his natural endowments in religious matters.

(3) Ephesians 4. 7-16. "Unto every one of us is given grace according to the measure of the gift of Christ", v. 7. Once again, "every one" is stated, while in verse 11 distinguishing names are given to the gifted ones. Note that the Risen Lord gives the gifts, so the gifted ones are responsible to Him.

It is humbling to realize that the three Persons of the Trinity are engaged in this distribution of gift to believers.

(4) 1 Peter 4. 9-11. "As every man hath received the gift, even so minister the same one to another, as good stewards of the manifold grace of God". A short list is then given.

READING: **2 Samuel 19. 31-40**

AN OLD DISCIPLE

WHEN A BELIEVER is elderly, it may be very difficult to do much; this applies to the ordinary affairs of daily life, or to the Lord's service and to assembly meetings. God knew that this was so; hence the Levites were allowed to serve around the tabernacle only until they were fifty years of age, Num. 8. 25. The more elderly amongst the Lord's people need therefore to be encouraged at this stage of their lives.

Of course, the Lord Jesus Himself never appeared to be old when He was here on earth; He grew up from childhood, and His age was thirty to thirty-three during His ministry prior to His death on the cross. Many verses in Hebrews show this eternal agelessness of the Lord: "thou remainest", 1. 11; "thou art the same, and thy years shall not fail", 1. 12; "neither beginning of days, nor end of life", 7. 3; "for ever, sat down on the right hand of God", 10. 12; "the same yesterday, and to day, and for ever", 13. 8.

Consider some characters who were old.

Barzillai, 2 Sam. 19. 32. He "was a very aged man", and eighty years old; also he was "a very great man". But he was deaf and had no sense of taste, v. 35. When David fled from Jerusalem, he had brought many things to the king to sustain him, 17. 28-29, but when David returned, owing to his age, Barzillai was unable to accompany him to Jerusalem. Truly, he had done what he could. The elderly may not be able to do much, but they can offer the Lord the devotions of their hearts.

Anna, Luke 2. 36. She was "of a great age", stated to be about eighty-four years. She departed not from the temple, but (i) served God with prayers night and day, and (ii) spoke to others of the Lord. Her witness was still strong.

Mnason, Acts 21. 16. He was "an old disciple", incidentally the last time the word "disciple" appears in the N.T. He was with Paul on the journey to Jerusalem, and Paul would lodge with him there. Hospitality could still be shown.

Paul, Philem. 9. The apostle calls himself "Paul the aged", as he was a prisoner in Rome. Yet he could be full of thanks, prayer and rejoicing for Onesimus and Philemon. Paul was restricted, yet his heart was still full of spiritual things.

Of course, none can now attain the aged vitality of Moses!

June 20th

READING: Acts 1. 1-26

HISTORICAL NAMES AND TITLES

IN THE Gospels and Acts, in purely historical descriptive passages, the Lord is referred to by His Name Jesus. Men did not address Him by that Name (with few exceptions, Mark 10. 47); "Sir" (namely, "Lord") and "Master" were the usual titles. But there are a few occasions when "Lord" rather than "Jesus" is used in a descriptive passage. When counting the number of occasions, it is necessary to check manuscript amendments.

Matthew's Gospel. On no occasion is "Lord" used; rather the Name "Jesus" is always employed.

Mark's Gospel. Always "Jesus" except two occasions: "after the Lord had spoken unto them . . . the Lord working with them", 16. 19, 20.

Luke's Gospel. Eight times "Lord" is used rather than "Jesus". "When the Lord saw her", 7. 13; ("the Lord said", 7. 31, is omitted entirely in the R.V.); "the Lord said" to the Pharisees, 11. 39; "the Lord said" to Peter, 12. 42; "The Lord then answered him", the ruler of the synagogue, 13. 15; "the Lord said" to the disciples, 17. 6; "the Lord said" to the Pharisees, 18. 6; "the Lord said" to Peter as Simon, 22. 31; "the Lord turned, and looked upon Peter", 22. 61.

John's Gospel. There is only one occasion in a descriptive passage where "Lord" is used and not "Jesus": "after that the Lord had given thanks", 6. 23.

The Acts. This phenomenon is continued in The Acts. The Name "Jesus" is used in 1. 1, 11, 14, 16. But a point of separation is reached in 2. 36, "God hath made that same Jesus, whom ye have crucified, both Lord and Christ", 2. 36, for after that the title "Lord" is used in historical passages. "The Lord added to the church", 2. 47; "and to him (Ananias) said the Lord in a vision", 9. 10; "the Lord said" to Ananias, 9. 11; "the Lord said" to Ananias, 9. 15; "whose heart (Lydia) the Lord opened", 16. 14; "the Lord spake to Paul in the night by a vision", 18. 9; "the night following the Lord stood" by Paul, 23. 11.

In these days, there may appear to be an unspiritual overusage of the Name "Jesus" on every occasion, which does not seem to be justified by the testimony of Scripture. Each believer must make up his mind before the Lord as to the Name or title he should use in worship, prayer, preaching or personal testimony.

June 21st

READING: **Joshua 10. 1-15**

THE LONGEST DAY

TODAY IS the longest day, the earliest rising of the sun and the latest setting of the sun. Before this date, the days have been getting longer; after this date, the days will be getting shorter. This is God's doing, for He promised that "summer and winter" shall not cease, Gen. 8. 22. If the earth's axis were not tilted, we would be living in a strange world indeed! We always like long days, for we are children of the day and not of darkness. Can you remember the 1940's and the 1950's when there was "double summer time" in operation?; the days seemed even longer then, with the sun not setting until 10 30 p.m. June 6th 1944 was called "Earth's longest day", but further north within the arctic circle, the summer sun never sets, and a day lasts for months.

In the Old Testament, the longest day is found in the book of Joshua. Here was a battle with the Amorites, and the battle could not be completed within one day. So Joshua said, "Sun, stand thou still", and "the sun stood still", Josh. 10. 13, until the battle was over. "The sun stood still in the midst of heaven, and hasted not to go down about a whole day"; this day was unique, v. 14. An amazing explanation has been given by a scientist, not to disprove the Biblical story, but to offer a physical reason why the earth's axis should have behaved in such an unusual manner.

But this phenomenon never happened again, yet one of God's prophets looked forward to a better event in the future. "And it shall come to pass in that day, that the light shall not be clear, nor dark: but it shall be one day known to the Lord, not day, nor night: but it shall come to pass, that at evening time it shall be light", Zech. 14. 6-7. This is describing the new conditions of the millennial day, and no doubt spiritual conditions are also being described. Revelation 21. 23 says, "the city had no need of the sun . . . the Lamb is the light thereof", adding, "there shall be no night there", v. 25; 22. 5.

When the Lord Jesus was here on earth, it was not all day although He was the Light of the world. There was a night scene when Judas went out, John 13. 30. When the Lord died on the cross, there was His longest night and the shortest day, prior to the never fading eternal day in which we also shall partake.

June 22nd

READING: **2 Timothy 2. 1-26**

MEN OF THE LAST DAYS

THE SECOND Epistles are often referred to as Epistles of the last days. Certainly 2 Timothy has this character, and since we believe that we are living in the last days prior to the Lord's return, we should take heed to the message that the apostle Paul is bringing to us. For men who were then antagonistic to all spiritual things are also abroad today, seeking to damage the truth by their doctrines and practices.

In particular, Paul lists four pairs of names, each of which demonstrates a certain turning away from the truth.

Phygellus and Hermogenes, 2 Tim. 1. 15. These illustrate the fact that "all they which are in Asia be turned away from me". They *turned from the truth*, and this is *religious error*. Here are men who refuse to believe that Paul was inspired by the Spirit, so they can turn away from anything that they dislike in his teaching. The antidote is, "Hold fast the form of sound words, which thou hast heard of me", v. 13.

Hymenaeus and Philetus, 2 Tim. 2. 17. Here were men who "concerning the truth have erred, saying that the resurrection is past already", v. 18. Thus they *corrupted the truth*, and this is *academic error*. For they argued rationally instead of spiritually, refusing to believe in a bodily resurrection of the future, relegating it to the past in a spiritual sense only. The antidote is "rightly dividing the word of truth", v. 15, embracing truth and discarding the religious theories of men.

Jannes and Jambres, 2 Tim. 3. 8. Here are men who "resist the truth: men of corrupt minds, reprobate concerning the truth". Here were men like the magicians, who *resisted the truth*, and this is *heretical error*. They copy, but everything is false. The antidote to this is, "continue thou in the things which thou hast learned", v. 14.

Demas and Alexander, 2 Tim. 4. 10, 14. They had forsaken Paul, and had done him much evil. Thus they *forsook the truth*, and this is *carnal error*. Demas loved the liberty of the world, rather than the narrow path of discipleship; Alexander plotted against Paul so as to throw off his words. The antidote to this is to be like Luke who remained with Paul, v. 11, and like Mark who was profitable for the ministry.

174

June 23rd

READING: Colossians 4. 3-18

ARISTARCHUS, PAUL'S FELLOW

THE CONVERSION of this man shows that this is not a passing phase, here today and gone tomorrow. It is impossible to remain the same as before one's conversion. Else one would be like the seed in Matthew 13. 2-9; the stony places and the thorns cannot produce any fruit from the good seed. As we examine the career of Aristarchus, it is obvious that he could never have dreamed what would happen to him in the years after his conversion.

He had lived in Thessalonica, Acts 20. 4. This man served idols, 1 Thess. 1. 9; he had been a Gentile who knew not God, 4. 5; the vengeance of God rested on those who knew Him not, 2 Thess. 1. 8; a man without hope and without God.

An evangelist came to Thessalonica, Acts 17. 1. Paul preached that Christ had to suffer and to rise from the dead, v. 3, leading to a great multitude of Greeks believing. No doubt Aristarchus made a Christian profession at that time, and although Paul had to leave quite quickly, yet he had made such a good impression, that the converts had to go forward.

The effects on the converts, and on Aristarchus in particular. His was a "work of faith, and labour of love, and patience of hope", 1 Thess. 1. 3. He became a follower of Paul and of the Lord Jesus, 1. 6; he received the Word, not as the word of men, but as the Word of God, 2. 13. This good beginning enabled Aristarchus to go forward with a call to unexpected service, as the verses containing his name specifically show.

Paul's fellow-traveller, Acts 19. 29. He went where God wanted him to go. In danger in Ephesus, he was one of Paul's "companions in travel". He then went with Paul to Corinth, and back to Macedonia, 20. 4. Later he was with Paul and Luke during the shipwreck, 27. 2.

Paul's fellow-worker, or "fellowlabourer", Philem. 24. He had learnt to do what God wanted him to do; he could be described as a beloved brother, a faithful minister, a faithful brother, and a servant of Christ. He was a fellow-worker "unto the kingdom of God", being a comfort to Paul, Col. 4. 11.

Paul's fellow-prisoner, Col. 4. 10. He was what God wanted him to be. He had suffered in Thessalonica, in Ephesus, and during the sea voyage. Now he suffered with Paul in Rome, being a comfort to Paul. What a difference conversion makes!

June 24th

READING: **Matthew 4. 1-11**

THE TEMPTATION OF THE LORD

THE PERFECTION of the Son had always been known to the Father; hence His declaration, "This is my beloved Son", showing that the Lord's baptism had nothing in common with a baptism unto repentance. Yet before the commencement of the Lord's ministry, Satan himself had to learn of His perfection, and this occurred when the Spirit led Him into the wilderness.

The three temptations answer to physical possessions, religious arrogance, and political power. Truly the Lord would possess all things; He would be the pre-eminent One amongst His people, and He would be King over all the earth; but not by the means that Satan presented. We can note great contrasts between the Lord and certain Old Testament characters.

(1) *Physical possessions.* In the wilderness, the Lord had nothing, but stones and bread were not to be His possession at the instigation of Satan, in spite of bodily need. Truly the Lord was greater than Solomon. At the beginning of his reign, Solomon did not ask God for "riches, wealth", 2 Chron. 1. 11, but later, when in a position of power, he ensured that he gained everything. 1 Kings 10. 14-29 shows Solomon in the pre-eminence of his possessions. But the Lord would have nothing when He was engaged in His service here below, Matt. 8. 20.

(2) *Religious arrogance.* In the temple in Jerusalem, the Lord had no religious status amongst the priests who loved position, power and pomp over the people who looked up to them in their arrogance. There was no possibility of the Lord taking a pre-eminent position on the temple's pinnacle, to be seen by the people with Psalm 91. 11-12 apparently fulfilled to untutored minds. How the Lord contrasted with Jeroboam in 1 Kings 12. 27-33, who arranged religious pomp and ceremony to satisfy the people and himself with pre-eminence.

(3) *Political power.* The kingdoms of this world consisted of Rome and its subordinate states, being the political glory of man. Such man-made power could not possibly be given to the Lord; only in Revelation 11. 15 will the kingdom of the world, completely cleansed, become the kingdom of the Lord. In the Old Testament, the outstanding example of political power is seen in Nebuchadnezzar, 2 Kings 24-25; Dan. 4. 30, but his kingdom was destroyed. How distinct was the Lord in all His perfection!

June 25th

READING: Acts 7. 51-60

THE STANDING LORD

THE LORD is sometimes seen as seated: seated for teaching, Luke 5. 3; and now in heaven in the dignity of divine exaltation, Heb. 1. 3. But He is often described as standing, One ready for action, or else actually engaged in work. Let us note some of the occasions when the Lord is seen as standing.

To read. In the synagogue in Nazareth, He "stood *up* for to read", Luke 4. 16, selecting the passage in Isaiah 61. 1-2. After that He sat down to speak to the congregation.

For healing. In the house of the mother of Simon's wife, He "stood *over* her". Thus he rebuked the fever, and healed her, with divine authority manifested in His standing position.

Waiting to teach. In Luke 5. 1, He "stood *by* the lake", ready to teach when in the boat, where He sat down.

Waiting to heal. Blind Bartimaeus had called for mercy, and "Jesus stood *still*", Mark 10. 49. The Lord called for the man, whose faith enabled the Lord to heal him.

As accused. In Matthew 27. 11, the Lord "stood *before* the governor"; mostly the Lord said nothing. He was dumb as a sheep before His shearers.

To reveal Himself. Mary was weeping for sorrow, looking towards the tomb, but the Lord was behind her "standing", John 20. 14. All He had to do was to call her name, and she knew Him immediately. Her weeping gave place to rejoicing.

Ready to intervene. Men were ready to put Stephen to death, but he saw "the glory of God, and Jesus standing *on* the right hand of God", Acts 7. 55. Here was the Son of man standing, in the position He will adopt when coming in glory and judgment, when He intervenes in that coming day.

To comfort. Now in prison, certainly Paul needed comfort, and the Lord provided this one night as He "stood *by* him", Acts 23. 11. See also 2 Timothy 4. 17.

His rights for judgment. John saw that *in the midst of* the throne "stood a Lamb as it had been slain", Rev. 5. 6.

Awaiting His return. John saw that "a Lamb stood *on* the mount Zion", Rev. 14. 1.

This is just one posture taken by the Lord on appropriate occasions. The Lord's people must learn to adjust their posture in service according to the nature of each occasion.

June 26th

READING: **2 Corinthians 1. 13-24**

GOD IS WITNESS: PAUL'S COMING

GOD IS witness. Do we believe this? "The eyes of the Lord are in every place, beholding the evil and the good", Prov. 15. 3. The unsaved certainly do not realize this; some of the churches in Revelation 2-3 could not have realized that the Lord was walking among the golden lampstands, discerning what was taking place in their service. Even Nathanael could not have known that the Lord could see him under the fig tree before this fact was made known to him, John 1. 50. And of course it is the same now; the Lord's people should rejoice in the fact that the Lord is the faithful Witness. Certainly Paul fully realized this fact, as he stated several times in connection with his movements in the Lord's service.

(1) *Having come*. Looking back on his stay in Thessalonica, the apostle stated that his entrance in to them was not in vain. He had been put in trust with the gospel, and he outlined his behaviour as he preached this gospel. He would not please men, but God; he would not use flattering words; he did not seek glory from men. These were no empty words, since he added, "God is witness", 1 Thess. 2. 5.

(2) *Unable to come*. The apostle Paul had great affection for the Philippians, ever since the gospel took root in that city. Many years afterwards, when he was a prisoner in Rome, Paul could still long after the Philippians; his prayers and thanksgivings to God were always on their behalf. These were no empty words, since he added "God is my record", Phil. 1. 8.

(3) *Not to come*. Paul had written the first Epistle to the Corinthians in order to correct them. He was unwilling to come to Corinth until he had heard that they had repented having read this Epistle. He had wanted to come indeed, 1 Cor. 4. 19, but refrained so as "to spare" them in his exercise of the rod of discipline. These were no empty words, since he added "I call God for a record", 2 Cor. 1. 23.

(4) *Desire to come*. In Corinth, Paul wrote to the believers in Rome. He thanked God for them, and prayed to have a prosperous journey to them by the will of God. He longed to see them, so as to impart "some spiritual gift, to the end that ye may be established". These were no empty words, since he added "God is my witness", Rom. 1. 9.

178

June 27th

READING: **Leviticus 10. 1-20**

TWO PAIRS OF UNSAVOURY PRIESTS

ORIGINALLY, the intention had been that Israel should be "a kingdom of priests", Exod. 19. 6. But the sin of the nation in the matter of the golden calf, and the faithfulness of the Levites to remain on the Lord's side, 32. 26, caused God to choose only the sons of Aaron to be priests, with Aaron as the high priest. Aaron had four sons, Eleazar, Ithamar, Nadab and Abihu. The line of the high priests continued only through Eleazar, Num. 20. 25-28. Not all the priests were faithful, and two pairs stand out in particular for waywardness.

Nadab and Abihu. In just the same way as sin entered the early church in Jerusalem through the greed and lying of Ananias and Sapphira, bringing down the immediate intervention of God, Acts 5. 1-11, so too in the early days of the tabernacle. Aaron and his four sons had been consecrated, with the glory of God appearing in divine approval, Lev. 9. 23, but immediately afterwards it would seem that Nadab and Abihu were drunk, 10. 9. Consequently, with no restraint on the activity of the flesh, they offered foreign incense before the Lord contrary to the commandment that Aaron should offer incense, Exod. 30. 7-9. Hence God intervened immediately, and the glory and fire of divine satisfaction turned into the fire of judgment, Lev. 10. 1-3. God will be sanctified. Consequently, only two sons remained, and the high priestly line would extend through Phinehas, son of Eleazar, Num. 25. 11-13.

Hophni and Phinehas. These two sons of Eli were indeed priests, but Eli was not the true high priest, since he was of the line of Ithamar. They were called "sons of Belial", 1 Sam. 2. 12. They engaged in service merely to satisfy the natural cravings of the flesh. In the Levitical ceremony, only the Passover lambs could be roasted; the sin offerings had to be boiled and eaten. But these two priests loved roast meat and not boiled meat, so they either stole the meat before it was boiled, or they extracted it from the boiling pot. This is described as sin that was "very great before the Lord", and the offering was abhorred, 1 Sam. 2. 12-17. God intervened, and they were both slain in battle, 4. 17. God is not mocked.

All believers are priests to the Lord today. What do we offer, and how do we offer? In spirit and in truth?

June 28th

READING: **Matthew 1. 18-25**

THE DEITY OF CHRIST

THE GREAT foundation doctrine held by all Christians is the truth of the Deity of Christ. Non-evangelicals may argue about it, and heretics may deny it altogether, but the Lord's people know the truth. Their salvation rests upon the Deity of the One who accomplished it. Yet many believers are unable to make use of the Scriptures that prove beyond doubt the validity of their faith, particularly when confronted with the smooth persuasion of the heretic or the theological unbeliever.

Let us select some of the major texts that cannot be gainsaid except by very illogical argument.

When the Lord was here, even unbelievers knew that His statement, "My Father worketh hitherto, and I work", John 5. 17, implied His Deity, "equal with God", and that is why they persecuted Him. The same is found in John 10. 33, "because that thou, being a man, makest thyself God", no doubt referring to the same event as in John 5. 17.

Matthew knew better than men, when he interpreted both the angel of the Lord and the prophet Isaiah, with inspiration also added to support his claim: "they shall call his name Emmanuel, which being interpreted is, God with us", Matt. 1. 23. Hence Matthew knew that the One called "Jesus" was also God with us.

To believers, "the Word was God", John 1. 1, is absolute truth. We admit that there is no definite article before the word "God", so heretics readily translate this as "the Word was a God". This would be a difficulty had the writer John not solved the problem with another text that contains the definite article "the" before the word "God". The great confession of Thomas, "My Lord and my God", John 20. 28, though not containing the word "the" in English, certainly contains it in Greek; the confession reads "The Lord of me and the God of me" literally. So Thomas knew that the Lord Jesus was "the God"; so did John who recorded this, for had it not been true he would not have recalled something so misleading, and the same can be said about the Spirit of inspiration. Write a reference to this confession in your Bible against John 1. 1, so you can always refer to this positive truth if heretics resist you.

"God was manifest in the flesh", 1 Tim. 3. 16, has more authority than modern translations admit, for they reject it!

READING: **Revelation 1. 4-20**

UNTO HIM

THERE ARE quite a number of occasions when the New Testament writers burst forth into a doxology of praise to God, the special subject matter of their writing causing this outburst of praise. In particular, there are three great "unto Him" verses, and a fourth one "to Him".

(1) *The past.* "Unto him that loved us, and washed (or loosed, according to other Greek manuscripts) us from our sins in his own blood, and hath made us kings and priests unto God and his Father; to him be glory and dominion for ever and ever", Rev. 1. 5-6. This loving and washing (or loosing) are divine acts of the past, though of course love persists to the present and for ever. These results of His sacrifice should call forth eternal praise, commencing now from redeemed hearts.

(2) *The present.* "Now unto him that is able to do exceeding abundantly above all that we ask or think . . . unto him be glory in the church by Christ Jesus", Eph. 3. 20-21. The reason for this outburst of praise to the One who can answer prayer is because of the prayer expressed in verses 14-19. To know the love of Christ which passes knowledge requires the power of God in the soul: He is able to make this love known.

(3) *The present.* "Now to him that is of power to stablish you according to my gospel, and the preaching of Jesus Christ . . . to God only wise, be glory through Jesus Christ for ever", Rom. 16. 25-27. This is Paul's final conclusion to the Epistle to the Romans, a masterpiece of the presentation of the gospel in every aspect. Having written so much, Paul did not heave a sigh of relief that the task was over, but his heart was taken up with praise because of the truth he had been expounding. The other doxology in this Epistle is "For of him, and through him, and to him, are all things, to whom be glory for ever", 11. 36.

(4) *The future.* "Now unto him that is able to keep you from falling, and to present you faultless before the presence of his glory with exceeding joy, to the only wise God our Saviour, be glory and majesty, dominion and power, both now and ever", Jude 24-25. How else could Jude conclude an Epistle that is so full of the activity of ungodly men in the last times? It could only end with a doxology extending to eternity.

June 30th

READING: Luke 13. 1-17

DISASTER AND TRAGEDY

AS THE AUTHOR writes this in the second week of March, there is still national shock at the sudden and unexpected sinking of the ferry Herald of Free Enterprise outside Zeebrugge in Belgium in the early evening of March 6th 1987. Whereas several hundred people were rescued, yet many bodies have been recovered, and many are still entrapped in the ship, to remain there until salvage operations are complete. Disaster strikes suddenly; it always has done so, either (i) the deliberate work of men in terrorism and war, (ii) the accidental effects of faster travel and larger buildings, or (iii) due to "natural" causes such as floods, earthquakes, volcanic eruptions, storms or clouds of poisonous gas. Thus in Matthew 8. 24, there was a great tempest, but both ship and occupants were saved miraculously. In Acts 27. 41-44, the ship was broken up, but all people on board were saved in the purpose of God. On other occasions, God mysteriously allows an event of great damage and tragedy to take place without intervening.

Luke 13. 1-3 was a horrible event enacted by Pilate. He had ordered the massacre of some Galilaeans because of their movement against the Romans. At the temple altar, Pilate had even mingled the victims' blood with that of the animal sacrifices. But the Lord made it clear that these Galilaeans were not worse sinners than others. Repentance was the lesson, else all would perish, no doubt referring to the destruction of the temple by the Romans in A.D. 70 with great loss of life.

If verse 1 was a calamity caused by men, then the fall of the tower in Siloam killing 18 men, was an "accident". This tower may have been part of the waterworks and aqueduct being built by Pilate with temple money. If Jewish workmen were being paid with temple money, then this was God's judgment upon them, thought the Jews! But no; such accidents are the portion of men in all walks of life. The lesson again was a call to repentance. "Likewise" may refer to the fall of the temple stones in A.D. 70 when it was destroyed by the Romans.

Indeed, dreadful accidents and events do bring tragdey into the homes and lives of those immediately concerned; may the Lord reveal Himself to them. But for the majority of men, the lesson is a call to repentance, else worse judgment will fall.

July 1st

READING: **Deuteronomy 31. 7-27**

JOSHUA THE MAN OF THE TABERNACLE

IN THE Old Testament, the Levites were occupied with the sanctuary service. Men of the other tribes had only to appear before God three times a year. Now Joshua was not of the tribe of Levi, rather of Ephraim; yet he was occupied with the tabernacle under many different circumstances.

(1) *Service Contemplated*. In Exodus 25-32 God revealed to Moses the details of the tabernacle. As a young man, Joshua was Moses' minister, 24. 13, and he accompanied Moses up mount Sinai; in 32. 17 he was with Moses as he came down the mount; we like to think that he heard something of the details of the tabernacle as given to Moses. Today, young believers should behold the plan of God for a local church, and to appreciate it thoroughly before being a public servant in a local church.

(2) *Service Consecrated*. There was a temporary tabernacle originally, and "Joshua, the son of Nun, a young man, departed not out of the tabernacle", Exod. 33. 11. This tabernacle was in the outside place, while men preferred to remain in their tent doors. Today, young believers should realize that a local church is outside the organizations of men, and there they should abide engaging in the fellowship of prayer and the breaking of bread.

(3) *Service Contracted*. Forty years later, evidently after long years of preparation, Joshua received from God his call to service. He and Moses had to present themselves in the tabernacle, so that God could give him a charge, Deut. 31. 11-15; only then did he know what his work for the Lord would be. Only because he was interested in the tabernacle could there be a divine call to service. See Acts 13. 1-4 for Paul's call.

(4) *Service Conducted*. The crossing of the Jordan and the capture of Jericho were achieved with the ark of the covenant from the tabernacle. Moreover, the tabernacle was erected at Shiloh, where distribution of the land by lot took place, Josh. 18. 1. Today, all service should be accomplished in fellowship with the local church.

(5) *Service Concluded*. At the end of his life, Joshua wrote the book of the law by the sanctuary of the Lord, Josh. 24. 26; today, a believer should faithfully end his life as he had begun. Thus one can finish one's course with joy, and look back on years spent for the Lord and His glory.

July 2nd

READING: **1 John 2. 1-17**

ALL THINGS NEW

"BEHOLD, I make all things new", Rev. 21. 5, is God's declaration for eternity. But there are many aspects of the believer's blessings that are already new.

(1) *New Creation*, 2 Cor. 5. 17, or "a new creature" as the A.V. puts it. Paul is writing about any individual believer. And whereas the world of sin and darkness still surrounds a believer, yet his interests, occupation and his affections are to be centred on different things. The new birth ensures that, to a believer, "old things are passed away; behold, all things are become new". The act of living has a different direction: "unto him which died for them, and rose again", v. 15. Thus a new creation should be occupied only with those new things that pertain to a new creation.

(2) *New Covenant*, Heb. 8. 8-13. The first covenant needed the cooperation of two parties, God and man. But the law only showed up sin, so a new covenant was required. In mercy, this was promised to Judah and Israel in Jeremiah 31. 31-34, and this was a one party covenant; only God was involved. Its basis was only "the blood of the new testament, shed for many for the remission of sins", Matt. 26. 28. This same basis, the blood of Christ, has brought believers into the same blessing of the forgiveness of sins.

(3) *New Commandment*, 1 John 2. 8, "a new commandment I write unto you". John had just mentioned the old commandment, v. 7. This new commandment is also found in John 13. 34, a Gospel that John had just written. We feel that the old commandment was to walk in the light of Christ, even as He walked, 1 John 2. 6. But many things John had not taught, until inspiration gave him a fresh knowledge of the Lord's teaching. This enabled him to present a "new commandment" to his readers, which was that believers should love their brothers, vv. 9-11. This corresponds to the new commandment issued by the Lord to His disciples in John 13. 34.

(4) *New City*, Rev. 2. 12. "I will write upon him the name of my God, and the name of the city of my God, which is new Jerusalem". This was the promise to the church at Philadelphia. This is a future blessing, when the church, as the new city, will descend for millennial administration.

READING: **1 Chronicles 25. 1-31**

THE GROWTH OF ASAPH AS A SINGER

ALL BELIEVERS should "offer the sacrifice of praise to God continually", Heb. 13. 15. But the ability to lead an assembly in worship is not acquired by young believers immediately upon conversion. Development is necessary, and typically we can trace this in the growth of Asaph in the Old Testament.

David appointed three families of singers, who could trace their descent from Levi. They were called "workmen", since their service was really work for the Lord, 1 Chron. 25. 1. They were "separated for the service", and "instructed in the songs of the Lord", v. 7. The meanings of the three families are important: Asaph means "one who gathers"; Jeduthun, "a choir of praise"; and Heman, "faithful". Today, a gathering of the Lord's people should be faithful in its acts of praise. There were originally 288 singers, "the small as the great, the teacher as the scholar", vv. 7-8. Today all are included, regardless of spiritual age, and regardless of status (teacher or learner). Asaph's growth should be a lesson for us all.

Originally, Asaph merely sounded with cymbals of brass, 1 Chron. 15. 19, but (i) he was in the right company, for there was Chenaniah a skilful instructor, vv. 22, 27, and David under whose influence he came, and (ii) he was in the right place, for this ascent of the ark up mount Zion speaks of the ascension position of Christ in glory, Eph. 4. 8.

The next stage is found in 1 Chronicles 16. 7, after the ark had been safely placed in the new tabernacle on Zion. David knew that there was to be continual praise on mount Zion, and he delivered a psalm to one whom he trusted, namely Asaph. So Asaph used a ready-made psalm composed by the sweet psalmist of Israel. Today, young believers should be able to enter into the meaning of worship expressed by more mature brethren. This ready-made psalm is full of spiritual instruction as to what is suitable in worship; see our remarks on page 76.

The final stage in Asaph's growth is found in Psalms 73-83, for here are eleven psalms actually composed by Asaph, showing that he now had the ability to lead in praise after suitable instruction and learning by the example of others. He had developed from receiving to producing. Even today, God is not honoured by silent hearts; we must be productive sweet singers.

July 4th

READING: **Revelation 3. 14-22**

THIRTY-TWO YEARS AT LAODICEA

THIS IS quite a long time in the experience of a local church, and things can happen that should not happen, thereby altering its character completely.

The city of Laodicea was not far from Colosse, and when Paul wrote to the Colossians from Rome, he also had the church at Laodicea in mind. He wrote, "For I would that ye knew what great conflict I have for you, and for them at Laodicea, and for as many as have not seen my face in the flesh", and "I bear him record, that he (Epaphras) hath a great zeal for you, and them that are in Laodicea . . . Salute the brethren which are in Laodicea . . . And when this epistle is read among you, cause that it be read also in the church of the Laodiceans; and that ye likewise read the epistle from Laodicea", Col. 2. 1; 4. 13, 15-16. Thus Paul had a great concern for these churches, and for all readers, his object being to "present every man perfect in Christ Jesus", 1. 28.

We may pick out three points that were of concern to Paul: (i) "unto all riches of the full assurance of understanding, to the acknowledgement of the mystery of God, and of the Father, and of Christ", 2. 2; (ii) "the Father, which hath made us meet to be partakers of the inheritance of the saints in light", 1. 12; (iii) "put off all these . . . put off the old man . . . put on the new man, which is renewed in knowledge after the image of him that created him", 3. 8-14.

But Paul knew of the spiritual dangers confronting them; men would be beguiling them "with enticing words", 2. 4. Epaphras therefore kept the Laodiceans in his prayers, 4. 12-13. But thirty-two years later, things had changed. Paul had departed this scene, though John remained. The roots and the foundations had been removed, 2. 7. They thought that they were still alright: they were rich, they could see, and they had the right clothes. But the discerning eyes of the Lord knew differently.

He claimed, (i) "thou art . . . poor", although they thought that they were rich, increased with goods, having need of nothing, Rev. 3. 17; (ii) "thou art . . . blind", now in darkness instead of the light; (iii) "thou art . . . naked".

But, after 32 years, what should have been? The value of true ministry should have preserved the church from failure.

July 5th

READING: **Hebrews 5. 1-14**

THE LORD BECAME

BOTH THE declaration of Scripture, and the words of the Lord Himself testify to the changelessness of His eternal Person. "Jesus Christ the same yesterday, and to day, and for ever", Heb. 13. 8; "Before Abraham was, I am", John 8. 58. Yet we must not overlook many statements of Scripture that, on account of His coming into Manhood, He became something, or participated in something, that had not been His portion before. It would be heresy to consider that He became God, that He became the Son, that He became the Word; rather this is His divine Person without beginning and without end.

In His lifetime. (i) "The Word was made (became) flesh", John 1. 14. Otherwise He could not have tabernacled visibly amongst His own as a real Man (rather than as a spirit, Luke 24. 37-39). In other words, He became what He had not been before in heaven. (ii) "Jesus Christ was made (became) a minister of the circumcision", Rom. 15. 8, for He came to the lost sheep of the house of Israel. (iii) "In all things it behoved him to be made like unto his brethren, that he might be (become) a merciful and faithful high priest", Heb. 2. 17. His priesthood was consequential upon His becoming Man.

In His death. (i) In the garden of Gethsemane, we read of the Lord, "being in an agony he prayed more earnestly", Luke 22. 44. The word for "being" is literally "becoming", an experience of soul through which He had not passed before. (ii) He "was made (became) in the likeness of men . . . and became obedient unto death", Phil. 2. 7-8. Here was the ultimate experience, descending into death, an experience through which He had not passed before. (iii) "Being made a curse for us", Gal. 3. 13. For the first time and the last time, He became a curse so that blessing might be ours instead.

His resurrection. (i) "The stone . . . is become the head of the corner", Matt. 21. 42. This refers to His exalted position, that derived from His rejection and death. (ii) "He became the author of eternal salvation unto all that obey him", Heb. 5. 9. This is His position now, relative to those that call upon Him for salvation. (iii) "Jesus, made (having become) an high priest for ever after the order of Melchisedec", 6. 20, an order consequent upon His ascension to glory.

July 6th

READING: **John 13. 1-30**

WEAKNESS IN UNDERSTANDING

WITHOUT APPEARING to be critical or uncharitable, many of the Lord's people can see much weakness in the life and service of many of their fellows, as assessed by the standards of Holy Scripture. This causes grief on the part of those who witness such weaknesses and failures. How much more the Lord Jesus! For He witnessed constantly many phases of weakness and failure in the lives of His disciples. These largely disappeared after the giving of the Holy Spirit, so we conclude that these weaknesses were manifested when the Lord was here because the Holy Spirit had then not been given to indwell men's hearts.

We may consider a few of these from the Gospels.

In Matthew 16. 22, Peter rebuked the Lord for stating that He had to be killed, and to be raised again. The Lord then rebuked Satan for having motivated Peter to be antagonistic to His words. Later, when speaking on the same subject, the Lord knew that the disciples' understanding was nil, and that His saying was hid from them, evidently brought about by Satan himself, Luke 18. 34. Indeed, He told Peter, "Satan hath desired to have you", 22. 31.

The apostles often showed a deep lack of understanding. For example, in Matthew 19. 23-26 they were amazed at the difficulty of being saved. In Luke 9. 53-56, with thoughts of judgment in their hearts, they could not understand the divine purpose that the Lord had come to save men's lives. In John 13. 6-8, Peter could not understand the meaning of the Lord washing the disciples' feet, while in 14. 8-9 Philip could not understand what it meant to see the Father. In 12. 16, they could not understand the application of Zechariah 9. 9 to the Lord riding into Jerusalem, while in Matthew 26. 31-33 Peter could not understand the necessity of the fulfilment of Zechariah 13. 7.

There was misunderstanding in Matthew 16. 5-12, when they could not perceive the meaning of false doctrine in the Lord's words about the leaven of the Pharisees. In the upper room, there was selfunderstanding. The Lord had given the sop to Judas, saying, "That thou doest, do quickly", but they thought that He had said something quite different, John 13. 24-29.

We shall revert to further aspects of weakness later.

July 7th

READING: 1 Samuel 14. 43-52

HE HATH WROUGHT WITH GOD

WHEN READING the Old Testament, it is good to pause at a phrase that brings to mind similar thoughts in the New Testament. Such a phrase occurs in verse 45, where concerning Jonathan we read, "he hath wrought with God this day", these being the words of the people to Saul who stated that Jonathan must die. The story is thus:

There was a battle with the Philistines. Jonathan and his armourbearer went over to the Philistines alone, saying, "it may be that the Lord will work for us: for there is no restraint to the Lord to save by many or by few", v. 6. Later he said by faith, "the Lord hath delivered them into the hand of Israel", v. 12. After the battle, Saul would have slain Jonathan for eating honey, but the people refused to allow the king to do so, saying, "he hath wrought with God this day". In other words, one's work must be accomplished with God, so that He can use the vessel to do His work. Else one's work is merely the work of the natural self, the work of man.

In the Lord's case, when He was here He moved entirely in keeping with the will of His Father. The Lord said, "thou, Father, art in me, and I in thee", John 17. 21, implying a mutuality of the divine mind in service. "The Father that dwelleth in me, he doeth the works", 14. 10, is an amazing statement, complementing the assertion that He did the works of His Father, 10. 37. The One wrought with the Other.

In the case of the service of the Lord's people, a similar principle applies. "The Lord working with them", is how the ascended Lord is seen in relation to His servants, Mark 16. 20. So when the servant does anything in the Lord's Name, His service is wrought with the Lord, and hence there are signs following. "We are labourers together with God", wrote Paul, 1 Cor. 3. 7-9, so Paul's work in the field and on the building site was really "God's husbandry . . . God's building", since He was giving the increase. Thus God is elevated above the workers. Elsewhere, Paul with others claimed to be "workers together with him", 2 Cor. 6. 1, so God beseeched men "by us", 5. 20. God works in His people to do His will and His good pleasure, Phil. 2. 13, demanding the faithful cooperation of the vessels in their work with God.

READING: **Romans 5. 1-21**

OBEDIENCE IN ROMANS

ROMANS is the Epistle that most of all deals with the free grace of God in the gospel, grace that displaces works as the operative means of acquiring salvation. Yet the words "obey, obedience" occur more times in the Epistle to the Romans than in other Epistles. Consider the following:

Reference to Christ. "By the obedience of one shall many be made righteous", Rom. 5. 19. There was obedience in the Lord's life: "I seek not mine own will, but the will of the Father", John 5. 30. There was obedience as He approached the cross: "not as I will, but as thou wilt", Matt. 26. 39. There was obedience when on the cross: "I come to do thy will", Heb. 10. 9, and He "became obedient unto death, even the death of the cross", Phil 2. 8.

Rererences to Paul. The apostle was obedient to the heavenly vision, Acts 26. 19, but references in Romans to obedience relate to the objectives of his preaching. Thus, "for obedience to the faith among all nations", Rom. 1. 5; faith is seen as obedience to the will of God. "To make the Gentiles obedient, by word and deed", 15. 18. The "mystery" was made known "to all nations for the obedience of faith", 16. 25-26. The reason why obedience is a necessary ingredient of the gospel is because God "commandeth all men every where to repent", Acts 17. 30. It is not a question only of having regard to the grace of God, but of submitting to the commands of God by obedience.

References to unbelievers. Not only in Romans, but also in other Epistles do we read of disobedience on the part of unbelievers. "By one man's disobedience", Rom. 5. 19; "they have not all obeyed the gospel", 10. 16. Elsewhere we read of wrath on "the children of disobedience", Eph. 5. 6; of those "that obey not the gospel of our Lord Jesus Christ", 2 Thess. 1. 8; of those who "stumble at the word, being disobedient", 1 Pet. 2. 8.

References to believers. Obedience under grace is a fundamental concept of the gospel: "ye have obeyed from the heart that form of doctrine which was delivered you", Rom. 6. 17, the "form" being a mould into which believers are shaped. This is also a testimony: "your obedience is come abroad unto all men", 16. 19.

July 9th

READING: **Isaiah 53. 1-12**

GOOD REPORTS

THIS IS the time of year when many young people at school are awaiting their reports on their summer examinations, and when students are waiting for their degrees of various classes based on their recent examinations. Reports can be good or bad; degrees can be first class, or merely a pass. A letter of commendation is really a spiritual report. The author has often had to write reports on students, reports as a referee for employers, and letters of commendation. In every case, it is essential to have something to write about.

There is a "good degree" for deacons, men who serve in a local church, 1 Tim. 3. 13; otherwise their service is not useful for edification. But the word "report" appears far more often.

To have to write a report on the Lord Jesus seems to go beyond what a mere author can do (though plenty of unbelievers willingly engage in this exercise, always with a view to criticising the Lord of glory). Yet Isaiah was called upon to write such a report; the whole of Isaiah 53 is full of the most blessed material. Yet, he asked, "Who hath believed our report?", v. 1. This is interpreted in John 12. 37-39 as implying that men did not believe the report; indeed, they could not believe. Paul adopts the same interpretation in Romans 10. 16, "they have not all obeyed the gospel. For Esaias saith, Lord, who hath believed our report?". So the best report given by divine inspiration can be rejected by men!

What about the Lord's people, and what about ourselves? What kind of reports are made about our spiritual character and service? We have many examples in the New Testament.

(i) Stephen with others: "seven men of honest report", Acts 6. 3; only then could they serve in financial matters. (ii) "Ananias . . . having a good report of all the Jews" in Damascus, 26. 12. (iii) Timothy was "well reported of by the brethren", 16. 2, and hence he could accompany Paul on the second journey. (iv) Paul: "by . . . good report", showing him to be an approved minister of God, 2 Cor. 6. 8. (v) Elders should have "a good report of them which are without", 1 Tim. 3. 7. (vi) Demetrius had a "good report of all men", 3 John 12. (vii) In the Old Testament, men of faith had "a good report", Heb. 11. 2. 39. What will our report be in heaven?

July 10th

READING: **Revelation 22. 6-21**

ETERNAL TITLES IN REVELATION

WE ARE not surprised that the eternal nature of Deity is made much of in Scripture. "From everlasting to everlasting, thou art God", Psa. 90. 2; "thou remainest", Heb. 1. 11. It is in Revelation that we find various groups of titles that reflect very clearly upon these eternal issues.

Alpha and Omega. These being the first and last letters of the Greek alphabet, the title shows the Lord as embraced in all the written Word of God. He is found in Moses, the prophets and the Psalms, Luke 24. 44. This title "Alpha and Omega" is first given in Revelation 1. 8, in the introduction to the vision. Then it appears in verse 11, as the Lord introduced Himself to John. Then we find the title in 21. 6, relating to the means of entrance into the eternal state. And finally in 22. 13, relating to present responsibility, with promised rewards for doing His commandments.

The Beginning and the Ending. The Lord is seen as the cause of all creation, and of its ultimate end. This title appears in the introduction to the vision, 1. 8, and partially in the letter to the Laodiceans, 3. 14. Then again, this title relates to the eternal state, 21. 6, no doubt referring to the passing away of the first heaven and the first earth, v. 1. Finally, the title appears in 22. 13, relating to present responsibility, no doubt so that believers should appreciate the transient nature of all physical things.

The First and the Last. Here is the Lord's pre-eminence as living, before creation's beginning and after its end. It appears in 1. 11, revealed to John on Patmos. It is also presented to John in 1. 17, when he had fallen at His feet as dead. It is the title used in the letter to Smyrna, 2. 8, and also in 22. 13, again relating to present responsibility.

Which was, which is, and which is to come (that is, always moving into the future). Grace and peace come from this Eternal One, 1. 4. The title appears in the introduction, coupled with the additional title, "the Almighty", 1. 8. It is applied to the One on the eternal throne in 4. 8, coupled with "Holy, holy, holy". When the Lord takes His great power for the millennial kingdom, the twenty-four elders use this title in praise, 11. 7. It is also used when the third bowl is poured out, 16. 5.

July 11th

READING: **Philippians 2. 1-11**

TEMPTATIONS: THYSELF — HIMSELF

WE ARE familiar with the three temptations through which the Lord passed in the wilderness These were direct temptations, when the Lord was directly facing the foe. But there were other temptations that men placed before the Lord Jesus, though the ultimate origin of these temptations was Satan himself in the background. We wish to draw attention to one temptation by Satan, and three by men, contrasting them with what the Lord actually did.

(1) In the second temptation in Matthew 4. 6, Satan said to the Lord, "*cast thyself* down". This would be a spectacular way of coming down, to be seen by men in wonder at the display of angelic power. Instead, Christ "*made himself* of no reputation, and took upon him the form of a servant, and was made in the likeness of men", Phil. 2. 7. This is how He actually came down, in lowly Manhood form as a servant.

(2) In Galilee, the Lord's unbelieving brethren suggested that He should go up to Jerusalem, saying, "*show thyself* to the world", John 7. 4. Namely, to display Himself as a worker of miracles for outward show. Instead, "he *humbled himself*, and became obedient unto death, even the death of the cross", Phil. 2. 8. This is the way in which the Lord would go to Jerusalem, humbling Himself unto death.

(3) When the Lord showed that He had to go to Jerusalem in order to suffer and to die, Peter said, "*Pity thyself*, Lord: this shall not be unto thee", Matt. 16. 22 marg. The Lord made it clear that Satan had caused Peter to say such a thing. But nothing could stop the ongoing outworking of the purpose of God. The work of salvation was accomplished thus: "once in the end of the world hath he appeared to put away sin by the *sacrifice of himself*", Heb. 9. 26.

(4) Even when the Saviour was on the cross, Satan worked through those who passed by. They said, "*save thyself*, and come down from the cross", Mark 15. 30. Again, nothing could thwart the working out of God's purpose. Instead, Paul wrote that the Son of God "*gave himself* for me", Gal. 2. 20.

Thus we have the record of temptations by Satan, by His brethren, by one of His disciples, and by the mob. In all cases He was faithful to the One who gave Him the work to do.

July 12th

READING: **Genesis 40. 1-23**

TWO BIRTHDAYS IN SCRIPTURE

THE CELEBRATION of a birthday, either of self or of another, should be a joyful event. This certainly is so in childhood, when the anticipated receipt of presents finally materializes, even though the child may have little or no understanding of what his actual birth really meant. But as age creeps on, birthdays change their character. Believers can look back, and trace the hand of God's goodness in their lives, "All the way my Saviour leads me, what have I to ask beside?". But unbelievers may sometimes treat the event as a licence for unrestrained revelling. Only two birthdays are recorded in Scripture, and there are many similarities between them: both were birthdays of kings, and they were thoroughly unpleasant involving murder. We can offer no suggestion as to why some good birthdays are not recorded to encourage us!

(1) *The birthday of Pharaoh*, Gen. 40. 20-22. Joseph was in prison in Egypt, a man who was a mere nothing in the eyes of Pharaoh. Joseph had interpreted dreams that Pharaoh's chief butler would be released for royal duties again, but that the chief baker would be hanged. Pharaoh's birthday took place three days later, with a feast to all his servants. Joseph's predictions then took place; Pharaoh had no compunction in committing murder, so the baker was hanged, while the butler was restored to a pre-eminent position. Alas that he forgot all about Joseph for a further two years.

(2) *The birthday of Herod*, Mark 6. 17-29. John the Baptist was in prison for denouncing Herod's immorality. On his birthday, Herod "made a supper to his lords, high captains, and chief estates of Galilee"; such corruption and feasting have been commonplace; see Dan. 5. 1-4. Thus Herodias' daughter was dancing before Herod, and asked for the head of John the Baptist. Herod was sorry, but for his misdirected oath he caused John to be beheaded in prison. By this means, Another was seen to have a pre-eminent position. For John had said, "He must increase, but I must decrease", John 3. 30. He was but a forerunner, and when the ministry of the Lord commenced, there was no room for men falsely to think that there was rivalry between John and the Lord. Thus John was removed, so that the Lord could have the pre-eminent position.

194

July 13th

READING: **1 Corinthians 1. 1-9**

GOD IS FAITHFUL: ARE WE?

IN VERSE 8 we read that "God is faithful"; namely, what He has promised He is able to perform, and He certainly will perform it in His own time. Thus the Lord Jesus "is faithful and just to forgive us our sins, and to cleanse us from all unrighteousness", 1 John 1. 9. He is described as "the faithful witness", Rev. 1. 5, and also to Laodicea as "the faithful and true witness", 3. 14. Additionally, when He comes in glory and judgment, He is called "Faithful and True", 19. 11. He is thus faithful in assessing what He sees in keeping with divine standards, as well as in meting out the proper and just judgment that suits the occasion.

But what about ourselves? We have faith, when we trust God; we are faithful when God trusts us. We have already looked at this subject in some detail on page 67, where several New Testament names were mentioned. But faithfulness to God was an Old Testament phenomenon as well, whether this word was used or not. When Miriam and Aaron complained against Moses, God spoke suddenly to them, saying "Moses my servant . . . is faithful in all mine house", and this was important since this statement is quoted in Hebrews 3. 5. In the days of Eli, when the priesthood was corrupt, God promised that He would raise up "a faithful priest", 1 Sam. 2. 35; this referred to Zadok, 1 Kings 2. 35. At the same time, Samuel was "established to be a prophet of the Lord" (strictly, "faithful to be a prophet"), 1 Sam. 3. 20 marg. In Nehemiah 7. 2, we find a "faithful man" who "feared God among many", while in 13. 13 we read of treasurers who were "counted faithful".

This designation of a servant of God as faithful is a divine assessment; it is no use a man claiming to be faithful if what he is doing runs contrary to scriptural principles. In Paul's case, he abandoned all that he stood for as an unconverted Jew, and the Jews would have counted him as unfaithful. But to Paul the divine assessment was of importance. He could look back, and ask himself why he was ever engaged in divine service. He supplies the answer: "I thank Christ Jesus our Lord . . . for that he counted me faithful, putting me into the ministry", 1 Tim. 1. 12. Thus overall, God was faithful: Paul knew that; and Paul was faithful: the Lord knew that.

READING: **2 Corinthians 9. 1-15**

UNSPEAKABLE

THIS WORD appears in English three times in the New Testament, though it is interesting to note that three different Greek words are used (each word appearing only once). The three occasions are:

(1) "Thanks be unto God for his unspeakable gift", 2 Cor. 9. 15.

(2) "How that he was caught up into paradise, and heard unspeakable words, which it is not lawful for a man to utter", 2 Cor. 12. 4.

(3) "Whom having not seen, ye love; in whom, though now ye see him not, yet believing, ye rejoice with joy unspeakable and full of glory", 1 Pet. 1. 8.

There are many reasons why things should be unspeakable. In daily life, not every experience, whether outward or inward, can be expressed in words. That is why there are those who are musicians, artists, mathematicians, etc. All have means apart from words with which to express their sentiments, emotions and knowledge. Thus in the three cases listed, the reasons why there were unspeakable words are (1) the amount exceeded what could be described, (2) there was no permission to express the words heard, and (3) the spiritual emotions are too full for words to be effective.

(1) Paul had been writing about the collection of money being made for the poor saints in Jerusalem; this was very "speakable" in the sense that it could be counted. Thus assembly accounts are very important, audited and distributed internally each year, with income and expenditure exactly balanced. But the riches of the One who became poor that we may be enriched, 2 Cor. 8. 9, are "unspeakable", namely cannot be counted up in words or figures. We may try to count our blessings, and are surprised at what the Lord has done for us.

(2) Paul's experience of hearing what was spoken in the "third heaven" is different from that of John, for he heard much that took place around the throne in Revelation. John recorded it fully, whereas Paul had to remain silent. Clearly these words were not for believers while on earth.

(3) The joy of salvation can certainly be experienced, though it may not be expressible, neither have we seen the Lord.

READING: Isaiah 26. 1-15

OTHER LORDS BESIDE THEE

ISAIAH CHAPTER 26 is remarkable. The great restoration chapters in Isaiah come essentially towards the end, but this restoration chapter 26 appears as a gem in the middle of the book. In particular, we concentrate on verse 13, "O Lord our God, other lords beside thee have had dominion over us: but by thee only will we make mention of thy name". The nation was looking back, to the years covered by the books of Judges and Kings, when national leaders of other nations held sway over them, and when idols dominated their religious experiences. Not that the Lord had been forgotten altogether; they wanted God and other lords "beside thee". In restoration and repentance, they look to the future, when the Lord "only" will dominate in their lives and hearts. In other words, they confessed that the true God had not been sufficient, and they wanted something else until they learnt the all-sufficiency of the One divine.

This lesson can be applied to the Lord's people today. As once unconverted, everything displaced the true God. Paul described the activity of the "other lords", writing of "idolaters . . . thieves, covetous", 1 Cor. 6. 9, with many other activities that displaced God entirely. The apostle provided another list in Galatians 5. 19-21, amongst which we find "idolatry". But the Christian profession of believers should be completely different: "What agreement hath the temple of God with idols? . . . Wherefore come out from among them", 2 Cor. 6. 16-17. But it is tragic when "other lords" still have dominion over some of the Lord's people.

When John wrote, "Little children, keep yourselves from idols", 1 John 5. 21, he could not have meant actual physical idols of the heathen. But there were plenty of distracting influences in those days that corresponded to idols. Thus he wrote, "Love not the world, neither the things that are in the world", 2. 15. Here were interests and careers that could displace the Lord Jesus. The teaching of the antichrists and the false prophets, 2. 19; 4. 1-3, could prove distracting if hearts tended to lean towards their assertions.

Paul warned against the danger of "not holding the Head", Col. 2. 19. He defined modern idolatry as "covetousness", and exhorted "flee from idolatry", Col. 3. 5; 1 Cor. 10. 14.

July 16th

READING: **Mark 8. 10-21**

THE LETTER-BOX OF YOUR HEART

THOSE WHO place gospel tracts through doors of people's homes will have noticed the great variety of letter-boxes fixed to these doors. Some are as difficult as possible to slip anything in; others are as easy as possible. And every form of graduation comes in between. The door may be open, so anything can get in. The box may be so low down; some boxes have two flaps, being a form of resistance. Others may have a heavy curtain or dirty jacket hanging inside as a form of resistance. Some have a heavy spring; others may be vertical and most awkward. Perhaps stuffed up with other things, or they may be too small even for a letter. The flap may be missing, presenting just a hole. It may be too rusty to open; it may be wide and large, but opening outwards. There may be no hole at all in the door. Poor postman! Poor evangelist with tracts to deliver freely! How they long for a proper box, opening inwards, easily, and at the right height.

What about the hearts of men? In grace, God loves to be able to deliver the gospel, but what does He find? Hearts that are similar to every letter-box we have just described. Think of them all; here we can present just a few.

The receptive heart. Here is a wide open door, without even a flap: a gullible soul who absorbs anything. They are "carried about with every wind of doctrine", Eph. 4. 14, and follow the "pernicious ways" of false teachers, 2 Pet. 2. 2.

The rusty heart. Such hearts are absolutely closed, and nothing can enter. There was "hardness of heart" because of unbelief, Mark 16. 14; Paul wrote of things that have not "entered into the heart of man", 1 Cor. 2. 9.

The resistive heart. The heavy spring or the curtain caused Stephen to say, "ye do always resist the Holy Spirit", Acts 7. 51; "these also resist the truth", 2 Tim. 3. 8.

The reluctant heart. The letter-box is too small, or there is a double flap; these men recognize that there is something in the gospel, but they do not want too much of Christ. "Have ye your heart yet hardened?", Mark 8. 17.

The responsive heart. Here is the ideal letter-box; "they have received" the words, John 17. 8; "ye received (the word) as it is in truth", 1 Thess. 2. 13.

July 17th

READING: **1 Kings 6. 21 to 7. 1**

PRIORITIES

IN ACTS 2. 25, Peter quoted from Psalm 16. 8, "I foresaw the Lord always before my face", or "I have set the Lord always before me". Note the word "always": not sometimes, or when it is convenient. The Lord Jesus had His priorities directed towards His God. David had the same exercise, at least, on occasions. He would not enter his house, or go to bed for sleep, until he had found out a place for the ark of God, Psa. 132. 3-5. There were those who served continually before the newly established tabernacle, 1 Chron. 16. 6, 37-40. But "all the people departed every man to his house", v. 43, as if their priorities were all wrong.

(1) In 1 Kings 7. 1, the word "But" is one of three in the record of Solomon's life. David had set his affection to the house of his God, 1 Chron. 29. 3, but Solomon seemed to have a different set of priorities. He had spent seven years on building the Lord's house, "but" he spent thirteen years building his own house. Can we understand that he showed more devotion, more interest, more care, energy and expense, with greater decoration, on his own house than on the Lord's house? Later, the people dwelt in "ceiled houses", while they allowed the house of the Lord to lie waste, Hag. 1. 4. But not so the Lord: He had not where to lay His head, yet the zeal of the house had eaten Him up. In Paul's case, he had "no certain dwellingplace", 1 Cor. 4. 11, yet he was daily concerned about the care of all the churches, 2 Cor. 11. 28.

(2) At the beginning of his reign, Solomon went up to Gibeon, where Moses' arkless tabernacle was sited, 2 Chron. 1. 3; "but" the ark was on mount Zion, v. 4. His priorities were wrong; he failed to recognize God's dwellingplace on mount Zion, and went to a traditional place, taking all the people with him; afterwards he could not bring them back very easily.

(3) Even at the beginning of his reign, Solomon had an Egyptian wife whom he could not bring to Jerusalem, because they were holy places where the ark had come, 2 Chron. 8. 11; such a lack of priority lasted to the end of his life. For then we read, "But king Solomon loved many strange women", 1 Kings 11. 1, contrary to the commands of God. So the spiritual side of Solomon's life was marred by his lack of priorities.

July 18th

READING: Acts 14. 21-28

WHO OPENS?

A GREAT PRINCIPLE is stated in Revelation 3. 7: the Lord is the One "that openeth, and no man shutteth; and shutteth, and no man openeth". Beware, therefore, lest a servant of God should seek to do opposite to the divine will. We can trace this principle of divine openings in the book of Acts.

Divine openings, physical applications. Divine intervention in physical matters was characteristic of those early days of the testimony. In Acts 5. 19, the apostles had been put in prison, "But the angel of the Lord by night opened the prison doors, and brought them forth". No wonder the chief priests were perplexed, v. 24, failing to see the same power as that which had rolled away the stone from the Lord's tomb, Matt. 28. 2, (not of course to let the Lord out, but to show that the tomb was empty). Again, when Peter was in prison in Acts 12. 10, the angel led Peter out, and the iron gate "opened to them of his own accord". When Paul and Silas were in prison, there was an earthquake and "all the doors were opened", Acts 16. 26. Paul left the prison, but returned until the next day when he was officially released. But God did not always intervene like this; neither does He today.

Divine openings, spiritual applications. When Peter was on the rooftop, he saw "heaven opened", Acts 10. 11, and he was granted a symbolic vision. (We find heaven opened also in Ezek. 1. 1 and Rev. 4. 1.) This vision enabled Peter to see that the gospel was also intended for the Gentiles, but in its fulness it was through Paul that God "had opened the door of faith unto the Gentiles", Acts 14. 27. (Paul used the idea of an open door in 1 Cor. 16. 9; 2 Cor. 2. 12; Col. 4. 3.) A different idea is found in Acts 16. 14, where the Lord opened Lydia's heart to Paul's gospel message.

Human openings. The physical act of opening the mouth in order to deliver a message often occurs, no doubt as an idiom, but we can see in the expression the wide-open mouth for clarity of speaking. Thus we read of Philip, 8. 35; Peter, 10. 34; Paul, 18. 14. One can also open in the sense of expounding the Scriptures to those for whom the Bible is a closed Book, 17. 3. We may also quote the case of a door not being opened, until they knew that Peter stood there, 12. 14.

200

READING: **Nehemiah 13. 1-12**

ABSENT — PRESENT

THERE IS an old proverb that says, "When the cat is away, the mice will play". It may be possible to act like this in spiritual things. It may be applicable to circumstances when the Lord is no longer present as He was in the days of His flesh. It may also be applicable when a believer knows that he is out of sight of the spiritual leaders of a local church.

After the return from Babylon, there was a period of 100 years during which the temple, the city and its walls were rebuilt. There was a time when Nehemiah was not present in Jerusalem, Neh. 13. 6. The result was that an enemy, Tobiah by name, dwelt in a room in the temple courts, vv. 7-8. The house of God was also forsaken, in that the Levites were not provided for, v. 11. The Gentiles sought access to sell things on the Sabbath day, and the Jews were marrying foreign wives, vv. 16, 23. But when Nehemiah was present again, he corrected everything, mentioning the "good deeds" that he had done for the house of the Lord, vv. 14, 22, 31. (Good done in relation to the house of God can also be found in 2 Chron. 24. 16 and in Psalm 122. 9.)

In Paul's case, he was absent, either when he was in prison, or when he left a place for further fruitful fields. Writing to the Colossians from prison in Rome, he recalled that he was "absent in the flesh", but that he was with them "in the spirit, joying and beholding your order", Col. 2. 5. Again, when in Ephesus, he was absent from the Corinthians, but present in spirit, and was able to judge, 1 Cor. 5. 3. Twice he mentioned this to the Philippians. In 1. 27, whether present or absent he wanted to hear of their affairs, while in 2. 12 both in his presence and in his absence he wanted them to work out their own salvation.

In the Lord's case, at the end of His life here, He prepared His disciples for the years of His absence: "I go away", He said in John 14. 28, and would devote His final hours of teaching giving the promise of the Holy Spirit who would empower them during His absence. When here, He exerted moral and spiritual control. But since, the world, the professing church and Christendom, and even believers have done dreadful things that would never have been done had He still been present. One look from the Lord, and believers should weep!

July 20th

READING: **Mark 9. 14-29**

WEAKNESS IN DEEDS

ON PAGE 188, we have considered the weakness that the apostles showed *in understanding* when the Lord was here; now we consider their weakness in deeds. On the whole, such weaknesses were not manifested after the Lord's ascension, evidently due to the presence of the power of the Holy Spirit that changed weakness into spiritual and moral strength.

Peter had been called by the Lord originally in John 1. 42, and he had witnessed the first miracle in Cana. Yet in Luke 5. 1-11, we find that Peter had returned to his occupation of fishing, having caught nothing all night. He confessed himself to be a "sinful man" on account of having departed from the Lord. Restoration was granted; from then on he would be one who would "catch men" with the message of truth.

Lack of faith was seen on several occasions; for example, during the storm when the Lord was asleep, Matt. 8. 24-27, and when Peter displayed great confidence yet not with the necessary faith to ensure that this confidence was spiritual and not natural, 14. 28-31. On another occasion, some of the disciples had been unable to cure a lunatick because of lack of faith, 17. 16, though the Lord had previously given them "power . . . to heal all manner of sickness", 10. 1.

Peter, James and John, the three apostles permitted to see the Lord in the heights of glory on the mountain top, and in the depths of suffering in the garden of Gethsemane, were men who had thoughts of judgment in their hearts. In Luke 9. 54, James and John were ready to command fire to come down from heaven to consume the Samaritans, while Peter with a sword cut off the right ear of the high priest's servant, John 18. 10. It was only after the giving of the Spirit that their ministry became filled with love for the souls of men unto salvation.

In the moments of great crisis, weakness was seen at its height; how graciously the Lord dealt with it. Peter was confident that he would lay down his life for his Master, John 12. 37. Shortly afterwards, all the disciples forsook Him and fled, Matt. 26. 56. Peter then followed the Lord "afar off", v. 58, and associated himself with the warmth and fellowship of this world, John 18. 18; this led to Peter denying the Lord three times. But all this changed from Acts 2 onwards!

July 21st

READING: **Luke 1. 28-37, 70-80**

THE HIGHEST

IN THE singular, this title refers to One divine, but in the plural it refers to the place where praise is expressed; in this sense, the word occurs four times in the N.T. When the Lord rode into Jerusalem in triumph, the multitude accompanying Him cried "Hosanna to the Son of David . . . Hosanna in the highest", Matt. 21. 9; Mark 11. 10; Luke 19. 38. They wanted their praises to be heard in higher places than merely on earth. When the Lord was born, the praises of the angels were, "Glory to God in the highest", Luke 2. 14. The following mention of "on earth" shows that "the highest" refers to the eternal praise to God around His throne in heaven.

But when the word is in the singular (spelt with a capital "H", "Highest", when it is a noun), it refers to the Person of God, to His most exalted status, to His pre-eminence, to the fact that He is high and lifted up. For example, Melchisedec is described as "priest of the most high God", Heb. 7. 1. And Stephen shows how much God is greater than any who may dwell in man-made temples, saying, "the most High God dwelleth not in temples made with hands", Acts 7. 48.

Gabriel foretold the Name of the Lord: "*Jesus*. He shall be great, and shall be called the Son of the Highest", Luke 1. 32. So Mary knew of the exalted status of the One who would be born, and who would have the throne. Again, the miraculous conception would take place because "the power of the Highest shall overshadow thee", v. 35. Later, at the birth of John the Baptist, his father Zacharias said, "thou, child, shalt be called the prophet of the Highest", v. 76. In a providential sense, the Lord's disciples are "the children of the Highest", 6. 35. It is clear that Luke used this title far more times than any other New Testament writer.

Alas, as with so many things that are holy and spiritual, men and Satan can use a title like this to their own ends. They copy this glorious exalted title. The unclean spirit in the man of the Gadarenes said, "What have I to do with thee, Jesus, thou Son of God most high?", Luke 8. 28. In Philippi, the damsel with a spirit of divination cried, "These men are the servants of the most high God", Acts 16. 17. We can be thankful that both man and damsel were liberated from demon possession.

READING: **1 Samuel 20. 11-29**

DAVID'S PLACE WAS EMPTY

DAVID HAD been in Saul's company as much as possible, as in 1 Samuel 18. 10; 19. 7, but there came a time when Saul's evil intentions against him caused him to leave Saul's table and flee, 20. 1. It was then on two days running that Saul noticed that "David's place was empty", v. 25. We admit that David had a perfectly legitimate reason for being absent!

Today, being present with the Lord's people gathered as a local church is also being present with the Lord. When there is a legitimate reason for absence, the Lord knows, and the believer involved can have a clear conscience, though perhaps sorrowful at having to be absent. Certainly, those present will easily recognize that he is absent, and that his place is empty. But when there is a bad conscience, or when there is no conscience at all, because there is no legitimate reason for absence, then something is seriously wrong spiritually with that believer. For absence can be habit-forming, perhaps leading to abandonment of the Word of God, of the Lord Himself, and of His people.

When Moses had taken the tabernacle outside the camp, Joshua at least remained faithful; others were content to be absent, and to remain at their tent doors, Exod. 33. 10. Later, the city of Jerusalem became the centre of worship, though those in the northern kingdom chose to be absent even on the three annual feasts when all males should have been present. When Hezekiah invited them to the Passover, many accepted, but many others refused to come to the place of God's choice, and mocked the messengers carrying the invitation, 2 Chron. 30. 10-11.

In the N.T., Peter had been with the Lord, John 2. 40-42, but later he had left Him, Luke 5. 1-11. For some reason, Thomas was absent from the upper room on the evening of the resurrection day: "But Thomas . . . was not with them", John 20. 24. In Acts 1. 15 there were about 120 gathered in the upper room, but should there have been more?, for over 500 had seen the Lord on one occasion, 1 Cor. 15. 6. Initially, there had been stedfastness in the gathering of the local church, Acts 2. 42, but later the rot had set in, and there were those who were "forsaking the assembling of ourselves together, as the manner of some is", Heb. 10. 25. Do we need these warnings?

July 23rd

READING: **Matthew 1. 1-17**

THE SON OF ABRAHAM

THIS STATEMENT appears in verse 1 of this genealogy, but the New Testament makes more of this concept in various contexts, from good to bad, from physical to spiritual.

(1) *The Pharisees.* What religious bigotry was demonstrated by the Pharisees, even when the Lord was present. They said in John 8, "We be Abraham's seed", "Abraham is our father", vv. 33, 39; Matt. 3. 9. How true physically, but such a parentage could never justify them spiritually. The Lord confirmed this physically, v. 37, but on a spiritual plane He said, "Ye are of your father the devil", v. 44. In other words, He showed where self-satisfied religious boasting leads, back to its source in the realm of darkness. Today, all men stand as individuals before God, and it is impossible to base any present status on what other men did in the past.

(2) *Paul.* The apostle looked back to the time when he was a Pharisee, boasting in being "of the stock of Israel, of the tribe of Benjamin, an Hebrew of the Hebrews; as touching the law, a Pharisee", Phil. 3. 5. Such privilege, stretching back to the Patriarchs, he counted but loss for Christ. False apostles claimed such a status, but to Paul it meant nothing: "Are they the seed of Abraham? so am I", 2 Cor. 11. 22.

(3) *Believers in a spiritual sense.* What is common between believers today and Abraham is that all are characterized by faith. This was Paul's theme, when he wrote, "the faith of Abraham: who is the father of us all", Rom. 4. 16, since he was "a father of many nations", not physically but on the ground of faith. Again Paul wrote, "they which are of faith, the same are the children of Abraham", Gal. 3. 7, because of righteousness imputed by faith.

(4) *The genealogy of Jesus Christ.* In Genesis 13. 15, promises were made "to thy seed for ever", not only to the nations. Paul re-interprets this to mean, "He saith not, And to seeds, as of many; but as of one, And to thy seed, which is Christ", Gal. 3. 16. Matthew 1. 2-16 traces the Lord's royal genealogy, while Luke 3. 23-34 no doubt traces it according to the flesh. For He "took on him the seed of Abraham", having partaken of flesh and blood, Heb. 2. 14-17, that through death He might destroy him that had the power of death.

July 24th

READING: Revelation 13. 1-18

THE ORIGIN OF THE BEASTS

THIS CHAPTER presents two beasts, the first in verses 1-10, and the second in verses 11-18. These two characters will dominate the world scene in the Mediterranean area both in a political and in a religious sphere of evil. It is interesting to trace the origin of these two beasts.

The first beast. In the book of Daniel we have several pictorial prophecies that show a succession of nations dominating in that part of the world. In chapter 2, there is the interpretation of the image of gold and other metals; in chapter 7 we have Daniel's vision of the four beasts. In particular, in verse 7 we have the fourth beast, nameless, but "dreadful and terrible, and strong exceedingly; and it had great iron teeth: it devoured and break in pieces". This was the fourth great empire, the Roman empire with its emperor, the nation that held sway when the Lord was here; its soldiers crucified the Lord of life and glory. The context of Daniel 7 traces this kingdom right up to the coming of the Son of man in glory. But the church fills a long "gap" not revealed in the O.T. So after the church has been taken to be with the Lord, this Roman kingdom rises to the fore again, so as to dominate when the Lord returns in glory. The first beast in Revelation 13 is seen in particular as the emperor, the one who "shall ascend out of the bottomless pit", 17. 8, and the one who shall "rise up out of the sea", 13. 1, namely from the nations. He is described as one "that was, and is not, and yet is". Long ago, some have suggested that Nero shall rise again, but this is without scriptural support.

The second beast, which we interpret as the religious beast of the future, the man of sin and the antichrist. John informs us that in his days there were many antichrists, 1 John 2. 18, though "antichrist shall come". Such men deny that Jesus Christ is come in the flesh, and oppose all divine authority. The antichrist will be a substitute for God on earth, and both Simon of Samaria and Herod were past types of this one to come, Acts 8. 10; 12. 22. In the future, he arises "up out of the earth", Rev. 13. 11, no doubt in Palestine, to seek to eliminate Christ. He is the "son of perdition", going to his own place like Judas previously, Acts 1. 25.

July 25th

READING: **Exodus 8. 25-32**

THE ABOMINATION OF THE EGYPTIANS

THIS EXPRESSION appears in three episodes in the books of Genesis and Exodus. It shows the attitude taken by the Egyptians to various activities of the Israelites. At the same time, we can see in these three paragraphs something of the attitude taken by men in the world towards the spiritual service and activity of God's people today.

(1) The expression in Exodus 8. 26. Pharaoh invited Moses to sacrifice to God "in the land", for he was determined not to let the people leave the land, v. 25. But Moses insisted upon taking a journey of three days into the wilderness. Worship was to be a private act, away from the world. The offering of a bull by the Israelites would be an abomination to the Egyptians, since bulls were Egyptian idols, and hence to them they were sacred. In this we see a picture of the fact that worship in spirit and in truth by God's people today must be completely different from the religion conducted by ritualists and unbelievers, some of whom use idolatrous practices.

(2) The expression in Genesis 46. 34. Joseph instructed his brethren how to explain their occupations to Pharaoh. They dealt with cattle and with their flocks of sheep. The Egyptians had their sacred bulls as idols, so could be pleased at men being occupied with cattle. Hence they had no time for the occupation of a shepherd, since he tended sheep; a shepherd was therefore an abomination to the Egyptians. Today, the occupation of a spiritual shepherd is of no value to the religious heirarchy that loves ecclesiastical administration rather than the spiritual care of the flock.

(3) The expression in Genesis 43. 32. The custom of the Egyptians was not to partake of a meal with the Hebrews, since that was an abomination to them. They would compromise their idolatrous religion if they had such fellowship with God's people. Thus the Lord Jesus presented Himself as the living Bread, but most men departed from Him, John 6. 51, 66. We must be careful in the application of this in the opposite direction; Peter learnt better in Acts 10. 28, though he fell backwards himself in Galatians 2. 12. God taught him that he could have company legitimately with the Gentiles, though "he withdrew and separated himself" when fear arose.

July 26th

READING: **1 Corinthians 16. 1-24**

EFFECTUAL, EFFECTUALLY

THE WORD "effectual" evidently means, capable of producing results. The word does not occur as relating to the Lord's life and service. If the word is used of His people's life and service, because the effects and results are divinely produced, then certainly the divine power in Christ that achieved so many mighty works can also be described as effectual.

For believers, the words occur seven times in the N.T.

An effectual door. "A great door and effectual is opened unto me", 1 Cor. 16. 9. As far as Paul was concerned, the cities he visited on his missionary journeys were doors opened by God. These doors were effectual, particularly as far as Ephesus was concerned (this is where Paul wrote the Epistle); the story of this effectual door is found in Acts 19, since God had opened the door of faith to the Gentiles, 14. 27.

Effectually working. "He that wrought effectually in Peter . . . the same was mighty in me", Gal. 2. 8. Paul knew that all evangelistic work to Jews and Gentiles was God's work, and only this caused it to be effectual. The natural power and ability of men cannot achieve spiritual results.

The effectual working making a minister. "I am made a minister . . . by the effectual working of his power", Eph. 3. 7. No man can make another man a servant of Christ; that would merely be a human ordination without power. But what is effectual is the choice, grace, gift and work of God.

Effectual service. "According to the effectual working in the measure of every part". All believers are gifted, and they all should work to the spiritual edification of other believers. Only this kind of service is effectual.

The effectual Word of God. "Ye received it not as the word of men, but . . . the word of God, which effectually worketh also in you that believe", 1 Thess. 2. 13. The word of political orators may move men naturally, but only the Word of God is effectual to move men spiritually.

Effectual faith. "That the communication of thy faith may become effectual", Philem. 6.

Effectual prayer. "The effectual fervent prayer of a righteous man availeth much", James 5. 16. An example is given of the double effective prayer of Elijah relating to rain.

208

July 27th

READING: Ruth 1. 1-22

THE HAND TO THE PLOUGH

IN THIS chapter, we read of the loyalty that a Moabite girl, Ruth, showed to Naomi her mother-in-law. She stands in complete contrast to Orpah, who had no further influence on the development of scriptural history. Believers today should never be like Orpah, who moved into a sphere of blessing for a while, but then returned to her people and her gods, v. 15. It is true that men sometimes say, "Lord, I will follow thee whithersoever thou goest", but really they refuse to put their hand to the plough, Luke 9. 57, 62. On the other hand, all believers have once put their hands to the plough, having separated themselves from the evils of non-evangelical religion. Temptation may enter, with the opportunity to return to the country from whence they came out, Heb. 11. 15, but the Lord enables us to desire a better, a heavenly country, v. 16.

Ruth's exercises should be ours towards the Lord.

(1) "Whither thou goest, I will go", Ruth 1. 16. A believer hears the divine call, "Follow me". Like those in Revelation 14. 4, we can "follow the Lamb whithersoever he goeth", without deviating backwards. When restoration is needed, He says to us, as He said to Peter, "Follow me", John 21. 19, 22.

(2) "Where thou lodgest, I will lodge". This is what happened to Andrew. He wanted to know where the Lord dwelt, and He invited him to "Come and see", John 1. 38-39. The result was that "he abode with him that day". Believers must not dwell in the tents of wickedness; rather they should be found with His people where He is to be found.

(3) "Thy people shall be my people". The Lord's people must recognize that their fellowship is with other believers. If otherwise, there is weakness in testimony; for "a friend of the world is the enemy of God", James 4. 4. Believers must appreciate going "to their own company", Acts 4. 23.

(4) "Thy God my God". No other lords have dominion over us, Isa. 26. 13. Rather, we believe the words of Christ, when He said, "my God, and your God", John 20. 17.

(5) "Where thou diest, will I die". Believers must confess practically that they have been crucified with Christ, Gal. 2. 20. Paul suffered as Christ suffered at the hands of men, as he was made conformable unto His death, Phil. 3. 10.

July 28th

READING: Ephesians 1. 1-23

FULNESS

THE WORD "fulness" in Scripture is very interesting. It refers to the complete capacity of a vessel that can be filled without leaking underneath. We are led to think of two objects, the vessel and its contents. When filled, it overflows, as the Lord said, "good measure, pressed down, and shaken together, and running over", Luke 6. 38. No leaks here; only overflowing at the top!

Natural fulness. "The earth is the Lord's, and the fulness thereof", Psa. 24. 1, said David. This refers to the contents of the earth, no doubt the things made during the third to the sixth day of the creation. Later, we read of the fulness of the sea, Psa. 96. 11.

Fulness relating to the Son. He was born "when the fulness of the time was come", Gal. 4. 4, namely when the law and the O.T. could be extended no further. The fulness of the Son in His ministry was overflowing to men, "of his fulness have all we received", John 1. 16. Paul stressed that the fulness of the Son related to Deity itself: the Father's pleasure was that "in him should all fulness dwell", Col. 1. 19, and "in him dwelleth all the fulness of the Godhead bodily", 2. 9. This was to counteract the Colossian heresy, showing the absolute Deity of Christ Himself.

Fulness in the present. As a missionary, Paul had no meagre gospel to present; in it was embraced all the counsel of God, and he was not ashamed to declare it. Writing to Rome, he said, "I shall come in the fulness of the blessing of the gospel of Christ", Rom. 15. 29. No short measure here; no hiding or keeping back part of its provisions. Entering into the fulness of Christ was part of the process of edification, Eph. 4. 13, while the church is seen as "his body, the fulness of him that filleth all in all", v. 23. The church is necessary to be part of His fulness; He is the Head, giving Him the right to possess the church as His fulness.

Fulness in the future. Paul writes of the fulness of the Jews, and then of the Gentiles, Rom. 11. 12, 25, namely, the totality of all converts. Certainly in the future, all converts will be gathered in one in "the fulness of times", Eph. 1. 10, marking an end of God's dealings with men on earth.

July 29th

READING: **John 4. 7-26**

CONTRASTS IN WORSHIP

THE NEW TESTAMENT is quite clear how God expects His people to approach Him in worship. However, many seem to think that it is a matter of convention, tradition and invention as to how worship is to be conducted spiritually, and such people appear to have no intention of exploring the Scriptures, so as to ascertain what God expects in worship. It is therefore good to notice how the Lord used the occasion of His encounter with the woman at the well, so as to present the divine will regarding the holy matter of worship.

Who worships? The Samaritans thought that their method taught by the false priest in 2 Kings 17. 27 was correct; the Jews thought that they were correct, merely having elaborated upon their Old Testament Scriptures. But the Lord spoke of "true worshippers", John 4. 23, namely, His people by faith.

Where does worship take place? The Samaritans had "this mountain", v. 20, mount Gerizim, upon which long ago a rival temple had been built; see Deut. 27. 12. The Jews worshipped in Jerusalem, John 4. 20, the place that God had chosen for His habitation. But the Lord introduced the blessed fact that a Person and not a place would be the true centre for worship, not on Gerizim nor in Jerusalem, John 4. 21.

Who is worshipped? The Samaritans could only worship a God known in the Pentateuch, though blurred by their false religion. The Jews worshipped the God revealed in the Old Testament, though He had been largely discarded as the Lord said, "in vain they do worship me", Matt. 15. 9. But the Lord introduced the blessed fact that the Father was to be worshipped, for He seeks worshippers, John 4. 23.

When does worship take place? The Samaritans and Jews had their ritual, the Jews having their daily, monthly, and annual times of sacrificial worship. But the Lord introduced something new, "the hour cometh, and now is", strictly referring to the time after His cross and resurrection when believers would be introduced to His Father.

How to worship? The Jews had their sacrifices, but the Lord introduced a completely new concept. He spoke of worshipping "in spirit and in truth", John 4. 23-24, because God is Spirit. So worship derives from the heart unto Him.

July 30th

READING: Luke 10. 17-24

THE LORD SAID PRIVATELY

WE NORMALLY think of the Lord addressing great multitudes who on occasions flocked to hear Him, perhaps from a hill side, from a boat by the sea shore, or within the temple courts. Alas, they often did not respond to His teaching, and even went backwards, John 6. 66. Sometimes, more was accomplished when just a few were listening to the Lord. There were occasions when prophets and kings wanted to know, but the Lord stated that they saw and heard nothing, v. 24. So the Lord took His disciples apart privately, and they were blessed on account of what they saw and heard. Note that only the privileged few could be there with Him; the choice was His. We sometimes enter huge office blocks, city halls, museums and stately homes, all with many doors marked "private". We think, What is going on behind those doors where we cannot enter?

Has the Lord taken us apart privately, so as to bless us with the special privileges of the Christian life, to see and hear Him? This would take place behind doors through which the unsaved cannot enter. Even physically, this may be behind the closed doors of our rooms, Matt. 6. 6. There are a number of examples in the Gospels. Thus in Mark 6. 31, the Lord took the disciples into a desert place apart, in order to rest; they went "by ship privately". As a result of their failure in healing a boy, the disciples "asked him privately" the reason for their failure, 9. 28. He explained the meaning of the parable of the wheat and tares in a house privately, having sent the multitude away, Matt. 13. 36. On the mount of Olivet, the disciples asked Him privately about future events and the end of the world, 24. 3. The great discourses in John 13-16 were all spoken to the apostles privately in the upper room and on the way to the garden of Gethsemane.

Many of the greatest events took place privately. The Lord's birth took place privately, and He was laid in a manger, witnessed only by the shepherds, Luke 2. 16. Only Peter, James and John witnessed the transfiguration, 9. 28. Again, only these three apostles were with the Lord in the garden of Gethsemane, Matt. 26. 37. Only a relatively few witnesses in Jerusalem were privileged to see the Lord in resurrection, yet from them sounded out the glorious truth of the gospel message.

July 31st

READING: **Philippians 1. 1-24**

PAUL'S CONSTANT THANKSGIVINGS AND PRAYERS

CHARACTERISTIC of most of Paul's Epistles are his constant thanksgivings and prayers for other local churches. It is useful to contemplate these, since they would enrich our own prayers with suitable topics, and would give us interest in the needs and blessings of other local churches. We can merely draw the attention of readers to some of these thanksgivings and prayers of Paul in some of his Epistles.

In Romans, Paul writes "without ceasing" he engaged in prayer for them, 1. 9. His prayer related to his journey to them, and his desire to establish them in the faith. He also thanked God for them all, that their faith was spoken of "throughout the whole world", v. 8. Conversely, he desired their prayers on his behalf, 15. 30-32.

In First Corinthians, Paul engaged in an amplified statement of the contents of his prayers. He commenced with, "I thank my God always on your behalf", 1. 4. In the following verses, it is difficult to decide exactly where the thanksgiving comes to an end. Certainly, Paul included the fact that they were enriched in all utterance and in all knowledge.

In Ephesians 1. 16, Paul ceased "not to give thanks for you, making mention of you in my prayers"; an extended prayer follows, reaching to the spiritual heights of the power of God in Christ. Conversely, the Ephesians were to engage in thanks "always", 5. 20, and in prayers "always", 6. 18.

In Philippians, Paul thanked God for every remembrance of them, 1. 3, 5. His prayers were "always . . . every", v. 4, and this prayer embraced their love and spirituality, vv. 9-11. In 4. 6, we find the converse, "in every thing by prayer and supplication with thanksgiving let your requests be made known unto God". Paul had a lot of time for prayer when in prison.

In Colossians, he was praying and giving thanks for them always, 1. 3. He stated that he did not cease to pray for them, v. 9, the following verses giving the substance of these prayers. Conversely, he desired their prayers, 4. 2-4.

The reader may also examine 1 Thess. 1. 2-3; 3. 10; 5. 17, 25; 2 Thess. 1. 3, 11; 1 Tim. 1. 12; 2. 1; 2 Tim. 1. 3-4; Philem. 4-6, 22. What an example lesson for believers today, when daily routine absorbs so much time throughout life.

213

August 1st

READING: **Acts 6. 1-8**

SERVICE OF LOCAL ADMINISTRATION

THROUGHOUT MOST of the Christian era, there has been great confusion on this subject. There is the question of responsibility in matters relating to finance, property, and other administrative duties. In Acts 6, it was not a matter of confusion; rather an orderly development under the hand of God is presented as the number of converts grew in Jerusalem. The matter came to a head with the "murmuring" of one kind of converted Jews against another kind. The apostles had done almost everything, including the distribution of finance. But no man can do more than what can be fitted into a working day, as in Moses' time, who worked as judge "alone", Exod. 18. 14.

Thus when Barnabas brought money, he "laid it at the apostles' feet", Acts 4. 37, knowing that they dealt with it, as well as engaging in evangelism and the ministry of the Word. So a subdivision of the work proved necessary, setting the New Testament pattern for all to follow afterwards. The Lord has gifted all His servants for spiritual work; He has given the gifts, and He guides His servants in the exercise of those gifts in their service. There is no selection committee amongst men to decide whether a believer should serve the Lord, how he should serve, where he should serve, and what he should do. This is the Lord's prerogative. These seven men in Acts 6 were men of that nature; they were full of faith and of the Holy Spirit, v. 5, with some being full of power doing great wonders and miracles, v. 8. *After* that, they engaged in administrative matters, and not *before*. Their spiritual abilities were the qualifications necessary for these other duties. Thus in the O.T., Chenaniah engaged in spiritual matters: he "was for song", and "instructed about the song, because he was skilful", 1 Chron. 15. 22, but later was engaged on administrative duties, for "the outward business over Israel", 26. 29.

Thus the seven were chosen by the church for these financial matters, as in 1 Cor. 16. 3; 2 Cor. 8. 19. Those chosen had the confidence of the believers, 2 Cor. 8. 18, 22. They continued in their spiritual work, Acts 6. 8; 8. 5, and their financial work was done in full fellowship with the elders, 11. 30.

Thus: spiritual work first, other matters second. The first is chosen by the Lord, the second by the local church.

August 2nd

READING: **1 Chronicles 9. 17-32**

PORTERS IN THE HOUSE OF GOD

APART FROM the priests, there were other Levites who were engaged in temple service. There were the singers, the porters and the treasurers. Today, all believers are priests, singers, porters and treasurers. As priests, believers are concerned with the most holy offering, Christ Himself, as they approach God in worship. As porters, believers are concerned with the maintenance of what is due to God.

In Numbers 8. 16-18, the Levites were chosen by God; they were wholly given unto Him. We find porters mentioned only in the so-called priestly books: 1 and 2 Chronicles, Ezra and Nehemiah. Initially, 212 were chosen by David, 1 Chron. 9. 22; 26. 1-19. All ages were included, "as well the small as the great", v. 13. Today, all believers, whether new converts or mature in old age, are called to this holy exercise of portership; it is God who calls to this service.

It is important to notice their character. Obededom was blessed of God, 26. 5; they were "mighty men of valour", v. 6; they were "able men for strength for the service", v. 8; they were "strong men", v. 9. We find such strength in N.T. verses such as 1 John 2. 14; 1 Pet. 5. 8-10; Eph. 6. 10.

The position that they occupied in their service was to have "the oversight of the gates of the house of the Lord", 1 Chron. 9. 23; they lodged around the house, v. 27, and wherever there was a gate, there the porters were stationed, 26. 13-18. They compassed king Joash, and were placed at the gates of the house of the Lord, 2 Chron. 23. 7, 19. No doubt those who had an ear to hear in Revelation 2-3 were porters, ready to do the Lord's bidding to keep the churches clean.

Their functions were varied. (i) They had to prevent anything unclean entering the house, 2 Chron. 23. 19. Today, every believer's heart is a gate, and he is personally responsible to see that he introduces nothing unclean into the local church. Elders must take heed to others as well. (ii) They were over the treasuries of the house, 1 Chron. 9. 26, and we must guard the holy things pertaining to the Lord Jesus. (iii) They were responsible for distributing the daily portion to the Levites, 2 Chron. 31. 11-14. Thus there should be a circulation of good things within a local church.

August 3rd

READING: **James 2. 1-5**

ASPECTS OF FAITH

VERSE 5 is a perfect gem; words are full of spiritual meaning, such as beloved, brethren, chosen, poor of this world, rich in faith, heirs, kingdom, promised, love. To dwell on these in turn would provide a feast of good things. James is writing about two kinds of practical faith: (i) "faith . . . with respect of persons", v. 1, and "rich in faith". To James, faith is something that works and grows; it influences every part of the believer's life. It is seen in relation to various parts of the body, mostly figuratively, though the physical members of the body cannot be immune from the influence of faith, else James would call that faith "dead".

Feet. Faith affects one's walk. We walk in the steps of the faith of Abraham, Rom. 4. 12. We walk by faith, wrote Paul elsewhere, 2 Cor. 5. 7, as we respond to the Lord's invitation to come unto Him for rest, Matt. 11. 28.

Hands. Timothy was responsible for "holding faith", 1 Tim. 1. 19. Faith had to be grasped firmly, and the grasp must never be relaxed. God gives power to those who believe, and this must be grasped, and not let go, John 1. 12.

Sense of taste. David exhorted the saints regarding taste: "O taste and see that the Lord is good: blessed is the man that trusteth in him", Psa. 34. 8. Similarly, writing of those who "believe in God", 1 Pet. 1. 21, the apostle wrote of tasting that the Lord is gracious, by partaking of the sincere milk of the Word, 2. 2-3.

Eyes. Several verses relate the eyes (spiritually) with faith. "Look unto me, and be ye saved", Isa. 45. 22; "blessed are they that have not seen, and yet have believed", John 20. 29; "looking unto Jesus the author and finisher of faith", Heb. 12. 2. Here is both the beginning and later progress.

Ears. "Faith cometh by hearing, and hearing by the word of God", Rom. 10. 17. The sheep who hear His voice are contrasted with those who believe not, John 10. 26-27.

The sense of touch. The woman said, "If I may touch but his clothes, I shall be whole". The Lord replied, "thy faith hath made thee whole", Mark 5. 28, 34.

The heart. We draw near with a true heart and in full assurance of faith, Heb. 10. 22. See also Ephesians 3. 17.

August 4th

READING: **Revelation 19. 11-21**

SMALL AND GREAT

THE EXPRESSION occurring in verse 18, "small and great", occurs many times in Scripture. Whether it refers to status, maturity or to age (naturally or spiritually), there are important lessons to be gleaned, since the expression occurs in so many different contexts.

(1) *Sin and judgment.* When Lot was in Sodom, the angels smote "both small and great" with blindness, Gen. 19. 11; in Asa's restoration, "small or great" would die if they would not seek the Lord, 2 Chron. 15. 13; with Jerusalem under judgment, "the great and the small" would die, Jer. 16. 6.

(2) *Testimony of the gospel.* Paul witnessed of the truth to "small and great", Acts 26. 22. Alas, many prefer to remain in the world than to repent, so we find that when Jerusalem was destroyed by Nebuchadnezzar, "all the people, both small and great" went into Egypt, 2 Kings 25. 26.

(4) *Blessings.* This is promised in Psalm 115. 13: "He will bless them that fear the Lord, both small and great". Thus the Lord took little children, and blessed them, Mark 10. 16.

(5) *Food.* Those converted, both small or great, must feed on the Word of God. Typically, such food was provided in the O.T. Thus in Josiah's restoration, "both small and great" heard the words of the book, 2 Kings 23. 2. In Hezekiah's restoration, he arranged the distribution of food to the Levitical servants, "as well to the great as to the small", 2 Chron. 31. 15.

(6) *Keeping out the evil.* A young man must cleanse his way, Psa. 119. 9. As pointed out on page 215, porters are responsible to maintain holiness in the house of God; these porters included "the small as the great", 1 Chron. 26. 13, and the same today. Youth is not excluded from this exercise.

(7) *Worship.* The Levitical singers for worship included "the small as the great", 1 Chron. 25. 8. Thus the temple children were such that, "Out of the mouth of babes and sucklings thou hast perfected praise", Psa. 8. 2; Matt. 21. 16.

(8) *The future.* There is the exhortation to praise God given to His servants, "both small and great", Rev. 19. 5, but others, "both small and great" receive the mark of the beast, 13. 16. At the battle of Armageddon, "both small and great" are judged, 19. 18, and also at the great white throne, 20. 12.

August 5th

READING: **Proverbs 9. 1-18**

MULTIPLYING AND INCREASING

OVER FORTY years ago, the author heard a preacher say that he read a chapter in the Proverbs every day, repeating the exercise every month. Certainly themes exist throughout the book, and these can only be explored by careful study, since so many verses appear to be "stand alone" verses, with no immediate development in the context.

Give a population of any country suitable food within a suitable environment, then it thrives; otherwise it will diminish. The same with any engine that needs fuel for its proper working. Similarly in spiritual things; life needs to be fed so that there may be an increase due to multiplication.

Proverbs 9. 9 contains this principle: "Give instruction to a wise man, and he will be yet wiser: teach a just man, and he will increase in learning". This is what we may call the man-ward aspect of multiplication. Teachers are visualized, so that the man who is taught may increase. We see here the necessity of taking in the Word of God. By this means, there is even the promise in verse 11 of days and years being multiplied. Thus more shall be given to him who has, so that he has more abundance, Matt. 13. 12. The five talents become ten talents, and the one pound becomes ten; see Matthew 25. 29 and Luke 19. 26 for the principle involved.

Now in Proverbs 10. 3 we have what we may call the God-ward aspect of multiplication. "The Lord will not suffer the soul of the righteous to famish"; the Lord provides, as Mary said, "He hath filled the hungry with good things", Luke 1. 53.

Proverbs 10. 4 presents a contrast, and can be applied to believers today: "He becometh poor that dealeth with a slack hand: but the hand of the diligent maketh rich". Give out to gain more spiritually! Proverbs 13. 7 should also be read in this connection. Paul knew this truth; he was poor yet made many rich, and he possessed all things, 2 Cor. 6. 10. Again, Proverbs 10. 5 continues the theme: "He that gathereth in summer is a wise son". Here is spiritual increase, gathered when material is plentiful. Verse 11 uses another metaphor; a well of water yields its constant increase, though sin can easily prevent such a flow of spiritual material. So may we be involved in our own increase, and also in that of others.

August 6th

READING: **1 Thessalonians 1. 1-10**

THE NECESSITY OF BEING AN EXAMPLE

WHEN WE consider the subject of being an example to others, that of the Lord Jesus comes to mind first of all. In the upper room, He said, "I have given you an example, that ye should do as I have done to you", John 13. 15. In spite of divine exaltation, what lowly service He engaged in, although He was their Lord and Master. There can be no room for the elevation of self, when one thinks of His example just before He suffered. For His suffering also constituted another example, "Christ also suffered for us, leaving us an example, that ye should follow his steps", 1 Pet. 2. 21.

Believers are responsible to be examples to others, and we may consider the following:

(1) *The local church.* Paul wrote to the Thessalonians, "so that ye were ensamples to all that believe in Macedonia and Achaia", 1 Thess. 1. 7, (Macedonia containing Philippi, and Achaia Corinth). They were an example in many ways: the gospel had come to them in power; they had become followers of Paul and of the Lord; their faithfulness was marked by affliction; their testimony spread abroad to "every place". How careful they must be, lest anything should mar their testimony, for men in the world were watching what was happening.

(2) *Elders.* In a local church, elders must be "ensamples to the flock", 1 Pet. 5. 3. Their shepherd care, their conduct, their service without remuneration, their service in feeding the flock, their lowly position without being "lords over God's heritage", are all points where example is necessary.

(3) *Paul.* The apostle knew his calling and responsibility, so he exhorted the Philippians to take note of others who followed him as an example, Phil. 3. 17. Do we rejoice when we see others walking as if following Paul who also followed Christ? He deliberately made himself an example so that the Thessalonians should follow him, 2 Thess. 3. 9.

(4) *Believers.* Timothy had to be "an example of the believers, in word . . . ", 1 Tim. 4. 12, and that in spite of his youth. Titus also had to show himself a pattern of good works, Titus 2. 7. Taken together, in these various cases, there were examples shown to the world, to the flock, to brethren, to believers and to young men.

August 7th

READING: Luke 19. 41-48

THE LORD AND THE TEMPLE

IN VERSE 44, the Lord had pronounced judgment upon Jerusalem; not one stone would remain upon another. This refers to the Roman destruction of the city in A.D.70, (but a similar expression in Luke 21. 6 refers to the temple). Then in verse 45, there is judgment on carnal religious gain in the temple courts. We then find several references to the temple which have important lessons for believers today.

A house of prayer. In verse 46, "My house is the house of prayer", the Lord quotes Isaiah 56. 7. There, God laid down conditions for obedience: His sabbaths had to be kept, with things chosen that please Him, v. 4. Israel would be a separated people, eunuchs would have a fruitful name, strangers would be His servants, the outcasts of Israel would be gathered. Then would God's house be a house of prayer. And today, prayer is effective when a man is righteous, James 5. 16, else prayer can be in vain.

A house of teaching. In Luke 19. 47, the Lord taught "daily in the temple", repeated in 20. 1. (That is, in the temple courts where the people assembled.) In verses 2-8, men wanted to know from whence the Lord's authority derived; He would not inform them, but the obvious implication is that it derived from heaven. Today, true teachers of Scripture have their authority to teach from heaven, and not from men.

A house of worship. "The stone which the builders rejected, the same is become the head of the corner", 20. 17, is quoted from Psalm 118. 22. There is thus a building up of stones and not a casting down. The Lord is seen as pre-eminent as the elevated Stone, and the context of Psalm 118 is that of worship: for in verses 21-29 there are thoughts of praise, rejoicing, sacrifice, and thanks.

A house of fellowship. In Luke 20. 42-43, "Sit thou on my right hand, till I make thine enemies thy footstool" is quoted from Psalm 110. 1, for here is mount Zion the dwelling place of God, with willing people in the beauty of holiness. The Lord is thus seen with His own people.

A house of giving. In Luke 21. 1-4, the Lord commends the widow who cast her two mites into the temple treasury.

Read these five features as also found in Acts 2. 42-45.

August 8th

READING: **1 Corinthians 4. 9-21**

DOVETAILING OF PURPOSE

PAUL WAS sending Timothy to Corinth, v. 17, but Paul would not come immediately, evidently waiting until he had seen the effect of this Epistle on the Corinthians. However, in verses 18-21, there is a three-fold intention stated (though we admit that two different Greek words are used, but in English the common word "will" links the thoughts together). These are:

"I will come to you".

"If the Lord will".

"What will ye?".

The apostle Paul planned for the future in his service, and so he knew that he expected to visit Corinth again. But others may have different intentions; you cannot force a man to do something if his intention is negative. Thus Paul sought to persuade Apollos to go to Corinth, but "his will" was not to come there and then, though he "will come" at a more convenient time, 1 Cor. 16. 12.

Yet Paul did not move according to his own will; when thinking of his future movements, he added "if the Lord will", and this was no empty phrase; he meant what he said. On other occasions, the divine will was negative, "not willing that any should perish", 2 Pet. 3. 9.

Yet the Corinthians were also involved; they had a will of their own, so Paul asked "What will ye?", namely, in what state of mind and discipline did they wish Paul to arrive? No doubt their will was almost irrelevant on account of the sinful practices existing in the local church. We find a negative will in Matthew 23. 37, "ye would not".

Such a three-fold will is necessary for any visit by a servant to a local church. The Lord's will overrules the intention of the servant and the desires of the members of the church. This three-fold manifestation was seen in Joppa in Acts 9. 36-41. The disciples desired Peter to come to them, v. 38; Peter was willing to go since he came to Joppa, and God's will was done since Tabitha was raised through Peter's prayer, v. 40. We find the same in Acts 18. 20-21.

We find the same in the Lord's life and service. He spoke of the Father's will, Matt. 26. 39; Heb. 10. 7; of His own will, John 17. 24; and the will of men, Matt. 20. 32.

READING: **Joshua 18. 1-10**

THE HISTORY OF SHILOH

SHILOH was about 20 miles north of Jerusalem; Gibeon was about six miles to the north-west, while Nob was one mile to the north. These were the places where the tabernacle was sited in the land. Two lines of interpretation can be traced, (i) the history of Christendom, and (ii) as far as the ark is concerned, the history of the movements of Christ up to the throne. We shall concentrate on (i).

The tabernacle was established at Shiloh, Josh. 18. 1, when the barrenness of the wilderness had been left behind, and when the fighting for the land was largely over. All Israel assembled there, and what a wonderful shadow this is of the original church in the Acts. The wilderness of unconverted days is left behind, and fellowship is enjoyed at the place where God has been pleased to place His Name. Possessions were distributed at Shiloh; indeed, the Lord's people in a local church have an abundance of spiritual possessions in Christ.

Unfortunately, errors of almost every kind arose later.

Imitation. Some of the tribes then left Shiloh, 22. 9, to set up their homes on the east of Jordan, at the same time erecting an altar there, giving every kind of excuse and reason for so doing. They thought that an "altar of witness" was better than the land of the Lord's possession, v. 19. Such similarity can be seen in the initial growth of Christendom.

Idolatry. Judges 17-21 presents a tragic story. Idolatry and evil grew in the north, and we read that this continued "all the time that the house of God was in Shiloh", 18. 31.

Intrigue. Hannah was a faithful soul at Shiloh, almost a remnant of faithfulness, 1 Sam. 1. 3, 9, while all around there was religious intrigue carried on by Eli and his sons, for Eli was usurping the function of high priest. Evil was now attacking the very centre, and reminds us of Diotrephes who wanted the preeminence, 3 John 9-10.

Iniquity. Ths sons of Eli introduced evil in Shiloh, but the Lord revealed Himself there to Samuel, 1 Sam. 3. 21. It was in the subsequent battle with the Philistines that the Lord forsook the tabernacle of Shiloh, Psa. 78. 60, never to return, using the event in Jeremiah 7. 12 to show what He would do to the temple. We see the climax of Christendom here, Rev. 17. 16.

August 10th

READING: **Hebrews 12. 18-29**

TWO COVENANTS INTRODUCED BY EARTHQUAKES

BAD EARTHQUAKES present a destructive tragedy, bringing with them much loss of life. In September 1962, there was the worst earthquake in Persian history, with over 10,000 people killed. In 1755 there was a bad earthquake below the sea near Lisbon, engulfing the city with a forty-foot wave that even caused the level of Loch Ness to rise and fall for an hour. It is interesting to note that many of the active earthquake regions are situated in parts of the world where the gospel has had but little impact, such as the middle east, the far east and parts of South America.

The first or old covenant was introduced by earthquakes, as in Exodus 19. 18 when the whole of mount Sinai "quaked greatly". Hebrews 12. 18-21 describes the fear that this induced in the people, including Moses. Earthquakes were used by God as a sign of impending judgment, Isa. 29. 6. Again in Amos 1. 1-2, "The Lord will roar from Zion" was stated "two years before the earthquake", and Josephus writes that this divided the mountain west of Jerusalem into two parts, one moving 500 yards, though this appears historical speculation.

At the introduction of the new covenant, an earthquake occurred when the Lord Jesus died, Matt. 27. 51, causing the centurion's heart to change when he confessed, "Truly this was the Son of God", v. 54. Again, there was a great earthquake when the stone was rolled away from the tomb, 28. 22. In subsequent missionary work, God intervened in Philippi; an earthquake occurred when Paul was in prison, Acts 16. 26.

In the future, "earthquakes in divers places", Mark 13. 8, will demonstrate the approach of the end of the age, as will wars, the rise of false Christs, and many other perils. The prophetic Scriptures give us more details. An earthquake will cause the division of the mount of Olives, Zech. 14. 4-5; God has stated that He will shake not only the earth but also the heavens, Hab. 2. 6-7; Heb. 12. 26-27. In Revelation 16. 18 there is described "a great earthquake, such as was not since men were upon the earth, so mighty an earthquake, and so great", causing the cities of the nations to fall.

But we can be thankful that we have a kingdom that cannot be moved, enabling us to serve God acceptably, Heb. 12. 22.

223

August 11th

READING: **Matthew 2. 1-12**

THE BRINGING OF PRESENTS

THERE ARE traditional times of the year when presents are exchanged with relations and friends. There are quite a number of occasions in the Scriptures when gifts were presented, and not all can claim to have been wholesome occasions. We shall pick a few out here, so that the reader can see what was involved in this deep-rooted practice.

Word Declared. Ezra was reading the words of the law to the people, and its meaning was explained, Neh. 8. 8. The people wept, but were encouraged by Nehemiah to eat and drink, "and send portions unto them for whom nothing is prepared", v. 10. Evidently here were gifts presented to the poor, and this led to rejoicing during the feast of tabernacles.

World Defeated. When the Jews had slain Haman's sons, there were days of rejoicing during which they engaged "in sending portions one to another", Esther 10. 19, 22.

Witnesses' Death. In the future, God will have His witnesses, though they will be mishandled even to death, Rev. 11. 7. Because of this, and before their resurrection, men will rejoice, "and shall send gifts one to another", v. 10. Thus men of good heart and men of evil heart can both send presents, either rejoicing in good or in evil.

Work Diminished. The king of Babylon sent a present to Hezekiah, Isa. 39. 1-2, who was "glad of them". The healing hand of God was disregarded by Hezekiah having fellowship with the enemy. Men brought "every man his present" to Solomon, 1 Kings 10. 25; this is *Wealth Developed*. Both the men of Judah and of the Philistines brought presents to Jehoshaphat because of the establishment of his kingdom, 2 Chron. 17. 5, 11; this is *Welcomed Dominion*.

Worshippers' Devotion. The wise men who came to Bethlehem to present gifts to the One born King of the Jews came in a spirit of worship, Matt. 2. 11. The gold implies worship as to His Kingship; the frankincense as to the fragrance of His Person, and the myrrh as to His sufferings.

Wonderful Deliverance. We are recipients from God of His great gift which is called "unspeakable", 2 Cor. 9. 15.

When we give presents, may it be with a spiritual sense of goodness in our hearts, doing it as unto the Lord.

August 12

READING: 1 John 2. 1-29

LITTLE CHILDREN

JOHN WAS an old man when he wrote his Epistles. Most of those to whom he was writing were therefore younger, and also younger in the faith. He could therefore look at them through maturer eyes, and so he addressed many of them with the deep affection involved in the description "Little children". We recognize that two different Greek words are involved, but that does not affect our selection of the nine times in which this name is used (in English) in the A.V. These are 2. 1, 12, 13, 18, 28; 3. 7, 18; 4. 4; 5. 21.

(1) *Sins forgiven.* "I write unto you, little children, because your sins are forgiven you", 2. 12. It is the blood of Jesus Christ that cleanses from all sin, 1. 7.

(2) *That ye sin not.* "My little children, these things write I unto you, that ye sin not", 2. 1. We know that we sin, but we must not practise sin as a regular feature of life.

(3) *The Father known.* "I write unto you, little children, because ye have known the Father", 2. 13. As Paul remarked, "I known whom I have believed", 2 Tim. 1. 12.

(4) *Loving in truth.* "My little children, let us not love in word . . . but in deed and in truth", 3. 18. Thus the Lord did not only talk about forgiveness, but He worked this out on the cross by dying for our sins.

(5) *Abiding in Him.* "Little children, abide in him", 2. 28; thus a flower abides in the plant so as to maintain life. Only then are we taught by God, and not by the antichrists.

There are also four occasions when warnings are given, so necessary in all ages when men lie in wait to deceive.

(6) *Let no man deceive you*, 3. 7. There were those who taught that it was in order to practise sin, but such men are of the devil and not of God.

(7) *The last time.* "Little children, it is the last time", 2. 18, because antichrists were abroad in the world, a herald of the antichrist himself of the last days.

(8) *Overcomers.* "Ye are of God, little children, and have overcome them", 4. 4. It is essential to hold the truth that the Lord Jesus came in the flesh; this is overcoming.

(9) *Free from idolatry.* "Little children, keep yourselves from idols", 5. 21, from being absorbed with material things.

August 13th

READING: **2 Chronicles 34. 1-21**

FAITH BEFORE THE END TIMES

JOSIAH REIGNED over 800 years after Moses, and 400 years after David. The Jewish nation had gone astray beyond remedy, and the faith of king Josiah was the one light in a dark scene before the monarchy came to an end, and the nation was taken into captivity. It is the same today; 2,000 years will soon have passed after the Lord's life on earth, and darkness reigns everywhere except in the testimony of His people prior to the end times. The apostolic doctrine has been abandoned, except by those who love the truth.

Right from the beginning of his reign, Josiah went back to the one (David) who had originally prepared for the temple, 2 Chron. 34. 2. For ourselves, right from the time of our conversion, we return to the Lord who had said, "I will build my church", Matt. 16. 18.

It was just before the end that Josiah did this. Because of the evil of king Manasseh, God had said, "I am bringing such evil upon Jerusalem . . . I will forsake the remnant of mine inheritance, and deliver them into the hand of their enemies", 2 Kings 21. 11-15. Josiah knew this; do we, in the end times before the Lord comes? There were reforms, but in all things the nation turned unto God "feignedly", Jer. 3. 10; Josiah was but a remnant. The same today; men seek reform, but God sees the heart, and knows those who are His. Again, faithful men sought to repair the Lord's house, 2 Chron. 34. 9-12, and today also, faithful men seek to hold to the truth relating to the local church and its service. But Josiah would not see the forthcoming judgment, vv. 27-28; neither will believers today, for they will be raptured prior to God's dealings in judgment upon men in their darkness and unbelief.

Note the things that Josiah regained. The ark was given its rightful place, 35. 3, (Christ has the pre-eminence today); the priests had their rightful service, v. 2, (today, all believers should recognize their priesthood); the words of the book were read, 34. 30, (the Scriptures are valued); the passover was killed, 35. 6, (the Lord's Supper is observed); God spoke of the future, 34. 24, (we value prophecy today).

Moreover, Josiah went back to David, Solomon, Moses, Asaph, Samuel, 35. 4, 6, 12, 15, 18. Do we go back to the N.T.?

August 14th

READING: Luke 22. 7-20

WE WITH HIM; HE WITH US

BOTH MATTHEW and Luke record the establishment of the Breaking of Bread, but there are differences in the accounts: in particular, note "he sat down, and the twelve apostles with him", Luke 22. 14, and "he sat down with the twelve", Matt. 26. 20. In Luke, He was there, and the disciples sat down with Him; in Matthew, the disciples were there, and He sat down with them. The difference is profound. In the O.T. men approached God in a physical sense (this answers to Luke); in the N.T. the Lord is found with His people (this answers to Matthew). Faith perceives the difference, but a religion of sight and touch really takes the O.T. position. Consider the difference as seen in several scriptures.

In the Old Testament, men approached God. Thus Moses "drew near . . . where God was", Exod. 20. 21; in 19. 17 he brought the people to meet with God. In 33. 7, men who sought the Lord went out to the tabernacle. Later, the people had to come to the place that God would choose, Deut. 12. 5. In David's time, men said, "Let us go into the house of the Lord", Psa. 122. 1. Even in the future, men will go up to Jerusalem to worship the King, Zech. 14. 16. And this method of approach spills over into the New Testament, for both the shepherds and the wise men moved physically to find the Lord Jesus. It all answers to Ezekiel 48. 35, "The Lord is there".

In the New Testament, the Lord introduced faith rather than sight. The Old Testament method was altered, so that Matthew 26. 20 introduces what is new. For in 18. 20, two or three gather in His Name, and then He is found in their midst (a specialized context, we agree, but there is a general principle for all gatherings). After the Lord's resurrection, twice the disciples were gathered in the upper room, and on those occasions, the Lord came where they were, and presented Himself alive, John 20. 19, 26. This promise to come was made by the Lord in John 14. 23. It was enacted again in Acts 2. 1; the Spirit came to where they were gathered together.

We conclude by observing that the O.T. *types* are still used in the N.T. with a *new* meaning. Thus we have "boldness to enter"; "let us draw near", "ye are come to mount Sion", Heb. 10. 19, 22; 12. 22.

READING: **Revelation 12. 1-5**

A NEW LOOK AT CHRISTMAS

IT IS certainly not necessary to consider the birth of the Lord Jesus only at so-called Christmas time. This time of rejoicing is permanently on the pages of Scripture to be read at all seasons. But there is another side of the story that is usually overlooked, at least by those who have no interest in knowing exactly what was taking place. For Satan was active when the Lord was born, and Revelation 12 explains what was happening before and afterwards. How different from Luke's account, where grace was revealed from heaven, where loving family details are given, and where the shepherds rejoiced.

The mention of "heaven", Rev. 12. 1, takes our minds to the purpose of God. The woman clothed with the sun refers to the nation of Israel with the glory of God. As the sun lightens the moon, so there was the Light to lighten the Gentiles. The twelve stars answer to the twelve tribes, and their administrative calling; (note these concepts in Genesis 37. 9, in Joseph's dream).

This woman was "with child", namely, the nation was destined to bring forth Christ as pertaining to the flesh; "unto us a child is born", Isa. 9. 6, One who "was made of the seed of David according to the flesh", Rom. 1. 3. This woman was "travailing in birth", referring to all the sufferings of the nation from Joseph's time in Egypt. For they were often in bondage to the nations around, and finally they were under Rome's dominion. The "red dragon" refers to the old serpent, the devil and Satan. The description of his heads and crowns is the same as that of the beast in Revelation 13. 1, showing what is the motivating power behind the future emperor. The "stars of heaven" answer to those opposed to the Lord, the heathen, kings and rulers of Psalm 2. 1-2. Being ready to devour means that Satan was ready to motivate Herod to seek to destroy the Lord Jesus after His birth.

Thus the "man child" was finally brought forth, ultimately to rule with a rod of iron, Psa. 2. 9; Luke 1. 32-33. Satan wanted to remove such authority. But He was "caught up unto God, and to his throne". Satan's plans were thwarted! There is no mention of His death and resurrection, only His ascension; these other topics are found elsewhere in Revelation.

August 16th

READING: **Corinthians 5. 1-21**

THE JUDGMENT SEAT OF CHRIST

THE JUDGMENT SEAT of Christ, for believers after their resurrection, is quite different from the judgment of the great white throne for unbelievers. The only judgments through which believers pass are (i) God's governmental hand for discipline and correction now, and (ii) the future judgment seat of Christ. Believers have no fear about this, since divine love has provided to the uttermost for the forgiveness and removal of sins. But the thought of the future encourages us to put things right here and now. At that future occasion, both the conduct and service of the Lord's people will be under review, both in motivation and in outworking.

Conduct – its motivation, Rom. 14. 10-13. "*Why* dost thou judge thy brother? or *why* dost thou set at nought thy brother?". In other words, have you judged or stumbled a brother, and why? Have you helped others, or hindered them, and why? All must give account before God, and these inner motives that control will be probed if they have resulted in damage spiritually to other believers.

Conduct – its outworking, 2 Cor. 5. 9-10. As Paul wrote, "We labour . . . that every one may receive the things done in his body, according to that he hath done, whether it be good or bad". Our deeds will be assessed, so what we do now should be compatible with an abundant entry into the everlasting kingdom.

Service – its motivation, 1 Cor. 4. 5. Speaking of the servants of Christ, Paul writes, "until the Lord come, who will bring to light . . . and will make manifest". A minister must be faithful, v. 2, for the counsels of the hearts will be manifested before that judgment seat. Why do we do what we do in our service? To follow the standards and objects of the day? Merely to follow others so as to be popular? Or to remain faithful, and thus to serve perhaps in a small corner?

Service – its outworking, 1 Cor. 3. 13-15. Every man's work shall be tried by the searching gaze of Christ. This is called a fire, and the kind of service that has built upon Christ as foundation will be that of extreme value.

As a result of this judgment seat, works and motives that have been unworthy of Christ will be removed. What is left will be fully eligible for reward, Rev. 22. 12; 2 Tim. 4. 8.

READING: **Daniel 6. 1-24**

DANIEL, A MAN WHO WAS SAVED

THE BOOK of Daniel is full of detail, but unless a careful study is made, the general reader will know only a few portions of the book, namely the historical parts rather than the prophetical parts. Unbelievers relegate the book of Daniel to mere historical myth, but the Lord Jesus made reference to "Daniel the prophet" and "the abomination of desolation" (an idol), Matt. 24. 15, while Hebrews 11. 33 speaks of the stopping of "the mouths of lions", referring to Daniel 6.

This event took place when Daniel was an old man, say about 85 years of age. He still manifested courage and faithfulness, for the king had decreed that those who prayed to God should be cast into the den of lions. Knowing this, Daniel prayed three times a day towards Jerusalem. He was seen to do this, so suffered the inevitable consequences. Yet in the morning, he testified, "My God hath sent his angel, and hath shut the lions' mouths, that they have not hurt me", v. 22. Thus he was unharmed, "because he believed in his God", v. 23. Hence he prospered, while his enemies were themselves cast in, v. 24.

Such a story is full of similarities to our position today, for the world is a den, where "your adversary the devil, as a roaring lion, walketh about, seeking whom he may devour", 1 Pet. 5. 8. We must be "stedfast in the faith", v. 9. When the Lord Jesus was here, Satan as a lion attacked Him, but He said "It is written". Satan adopted many methods with which to devour Him, and he arranged for men to desire to crucify Him; the Lord said, "Save me from the lion's mouth", Psa. 22. 21, and He was saved through resurrection.

For us, we are somewhat like Paul, with lions surrounding us on occasions. He could declare, "I was delivered out of the mouth of the lion", 2 Tim. 4. 17. Because the Lord was delivered, so were Paul, Daniel and ourselves in God's good time. But the converse is also valid. As Daniel's enemies were cast into the den, it is written of unbelievers that all that remain of them from the mouth of the lion are "two legs, or a piece of an ear", Amos 3. 10-12. In other words, Satan devours unbelievers, from which there is no escape if the gospel is refused. Let us have faith like Daniel, when we are delivered for ever, else men are devoured for ever.

August 18th

READING: **Exodus 28. 26-38**

PERPETUAL SERVICE

IN THE CONTEXT of the tabernacle, eight times in the book of Exodus there appears a word variously translated "always, perpetual, continual". It is important to note these, for the lesson applied to believers today relates to the continuity of their own service for the Lord.

Three times it relates to the sanctuary. "Thou shalt set upon the table showbread before me *alway*", Exod. 25. 30; "that they bring thee pure oil olive beaten for the light, to cause the lamp to burn *always*", 27. 20; "he shall burn incense upon it, a *perpetual* incense before the Lord throughout your generations", 30. 8.

Three times it relates to the priest. "Aaron shall bear the names . . . when he goeth in unto the holy place, for a memorial before the Lord *continually*", 28. 29; "the Urim and the Thummim . . . upon his heart before the Lord *continually*", 28. 30; the blue lace with "Holiness to the Lord" "shall be *always* upon his forehead", 28. 38.

Two times it relates to sacrifice. "Two lambs of the first year day by day *continually*", 29. 38; "a *continual* burnt offering . . . at the door of the tabernacle", 29. 42.

Note that these are all described as "before the Lord".

The *table* speaks of spiritual food, the words of the Lord Jesus and the apostles' doctrine which the believers "continued" in, Acts 2. 42. The *light* speaks of the Spirit, who was sent to abide with believers "for ever". The *incense* refers to the worship and prayers of the saints, Rev. 5. 8; 8. 4; Paul gave thanks in his Epistles, "always", Col. 1. 3. The *names* refer to prayers being taken in before the Lord; this was Paul's exercise, he "did not cease to pray for you", Col. 1. 9. The *Urim* and *Thummim* was the means whereby God gave guidance to His people; in Paul's case, he spoke of his care of all the churches "daily", 2 Cor. 11. 28. *Holiness* has been perfected "for ever", Heb. 10. 14. Finally, the *lambs* speak of the sacrifice of worship; by Him we offer the sacrifice of praise to God "continually", 13. 15, reminding us of the fact that they "continued" in the Breaking of Break, Acts 2. 42.

So the N.T. responsibilities of the Lord's people today are parallel to the O.T. responsibilities of the priests.

READING: **1 John 2. 18-29; 4. 1-6**

ANTICHRISTS AND THE ANTICHRIST

PREVIOUSLY IN chapter 2, John had been writing about the world. Now he considers another prevalent danger, namely antichrists and their doctrine. For John, the period was that prior to the Lord's return, characterized by many antichrists; there are more today throughout Christendom. First of all, these men seemed to have been associated with a local church, but their character and activity pointed forward to the one antichrist of the future; all are opposed to Christ.

Relating to the future, many men shall come saying, "I am Christ", deceiving many, Matt. 24. 5. There shall arise false Christs, and will be advertised as "here is Christ", vv. 23-34; but "believe it not". In 2 Thessalonians 2, Paul wrote a lot about this man of the future; he would be "that man of sin" and "the son of perdition", v. 3. He would show "himself that he is God", v. 4; he is called "that Wicked", v. 8, while he will be engaged in "the working of Satan with all power and signs and lying wonders", v. 9. Revelation 13. 13-14 presents the man as doing "great wonders . . . and deceiveth them that dwell on the earth by the means of those miracles".

There were precursors of this man of sin in The Acts. Simon of Samaria asserted that he himself "was a great one", Acts 8. 9-11, while people claimed of Herod, "It is the voice of a god, and not of a man", 12. 22. Peter wrote that there will be such men, engaged in "denying the Lord", 2 Pet. 2. 1; Jude 4. Today, there are men who deny the Sonship of Christ, His Deity, His miraculous birth, His perfection in Manhood, the meaning of His sacrifice, and His resurrection, with many engaging in idolatry. Many such men strut throughout the pages of history.

According to John, they went out into the world, 1 John 2. 19; 4. 1, this being the beginning of Christendom with all its false religious ramifications. (Note, in Acts 20. 29, false men as grievous wolves came into the local church.) But it is stated that they were not "of us", contrasting with "one of you", Col. 4. 9, 12. A true brother "of us" would continue always, but a man "not of us" is not a true member of the body of Christ, so his proper position is locally outside. In fact, their desertion proved that such men were not of the saints, as in John 6. 66, where many went backwards from the Lord.

August 20th

READING: **Psalm 84**

THE DESIRE OF AN EXILE

HERE IS an exile outside Jerusalem, contemplating the blessings of those who are able to dwell in the house of God, v. 4. We can visualize the armies of the enemy surrounding Jerusalem, so that the exile cannot reach the place of God's choice. Even a sparrow could easily fly over the armies to gain her destination, but the exile could only live with his thoughts of previous blessings, recognizing that the Lord's tabernacles are "aimiable", with his soul fainting for the courts of the Lord. Paul had this exercise towards the local churches, for when in prison in Rome he wrote the so-called Prison Epistles, and John also, an exile on Patmos, wrote to the seven churches the messages from the Lord Jesus. David felt like an exile sometimes, for he contemplated an army encamped against him, Psa. 27. 3; yet his desire would be to dwell in the house of the Lord all the days of his life, and to behold the beauty of the Lord, v. 4. We also are exiles in a strange land, far from our heavenly home; the Father's house may seem afar off, but we have the privilege of sharing fellowship with those like-minded, and entering into the joys of worship and service in a local church. Our affections for this should be as deep-seated as those of the psalmists.

The title to Psalm 84 states that it is "for the sons of Korah". Korah was a rebel, denying the authority of Moses; he and others stood in their tent doors, Num. 16. 27, until the earth swallowed them up; yet grace reigned, for "the children of Korah died not", 26. 11, and they ultimately became keepers of the gates of the tabernacle, 1 Chron. 9. 19. What a transformation! No wonder the exile contrasted the "tents of wickedness", Psa. 84. 10, (Korah's tents), with the holy occupation of being "a doorkeeper in the house of my God", (the tabernacle gates). So the aspirations of the exile contrast with the unspiritual oppositions of men.

Today, all believers are exiles, though we should not labour under the disadvantages of Psalm 84. We should have the same exercises to gather in the Lord's Name, and under normal circumstances nothing should prevent us from doing so. The tents of wickedness that once formed our associations as unconverted are described in the N.T., 1 Cor. 6. 9-11.

August 21st

READING: **Luke 22. 39-46**

CIRCLES OF NEARNESS

IN A PRACTICAL sense, not all believers are in the same state of nearness to the Lord Jesus, at least in as far as their affections are concerned. We may consider this matter as a series of circles, the Lord being at the centre, with His people at varying distances from Him in their affections.

The garden of Gethsemane. Judas had been removed, morally and spiritually being at an infinite distance from the Lord. The other eleven apostles were differently placed. As soon as the Lord had come to the garden, He said to eight of them, "Sit ye here", Matt. 26. 36. They formed the outer ring of fellowship. Peter, James and John were taken further into the garden, v. 37; these formed the inner circle. But the Lord Jesus Himself "was withdrawn from them about a stone's cast", Luke 22. 41, or "he went a little further", Matt. 26. 39. The blessed Lord was therefore in the centre, alone in prayer with His Father prior to His crucifixion. Afterwards, He united the eleven again, before the outsider Judas arrived to betray Him. Where would we have been? Where are we today? Which circle do we adhere to? We can see such circles on the other occasions when Peter, James and John were taken apart alone with Him.

The throne in Revelation 4-5. There was One seated on the throne, Rev. 4. 2. There was the Lamb in the midst of the throne, 5. 6. There is divine pre-eminence at the centre, before we note the circles surrounding the throne. There were the twenty-four elders, no doubt referring to the Lord's people as members of His church. There were the four living creatures, no doubt heavenly attendants of the throne. Then there were the many angels, and ten thousand times ten thousand round about the throne, 5. 11. Finally, we find "every creature which is in heaven, and on the earth, and under the earth", v. 13. This is the great series of circles of the future, with our portion nearest to the Lamb of God.

Love. There is a wide expanse to which divine love reaches, commencing with the Centre. "The Father loveth the Son", John 3. 35; 5. 20; 17. 24. Then Paul declared "the Son of God, who loved me", Gal. 2. 20. There follows an expansion from the individual to the church, "Christ also loved the church", Eph. 5. 25, followed by love to the world, John 3. 16.

August 22nd

READING: **Hebrews 10. 1-18**

A BODY PREPARED

WHEN THE Lord Jesus stepped into Manhood, the Holy Thing that was born was physically real. Later some denied this, and today many false theories are held by those who advance heresy under the guise of a superior philosophy. There are several aspects of the body of the Lord stressed in the Scriptures.

His physical body. The Lord did not have a human body before His incarnation; rather a body was prepared that would be infinitely holy, the vessel of the divine Occupant, a temple, John 2. 21, and prepared for sacrifice. He was made in the likeness of men, Phil. 2. 7, partaking of flesh and blood, Heb. 2. 14. In His resurrection, His disciples thought that He was a spirit, Luke 24. 37, but He stressed that He had flesh and bones unlike a spirit. If David was "fearfully and wonderfully made", Psa. 139. 14, how much more the body of the Lord Jesus, miraculously conceived and without sin.

His mystical body. In Ephesians 1. 22, the church is called "his body, the fulness of him that filleth all in all". The reason why the term "body" is applied to the church in its glorious totality is because the Lord is its Living Head, with absolute authority to control. Just as our heads control our bodies through the nervous system, so spiritually the Lord Jesus as Head controls His body the church. This concept reaches also to the local church in the matter of service, a metaphor that Paul describes in 1 Corinthians 12. 14-30 in relation to the differing functions of the members.

His glorious body. On the mount of transfiguration, the Lord's pre-resurrection body was transfigured before the apostles, when His face shone as the sun, and when His clothes permitted the whiteness of the light to penetrate through, Matt. 17. 2. Now His post-resurrection body as ascended is described as "his glorious body", Phil. 3. 21. By grace, our bodies will be fashioned like unto His glorious body.

A symbolical body. "This is my body", said the Lord in the upper room, 1 Cor. 11. 24, speaking of the bread by which we remember Him on the Lord's Day. By means of the bread and the cup, we show forth His death until He come, as we engage in this act of worship. Scripture knows nothing of the idolatrous theory that the bread actually becomes His material body!

August 23rd

READING: **1 Corinthians 3. 1-10**

NATURAL, CARNAL, SPIRITUAL

THE SCRIPTURES often divide all mankind into classes; for example, Jews, Gentiles, the church of God, 1 Cor. 10. 32; those who believe and those who do not believe, John 3. 18. In 1 Corinthians 2. 14 to 3. 3 the Spirit through Paul has divided men into natural, carnal and spiritual. It is important to consider each class separately, for "carnal" and "spiritual" both refer to Christians in the context.

Natural men. These are those who have been blinded by the evil one, those without hope and without God. They see the cross of the Lord as mere irrelevant history, being, in fact, enemies of the cross of Christ; some would seek to crucify the Lord afresh. They reject inspiration, and treat the Word of God merely as if it were the word of men, treating it by the method of destructive criticism. They may seek to meddle with the church of God, even using it for their own en !~, and acting as false prophets like Jezebel, Rev. 2. 20.

Carnal men. These are "babes" not experiencing the presence and power of God, 1 Cor. 3. 1; those who have gone back from any maturity to which they may have attained; those who are saved, but do not perceive the relevance of the cross of Christ in daily life, having forgotten the meaning of their baptism; those who do not avail themselves of the food of the Word of God, being barren and unfruitful, and often holding false doctrine through man-made arguments, 1 Cor. 15. 12. They work for self, producing merely the wood, hay and stubble, taken up with the world and not with Christ. They walk "as men", hardly distinct from unbelievers in the world, 3. 3.

Spiritual men. Here are established Christians with the mind of Christ. Showing the new man, they have presented their bodies to God. They preach Christ crucified, and not the doctrines of men, knowing that they are the fruit of the travail of His soul. They feed upon the Bread of Life from the Word of God, valuing this as inspired by the Spirit. In their service, they seek to be true and loyal, devotedly building on the one foundation those precious things as "gold, silver, precious stor.~". They are labourers together with God, doing all things in the Name of the Lord Jesus.

We should assess our own standards in the things of God.

August 24th

READING: **Isaiah 61. 1-6**

THE SPIRIT AND THE LORD IN ISAIAH

THE OLD TESTAMENT references to the Lord Jesus are not given "by measure", rather they are pressed down and running over. For many of the Lord's people, such unexplored territory yields holy details concerning the mind of God. For example, the Trinity is seen in Isaiah and in the New Testament portions deriving from it.

Thus in Isaiah 6, we have Jehovah, with the acclamation "Holy, holy, holy". But in John 12. 40-41, this refers to Christ, when Isaiah "saw his glory". And in Acts 28. 25, it is seen as the Holy Spirit who was speaking.

Similarly, the references to the Spirit and Christ show the voice of the Trinity, and also embrace the four Gospels.

Isaiah 61. 1 gives us the voice of the Lord Jesus, "The Spirit of the Lord God is upon me". This takes our minds to *Luke's Gospel*, and to 4. 18. We read of the Spirit coming upon Him at His baptism, and driving Him into the wilderness; this anointing was for service. He came in the power of the Spirit into Galilee for the commencement of His ministry. The Gospel ends with the Lord explaining the things written in the prophets concerning Him, and this must have included Isaiah.

Isaiah 11. 2 gives us the voice of the Spirit of prophecy, "the spirit of the Lord shall rest upon him". In fact, we find in these verses the seven-fold Spirit. The Lord is described in relation to "a rod out of the stem of Jesse". The royal line is envisaged, and so corresponds to *Matthew's Gospel*, where the Lord is seen as "the son of David", Matt. 1. 1.

Isaiah 42. 1 presents us with the voice of God, "Behold my servant, whom I uphold; mine elect, in whom my soul delighteth; I have put my spirit upon him". This takes the mind to *Mark's Gospel*, where the Lord is presented as the Servant. Verses 1-3 are quoted in Matthew 12. 18-20, where the Lord withdrew Himself from the criticism of the Pharisees, but had mercy on those who were in need and out of the way.

Isaiah 48. 12, 16 takes our minds to the beginning, to the First and the Last, "the Lord God, and his Spirit, hath sent me". This refers to the eternal One in *John's Gospel*, where He is seen as the One sent from the Father. This is translated in the R.V. as "the Lord God hath sent me, and his Spirit".

August 25th

READING: Zechariah 14. 1-9

AT EVENING TIME IT SHALL BE LIGHT

AT THIS time of the year, the evenings are beginning to draw in, and the nights become longer. Most of us do not like this, since the long nights of winter will last for many months to come. We have examined some aspects of this on page 173. During the last war and afterwards, summer time was kept during the winter, with double summer time during the summer months. Thus the sun did not set until well after 10 30p.m.! There are suggestions in the present day to keep summer time during the winter months; we all prefer light in the evenings when we are awake, rather than in the mornings when we are asleep. But not everything in God's creation likes the light; many garden insects are found in the darkness under stones, and rapidly run from the light when disturbed. Again, not all men can enjoy the light. Within the arctic circle the winter months form one permanent night of darkness. Coal miners who work day shifts do not see daylight during the winter months. Blind people are permanently in a world of darkness.

These physical ideas are used much in the Bible with a spiritual meaning. Generally, men are like those insects that prefer the darkness, as the Lord said, "men loved darkness rather than light, because their deeds were evil", John 3. 19.

Although the Lord was the true Light, yet He endured the darkness of the cross. The two on the Emmaus road were concerned about the unknown One continuing His journey in the dark, "Abide with us: for it is toward evening, and the day is far spent", Luke 24. 29. The church at Troas could not function spiritually without the use of physical light: "there were many lights in the upper chamber", Acts 20. 8.

But God changes darkness to light. That coming day shall not be day nor night; "at evening time it shall be light", Zech. 14. 6-7. The gospel message has this effect on the hearts of men; "the people which sat in darkness saw great light . . . light is sprung up", Matt. 4. 16. Paul described his own preaching as turning men "from darkness to light", Acts 26. 18. Peter wrote of the same effect, "who hath called you out of darkness into his marvellous light", 1 Pet. 2. 9.

Finally, in that great millennial city, "there shall be no night there", Rev. 21. 23, 25.

READING: 1 Thessalonians 4. 13-18

THE ARCHANGEL

THE READER may not have noticed that the word "angel" also appears in the middle of the words "evangel, evangelistic, evangelize, evangelist". The reason is that the word "angel" means messenger; thus both John the Baptist and his disciples are called by this word "angel" (messenger), Luke 7. 24-27, as were some of the Lord's disciples, 9. 52. But usually, the word refers to heavenly beings, including those special ones who were sent down to earth with divine messages for men. Thus the words "gospel, evangel" mean "a good message".

There are ranks of angels in heaven, though some had sinned and are awaiting judgment, 2 Pet. 2. 4. Additionally, there is the archangel, of the highest rank for special service. This title appears only twice in the Scriptures, 1 Thess. 4. 16 and Jude 9, and only one archangel is named, "Michael", Jude 9; Gabriel, though important, is not called an archangel. Michael means "Who is like God?", a leader who recognized the uniqueness of God, and Gabriel means "God is my strength". The following facts should be noted:

For Daniel, Dan. 10. 13, 21. A vision from God had been granted to Daniel through an angel who had been thwarted for twenty-one days, until "Michael, one of the chief princes, came to help me". Michael supported the angel in the fight against Persia and Greece, v. 20.

For the body of Moses, Jude 9. "Michael the archangel" contended with Satan about the body of Moses, but would only say, "The Lord rebuke thee". No doubt this concerned the retrieval of the body of Moses, so as to appear on the mount of transfiguration, for his body had been placed in an unknown grave, Deut. 34. 6, though it was not unknown to Michael.

At the rapture, 1 Thess. 4. 16. Angels watch over us now, but at the ascent to heaven, the voice of the archangel and the trump of God (the voice of Christ, Rev. 1. 10) will identify Michael superintending the ascent of the saints.

The casting out of Satan, Rev. 12. 7-9. Michael is named as responsible for the casting out of Satan from his kingdom in the air to the surface of the earth in that coming day.

For Israel, Dan. 12. 1. Michael stands for Israel in the future time of trouble, the great tribulation.

August 27th

READING: **Exodus 31. 1-11**

THE LORD'S SERVANTS

THE LORD had completed giving to Moses the details of the construction of the tabernacle; He finally gave the names of the two principal builders of the structure. A special structure needed special builders, fully equipped for their task. God did not leave it to Moses to make the selection; rather two men were named by God, Bezaleel and Aholiab. These men were of a special character; they were filled "with the spirit of God, in wisdom, and in understanding, and in knowledge", v. 3. This recalls what is said of the Lord Jesus in Isaiah 11. 2; for there rested upon Him "the spirit of wisdom and understanding . . . the spirit of knowledge".

After Moses had come down from the mount, and when the trouble brought about by the golden calf had been resolved, Moses told the people about God's choice, and he repeated the information about the filling of these men, Exod. 35. 30-35.

The work was then commenced by these two named men, 36. 1, together with every wise hearted man also equipped by the Lord. The completion of this work by these two named men is given in 38. 21-23: "Bezaleel . . . made all that the Lord commanded Moses. And with him was Aholiab".

We can say similarly: Moses was a type of Christ, Bezaleel of Paul, and the wise hearted people of all believers. On high in ascension glory, the Lord received the Spirit to shed forth upon His people, Acts 2. 33. "I will build my church", said the Lord Jesus, but He was going to equip His servants with wisdom and knowledge in order that they should work effectively, 1 Cor. 12. 8. In particular, Paul worked like Bezaleel. It was the Holy Spirit who selected Paul and sent him forth, Acts 13. 3-4; there was no self-choice in the matter. As Paul wrote, "he gave some, apostles", Eph. 4. 11, knowing that he had received his ministry from the Lord Jesus, Acts 20. 24. As for the doing of the work, he was a wise masterbuilder, 1 Cor. 3. 10. Many others then joined in the work as exercised by the Lord, building on the one foundation that Paul had laid. But Paul outshone all of them, for he laboured "more abundantly than they all", 15. 10. Yet as Bezaleel was working for and with Moses, so for all believers today; we work with the Lord, and He with us, Mark 16. 20.

240

August 28th

READING: **Jeremiah 33. 1-14**

THE VOICES OF THE BRIDEGROOM AND THE BRIDE

NO DOUBT not all believers have read the book of Jeremiah with any appreciation as to its overall structure. It is good to have a framework, upon which to hang one's understanding of a long complicated book. Forbid the thought that the chapters are completely mixed up with no spiritual order behind them.

Certainly the order is not historical order. There are five main sections, and in the first four sections, historical order is preserved through each section. The theme of bride and bridegroom appears several times in the book. The five sections are as follows:

(1) Chapters 1-18. Divine examination of Jerusalem in departing from her true Husband to false idols.

(2) Chapters 19-24. Two alternatives for Jerusalem in the closing days: the way of life or the way of death, 21. 8.

(3) Chapters 25-34. Alternative 1. For those who leave Jerusalem, the promise of restoration through the new covenant.

(4) Chapters 35-44. Alternative 2. For those remaining in the city, their final judgment and their worse state in Egypt.

(5) Chapters 45-52. Divine judgment foretold on the nations who were false lovers of Jerusalem leading her astray.

After recalling a catalogue of sins, the relationship between Jerusalem and her true Husband had been broken. As a result, there would cease "the voice of gladness, the voice of the bridegroom, and the voice of the bride", Jer. 7. 34.

The divine examination of Jerusalem continued, and once again God asserted that the bridal relationship would cease, "I will cause to cease . . . the voice of mirth, and the voice of gladness, the voice of the bridegroom, and the voice of the bride", Jer. 16. 9. Both these come in the first section.

The quotation occurs again in the third section prior to the restoration promises. Sin is again under scrutiny, and God asserts, "I will take away . . . the voice of the bridegroom, and the voice of the bride", 25. 10. Note the other things to be taken away in this verse. See also Revelation 18. 23.

The new covenant had been promised, 31. 33. Then the things taken away could be restored, "the voice of joy, and the voice of gladness, the voice of the bridegroom, and the voice of the bride", 33. 11. Mercy restores many other things as well!

August 29th

READING: **2 Corinthians 2. 1-17**

OPEN DOORS

ON PAGE 200, we considered the opening of doors, mainly physically. There are further thoughts that can be expressed on this subject, which is of importance to God's people today.

In Isaiah 61. 1, there had been promised that liberty would be proclaimed to the captives, and "the opening of the prison to them that are bound". In the context, this refers to the captivity of Zion, but it has a wider implication, for the Lord quotes this of His ministry in Luke 4. 18, "to set at liberty them that are bruised". This was accomplished physically on several occasions in the Acts. Thus the angel of the Lord opened the prison doors by night to release the apostles, 5. 19, leading to further testimony in the temple courts. Peter was released from prison, 12. 10, leading to fellowship and prayer in the Jerusalem church. Paul and Silas were released in Philippi, 16. 26, leading to testimony in the gospel and the baptizing of the jailor's household.

In spiritual matters, the open door speaks of arrangements made by God for the successful prosecution of His will in the service of His people. When He arranges for an open door, He has a key so that no man can shut and no man can open contrary to His will, Isa. 22. 22; Rev. 3. 8.

After the first missionary journey, Paul reported to the church at Antioch how God "had opened the door of faith unto the Gentiles", Acts 14. 27. It was through much tribulation that Paul and Barnabas went from city to city, 14. 6 showing that in reality they had to flee from city to city, and by this means they preached the gospel in new places. Paul regarded this as God's open door, rather than persecution.

On his third journey, in Ephesus Paul wrote that "a great door and effectual is opened unto me", 1 Cor. 16. 9; he would therefore tarry, as he watched the Word of God growing and prevailing for three years, Acts 19. 20; 20. 31. Again on his third journey, there was an open door in Troas, but he was unable to take advantage of it, 2 Cor. 2. 12, though he spent a week there later, Acts 20. 6.

In prison in Rome, there was no miraculous release, but he sought "a door of utterance", Col. 4. 3. The gospel was thus furthered, Phil. 1. 12; Acts 28. 30-31.

242

August 30th

READING: **Psalm 3. 1-8**

THE EVENING AND THE MORNING

THIS PHRASE occurs six times in Genesis 1. The creation of the next day had its roots in a previous night. The new creation now arises from the night of the cross of the Lord Jesus; the millennial day of the Sun of righteousness arises from the previous night of the Son of man. Psalms 3-8 contain a panorama of a morning, evening, night, midnight, dawn and second morning. And this is not surprising, since Psalm 1 commences with the godly man meditating on God's law "day and night", v. 2. Consider the following verses:

Morning. "I laid me down and slept; I awaked; for the Lord sustained me", Psa. 3. 5, said David when he was troubled by his enemies. Typically, we see the Lord Jesus before His cross, early in the morning still in safety, teaching in the temple courts although surrounded by enemies, Luke 21. 38.

Evening. The evening approached, and David anticipated sleep again, "I will both lay me down, in peace, and sleep", Psa. 4. 8. Each evening, the Lord went out to the safety of Bethany and the mount of Olives.

Night. "My voice shalt thou hear in the morning, O Lord; in the morning will I direct my prayer unto thee, and will look up", Psa. 5. 3. During the night of the cross, the Lord anticipated the morning of resurrection; there was the glory to follow, and the joy set before Him, Heb. 12. 2. .

Midnight. "In death there is no remembrance of thee: in the grave who shall give thee thanks? I am weary with my groaning; all the night make I my bed to swim", Psa. 6. 5-6. Of course we cannot apply all these ideas directly to the Lord, yet He did go down into death and was placed in the tomb. It was an experience that He had not tasted before, and one that He will not taste again.

Dawn. "Arise, O Lord . . . lift up thyself . . . awake for me to the judgment that thou hast commanded", Psa. 7. 6. We find here the approach of the dawn, the approach of the first day of the week, very early in the morning. These were David's words, often anticipating judgment, but the Lord arose with mercy before Him, though judgment will ultimately follow.

Second morning. "Crowned him with glory and honour", 8. 5, the millennial day of dominion over all God's creation.

August 31st

READING: **Luke 10. 38 to 11. 1**

THE TITLE LORD

THIS TITLE "Lord" that men ascribed to the Son of God is the one that is mostly used in the four Gospels. In these days when some use another Name on a popular (and to us, repeatedly irreverent) level, it is important to notice this fact, and to ask ourselves, Do we use this title?, thereby owning His authority and our personal need. (On a few occasions, when spoken by unbelievers, the title is translated "Sir" with no implication of Deity involved.) For believers, when Deity is implied in the title, we know that it is only by the Spirit that this title can be used, 1 Cor. 12. 3. In a future day, some will use the title in a state of despair, "Lord, Lord", Matt. 7. 22, but He will confess that He never knew them. Let us consider some examples of the use of this title, and the reader can assess why this title was employed.

The disciples awoke the Lord in the boat during the storm, saying, "Lord, save us: we perish", Matt. 8. 25. In another storm scene, Peter, walking on the water and beginning to sink, cried, "Lord, save me", 14. 30. Even the Gentile woman, whose daughter was vexed with a demon, cried, "O Lord, thou Son of David . . . Lord, help me", 15. 22-25. During the last night, all the disciples at the table with the Lord asked, "Lord, is it I?", 26. 22.

After the transfiguration, at the bottom of the mountain, the father of the boy said, "Lord, I believe; help thou mine unbelief", Mark 9. 24.

When men started to make excuses as to why they should not follow Him, they said, "Lord, I will follow thee . . . Lord, suffer me first to go and bury my father", Luke 9. 57-61. In the home in Bethany, Martha said, "Lord, dost thou not care?", 10. 40. Then the disciples asked, "Lord, teach us to pray", 11. 1. Later, when the question of forgiveness was raised, they requested "the Lord, Increase our faith", 17. 5.

There were but a few who remained with Him; Peter asked, "Lord, to whom shall we go?", John 6. 68. In John 11, many times this title is used; at the entrance to the tomb, Martha said, "Lord", with contradiction in her voice, 11. 39.

At his conversion, Paul started with the right title, "Lord, what wilt thou have me to do?", Acts 11. 6.

September 1st

READING: **Romans 16. 1-27**

IN THE LORD

YESTERDAY, we considered a selection of occasions in the Gospels when men and women rightly called the Lord Jesus by His title "Lord". Such a confession is no empty form of words, it should arise from the heart, but corresponding deeds arise from the heart as well. Thus the expression "in the Lord" is a familiar one, particularly in the Epistles, and demonstrates the subjection of a believer to the will of the Lord in his life. We consider some of the occasions when it is used.

In Romans 16. 1-2, Paul commends "Phebe our sister", who served in the church at Cenchrea. The church at Rome was exhorted to "receive her in the Lord", to accept her as one doing the will of the Lord. In verse 12, we read of Tryphena, Tryphosa and Persis who "labour in the Lord"; their service was not according to the objectives and methods of men, but fully in keeping with the will of the Lord. In verse 22, Tertius greeted the church "in the Lord"; that is, his greetings came from a heart and life subject to the Lord's will, so here was no ordinary greeting that the world would engage in, rather it was a heart-felt spiritual greeting.

There were those described by Paul as "faithful in the Lord"; we may mention Timothy, 1 Cor. 4. 17, and Tychicus, who is twice described like this, Eph. 6. 21; Col. 4. 7. Tychicus had the spiritual duty of carrying the Epistles from Paul in Rome to these destinations, as well as conveying exact news of Paul's state. Only a man subject to the will of the Lord could Paul trust with this task. We are also "in the Lord" when we can be trusted with the task of propagating Paul's Epistles exactly and without change or diminution.

A difference of opinion between two sisters in Philippi could only be resolved by being "of the same mind in the Lord", Phil. 4. 2. Thus they should have the mind of Christ, thereby ending differences of opinion. Paul exhorted the whole church at Philippi to "stand fast in the Lord", v. 1.

On very practical levels, believers must recognize elders in a local church, those who "are over you in the Lord", for this is a divinely-given function, 1 Thess. 5. 12. Marriage must be "in the Lord", 1 Cor. 7. 39, namely, not just to any partner, but to one mutually submissive to the same Lord.

READING: **Jude 8-25**

BUT, BELOVED, REMEMBER YE THE WORDS

THE CHRISTIAN life consists of looking to the future, to that blessed hope. In our service, we are also occupied very much with the present. But in many cases we also look back and contemplate the past; that is where the word "remember" often occurs. This is not a matter of mere past history, however valuable and interesting Biblical history can be. Rather we remember with a view to its effects in the present.

The best-known remembrance is that of the Lord's Supper, when the Lord said of the bread, "this do in remembrance of me", Luke 22. 19; 1 Cor. 11. 24, and also of the cup, "in remembrance of me", v. 25. It may be that some believers seldom remember anything other than this during the week. But there are many other things that we are exhorted to remember.

"Remember the word that I said unto you, The servant is not greater than his lord", John 15. 20. This was spoken earlier that evening in 13. 16, and shows that *every* remark of the Lord must be remembered and not overlooked.

"Remember the words of the Lord Jesus, how he said, It is more blessed to give than to receive", Acts 20. 35. This is remarkable, since this statement of the Lord does not appear in the four Gospels. It had been passed on by mouth, and has become enshrined in the written Scriptures. Nothing like that exists today; all truth that we have is recorded in the Scriptures. There is no passing on of verbal tradition, for this becomes altered, but what is written remains unaltered.

Referring to the man of sin, Paul wrote, "Remember ye not, that, when I was yet with you, I told you these things?", 2 Thess. 2. 5. We too must remember past ministry given by the Lord's servants; some stands out as of extreme value. Some of us may have happy memories of ministry heard 40 years ago!

Regarding false doctrines of the last times, and their correction from Scripture, Paul wrote, "If thou put the brethren in remembrance of these things, thou shalt be a good minister of Jesus Christ", 1 Tim. 4. 6. Thus teachers are responsible to be corrective in their ministry; what is heard must be remembered so as to lead to faithful living.

Finally, we must remember the words spoken by the apostles regarding the last times, Jude 17; 2 Pet. 1. 12, 15.

September 3rd

READING: **2 Chronicles 5. 1-14**

THINGS DEDICATED FOR THE HOUSE

WHEN THE TEMPLE was finished, it was empty, until Solomon brought in all that was suitable for God's presence, for God's house would be filled.

The house had been built according to divine instructions: David gave these instructions to his son, for he had received them by the Spirit, 1 Chron. 28. 11-12, 19, "the Lord made me understand in writing by his hand upon me". Today, Paul had the pattern of the church by the Spirit, but it is passed on to us by writing, namely in the inspired Scriptures. With such a vast undertaking before him, Solomon felt his weakness, "who am I then, that I should built him an house?", since he was "young and tender", 2 Chron. 2. 6; 1 Chron. 29. 1. Truly, the Lord must built the house, else natural labour is in vain, Psa. 127. 1, while Paul claimed, "I can do all things through Christ which strengtheneth me", Phil. 4. 13.

It is stressed that what was brought in was (i) the things that David had dedicated, and (ii) the ark that Moses had made, 2 Chron. 5. 1, 5. Nothing new was brought in. In the newly founded church, only the apostles and prophets were used by God to bring in new things. The silver and gold speak of the character of service that glorifies God, 1 Cor. 3. 12; the instruments speak of the means and abilities in service; the treasures speak of that which is laid up in heaven.

Where did David get the things from that Solomon dedicated to the Lord? (i) Of his "own proper good", 1 Chron. 29. 3, namely his own possessions (strictly from the Lord) that David redirected to the house. Today, this can refer to both material and spiritual possessions; all are held in trust for the Lord to use in His service. (ii) Other people had willing hearts, and gave precious stones, vv. 8, 14. Bringing to the service of a local assembly is not left to just one or two; all are intimately concerned. (iii) David's possessions on account of his being king, v. 2. These are distinguished from his personal possessions. A special calling in God's service enables some today to bring special material for the edification of the saints. (iv) Spoil gained in battle was dedicated to the Lord, 18. 11. Spiritual soldiers thus gain much for the Lord, 1 Tim. 6. 12; 2 Tim. 2. 1-4; 4. 7.

September 4th

READING: **Acts 4. 23-37**

ASSEMBLED TOGETHER

IN MATTHEW 18. 20, the Lord spoke of being gathered together in His Name. The verb used here corresponds to the noun "synagogue"; in the N.T., the verb is *not* used for gatherings in a Jewish synagogue, but it is used seven times for the gatherings of a local church. It is therefore important to note what these seven occasions refer to.

(1) *The Breaking of Bread*. When the disciples "came together to break bread" in Troas, Paul used the time up to midnight to preach to them, Acts 20. 7. The breaking of bread itself is an act of worship, as each believer partakes of the emblems in memory of the Lord Jesus.

(2) *A Prayer Meeting*, Acts 4. 31. "When they had prayed, the place was shaken where they were assembled together". Here is a prayer where Scripture was quoted before prayer was made, after which the prayer was answered.

(3) *A Teaching, or Ministry Meeting*, Acts 11. 26. Paul was brought to Antioch, and "a whole year they assembled themselves with the church, and taught much people", Acts 11. 26; this was the only way for individual and collective growth in the faith. This was not a case of: give it easily and receive it easily, for true learning means a deep digging of Scripture.

(4) *Bible Reading*, Acts 15. 30. Paul and others came to Antioch from Jerusalem; they "gathered the multitude together", and read a letter from Jerusalem. See Col. 4. 16. Today, we read the Scriptures, and study it by mutual conversation.

(5) *A Missionary Meeting*, Acts 14. 27. Having returned to Antioch at the end of their first journey, they "gathered the church together" to explain all that "God had done with them". All success must be recognized as coming through God working.

(6) *An Elders' Meeting*, Acts 15. 6. "The apostles and elders came together for to consider of this matter". There are occasions when some matters need to be discussed, firstly at least, out of the hearing of the rest of the church. The elders form a distinct group within a church, Acts 20. 17, and it is right for them to gather to consider the work that the Lord has laid upon them.

(7) *A Discipline Meeting*, 1 Cor. 5. 4. "When ye are gathered together". A list is given as to when a brother can be put outside a local church, v. 11, but be careful if one adds to this list!

READING: **Mark 6. 32-44**

THE LORD LOOKED UP TO HEAVEN

THE LORD JESUS possessed eyes as we do; what did He see? In Luke 6. 20, He lifted up His eyes on the poor of the flock; in Revelation 2. 18, His eyes were like a flame of fire in their discernment, causing Him to say, "I know thy works". But there were other occasions when the Lord looked upwards even to heaven; this is suggestive of eyes more than physical, for He could perceive things unseen in the heavenly realm where the Father dwelt. In our case, faith has spiritual eyes which can perceive things unseen. The sinner cannot lift up his eyes to heaven, Luke 18. 13, yet the believer can say, "Unto thee lift I up mine eyes", Psa. 123. 1. But in the Lord's case, we have the following four instances.

(1) *Relating to Conversion.* Just before the miracle of the raising of Lazarus, "Jesus lifted up his eyes, and said, Father, I thank thee that thou hast heard me", John 11. 41. As far as unbelievers are concerned, they are dead in sins, but the Lord looks to His Father so that they may receive life, being quickened and saved not by self but as the gift of God.

(2) *Relating to Confession.* The Lord was healing one that was deaf and could not speak properly. "Looking up to heaven, he sighed, and saith unto him, Ephphatha, that is, Be opened", Mark 7. 34. The man could now speak plainly, and the news was spread abroad. In our case, we are called upon to confess Him, Rom. 10. 10, and then He confesses us before His Father, Matt. 10. 32.

(3) *Relating to Comfort.* Certainly there was discomfort when 5,000 were hungry in the wilderness. But with a few loaves and fishes brought to Him, "he looked up to heaven, and blessed, and break", Mark 6. 41. Today, souls are comforted when fed with the Word of life; He looks to the Father that we may be fed with spiritual food.

(4) *Relating to Condition.* A few hours before He died, He "lifted up his eyes to heaven", John 17. 1. He was then praying for His disciples, that they should be kept from the evil, to sanctify them so that they could behold His glory. Has He looked to the Father that we too should have the blessings for which He prayed in this great prayer? May we expect the answer to this prayer, by entering into its provisions.

September 6th

READING: **Revelation 21. 22-27**

THE SUN

THE SUN is the most prominent body in the heavens, and it is obvious to all that it gives life, light and heat, without which the earth's surface would be a barren wilderness. Hence, on account of its prominence, men of all ages have been willing to treat it as a deity. Our popular word "Sunday" means "the day of the sun god". We read of some in the temple courts who "worshipped the sun toward the east", Ezek. 8. 16, something "which they have loved, served, sought, worshipped", Jer. 8. 2. Physically, the sun has its dangers too; it can be the source of forest and heath fires, and by means of its control over the weather it sometimes brings droughts. The sun causes day and night, and these shall not cease, Gen. 8. 22.

There have been strange events associated with the sun, that unbelievers would refuse to accept. Joshua's long day is an example, Josh. 10. 13, while in Hezekiah's day as a sign from the Lord the shadow cast by the sun on a sundial went backwards by ten degrees, 2 Kings 20. 9.

In a spiritual sense, the sun was eclipsed by greater events. The Lord has the true and absolute pre-eminence, so on the mountain top, "his face did shine as the sun, and his raiment was white as the light", Matt. 17. 2. By contrast, when He died on the cross, the sun hid its face, and "there was darkness over all the land", 27. 45.

Paul's conversion-experience was such that he saw a light "above the brightness of the sun", Acts 26. 13, that blinded him for a season, while John saw the face of the Lord "as the sun shineth in his strength", Rev. 1. 16.

In future judgments, the sun shall be darkened, Matt. 24. 29; Acts 2. 20. But ultimately, the Lord will be seen as "the Sun of righteousness", arising with healing in His wings, Mal. 4. 2, and hence the holy city of the future has no need of the natural sun, for "the Lamb is the light thereof", Rev. 21. 23. The natural sun remains for men on earth, since only when it ceases to exist will Israel cease to be a nation, Jer. 31. 36.

Today, in mercy, God causes the sun to shine on the evil and on the good, Matt. 5. 45; this is His providence. But in the future, the righteous shall "shine forth as the sun in the kingdom of their Father", 13. 43. We shall be like the Lord!

September 7th

READING: Luke 10. 25-37

WHO IS MY NEIGHBOUR?

SOME OF THE Lord's parables were designed to hide the truth, Matt. 13. 11-17, while others had a clear message for all to understand. The parable of the good Samaritan is of this latter type. Rightly we see in this parable a picture of the Lord Jesus who, so differently from the religious Jewish leaders around Him, did everything that He could to meet the spiritual needs of men in sin. That is what *we* see in this parable, but what was *the lawyer* intended to see?

The lawyer had introduced "thy neighbour" in verse 27, quoting from Leviticus 19. 18. The expert on the law wanted the Lord to interpret the meaning of "thy neighbour". A parable was all that was needed to do this clearly, but the lesson for the lawyer was that he should be a neighbour himself!

Jericho was a place of a curse, Josh 6. 17. Here was a man travelling backwards from Jerusalem to Jericho, like Abram from Bethel to Egypt, Gen. 12. 10, like Naomi from Bethlehem to Moab, Ruth 1. 1, and like some of the churches in Revelation 2-3. We have no hesitation is suggesting that the priest and Levite were also travelling down to Jericho, but that the good Samaritan was travelling to Jerusalem, although hostility would await him there. Only those who are facing in the right direction can offer help to those in spiritual need.

The Lord did not actually state who was the neighbour of the man who had fallen amongst thieves. He asked the question of the lawyer, and the answer was obvious. There was a man in need, and there was a man who met that need. The neighbour was the man who met that need. Hence, who was the lawyer's neighbour? Evidently *someone else* who met his personal need. So the lawyer had to recognize his own need, and see that there was a better than he who could meet that need; such had to be loved. The one who was helped had to love the one who had helped him. The parable did not present the matter the other way round, namely the love that the Samaritan had for the wounded man (though that love must have been genuine). Rather the Lord said, "Go, and do thou likewise". In other words, the lawyer had to act as the Samaritan, as a neighbour himself; only then could he know who was his own neighbour. Thus there were four neighbours: the Lord, the Samaritan, the lawyer, and his own neighbour.

September 8th

READING: **1 John 1. 1-10**

FELLOWSHIP

FELLOWSHIP in the Scriptures is not something that is half-hearted and fleeting; it is complete and lasting. It is so easy to talk about "having fellowship" or "being in fellowship", and applying this only to part of a believer's responsibility in a local church. We may give the word a technical importance, but really it means a sharing in common, a permanent bond of spiritual interests and priorities in the things of God. Consider the following aspects of fellowship:

Commencement. The bond of fellowship is formed by a relationship to the Father and His Son. This will distinguish Christian fellowship from worldly contacts such as clubs and associations. In 1 John 1. 3, the fact that the Son came into Manhood is the basis of "fellowship with us", the "us" being those who had witnessed His Manhood. But John adds that this fellowship is not only having things in common with the apostles (no doubt all of whom had passed away), but also with the Father and the Son, having minds and thoughts fashioned by the mind of Christ and by the divine will. Paul called this "the fellowship of his Son", 1 Cor. 1. 9.

Continuation. Fellowship is something continuous, as the early church "continued stedfastly in the apostles' doctrine and fellowship", Acts 2. 42. This took place after the baptism of those early believers; it was a new sphere of living.

Conditions. It is remarkable that these conditions as recorded in the N.T. appear to be very negative. There should be no fellowship with demons, 1 Cor. 10. 20, namely, with false religious practices. Righteousness has no fellowship with unrighteousness, light has no communion with darkness, 2 Cor. 6. 14. God's people are exhorted to come out of contact with mystery Babylon, being not *partakers* of her sins, Rev. 18. 4. There must be "no fellowship with the unfruitful works of darkness", Eph. 5. 11. This corresponds to 1 John 1. 6, "If we say that we have fellowship with him, and walk in darkness, we lie, and do not the truth". We walk in the light.

Cooperation in service. We must show the "right hands of fellowship", Gal. 2. 9, in God's service. There is "fellowship in the gospel", Phil. 1. 5, and practically "the fellowship of the ministering to the saints", 2 Cor. 8. 4.

READING: **Psalm 8**

SMALLNESS

GOD IS God of things great and small in His universe, whether we think of the vast nebulae at vast distances from the earth, or the almost infinitesimal particles that compose the atoms of God's creation. As far as we know, David did not have revealed to him these great discoveries of modern times, yet clearly he knew something, and that led him to ask, "What is man?", as if seemingly he was insignificant when contrasted with greater things. Yet man was visited by God, who had dealings with man in ways far above God's visitations on other parts of His creation. Man may be small, yet he fills an important part in God's purpose. It is good therefore to note how God takes up things that are small, even "things which are not", 1 Cor. 1. 28, so that no flesh should boast. Indeed, the weak things chosen by God are intended "to confound the things which are mighty", v. 27, and this includes the mighty beasts of the world empires described in Daniel 7.

The manna in the wilderness was "a small round thing", yet God used this to feed a mighty nation for forty years until it ceased, Exod. 16. 14. David was the youngest son of Jesse, and Goliath was a giant, but faith in God provided David the victory when only one pebble out of five was used in his sling, 1 Sam. 17. 49. A little maid was used to initiate circumstances for the healing of Naaman, 2 Kings 5. 3. "Seek them not" said the Lord to one who might have sought great things for himself, Jer. 45. 5. Bethlehem was "little among the thousands of Judah", Mic. 5. 2, yet here was a town from which the Ruler in Israel would come forth. There were only five loaves and two fishes, Matt. 14. 17, yet that was sufficient for the Lord to feed the 5,000.

No wonder conversion is likened by the Lord to "little children", Matt. 18. 3. The Lord looked upon His disciples, and viewed them as a "little flock": through them all service would be worked out, Luke 12. 32. In his service, Paul regarded himself as "the least of the apostles", 1 Cor. 15. 9, and "less than the least of all saints", Eph. 3. 8; such a man God could used mightily! God gives grace to the humble, and they shall be exalted in due time, 1 Pet. 5. 5-6, but the mighty are put down, and the rich sent empty away, Luke 1. 52.

September 10th

READING: 1 Corinthians 7. 16-24

THE UNIVERSAL APPEAL OF FIRST CORINTHIANS

IT IS not correct to say that the Corinthians were so much in the wrong that they deserved the Epistle that Paul wrote to them, but it has nothing much to do with us. Neither is it correct to state, "That is Paul", again as if it has nothing much to do with us. Rather the point is that all Scripture is profitable, and when writing this Epistle Paul had its universal value very much before his mind. This is evident from many verses in the Epistle, and it must therefore have been in the mind of the Spirit of inspiration. The point is that, if some part of the N.T. proves to be too pointed for some believers of the modern generation, then they can easily reject it from their "more enlightened" understanding. We may thus consider briefly the proof of its universal appeal.

Paul addressed the Epistle, not only to the church of God at Corinth, but to "all that in every place call upon the name of Jesus Christ our Lord, both theirs and ours", 1 Cor. 1. 2. So Paul himself knew that the Epistle would be read far and wide, the Lordship of Christ being the common bond between churches.

In 1 Corinthians 4. 17, Paul states that both he and Timothy had a united policy regarding what is taught in the churches; "as I teach every where in every church". In other words, no church is outside the range of Paul's teaching, and any servant like Timothy must restrict his teaching to what is found in the Scriptures. Nothing else can be valid.

In the context of 7. 17, Paul states that every man has his proper calling from God in many spheres. Believers must not go outside this calling, and he insists that he has ordained this truth in "all churches". None is exempt.

In 1 Corinthians 11. 2-16, Paul argues successfully why men should have their heads uncovered and why women should have their heads covered in a gathering of the church. He suspected that some would be contentious about the matter, but "the churches of God" have no custom to be contentious.

What Paul writes "are the commandments of the Lord", and hence are applicable at all times, 14. 37. The word was not restricted to Corinth only, v. 36.

Paul's exhortations were intended not for Corinth only, but for "the churches of Galatia" as well, 16. 1.

September 11th

READING: **Zechariah 14. 16-21**

NO MORE THE CANAANITE IN THE HOUSE

WHAT A GLORIOUS prospect in the day yet to come, when there shall be "no more the Canaanite in the house of the Lord of hosts". When the details of the tabernacle were given, all was to be "Holiness to the Lord", Exod. 28. 36, but later the Canaanite in every form of unholiness was introduced by men into the house. Thus Nadab and Abihu introduced strange incense, Lev. 10. 1. Solomon introduced idols on the mount of Olives, the nearest place that he dared introduce them, 1 Kings 11. 1. The sons of Athaliah had broken up the house of God, and had bestowed the dedicated things to Baalim, 2 Chron. 24. 7. Hezekiah caused all the idolatrous refuse to be taken out of the house of the Lord, 29. 5, 16. Josiah did the same thing later, for the house was full of the vessels made for Baal, 2 Kings 23. 4-6. Asaph complained that the enemy had done wickedly in the sanctuary, Psa. 74. 3, and that the holy temple had defiled by the heathen, 79. 1. The Lord knew that "strangers are come into the sanctuaries of the Lord's house", Jer. 51. 51, and that the heathen had entered into the sanctuaries, Lam. 1. 10. Even the priests had polluted the sanctuary, Zeph. 3. 4. For example, the priest Eliashib prepared a room in the house for Tobiah the Ammonite and his possessions, Neh. 13. 4-8. What a catalogue!, and many other examples can be found in the O.T. If the reader has time, he should read the whole of Ezekiel 44. How thankful we must be that, in the future, the Canaanite will be entirely kept out.

Alas, in the present day, the Canaanite can be found in local churches; each of these should be a holy temple, 1 Cor. 3. 17. But false men and deeds have sometimes found it easy to enter. In Acts 5. 1-6, Ananias had tempted the Holy Spirit by lies to the apostles. There emerged false teaching by certain Pharisees which believed, 15. 5. The world had come into the Corinthian church, meaning that some believers were walking "as men", 1 Cor. 3. 3. False brethren had bewitched the Galatians, Gal. 2. 4; 3. 1. There were those who were spoiling the Colossians with philosophy and the tradition of men, Col. 2. 8. Some were being deceived, 2 Thess. 2. 2-3, while there were "things that are wanting" in Crete, Titus 1. 5. Hence may we beware, Acts 20. 28-30.

September 12th

READING: **John 20. 11-31**

"MY LORD"

ALREADY ON pages 244 and 245 we have considered the title "Lord" and the believer's position "in the Lord". We may now consider the actual profession "my Lord" that appears five times in the N.T. It represents an individual confession of ownership, the believer owing the Lord, and the Lord owning the believer. More particularly, on page 100 we have considered the Lord's possession, exemplified by His word "My".

(1) *Lord prior to His birth*, Elizabath to Mary: "whence is this to me, that the mother of my Lord should come to me?", Luke 1. 43. It was because she was filled with the Holy Spirit that she could make such a statement. Only by faith could she know that the Lord would soon appear in the flesh, and she also knew the power of the Lord, both in herself and in Mary, vv. 25, 43.

(2) *Lord in death*, Mary Magdalene to the unrecognized Lord who she thought was still dead. "They have taken away my Lord, and I know not where they have laid him", she said, John 20. 13. She still confessed Him as Lord, even though she thought that He was dead. Her recognition of Him as "Master" changed to "Lord" when speaking to the disciples, vv. 16-18.

(3) *Lord in resurrection*, Thomas directly to the Lord: "My Lord and my God", John 20. 28. In the upper room after the first appearance, Thomas had not believed the apostles' testimony, but at the second appearance there was nothing else that he could do but humbly to undo his faithlessness by this great confession directly to the Lord. After such a confession of Deity and absolute authority, a man cannot be the same again!

(4) *Lord in ascension*, spoken by David, and quoted by the Lord, then by Peter and by the writer of the Epistle to the Hebrews: "The Lord said unto my Lord, Sit thou on my right hand, till I make thine enemies thy footstool", Psa. 110. 1; Matt. 22. 44; Mark 12. 36; Luke 20. 42; Acts 2. 34-35; Heb. 1. 13. All believers can confess that *their* Lord has been exalted to such heights of glory and authority.

(5) *Lord in the heart*, written by Paul to the Philippians: "I count all things but loss for the excellency of the knowledge of Christ Jesus my Lord", Phil. 3. 8. Here is no religious attainment, but one in subjection to the divine authority.

September 13th

READING: **1 Peter 3. 12-22**

THE OUT AND IN OF BAPTISM

A WEB of confusion has been woven by tradition in many minds regarding baptism. Such minds may get very angry if it is shown that Scripture is different from tradition. Baptism does not save in the sense of conversion. It certainly does not replace the value of the blood of Christ that cleanses from all sin. As verse 21 puts it, baptism does not put away the filth of the flesh; rather it is a signpost pointing away from the past activity of the flesh, to the opposite pathway according to God's will. That is what Acts 22. 16 means, "arise, and be baptized, and wash away thy sins". Practically, Paul (as Saul) would eliminate the practice of pre-conversion sin. We may mention four O.T. illustrations.

(1) *Noah.* Eight souls being saved by means of the ark in the days of Noah is a picture of baptism, 1 Pet. 3. 20. Noah was taken out of the world dominated before the flood by sin to a new world afterwards, and that by means of water. This answers to Romans 6. 4, where we are buried with Christ "by baptism into death", and then we walk in newness of life.

(2) *Red Sea.* After the Passover redemption by blood, almost immediately the children of Israel came out of Egypt through the Red Sea, so as to journey to the promised land. In 1 Corinthians 10. 2, Paul wrote that they "were all baptized unto Moses in the cloud and in the sea". This wrought a change; for they were to be worshippers in the wilderness. It was the same in Acts 2. 42; having been baptized, they continued stedfastly in fellowship and Breaking of Bread.

(3) *Crossing of Jordan.* Twelve stones were left in the river Jordan, Josh. 4. 9, while another twelve from the Jordan were taken to the other side, vv. 1-3, 20-24. This is a picture of baptism; the old man was left in death, while the new man manifests the new life in Christ.

(4) *Jonah.* Jonah went down into the depths, and was brought up again to live a new life. This also is a type of baptism, where we see the thoughts of "in" and "out".

There is a warning. Afterwards, Noah got drunk, Gen. 9. 21; there was murmuring after the things of Egypt, Exod. 16. 3; Achan stole from Jericho, Josh. 7. 1; Jonah still grumbled, Jon. 4. 1. In all this, where was the out and in of baptism?

257

September 14th

READING: **1 Kings 8. 1-11**

THE CONTENTS OF THE ARK

VERSE 9, "There was nothing in the ark save the two tables of stone", must be contrasted with Hebrews 9. 4, "the ark of the covenant . . . wherein was the golden pot that had manna, and Aaron's rod that budded, and the tables of the covenant".

The facts. The two stones containing the commandments were placed in the ark, Exod. 25. 16; 40. 20. This is God's side of the covenant, the standard demanded of men in keeping with His holiness. Man's side is seen in Romans 7. 10, where the commandment, ordained to life, was found to be unto death.

In Exodus 16. 32, a pot had to be filled with manna, to be laid up before the Lord. This was to be a memorial in years to come, the bread of life that God had provided for the people in the wilderness.

In Numbers 17. 8, God chose Aaron's rod that had budded and produced almonds in the tabernacle; this rod of life had to be laid up before the testimony as a token, v. 10. This speaks of Christ's authority as risen, choosing His servants to serve Him in the sanctuary, away from the scenes of rebellion.

Moses had to write "the words of this law in a book", and this was placed "in the side of the ark", Deut. 31. 24-26; this would be a witness against the people and their rebellion.

Interpretation. But when the ark was brought into the temple by Solomon nearly 500 years later, all the contents had disappeared except the tables of stone. According to the record, the only time when the ark had been in the enemies' hands was when the Philistines captured it, 1 Sam. 5. 1, and then returned it with items of gold, 6. 5, 8, 15, being relics of idolatry. It appears that they stole the miraculous manna and rod that budded. In other words, they wanted life and not death, so left the unkeepable tables of stone. The children of Israel thus had only that which spoke of death.

It is the same today. Christ as the Life is not desired, and men speak only of His moral qualities. They prefer to be under the law (although they cannot keep the law), and reject the concept of life coming through faith in His Name. They have no desire for the Bread of Life, John 6. 35, and the fact that His Lordship and authority show up the rebellion in the hearts and lives of men. May we appreciate all the contents of the ark!

September 15th

READING: **Psalm 132**

RESTORATION OF THE CONTENTS OF THE ARK

YESTERDAY WE saw that the contents of the ark, except the tables of stone, had been removed, and when the ark was brought by Solomon into the temple at its dedication, 1 Kings 8. 9 states that there was "nothing in the ark" except these tables of stone. Then Solomon spoke his great dedicatory prayer. In particular, the closing verses of this prayer, 2 Chron. 6. 41-42, are similar to Psalm 132. 8-10, which we believe was spoken by Solomon on this occasion. Solomon recalls the past, vv. 1-7; he prays in the present, vv. 8-13; he quotes the Lord's reply for the future, vv. 14-18. The psalm concerns the ark, the rest of God, and the throne.

The types and shadows that looked forward to Christ were gradually removed during O.T. times by various means. But the book of Revelation is full of references to the tabernacle symbolism, showing that there is a restoration in the future of that which had been done away (spiritually, of course). And this is also found in the O.T., for Psalm 132 contains oblique references to the restoration of what had been lost.

The ark was restored, as Josiah later commanded the ark to be placed in the house in Jerusalem, 2 Chron. 35. 3. As Solomon said, "in it have I put the ark", 6. 11. This corresponds to the Lord Jesus being given His rightful place from hearts and lives that previously had been going astray.

In Psalm 132. 12, we read, "If thy children will keep my covenant and my testimony that I shall teach them"; this refers to the two stones of the covenant, but it looks forward to the new covenant, for God will put His laws in their mind, and will write them in their hearts, Heb. 8. 10. The old stones would give place to a new covenant in Christ.

In Psalm 132. 15, God has promised, "I will satisfy her poor with bread". Here is the replacement of the manna in the golden pot. No longer hidden within the ark, but available for all the poor of God's people, for to them He has sent His Son to be the true Bread from heaven, John 6. 32.

In Psalm 132. 17, God will make the horn of David to bud. A horn refers to power, as in 1 Kings 22. 11. The line of David would bud when the Lord Jesus came forth, and in Him there is restoration, for He has all power and life.

September 16th

READING: **Matthew 11. 20-30**

"MY FATHER"

WE HAVE considered the believer's profession "my Lord" on page 256; it is good now to consider the Son's profession "my Father". The title "Father" appears about fifty times in the four Gospels. "Your Father", spoken by the Lord, appears fifteen times in Matthew, Mark and Luke, but this does not appear in John's Gospel until after the resurrection, 20. 17.

But the Lord's usage of the intimate title "My Father" comes in fourteen times in the Gospels, in contexts showing the mutual activity behind this intimate relationship. Thus He said to the Jews, "My Father worketh hitherto, and I work", John 5. 17, implying His Deity. We may consider some of these.

What is given to the Son. In what appears to be an explanation of a prayer, He said (and was heard by His disciples), "All things are delivered unto me of my Father", Matt. 11. 27. He said to the people, "as my Father hath taught me, I speak these things", John 12. 28. Speaking of His sheep, He said, "My Father, which gave them me, is greater than all", 10. 29. Outside the Gospels, He said to the church at Thyatira, "as I received of my Father", Rev. 2. 27.

The Father's activity towards the Son. The Son sought not His own glory, but said, "it is my Father that honoureth (glorifieth) me", John 8. 54. Because He would lay down His life, He stated, "Therefore doth my Father love me", 10. 17, and in resurrection He said, "as my Father hath sent me, even so send I you", 20. 21. These three quotations show activity of the Father directed towards the Son.

The Father's activity towards His people. Concerning the revelation that Peter had about the Son, the Lord declared that this came from "my Father which is in heaven", Matt. 16. 17. If two or three would agree in prayer, "it shall be done for them of my Father which is in heaven", 18. 19. Speaking about a privileged position in heaven, He said, "it shall be given to them for whom it is prepared of my Father", 20. 23. In John's Gospel, the Lord declared, "my Father giveth you the true bread from heaven", 6. 32. In the same discourse, He said that no man could come to Him "except it were given unto him of my Father", 6. 65. Finally, He taught that "he that loveth me shall be loved of my Father", 14. 21. How the Lord valued this relationship!

September 17th

READING: **Hebrews 11. 1-19**

AN OPPORTUNITY TO HAVE RETURNED

IN THE ORDERLY progress of revelation from Genesis to Revelation, God went forwards. In His dealings with men, and the outworking of His purpose, He went forwards, as seen in the order adopted in Hebrews 11. In Ezekiel 1. 12, the cherubim "went every one straight forward"; where the spirit was to go, they went. In the Lord's case, "he stedfastly set his face to go to Jerusalem", Luke 9. 51, in keeping with Isaiah 50. 5, "neither turned away back". The Lord enunciated the general principle for those who take up their cross to follow Him, "No man, having put his hand to the plough, and looking back, is fit for the kingdom of God", Luke 9. 23, 62.

We see this principle worked out in the experience of Abraham. He came out of Ur of the Chaldees, Heb. 11. 8, and after that he was one of the pilgrims and strangers on earth, with no desire to go back to his original sphere of idolatry without God, "if they had been mindful of that country whence they came out, they might have had the opportunity to have returned", v. 15. Rather, his eye was always forwards to the unseen promises of God. In practice afterwards, God's people were not always so faithful.

Soon after the exodus from Egypt, the children of Israel were mindful of the flesh pots in Egypt, and were dissatisfied with their wilderness conditions, Exod. 16. 3. Later, in the wilderness, they were mindful of "the fish, which we did eat in Egypt freely", Num. 11. 5, being dissatisfied with the manna which God provided. Then, having heard the report of the spies, they demanded, "Let us make a captain, and let us return into Egypt", 14. 4. At the end of the wanderings, God stated that any future king was not to "cause the people to return to Egypt", Deut. 17. 16. Stephen summed this up, "in their hearts (they) turned back again into Egypt", Acts 7. 39.

We find similar things in the N.T. Peter had been brought to the Lord in John 1. 42, but afterwards had returned to his fishing practice, Luke 5. 8-11. The Galatians were building again the things they had once destroyed; Paul would not do this! The Hebrews were returning to Jewish ceremony. But Paul always desired to forget those things that were behind, so as to reach forward to the things that are before, Phil. 3. 13.

261

September 18th

READING: Acts 21. 1-17

THE EVANGELIST

THIS WORD "evangelist" describes certain believers with a certain spiritual gift and calling from the Lord. To our ears, it is a very familiar word, yet it occurs only three times in the N.T. The cognate words "gospel" (or evangel) and evangelize (or, to preach the gospel, etc.) occur far more frequently, as a concordance will show. An evangelist is a man who announces the good tidings, these good tidings having originated from God and not from man, Gal. 1. 1-12. We shall examine the three times the word "evangelist" occurs.

(1) *Men with a gift.* In Ephesians 4. 11, Paul has provided a short list of names attached to gifted men in the church. He makes it quite clear that the Giver is the Risen Lord who has ascended on high. Men do not choose "apostles, prophets, evangelists, pastors and teachers", neither do they equip them for their sphere of service. The Lord Jesus also was an Apostle, Heb. 3. 1; He was a Prophet, as when He said, "No prophet is accepted in his own country", Luke 4. 24; He was a Pastor as the Good Shepherd, John 10. 14; He was a Teacher, "I then, your Lord and Master (Teacher)", John 13. 14. But He was never called an Evangelist, although He preached the gospel on many occasions, Mark 1. 14. We wonder why He was never called an Evangelist (perhaps to avoid confusion with the word "angel" that is clearly embedded in the word itself, though this is not an exact embedding in the corresponding Greek nouns).

(2) *Philip the evangelist.* On his journey to Jerusalem with a large sum of money from the Gentile churches, Paul and his company "entered into the house of Philip the evangelist" in Caesarea, Acts 21. 8. Twenty-seven years before, Philip had been chosen to deal with financial matters in Jerusalem, 6. 5, a man already gifted in spiritual things. He evangelized in Samaria, and baptized the eunuch, 8. 36-39. He testified to many or to few, and retained his gift for many years.

(3) *Timothy.* One of Paul's last exhortations was, "do the work of an evangelist", 2 Tim. 4. 5. And this in spite of the fact that men would not endure sound doctrine, turning their ears from the truth, vv. 3-4. Such faithful men may well be as sheep amongst wolves.

262

September 19th

READING: Luke 10. 38-42

THE VILLAGE OF BETHANY

THIS VILLAGE of Bethany, meaning a house of dates or figs, lay on the eastern slopes of the mount of Olives; the city of Jerusalem lay on its western side. Whereas there was no place in Jerusalem where the Lord could stay, yet there was a home in Bethany where hospitality was offered. We may note the following points about this village.

(1) *Serving, Sitting*. Bethany was a "certain" village, and Martha a "certain" woman, Luke 10. 38. The difference between the occupations of Mary and Martha is noteworthy; one was the woman of the heart, the other of the hands. Both were necessary; the Lord provided the word for Mary, and Martha provided the food for the Lord.

(2) *Sickness, Salvation*. Lazarus "of Bethany", John 11. 1, was sick and died. The faith of both Martha and Mary was tested. Both confessed that if the Lord had been with them, then Lazarus would not have died. But only Martha confessed that He was "the Christ, the Son of God", v. 27. No doubt she learnt this on the previous occasion, although she had been serving rather than listening to His word.

(3) *Supper, Spikenard, Serving*. Six days before the Passover, the Lord was invited to a supper at this hospitable home in Bethany, John 12. 1. Martha again served, but Mary anointed the Lord's feet with spikenard. Judas grumbled as a thief, and would have loved to have had the money instead.

(4) *Sending, Sitting, Song*. The Lord sent two disciples to the village to fetch a colt, and then He rode in triumph as King into Jerusalem, acclaimed in song by His disciples, Mark 11. 1. But in Jerusalem, His throne would be a cross.

(5) *Sleeping, Safety*. During the last week, the Lord passed the nights in the safety of Bethany, Mark 11. 12; Luke 21. 37. "I will both lay me down in peace, and sleep: for thou, Lord, only makest me dwell in safety", Psa. 4. 8.

(6) *Sacrifice, Supper*. Two days before the Passover there was another supper in Bethany, Matt. 26. 2, 6. This time the Lord's head was anointed, but the disciples grumbled.

(7) *Separation*. Acts 1. 12 informs us that the Lord ascended to heaven from Olivet, but the place was Bethany, Luke 24. 50; "he was parted from them . . . into heaven".

September 20th

READING: **Joshua 1. 1-9**

THE STUDY OF THE SCRIPTURES

JOSHUA WAS responsible to meditate day and night in the book of the law, Josh. 1. 8. By this means there would be good success and prosperity in his service. Likewise the godly man in Psalm 1. 2 delighted to meditate day and night in the law of the Lord, leading to prosperity in all that he did. In the N.T., the Lord exhorted men to "Search the scriptures", John 5. 39, while the Bereans "searched the scriptures daily", Acts 17. 11, in order to test Paul's doctrine about Christ in the light of the O.T. Scriptures. Conversely, a lack of Bible study leads to barrenness and weakness in worship and service.

Certainly teachers are supplied by God in local churches, Eph. 4. 11, but there must also be diligent study at home. The Holy Spirit has been sent to guide into all truth, John 16. 13; thus a brother who appears to be a mine of information at a Bible Reading has spent long hours of work at home. There can be distractions at home, in which case the study of the Scriptures is the first thing to suffer. But may there not be materialistic pursuits for one's own pleasure, when one can be occupied with the things that are seen, 2 Cor. 4. 18.

There may be no incentive to study; this can be overcome by sensing the necessity of study and the blessings that flow from it. Job said, "I have esteemed the words of his mouth more than my necessary food", Job 23. 12. There is a spiritual appetite when one has this valuation of the Word of God. Also Bible study must not be superficial; a quick reading each morning is not real study; time and experience are necessary to seek out the meaning and application of each verse. Thus the Jews knew not "the voice of the prophets", although they were read each Sabbath day, Acts 13. 27. Again, Bible study is not academic, as may be found in a theological college, and as demonstrated by the N.T. scribes and lawyers. Instead, may we say, "I have more understanding that all my teachers", Psa. 119. 99, because the Spirit "communicates spiritual things by spiritual means", 1 Cor. 2. 12 *lit*.

Start learning the Scriptures when one is young, and this will lead to prosperous service later. For example, Timothy started to learn the Scriptures as a child, 2 Tim. 3. 15, and then he commenced to serve with Paul later, Acts 16. 11-3.

September 21st

READING: **Ephesians 6. 1-9**

PARENTS AND CHILDREN

THERE ARE good parents and bad parents, good children and bad children. Obviously these can be combined in four ways, and examples can be given from the Scriptures that illustrate these four possible combinations of parents and children.

(1) *Bad parent, bad child.* We may mention the various kings of the northern kingdom, namely Israel. The kingship passed from family to family, but sometimes a son was proclaimed king when his father died. The first king was Jeroboam, who reigned for twenty-two years; his son Nadab was king after him, 1 Kings 14. 20. Jeroboam is described by God as "(thou) hast done evil above all that were before thee", v. 9, while his son Nadab is described as: "he did evil in the sight of the Lord, and walked in the way of his father, and in his sin wherewith he made Israel to sin", 15. 26. The bad influence of the idolatrous father passed on to the son.

(2) *Bad parent, good child.* Ahaz king of Judah was awful in the extreme. He made molten images, 2 Chron. 28. 2; he took away a portion from the house of the Lord, v. 21, and shut up its doors, v. 24. But his son Hezekiah, although brought up in this idolatrous atmosphere, did "right in the sight of the Lord", 29. 2; he opened the doors of the house, and cast out all the evil contained therein, vv. 5, 16.

(3) *Good parent, bad child.* Many examples will come to the mind of the reader, something that some Christian parents have to sustain when their children depart from the truth of the Lord Jesus. Aaron was a man sanctified for divine service by blood, Lev. 8. 30. His two sons Nadab and Abihu passed through the same ritual, but their hearts were far from the commandments of the Lord. In a state of drunkenness, they offered foreign incense to the Lord, and this led to their death before the Lord, 10. 1-2.

(4) *Good parent, good child.* We think of the unfeigned faith that dwelt in Eunice, the mother of Timothy, and which later was found in her son Timothy as well, 2 Tim. 1. 5. He had known the Scriptures from a child, 3. 15, and had been saved, not through works but according to God's purpose and grace, 1. 9. He had to learn to be a good soldier of Jesus Christ, 2. 3, continuing in the things he had learnt, 3. 14.

September 22nd

READING: **1 Peter 2. 1-8**

FEATURES OF A SPIRITUAL HOUSE

ACCORDING TO the Holy Spirit through Peter, we are "built up a spiritual house", 2. 5. The particular object in these verses is that the living stones should "offer up spiritual sacrifices". But there is a range of features that pertain to a spiritual house, and we may consider some of these.

A place of sonship. In a spirit of repentance, the prodigal son returned to his father's house, Luke 15. 20. The best robe speaks of the beauty of sonship, while the ring speaks of dignity and authority. Children (in 1 John) imply beginnings; sons (in Paul) imply endings, brought to glory.

A place of worship. The tomb in John 11 led to the table in the house at Bethany, 12. 1-3. In Lazarus, Martha and Mary we can see witness, work and worship.

A place of unity. A house divided against itself cannot stand, said the Lord Jesus, Matt. 12. 25. Hence the unity of believers in local churches should be a matter of great importance. Thus Paul exhorted the Corinthians to "speak the same thing, and that there be no divisions among you", 1 Cor. 1. 10, while in Ephesians 4. 3-6 he wrote of the necessity of keeping the unity of the Spirit.

A place of sacrifice. After Solomon's dedication of the temple, God appeared to him in a dream, saying, "I have heard thy prayer, and have chosen this place to myself for an house of sacrifice", 2 Chron. 7. 12. This is to be done today "continually", Heb. 13. 15. Note how Job worshipped God, in spite of calamities that were falling around him, Job 1. 20.

A place of prayer. Through Isaiah, God said, "mine house shall be called an house of prayer for all people" ("house of prayer" is mentioned twice in the verse), Isa. 56. 7. Prayer is not just for an emergency, though it was in the house of Mary in Jerusalem in Acts 12. 12, where many were praying together.

A place of holiness. "Holiness becometh thine house, O Lord, for ever", Psa. 93. 5. Reverence in God's presence is of paramount importance: "the temple of God is holy, which temple ye are", 1 Cor. 3. 17.

A place of evangelism. The Lord claimed in a parable, "my house may be filled", Luke 14. 23, and that by the gospel message of invitation. This happened in Acts 10.

September 23rd

READING: **Isaiah 1. 1-31**

SURVEY OF ISAIAH

IT IS GOOD to have a survey of a Bible book, whether the book is long or short. In reading the book through, we then have a framework on which to build our understanding of the progress of thought through the book. However dreadful many chapters of the prophets may be, the usual objective is to introduce ultimate restoration. In Isaiah, the restoration is of Zion, in Jeremiah of affections, in Ezekiel of God's glory, and in Daniel of Christ's kingdom and authority.

Isaiah testified for God during troublous times, when God's judgment was falling on the northern kingdom through the Assyrian invasion, and when its effects upon Jerusalem were also being felt throughout Judaea. We may summarize the prophecy of Isaiah as follows:

Chapters 1-12. Here spiritual lessons are drawn from the Assyrian invasion. The sin of Judah is detailed, yet with many prospects of restoration, the glories of Messiah and the salvation of the inhabitants of Zion.

Chapters 13-27. It was the nations that surrounded Israel that led God's people astray. Here, these nations are subjugated, with Zion the centre of God's government.

Chapters 28-35. Here we have the moral invasion of Judah, with many fleeting glimpses of restoration scenes.

Chapters 36-39. These are purely historical chapters, showing how God effected the deliverance of Jerusalem from the invading Assyrians, and Hezekiah's recovery from sickness. In a prophetic sense, this history from the past is a picture of Israel's future deliverance from the great tribulation, and the nation's recovery from the spiritual death of unbelief.

Chapters 40 to 52. 6. Here is a growing crescendo of truth concerning restoration; we find mention of Cyrus, and certain prophetic details of the Lord's life.

Chapters 52. 7 to 63. Here we have the only basis of redemption, namely through Christ. Thus in chapters 54-62, we read details of the ultimate scope of millennial blessings, while in chapters 63-66 we have the application of these promises to the period when Isaiah was prophesying.

The fact that Isaiah is so often quoted in the N.T. is sufficient proof that it is also of value to believers today.

September 24th

READING: **2 Thessalonians 2. 1-12**

CHRIST AND ANTICHRIST CONTRASTED

IN THE FUTURE, prior to the manifestation of Christ as King of kings and Lord of lords, there will be manifested the political beast, the false prophet or the antichrist, and Mystery Babylon. In a measure, these may be working in the present, but their fully-developed nature will only be active after the rapture when the church is taken. We will extract various words from this chapter applying to the antichrist, the man of sin, and provide complete contrasts in verses that show the holy nature and life of the Lord Jesus.

Verse 3. "Man of sin": *contrast*, "this man hath done nothing amiss", Luke 23. 41. "Revealed": *contrast*, "in the day when the Son of man is revealed", 17. 30. "Son of perdition": *contrast*, "the Son of the living God", Matt. 16. 16.

Verse 4. "Opposeth": *contrast*, "not as I will, but as thou wilt", Matt. 26. 39. "Exalteth himself": *contrast*, "Him hath God exalted with his right hand", Acts 5. 31. "Above": *contrast*, "far above all principality, and power, and might, and dominion", Eph. 1. 21. "Worshipped": *contrast*, "they . . . fell down, and worshipped him", Matt. 2. 11. "In the temple": *contrast*, "in the day time he was teaching in the temple", Luke 21. 37. "That he is God": *contrast*, "he that hath seen me hath seen the Father", John 14. 9.

Verse 7. "The mystery of iniquity": *contrast*, "I always do those things that please him", John 8. 29. "Doth already work" but worse in the future: *contrast*, "I must work the works of him that sent me", John 9. 4.

Verse 8. "That Wicked (one)": *contrast*, "The Holy One and the Just", Acts 3. 14. "Whom the Lord shall consume": *contrast*, "thou remainest . . . thou art the same, and thy years shall not fail", Heb. 1. 11-12.

Verse 9. "Whose coming is after the working of Satan", *contrast*, "the Father that dwelleth in me, he doeth the works", John 14. 10. "All power and signs and lying wonders": *contrast*, "a man approved of God among you by miracles and wonders and signs", Acts 2. 22.

The description of the antichrist is limited in the number of verses devoted to him in the N.T., but as far as Christ is concerned, the verses above can be multiplied many-fold.

September 25th

READING: **Jeremiah 36. 1-26**

THE STORY OF A COLD DAY

THE PROPHET Jeremiah had been preaching for 22 years, when he had the command from the Lord to write in a book all the words that the Lord had spoken through him over the years, v. 2. The people would then know that they had to turn from their evil, so that God could forgive their iniquity, v. 3.

Baruch wrote the book from the mouth of Jeremiah, v. 4, and then he had to go and read these words in the temple, words that are described as "the words of the Lord", v. 6. This is how the Word of God gets around. A man named Michaiah heard these words, and went and told the princes all that he had heard, vv. 11-12. They were fearful when they heard the reading, and determined to tell the king, suggesting that Baruch and Jeremiah should hide, vv. 16-17.

The princes told the king about the words of the book, though they did not take the book with them, v. 20. So Jehudi fetched the book, and started to read it before the king who was sitting in his winterhouse before the fire. After three or four pages had been read, the king without any fear took the roll and cast it into the fire, "until all the roll was consumed", v. 23. Three of the princes protested to the king, but he would not listen to them, v. 25.

The king sought to punish Baruch and Jeremiah, "but the Lord hid them", v. 26, and instructed another copy to be made, with additional material, v. 32. This is the book of Jeremiah that we have today, showing the preserving hand of God who has preserved the Scriptures even to the present day, through periods of attack when Bibles were destroyed and burnt.

This story is very similar to that of the Lord Jesus as the Word of God. He came for men to see and hear, with the message that men should repent so as to be forgiven. Until one cold night, when Peter denied the Lord before a fire, when men sought to kill the Lord by crucifying Him on the cross. But the Word appeared again in resurrection, not now to the Jewish authorities, but to the chosen few, and He lives in heaven for evermore, where no attacks can reach Him there.

So these events effectively happened twice, to the written Word of God, and to the Lord Jesus as the Word of God. Today, believers have both, which cannot be taken away.

September 26th

READING: **Romans 11. 26-36**

OF HIM, THROUGH HIM, TO HIM

CHAPTERS 9-11 show how God will take up again His earthly people, and the means that He will use caused Paul to end this section with words of wonder and praise. Therefore Paul wrote, "For of him, and through him, and to him, are all things", v. 36, referring to the Source, the Channel and the Return; this is like the circulation of the waters: the rain comes down from the skies, the water runs to the seas, and evaporation takes place with the vapour returning to the skies again. "Source, Guide and Goal of all that is" is how one translation renders it as a paraphrase.

Considering verses 34-35, we note that "the mind of the Lord" refers to the Source; the absence of any counsellor to the fact that He works all things according to His will as the Channel; and that none has given first to Him refers to the fact that all things ultimately Return to Him.

The application to the Jews appears in chapter 11. The Source: "his people which he foreknew", v. 2. The Channel: "God is able to graff them in again", v. 23; "There shall come out of Sion the Deliverer", v. 26. The Return: "I have reserved *to* myself", v. 4.

We can also see an application to the Lord. The Source: "I seek not mine own will, but the will of the Father which hath sent me", John 5. 30. The Channel: "The Son can do nothing of himself, but what he seeth the Father do", v. 19. The Return: "I have glorified thee on the earth", 17. 4; "And now come I to thee", vv. 11, 13. In other words, He came down and returned in keeping with the divine purpose, being a Channel of the works of God while He was here on earth.

We can also apply these principles to the service of God's people today. The Source: "Possessing all things" wrote Paul, recognizing that all things came by grace from on high, 2 Cor. 6. 10. Thus he stresses that gifts for service come through the Holy Spirit, 1 Cor. 12. 11. The Channel: "I can do all things through Christ which strengtheneth me", he wrote to the Philippians, showing the ability that he had to conduct his service for the Lord, Phil. 4. 13. The Return: "God is my witness, whom I serve with my spirit in the gospel of his Son", Rom. 1. 9. May we serve under the same principles!

September 27th

READING: **Matthew 23. 37 to 24. 3**

INTEREST IN DISCARDED THINGS

AT THE END of chapter 23, the Lord departed from the temple courts in Jerusalem for the last time. The cold ritual and behaviour of the priests could not be tolerated any longer; the temple itself was "your house", and could not be recognized as God's house, for this was Herod's masterpiece, the will of God having been lacking in its building. The flesh had taken over the sacrifices, feasts and worship of the O.T. Divine judgment therefore fell upon the place, and it would be left "desolate", as a barren wilderness with nothing for God.

This was nothing new, had the disciples had their minds taught by their own O.T. Scriptures. Moses' tabernacle had ultimately been forsaken by God because of idolatry in Eli's day, Psa. 78. 60. Solomon's temple suffered a greater judgment, for it was burnt by Nebuchadnezzar, 2 Kings 25. 9.

Consequently if Jerusalem would not have the Lord Jesus, then He would ensure that they would not have their temple after its destruction by the Romans in A.D.70.

Thus in Matthew 24. 1, the Lord departed, but the disciples lingered before a building so magnificent in its design and construction, and they wanted to involve the Lord also in the physical examination of the temple. However, they were in good company, if not a mistaken company, for Solomon before them had brought up the forsaken tabernacle at the dedication of the temple, 2 Chron. 5. 5, though what he did with it we are not told (perhaps he stored the parts in one of the rooms built around the outside of the temple).

The Lord Jesus wanted His disciples to make a complete break with a religion of the flesh. Consequently, He foretold its fate: "There shall not be left here one stone upon another, that shall not be thrown down", Matt. 24. 2. We are therefore exhorted to set our affections on things above, not on things on the earth, Col. 3. 2. This may be difficult for believers, particularly new converts. But Paul made a complete break with the system of Jewish religion in which he had been brought up; in his affections and interests he had discarded it, and would not build again the things that he had destroyed, Gal. 2. 18.

On the mount of Olives, the Lord then turned their thoughts to a greater destruction at the end of the age, Matt. 24. 3.

September 28th

READING: **Galatians 1. 1-24**

DIVINE WORK, NOT MAN'S

THE CROSS of the Lord Jesus should teach us to obliterate ourselves when engaged in the Lord's service. All about our service really pertains to the Lord: "the Lord working with them", Mark 16. 20. But this is a hard lesson to learn, particularly when a believer feels himself to be so active and outgoing. But the doctrine behind this "all of Christ, and none of self" must first of all be appreciated, so we may consider a few points from the Scriptures.

(1) Paul states that his apostleship was "not of man, neither by man, but by Jesus Christ, and God the Father", Gal. 1. 1; the same applies to all spiritual gifts and positions of responsibility in a local church. Such gifts and positions are therefore used solely for Him and His glory; the flesh must be absent, together with personal glory so often sought for.

(2) As Paul viewed his work, he wrote, "I laboured more abundantly than they all: yet not I, but the grace of God which was with me", 1 Cor. 15. 10. His great successes were solely due to the divine working through him. The servants are nothing, but "God that giveth the increase", 3. 7.

(3) The gospel that Paul preached "is not after man . . . but by the revelation of Jesus Christ", Gal. 1. 11-12. He did not seek help from the other apostles, but he taught what he had received from heaven itself; this gave him authority.

(4) All Paul's teaching had the same character; it was "not as the word of men, but as it is in truth, the word of God", 1 Thess. 2. 13. For this reason, his teaching worked effectually, else it would be mere oratory and persuasion.

(5) In matters pertaining to obedience, one's pathway is clear when the authorities make conditions contrary to the Word of God. "We ought to obey God rather than men", Acts 5. 29, so there is a ladder of priorities in obedience.

(6) In all activity of life, there is a general principle, "whatsoever ye do, do it heartily, as to the Lord, and not unto men", Col. 3. 23.

(7) Stephen said, "the most High dwelleth not in temples made with hands", Acts 7. 48. This is because the Lord is a minister of the sanctuary and of "the true tabernacle, which the Lord pitched, and not man", Heb. 8. 2.

September 29th

READING: **Luke 4. 1-13**

THE LORD'S GLORY IN THE GOSPELS

THIS READING in Luke 4 is really a contrast to our main subject. Satan thought that he had the glory of all the kingdoms of the world to offer to the Lord, v. 6. But this glory was merely that of exalted man, and even that was not Satan's to offer. In reality, the kingdoms will be cleansed when the Lord comes in glory, and then the kingdom of this world will become the kingdom of the Lord, Rev. 11. 15. But other verses in the Gospels trace the Lord's glory, and we may mention some of these in an ordered presentation.

Before He came. The Lord in His prayer made mention of the glory that He had with the Father before the world was, John 17. 5. When Isaiah saw the glory in Isaiah 6, it was really the glory of Christ that he saw, John 12. 41.

At His birth and as a Child. When the Lord was born, the angel of the Lord came upon the Shepherds, and "the glory of the Lord shone round about them", Luke 2. 9. The heavenly host praised God by saying, "Glory to God in the highest", v. 14. A few days later, Simeon in Jerusalem referred to the Babe in his arms as "the glory of thy people Israel", v. 32.

In His life here below. The apostle John wrote, "we beheld his glory, the glory as of the only begotten of the Father", John 1. 14. Miracles manifested forth His glory, as in Cana of Galilee, 2. 11, and as in Bethany when Lazarus was raised, 11. 4, 40. There was a physical manifestation of His glory on the mountain top, when His face shone as the sun, Matt. 17. 2; Moses and Elijas also appeared in glory.

His glory now. The glory given the Son by the Father is further distributed to His people; this glory is that which is consequential upon His Manhood, it cannot be the unique glory of Deity, John 17. 22. Also the Son expressed His desire that His own people should behold His glory, by faith now, but face to face in the future, 17. 24.

In the future. Prior to the transfiguration, the Lord declared that He, the Son of man, would come "in the glory of his Father", Matt. 16. 27. He elaborated upon this in His prophetic discourse, "The Son of man coming in the clouds of heaven with power and great glory", Matt. 24. 30. Mark 10. 37 also speaks of His right hand and left hand in glory.

READING: **Psalm 16. 1-11**

THE LORD'S LIFE IN THE PSALMS

IF THE New Testament were not in existence, what would we know about the Lord Jesus? If we had the capacity to search through the Old Testament, extracting all the verses that speak of His Person, life and death, we could arrange it all in order like another Gospel. For the Lord did that once, "And beginning at Moses and all the prophets, he expounded unto them in all the scriptures the things concerning himself", Luke 24. 27, 44-47. If we restrict ourselves only to the Psalms, we can make certain progress in tracing mainly the story of the cross and resurrection.

Psa. 69. 9 = John 2. 17, "the zeal of thine house hath eaten me up", His consuming passion for holiness in divine things.

Psa. 8. 2 = Matt. 21. 16, "Out of the mouth of babes and sucklings"; praise did not come from temple or synagogue.

Psa. 41. 9 = John 13. 18, "which did eat of my bread, hath lifted up his heel against me", announcing the traitor.

Psa. 2. 1-2 = Acts 4. 26-27, "Why do the heathen rage?", showing the kinds of men associated with His crucifixion.

Psa. 22. 16 = Matt. 27. 35, "they pierced my hands and my feet" implies "And they crucified him".

Psa. 22. 18 = Matt. 27. 35, "They . . . cast lots upon my vesture", one of the details of the crucifixion story.

Psa. 22. 1 = Matt. 27. 46, "My God, my God, why hast thou forsaken me?", referring to the absolute depth of sufferings of Christ in the hours of darkness.

Psa. 69. 21 = John 19. 28, "in my thirst they gave me vinegar to drink", a repercussion of crucifixion.

Psa. 31. 5 = Luke 23. 46, "Into thine hand I commit my spirit", showing the last moments before He died.

Psa. 34. 20 = John 19. 36, "He keepeth all his bones: not one of them is broken", something that had to be fulfilled.

Psa. 16. 10-11 = Acts 2. 27-28, "thou wilt not leave my soul in hell", referring clearly to the inevitability of the resurrection of Christ.

Psa. 118. 22-23 = Matt. 21. 42, the refused Stone becoming the Head of the corner, the Lord exalted in resurrection.

Psa. 110. 1 = Matt. 22. 44, "Sit thou on my right hand", showing the ascension position of the Lord even now.

October 1st

READING: **Acts 1. 15-26**

THREE YEARS

WE HAVE already discussed on page 2 the period of three years during which a student is away from home engaged in his studies, showing the spiritual responsibilities that rest upon him as a good servant of the Lord Jesus. We continue this theme today, since the beginning of October (or end of September) is usually the time when such studies commence.

We have read this passage in Acts 1 since in it Peter lays down the conditions and qualifications to be satisfied for a new apostle to be chosen to replace Judas. The occupation of the previous three years were vital for a man to take up special responsibilities in the service of the Lord. Several men had the necessary qualifications, of which the Lord chose one. Peter said, "of these men which have companied with us all the time that the Lord Jesus went in and out among us, beginning from the baptism of John, unto that same day that he was taken up from us, must one be ordained to be a witness with us of his resurrection", Acts 1. 22. In other words, during the previous three years, the one chosen must have been faithful in following the Lord. There could be no effective service had there not been prior faithfulness throughout the years of the Lord's ministry. He would thus know all about the details of the Lord's teaching; an almost blank mind cannot be chosen to serve the Lord.

The Ephesians were prepared for three years prior to Paul leaving them, when they would be alone to carry on their testimony according to his teaching. Recalling this period, Paul said, "I kept back nothing that was profitable for you", Acts 20. 20; he declared "all the counsel of God", v. 27. This period of preparation is described as "by the space of three years I ceased not to warn every one night and day with tears", v. 31. After these three years, the elders were equipped "to feed the church of God", v. 28.

As a young man in Babylon, Daniel studied for three years before having an examination before the king, Dan. 1. 5. He learnt much of the learning of Babylon, but not at the expense of the things of God. He lived faithfully for God, separated from obnoxious things, and came out top!, v. 20. He was then able to serve God until old age, because he started well.

October 2nd

READING: **Psalm 78. 65-72**

DAILY LIFE AS THE SCHOOL OF EXPERIENCE

THE LORD JESUS experienced many things in Manhood that He could not have experienced prior to His coming into this world; these experiences passed into His soul by means of the human body that was His in the days of His flesh. For example, His ministry of sympathy as High Priest; He served on earth amongst men so that He can now serve in heaven meeting the needs of His people here below. Similarly for believers now; our daily experiences in life should help in our spiritual work for the Lord. Daily lives form a school used by God for the formation of spiritual maturity and ability. We may quote 1 Timothy 3. 12: ministers must rule their children and houses well in order to be "deacons" serving the Lord. We wonder what experience Timothy passed through in order to have a good report by the local churches, Acts 16. 1-3.

The experience of Peter. Peter was a fisherman, Luke 4. 2; he knew all the difficulties and disappointments, all the hard work by day and night. The Lord called him (more than once) until he left his fishing to follow Him. As a result, He said, "from henceforth thou shalt catch men", v. 10. Thus Peter became an *evangelist*, gaining souls for Christ.

The experience of Paul. This man had been a studious Pharisee, gaining knowledge that made him an able exponent of the law. He also was a tentmaker, making structures suitable for dwelling purposes, Acts 18. 3. But he became a teacher of the things of the Lord, and also "a wise masterbuilder" in the local churches, 1 Cor. 3. 10, building spiritual temples rather than tabernacles. Thus he was a *teacher*.

The experience of David. He was the youngest son, keeping his father's sheep, 1 Sam. 16. 11; 17. 34. This led him to write Psalm 23, "The Lord is my shepherd". God took David from the sheepfolds, his school of experience, and caused him to "feed Jacob his people", feeding and guiding them as a spiritual shepherd, Psa. 78. 70-72. Thus he was a *pastor*.

The experience of Joseph. Even though he was young, he was made "overseer" over Potiphar's house, Gen. 39. 3, and he was faithful both morally and financially. Later Pharaoh said to him, "I have set thee over all the land of Egypt", Gen. 41. 41, 55. Thus typically he became an *elder*, 1 Tim. 3. 5.

276

October 3rd

READING: 1 Thessalonians 1. 1-10

YOUR WORK OF FAITH

IN 1 CORINTHIANS 13. 13, Paul wrote of "faith, hope, charity (love)"; these are active possessions of the soul, they are not passive, for they abide here and now. The idea that faith can work occurs three times in Paul's writings; this must not be confused with the false doctrine that works are necessary for salvation. But certainly good works follow salvation. Abraham was justified by faith when he believed God that he would have a son in his old age, Rom. 4. 3, 18-22; and then many years later he was justified by works when he was willing to offer up his son Isaac, James 2. 21-24.

(1) Galatians 5. 6, "in Christ Jesus neither circumcision availeth any thing, nor uncircumcision, but faith which worketh by love". The Galatians were returning to an old religion that had as its basis the works of the natural man, but in Christianity this is replaced by faith, working, love. Faith is the stimulus, love is the lubrication, and works are the final product. This love may be (*a*) Christ's love, for Paul wrote, "I live by the faith of the Son of God, who loved me", 2. 20, or (*b*) the believer's love, for by love we serve one another, 5. 13-14.

(2) 1 Thessalonians 1. 3, "remembering without ceasing your work of faith, and labour of love, and patience of hope in our Lord Jesus Christ". These works of faith can be seen in such verses as, "ye became followers of us, and of the Lord", v. 6; "ye were ensamples", v. 7; "from you sounded out the word of the Lord", v. 8; "the word of God, which effectually worketh also in you", 2. 13; "ye, brethren, became followers of the churches of God", v. 14. All this is faith in action, and shows what God expects from a working faith.

(3) 2 Thessalonians 1. 11, "the work of faith with power", this being part of Paul's prayer for them, that God would fulfil this manifestation of faith. Thus the works of faith are not works of self or of the flesh, but they are subject to the outworking of the Author of faith. Paul had just given thanks to God that "your faith groweth exceedingly", v. 3, and that he could glory in other local churches of the patience and faith of the Thessalonians, v. 4. Thus he desired that they should be established in every good word and work, 2. 17.

October 4th

READING: **1 Corinthians 14. 29-40**

MARKS OF THE SPIRITUAL MAN

THE SPIRITUAL MAN is named only three times in the N.T. by Paul. Many things are described as spiritual, such as meat, drink, Rock, gifts, body, blessings, songs, understanding, house, sacrifices, and so on. But are we spiritual?, namely, with our outlook and activity dominated by the Spirit given by the Risen Lord. The three times the spiritual man is described all relate to the fellowship and service of a local church.

(1) *Reception.* "He that is spiritual judgeth (discerneth) all things", 1 Cor. 2. 15. (The word "judge" is the same as "discern" in verse 14.) Paul is talking about the important question, How do believers know the mind of God? He asserts that it is impossible for the natural unsaved man to know anything about the things of the Spirit of God. But believers have received the Spirit so that they might know the things of God. They are therefore called spiritual, because they can discern spiritual realities. The Spirit teaches spiritual things, and uses spiritual means to do so. The means of the flesh are therefore absent from the methods of a spiritual man, who communicates spiritual things by spiritual means.

(2) *Regulation.* ". . . Spiritual, let him acknowledge that the things that I write unto you are the commandments of the Lord", 1 Cor. 14. 37. Spiritual believers recognize that their fellowship and service are regulated by the commandments of the Lord given, mainly, through the apostle Paul. The Corinthians were mishandling the gifts of the Spirit, and their service was all out of order. In chapter 14, Paul issues instructions from the Lord that are equivalent to commandments under grace; those who take heed are spiritual.

(3) *Restoration.* "If a man be overtaken in a fault, ye which are spiritual, restore such an one in the spirit of meekness; considering thyself, lest thou also be tempted", Gal. 6. 1. Many of the Galatians had been overtaken by the fault of going back to the law of Moses. A big outgoing dictator would only make matters worse. Only a spiritual man could discern the nature of the fault, and could present the liberty of Christ through the Spirit unmixed with men's ideas. No one else can help, so this brings humility, meekness, carefulness to the man who has to deal with the fault.

278

October 5th

READING: **Hebrews 12. 1-14**

CHRIST THE FIRST-LEADER

THE WORD translated "author" in verse 2 is a word that appears four times in the N.T., each time referring to the Lord Jesus in an exalted and pre-eminent status. The word itself combines two smaller words meaning first and to lead. Hence the word refers to someone who leads, or someone who originates something for someone else. The four occasions are:

(1) "To make *the captain* of their salvation perfect through sufferings", Heb. 2. 10.

(2) "Looking unto Jesus *the author* and finisher of our faith", Heb. 12. 2.

(3) "Ye . . . killed *the Prince* of life, whom God hath raised from the dead", Acts 3. 15.

(4) "Him hath God exalted with his right hand to be *a Prince* and a Saviour", Acts 5. 31.

The word is used of no other person in the N.T.; moreover, no unbeliever can understand what the title means. The first two quotations were written to believers, while the last two were spoken by Peter to unbelievers in Jerusalem.

Note the position of the Lord in the four contexts. And note too that His death is referred to in all four contexts.

(1) The Lord Jesus is seen as crowned with glory and honour, Heb. 2. 9, having passed through the suffering of death.

(2) He is seen as set down at the right hand of the throne of God, Heb. 12. 2, having endured the cross.

(3) God has glorified His Servant Jesus, having raised Him from the dead, Acts 4. 13, who had been killed by men.

(4) God has raised up Jesus, exalting Him with His right hand, Acts 5. 31-32, this One having been hanged on a tree.

The work of Christ is also seen in the four contexts, work that no exalted leader amongst men could ever achieve.

(1) The Lord is seen as bringing many sons to glory, and sanctifying them to be called brethren, Heb. 2. 10-11.

(2) He originates our faith, and is also the "finisher" of it, Heb. 12. 2.

(3) He originates our life, the One who was Life from eternity; "I give unto them eternal life", John 10. 28.

(4) He grants repentance and forgiveness of sins, giving the Spirit to those who obey Him, Acts 5. 31-32.

October 6th

READING: **1 Chronicles 13. 1-14**

UNITED DECISIONS

THE IDEAL local church is of one mind in the things of the Lord. When considering its avenues of service, it should be enabled to take united decisions in the fear of the Lord. Let us consider some scriptural examples, when there was one mind amongst God's people, in both O.T. and N.T.

The ark brought to Jerusalem. In 1 Chronicles 13. 1-3, David's exercise was deep and not hasty; he consulted first with many captains and leaders. He then explained his exercise to all Israel, "If it seem good unto you, and that it be of the Lord our God . . . let us bring again the ark of our God to us". Before he took this decision, David would not spend time in bed asleep, Psa. 132. 3-5. God's will was sought, and also the fellowship of all God's people. Alas, the method that David used was not according to God's will, and the project ended in temporary failure. The "due order" was not followed, 1 Chron. 15. 13. The second attempt was made with David knowing God's will regarding the carrying of the ark, v. 2.

Hezekiah's passover. Hezekiah's passover could not take place in the first month, since the priests were not sanctified sufficiently, 2 Chron. 30. 3. So he discussed the matter with the princes and people, v. 2, and decided to keep it in the second month (in keeping with the will of the Lord in Numbers 9. 10-11). This decision "pleased the king and all the congregation", v. 4. So they went back to the Word after years of departure under Ahaz. In fact, God gave them one heart to do the commandment by the word of the Lord, v. 12.

The letter from Jerusalem. After much discussion about the suggested necessity of keeping the law of Moses, Acts 15. 5, James suggested that a letter should be sent to the churches of the Gentiles about this matter. "Then it pleased the apostles and elders, with the whole church", v. 22, to send chosen men with the letter. Moreover, the letter itself contained a statement about this unanimity of thought, "it seemed good to the Holy Spirit, and to us", v. 28.

Note in all these three cases that the will of God was brought into the decision-making process. Moreover, in each case, one man (David, Hezekiah, James) had the idea, and the others then followed. See Acts 16. 9-10 for another example.

October 7th

READING: **John 6. 60-71**

THE LIVING GOD

WE SOMETIMES sing the hymn containing the line, "Change and decay in all around I see". How good it is, then, for believers to have a changeless eternal Object before the gaze of their faith, "him that liveth for ever and ever", Rev. 4. 10. We consider "the living God" under various aspects.

Thirsting after. In two Psalms, we find the psalmist thirsting after "the living God", 42. 2; 84. 2. This is no mere theory, rather an exercise that is heart-felt.

Divine relationships. Peter would not go backwards, but confessed the Lord as "that Christ, the Son of the living God", John 6. 68. On another occasion, he again confessed "the Christ, the Son of the living God", Matt. 16. 16, while others thought that He was merely John the Baptist, Elijah or one of the prophets. Paul later wrote of "the Spirit of the living God", 2 Cor. 3. 3.

Divine possessions. Men may see the various churches on earth as administrative units with organizing committees, but Paul viewed true local churches under the name "the house of God, which is the church of the living God", 1 Tim. 3. 15. He also viewed these local companies each as "the temple of the living God", 2 Cor. 6. 16, where He dwells amongst His people wholly separated from darkness, unrighteousness and infidels.

The effect on service. Paul visualized the Thessalonians as having "turned to God from idols to serve the living and true God", 1 Thess. 1. 9; such should be the object of gospel preaching today. It certainly is linked with the reception of salvation, for the blood of Christ purges our "conscience from dead works to serve the living God", Heb. 9. 14.

Trust. Paul's life was governed by the principle, "we trust in the living God", 1 Tim. 4. 10; Timothy also had to command and teach this. Again, those that are rich had to be exhorted not to "trust in uncertain riches, but in the living God, who giveth us richly all things to enjoy", 6. 17.

Unbelief. There can be an evil heart that departs "from the living God", Heb. 3. 12, if a religion of ceremony is desired. And unbelievers do not recognize that "It is a fearful thing to fall into the hands of the living God", 10. 31.

This is an impressive list, to which we all must take heed.

October 8th

READING: **2 Corinthians 1. 12-24**

ACKNOWLEDGEMENT

ACKNOWLEDGEMENT of what we hear and read is of great importance, for it implies that a practical repercussion flows from what enters the mind and heart. This applies to doctrine as well; if the doctrinal chapter on the resurrection (1 Cor. 15) is acknowledged, then the believer will be stedfast, unmoveable, his labour not being in vain in the Lord, v. 58. Otherwise the doctrine will merely be held academically, having no effect on the Christian life.

After four chapters dealing with service in a local church, Paul wrote, "If any man think himself to be . . . spiritual, let him acknowledge that the things that I write unto you are the commandments of the Lord", 1 Cor. 14. 37. Unspiritual men would refuse to acknowledge this! These are not commandments of the law, but of grace; they are the highest commandments of all, not Paul's but the Lord's, pertaining to the Lord's Supper and spiritual gifts.

After having mentioned the names of some faithful men, Paul wrote, "therefore acknowledge ye them that are such", 1 Cor. 16. 18. Those who were complaining had to recognize others who helped Paul. For example, in Numbers 12. 1 Miriam and Aaron complained about Moses. Rather, they had to acknowledge that Moses was faithful in all God's house, v. 7.

"We write none other things unto you, than what ye read or acknowledge; and I trust ye shall acknowledge unto the end", 2 Cor. 1. 13. In other words, Paul was writing essentially nothing that was new in these two Epistles, only what he had taught when he had been with them. As examples, the gospel and the Lord's Supper had already been taught, though he wrote about these subjects again, 1 Cor. 11. 23; 15. 1. He wanted them to acknowledge these things always, but were there some who refused to acknowledge these things any more?

To "acknowledge even to the end" is an important proof of one's salvation. The life proves the reality of faith, and this is the meaning of verses such as Hebrews 3. 6, 14.

"Ye have acknowledged us in part", 2 Cor. 1. 14. Paul knew that the Corinthian church was divided; some held to him and a minority did not. Chapters 1-9 were written particularly for the former, while chapters 10-13 for the latter.

October 9th

READING: **Leviticus 23. 4-16**

OVERALL SURVEY OF THE FEASTS

IN 1 CORINTHIANS 2. 6-10, Paul wrote of "the wisdom of God in a mystery"; those who crucified the Lord did not know this, but it was revealed to those who loved the Lord. As an example of this, we may consider the seven feasts in Leviticus 23, prophetical in nature, and there are direct or indirect references to these feasts in 1 & 2 Corinthians. These feasts can be interpreted as God's calendar, relating to Christ, the church, and to Israel. Thus, as to their *interpretation*, we can see that the first four spring feasts refer to Christianity, while the last three autumn feasts to restored Israel. But as far as *application* is concerned, we can see pointers to the present dispensation in all seven feasts.

(1) *The passover*, Lev. 23. 5, in commemoration of the deliverance of Israel from Egypt. Paul wrote, "Christ our passover is sacrificed for us", 1 Cor. 5. 7.

(2) *The firstfruits*, Lev. 23. 10, two days after the passover. Of the resurrection, Paul wrote that "Christ (is) become the firstfruits of them that slept", 1 Cor. 15. 20.

(3) *Unleavened bread*, Lev. 23. 6, lasting a week, so it has ongoing implications in life. Paul wrote, "let us keep the feast . . . with the unleavened bread", purging out "the old leaven" in the process, 1 Cor. 5. 7-8.

(4) *Pentecost, the feast of weeks*, Lev. 23. 15. This looked forward to the true "day of Pentecost" when the Spirit was given, Acts 2. 1. Paul wrote, "by one Spirit are we all baptized into one body", 1 Cor. 12. 13.

(5) *Trumpets*, Lev. 23. 24, referring to Israel's future regathering. Applied to believers today, Paul wrote, "the trumpet shall sound . . . we shall be changed", 1 Cor. 15. 52.

(6) *Atonement*, Lev. 23. 27, when Israel shall repent and have forgiveness. Since atonement means "to cover", Christ has done more in that He has taken sins away. Paul wrote, "he hath made him to be sin for us", 2 Cor. 5. 21.

(7) *Tabernacles*, Lev. 23. 34, speaking of Israel's peace and safety in the land during the millenniun. This lasted for a week, so has an ongoing application. Paul wrote, "that the power of Christ may rest upon me (may tabernacle, dwell upon me)", 2 Cor. 12. 9. Paul remained permanently in this feast!

October 10th

READING: **Romans 6. 1-13**

THE TESTIMONY OF BAPTISM

OF THE Lord's disciples, no one saw Him die on the cross except John and the women standing afar off. No one saw Him in resurrection, except his disciples (listed in various parts of the N.T.). Yet believers today must live in the light of His death and resurrection. We are blessed when we have faith, John 20. 29, but what does God allow us to see in addition to faith? Instead, we see a new convert being baptized in water, typically dying with Christ and being raised with Christ.

Thus all believers who have been baptized have been "buried with him by baptism into death", Rom. 6. 4; "we have been planted together in the likeness of his death", v. 5; "our old man is crucified with him", v. 6; we are "dead with Christ", v. 8. This act has been witnessed by many, for baptism is not a secret event, done out of sight of our fellow-believers.

And when we come up out of the water after baptism, Paul has described this by the phrases, "in the likeness of his resurrection", v. 5; "even so we also should walk in newness of life", v. 4; "we shall also live with him", v. 8. This typical act of being raised to a new life spiritually and morally has also been witnessed by many other believers.

This is the nearest that we get to seeing the death and resurrection of Christ; instead, we see a believer going the same way, water being used as a symbol of immersion into death. This is a new convert's testimony, not only of faith in Christ, but of his resolve, both before God and before men, to live a new life suitable for his resurrection standing in Christ. Evidently, the act of being baptized is something that should be done by conviction, and *not* by merely copying what has happened to other believers. Thus the eunuch was baptized because of his conviction, "what doth hinder me to be baptized?", Acts 8. 36.

Many years ago, when the author was selecting applicants for entry into university, one headmaster wrote of an applicant: "He tells me he is about to be baptized. This impresses me, because at this age I underwent the ritual in a spirit of recalcitrance and I did it to please my parents. He is doing so from conviction which is certainly not militant. He is a boy who has acquired a sense of values and of purpose".

October 11th

READING: **Isaiah 60. 1-22; 61. 1-3**

THE PLANTING OF THE LORD

METAPHORS ABOUND throughout the Scriptures, particularly in those parts that are not just plain history. Thus the psalms and prophets are especially rich in metaphors, and the reader can perceive that almost every verse of our reading contains pictorial representations, and very common things of daily life are used in these pictures. In particular, we can consider the subject of planting.

Life. The future restoration of God's earthly people will yield trees called "the planting of the Lord", 61. 3; "the branch of my planting", 60. 21. There were plenty of others, and the Lord Jesus spoke of these when He said, "Every plant, which my heavenly Father hath not planted, shall be rooted up", Matt. 15. 13. Those planted by God possess leaves that "shall not wither", Psa. 1. 3, but others are like the fig tree that withered away, Matt. 21. 19. The trees that God plants are like "a green olive tree in the house of God", Psa. 52. 8. Just before His crucifixion, the Lord referred to Himself as "a green tree", but the Jews were lifeless like a "dry" tree, Luke 23. 31.

Growth. In ordinary horticulture, a man may plant a seed, seedling, shrub or small tree, but he cannot make it grow. He may water it, and tend to its needs by removing weeds, but he cannot make it grow. The power of growth resides in natural laws outside his own competence. But when God plants, the whole of the plant or tree's growth depends upon Himself: "the work of my hands", Isa. 60. 21. Truly in matters spiritual, it is God "that giveth the increase", 1 Cor. 3. 7.

Position. He plants His trees where He will, according to the divine purpose revealed in Scripture. Thus the various trees will "beautify the place of my sanctuary", Isa. 60. 13; and we can but compare this with Acts 2. 47 where "the Lord added to the church" those who were being saved. In other words, to those who are likeminded in the faith, seeking to follow in fellowship and service according to God's Word.

Fruit. This is what God wants, fruit Godward, "that I may be glorified", Isa. 60. 21; 61. 3. Believers will show forth His praises, and serve at His altar, 60. 6-7. Morally, they will bring forth the fruit of the Spirit, Gal. 5. 22-23.

October 12th

READING: **Revelation 2. 18-29**

TILL I COME

TOGETHER WITH Laodicea, the church at Thyatira was the most unspiritual church that the Lord addressed in Revelation 2-3. Churches in such states could not possibly be waiting for the coming again of the Lord Jesus. And yet to the faithful ones in Thyatira, the Lord holds out the promise "till I come", v. 25, in keeping with His previous promise "I will come again", John 14. 3. There are five such phrases that refer to the period prior to His coming again.

(1) *Remaining*. Speaking to Peter about John, the Lord made His final recorded remark in John 21. 22, "If I will that he tarry till I come, what is that to thee? follow thou me". No believer knows whether he will be one of those who "are alive and remain unto the coming of the Lord", 1 Thess. 4. 15. But we must all act as if this may be so, for He will not tarry.

(2) *Retaining*. To the rest in Thyatira (the faithful ones) the Lord said, "that which ye have already hold fast till I come", Rev. 2. 25. These did not have the doctrine of the prophetess Jezebel, but were exhorted to retain steadfastly the truth that they had accepted. All believers are required to hold to truth and not to deviate from it as they wait for His return.

(3) *Remembrance*. One of the most important acts of service in the Christian life is that of breaking bread at the Lord's Supper. Paul wrote, "ye do show the Lord's death, till he come", 1 Cor. 11. 26. To have His return before the heart would keep believers from the deviations of Corinth, and all other subsequent deviations, relating to the Lord's Supper.

(4) *Reception*. Some wanted the kingdom of God immediately to appear, but the Lord would rather give "pounds" to His servants in His absence. All believers receive such gifts and abilities with which to trade spiritually, hearing His voice, "Occupy till I come", Luke 19. 13. In this intervening period, the Lord's service is an ongoing occupation for all believers.

(5) *Responsibility*. "Judge nothing before the time, until the Lord come, who both will bring to light the hidden things of darkness . . . and then shall every man have praise of God", 1 Cor. 4. 5. At His coming, the deeds and motives of His servants will be reviewed, and rewards will be distributed. Believers have a deep responsibility to faithfulness in His absence.

October 13th

READING: **2 Peter 2. 1-14**

THE DIVINE DESPOT

IN THESE DAYS, many nations talk of "democracy" in their political systems, otherwise there is one or another form of "dictatorship". The former listens to the voice of the people, the latter uses cruelty to retain the power of the few. But divine administration knows neither democracy nor dictatorship, for the authority and rule of Christ is quite distinct.

Divine Names used in the Scriptures are not always clear in translation. The usual title for Christ is "Lord" (*kurios*) implying His authority that is owned by His servants. But another title "Lord" is *despotēs*, showing the supreme authority that He wields amongst men, whether they recognize it or not. Let us consider some of the occasions when this title is used.

By Simeon. Knowing that he would see the Lord's Christ before his death, he recognized the Babe Jesus as He was brought into the temple. He said, "Lord (Despot), now lettest thou thy servant depart in peace", knowing that he had "seen thy salvation", namely, the Christ, Luke 2. 29-30. He thus owned the total authority of God, and he took the position of a bondslave before Him.

Relative to believers. Paul uses this word once only, in his last Epistle, 2 Tim. 2. 21, "sanctified, and meet for the Master's (Despot's) use, and prepared unto every good work"; (we prefer "Master" rather than "master", following J.N.D.'s translation). Here, at the end of his life, Paul refers to the deepest servant-Master relationship, the servant being totally committed to the absolute divine authority.

Relative to the world. When released from prison, Peter and John (with others) addressed God, "Lord (Despot), thou art God", Acts 4. 24, having absolute authority over those who crucified Christ. Towards the end of his life, Peter used the word again; false teachers would deny the Lord (Despot), 2 Pet. 2. 1, not realizing the absolute authority of the One whom they denied. Jude wrote the same thing, "denying the only Lord (Despot) God", Jude 4. The awful activity of these men is found in these chapters. Finally, those who are martyred during the future tribulation will wait for God to avenge their blood, prefixing their cry with, "How long, O Lord (Despot)", Rev. 6. 10, recognizing His absolute authority to deal with His enemies.

October 14th

READING: Exodus 25. 1-9

THE PATTERN SHOWED ON THE MOUNT

WHEN MOSES had to build the tabernacle and all its associated contents, he did not have a free hand to introduce his own ideas and designs. The same may be said about the fellowship and service of a local church. Six times there appears the concept of the pattern that was shown to Moses in the mount, and there are obvious lessons for believers today.

In Exodus 25. 9 and Hebrews 8. 5 are general commands: "See ... that thou make all things according to the pattern shewed to thee in the mount"; its accomplishment is recorded in Exodus 39. 43. "Make all" suggests obedience; "pattern" means God's design and not the best of man's design (Herod's temple followed the latter); "shown" indicates that the Word of God makes known the mind of God; "mount" provides the thought of a heavenly origin and not an earthly one.

"And look that thou make them after their pattern, which was shewed thee in the mount", Exod. 25. 40. This refers to the ark, the table and the lampstand, all in chapter 25. The ark implies the dwelling place of God. Today, God's dwelling place is a "holy temple", and the Lord's people are also built "together for an habitation of God through the Spirit", Eph. 2. 21-22. The table speaks of spiritual food available for the people of God, as when Paul taught the church at Antioch for a year, Acts 11. 26. The lampstand denotes the work of the Spirit of God, all service being accomplished by "that one and the selfsame Spirit, dividing to every man", 1 Cor. 12. 11.

"And thou shalt rear up the tabernacle according to the fashion thereof which was shewed thee in the mount" refers to the tent, its coverings and the boards, Exod. 26. 30. In the N.T., the establishment of a local church and its service comes from God; the Scriptures tell us what to expect. Paul as a wise masterbuilder laid the foundation, and other builders knew from his teaching what to build on the Lord Jesus, 1 Cor. 3. 10; these were all "the commandments of the Lord", 14. 37.

"As it was shewed thee in the mount, so shall they make it", Exod. 27. 8, refers to the altar of burnt offering. Here is the place of true worship; Paul introduced nothing new, since he had "received of the Lord" the details of the Lord's Supper, 1 Cor. 11. 23. "Spiritual sacrifices" are His choice, 1 Pet. 2. 5.

October 15th

READING: **Mark 10. 17-31**

THEY WOULD NOT; THEY WENT AWAY

THE SUBJECT to be considered today is very solemn, even negative in character. Yet it is something that preachers of the gospel have had to sustain for years; certainly the Lord experienced it during His ministry. Truly, preaching leads to salvation, Rom. 10. 13-15, 17, but in many other cases, "the word preached did not profit them, not being mixed with faith in them that heard it", Heb. 4. 2. Our subject is "Come unto me" in reverse, and there are many examples in the N.T.

The rich young ruler. This young man was interested in eternal life and morality, but he preferred the riches of this world to the riches of heaven, Mark 10. 17, 22. The result of the Lord's exhortation was that he was sad, and "went away grieved". Having left all, Peter thought that he was better, v. 28, but when tested, he fled and denied the Lord.

The ten lepers. In Luke 17. 13, the ten lepers were very interested in being cleansed. Only one of those who were healed could see that it was right to turn back and give glory to God. The others walked back to a religion shortly to be discarded. Today, salvation is possible, and either the convert follows the Lord or else he turns away and follows the ritual of a cherished religion, with no regard to the scriptural principles involved.

Many disciples. After His long discourse in John 6, the Lord ended by observing that the Spirit quickens (the A.V. and R.V. have "spirit", but J.N.D. has "Spirit"), but the flesh profits nothing, v. 63. The Lord's words were life, but most of the disciples would not appreciate this, so they "went back, and walked no more with him", v. 66. Only the apostles remained with Him, and Peter confessed Him as the Son of God.

Jerusalem. By His teaching, the Lord would have gathered the people of Jerusalem together, but "ye would not", Matt. 23. 37. Thus the house was left desolate, and the city was later trodden down of the Gentiles until its restoration.

Antioch. When the majority would not have Paul's words, he said, "ye put it from you", namely, the Word of God, Acts 13. 46. Effectively, they distanced themselves from the Word of God, and as a result Paul turned to the Gentiles who then "glorified the word of the Lord", v. 48.

October 16th

READING: **Hebrews 9. 16-28**

THE THREE APPEARINGS

WE WISH to draw the reader's attention to the fact that the verb "to appear" occurs three times at the end of this chapter: "once in the end of the world hath he appeared to put away sin by the sacrifice of himself", v. 26, (in the past); Christ entered "into heaven itself, now to appear in the presence of God for us", v. 24, (in the present); "unto them that look for him shall he appear the second time without sin (apart from the sin question) unto salvation", v. 28, (in the future). This is of great value, but it is remarkable in the sense that three different Greek words are used.

(1) Verse 26. The word "appeared" means to make clear, visible, manifest, opposite to be hidden, secret. (Our English words "fancy, phantom" have the same root, being something clear to the mind.) As in Mark 4. 22, "there is nothing hid, which shall not be manifested". Thus the Lord Jesus was publicly manifested as Man in the flesh for all to behold, yet with the object of putting away sin by the sacrifice of Himself. John uses the same word in his first Epistle: "he was manifested to take away our sins", 3. 5, 8.

(2) Verse 24. The word "to appear" means to make visible, represent. (Our English words "emphasis, emphasize" have the same root, as the titles of this page are in bold or emphasized type.) The word is used in John 14. 21, "I will love him, and will manifest myself to him". Thus the Lord Jesus has been raised, and now in heaven He is still active for us; before God He is emphasized as Saviour and Great High Priest on behalf of His people. Nothing can go wrong with the divine work that He now accomplishes for all believers.

(3) Verse 28. The word "appear" suggests a dramatic suddenness with light, as of a spiritual vision. (Our English words "optics, optical" have the same root, the science of dealing with light through telescopes or microscopes.) The N.T. uses this word for many miraculous appearings, such as when Moses and Elijah "appeared", Matt. 17. 3, and "suddenly . . . there appeared unto them cloven tongues like as of fire", Acts 2. 2-3. In Hebrews 9. 28, we have the Lord suddenly coming for His own people, thereby to complete the redemption of the body; suddenly "we shall be changed", 1 Cor. 15. 52.

October 17th

READING: Acts 20: 25-38

THE CALL OF ELDERS

ELDER, BISHOP, overseer are designations of the same man in a local church; in the N.T. there was always a plurality of such men in any local church. In the established church in the United Kingdom, bishops are selected by the Prime Minister from a short list provided by the ecclesiastical authorities, and sometimes the policy of the former may be different from that of the latter! But the N.T. is quite clear as to the divine method for the selection of overseers or elders; the hand of men and of politicians is entirely absent from the process. In N.T. days, the Roman authority chose the high priest in Jerusalem, but this was far removed from God's method in the O.T., and from the spiritual way in which elders are recognized in any local church.

Elders are made by the Holy Spirit, Acts 20. 28. In other words, the elders in Ephesus had been made by the Holy Spirit, and not by Paul, although he had been with them for three years. In just the same way as salvation is a divinely given blessing, and recognized by all recipients, so elders can similarly recognize the divine work. The Spirit would make no mere administrator an elder, but a man having a great sense of responsibility towards the local flock.

There must be personal and individual exercise: "If a man desire the office of a bishop, he desireth a good work", 1 Tim. 3. 1. The proper translation of "the office of a bishop" is merely "overseership"; work, not an office, is involved. He must assess himself in the light of the qualifications given in verses 2-7; he cannot pick and choose which of these many qualifications he may abide by. He must assess his motives; whether another elder is needed; the time he has available for this work; whether he is a personal worker, certainly not a committee man, and whether he is apt to teach.

The members of the church do not choose, but they must recognize such men, 1 Thess. 5. 12. They would not recognize a man seeking his own interests; one seeking reward for his service, 1 Pet. 5. 4; a dictator like Diotrephes, 3 John 9; a man acting like a false apostle, Rev. 2. 2; a stranger, John 10. 5; or a grievous wolf, Acts 20. 29. Existing elders would also be watching for well qualified men to join them.

October 18th

READING: **1 Samuel 16. 1-13**

BETHLEHEM THROUGHOUT THE SCRIPTURES

BETHLEHEM is not a town associated only with the birth of the Lord Jesus. The place occurs many times in both the O.T. and the N.T., and it is good to have an overall spiritual assessment of the place throughout the Scriptures. Its name means "house of bread", and it lies about six miles south of Jerusalem.

(1) *Place of Departing.* Tragedy marks the first reference in the O.T., for it was here that Rachel died in giving birth to Benjamin, Gen. 35. 16-20, from whom Paul stemmed, Phil. 3. 5.

(2) *Place of Desolation.* Having left Bethlehem years before, Naomi returned there possessing nothing except Ruth; she went out full, and returned empty, Ruth 1. 19-22.

(3) *Place of Discernment.* It was here that Samuel first of all failed to discern the Lord's anointed, but finally he discerned David as God's choice of king, 1 Sam. 16. 4, 12.

(4) *Place of David's Deeds.* Here David stayed until he was called to the battle with Goliath, 17. 15. He humbled himself and was then exalted later.

(5) *Place of Deceit.* Jonathan decided to tell Saul that David had returned to Bethlehem, 20. 6. This was a lie, for David would remain in safety outside Saul's house.

(6) *Place for Drink.* Three mighty men obtained water from Bethlehem's well for David, but he poured it out unto the Lord because of the danger sustained by these men, 2 Sam. 23. 14-17.

(7) *Place of Delivery.* Having arrived from Galilee, Mary gave birth to her firstborn, the Lord Jesus. A stable was used, since the enrolment caused havoc with accommodation, Luke 2. 4.

(8) *Place of Devotions.* The shepherds received the angelic message, and found "the babe lying in a manger", v. 16.

(9) *Place of Donations.* Later, the wise men from the east came to worship Him, opening their treasures, and presenting them to the Lord Jesus, Matt. 2. 11.

(10) *Place of Destruction.* Having failed to identity the Lord Jesus, Herod slew all children in Bethlehem to try to include the Lord in the net, but he failed, 2. 16.

(11) *Place of Division.* His teaching caused division, and the town of Bethlehem was brought into focus, John 7. 40-44.

(12) *Place of Despot.* The absolute Ruler was promised to come out of Bethlehem, Micah 5. 2.

October 19th

READING: **Colossians 4. 1-18**

ONE OF YOU

AN EXPRESSION such as "one of you" implies that one person is identified out of many who also can be identified. The word "you" does not define a vague company with vague boundaries, but a known company with known boundaries, with an inside and an outside. This company may be growing, but at any time this company forms a fellowship, each brother or sister having fellowship with all the others. Moreover, the idea of loyalty is implied — the one with the other, each one to the company as a whole, and each one to the Lord Himself.

We note a similar expression in the Gospels. In Bethany a supper was made for the Lord, and "Lazarus was one of them that sat at the table with him", John 12. 2. The primary object of the gathered company was the Lord; at the same time, the word "them" implies a definite boundary, and Lazarus was within that boundary. Similarly in Luke 24. 22; the two on the Emmaus road said to the Lord (as unknown), "certain women also of our company". This company was very restricted, consisting of the Lord's disciples. The "certain women" must have been "Mary Magdalene and the other Mary", Matt. 28. 1. Clearly all were known to each other.

The same observations apply to a local church or assembly, where likemindedness, fellowship and service are the portion of all members, each showing loyalty to the Lord and to the other believers. Thus Onesimus, a beloved brother recently converted, was "one of you", even though he had been unconverted when he had left Colosse. Paul knew that his outlook, character and objectives now matched those of the Colossian believers; they were the "you", while Onesimus was the "one", Col. 4. 9. Similarly, Epaphras is described as "one of you", vv. 12, 13. He had come to Rome to find Paul, and the apostle knew of his zeal for his home church, where all would pull together in their service for the Lord who was the one attractive Centre, enabling the "you" to be bonded together.

Thus Peter and John went "to their own company", Acts 4. 23; the converted Saul attempted to join himself to this company, 9. 26-27. In 11. 12, Peter came to the place where many were gathered praying; later Paul gathered the church at Antioch together, 14. 27. Do we view our church like this?

READING: **2 Corinthians 10. 1-18**

PAUL'S ABSENCES

THERE IS an English proverb that says, "When the cat is away, the mice will play". This certainly has happened in spiritual things. When a leader or an authority is not present for a season, then some men will take advantage of it, seeking to introduce their own ideas rather than those of the leader or authority. Thus when Nehemiah was away from Jerusalem, Tobiah the Ammonite was given a room in the temple courts, and the Levites were no longer carrying out their duties, Neh. 13. 1-12. Again, in John chs. 13-16 the Lord made final preparations for His disciples after His departure, dealing with subjects such as the Holy Spirit, prayer, fruitfulness, and His coming again. But these subjects have been largely discounted in following generations; men have introduced things that they would not have dared to do had He still been present on earth amongst them. The apostle Paul had divinely given authority, and he formed many local churches, but when he left them various difficulties and errors entered.

When Paul was absent from Corinth, they asserted that his letters were "weighty and powerful", though some could disregard them. However, they were glad to think that his presence would be weak, and his speech contemptible, so that they could disregard him face to face. But Paul made it clear that his presence would be as powerful as his letters in his absence, 2 Cor. 10. 8-11.

What a different attitude Paul could take with regard to the Colossians when he was in prison in Rome. He wrote, "though I be absent in the flesh, yet am I with you in the spirit, joying and beholding your order, and the stedfastness of your faith in Christ", Col. 2. 5. The Lord could not say this to all the seven churches in Revelation chs. 2-3.

Again in prison, Paul wrote to the Philippians, "whether I come and see you, or else be absent, I may hear of your affairs, that ye stand fast in one spirit, with one mind, striving together for the faith of the gospel", Phil. 1. 27.

As absent, Paul knew of the great moral disorder in Corinth; he wrote, "as absent in body, but present in spirit, (I) have judged already, as though I were present", 1 Cor. 5. 3. They had to carry out the proper measure of discipline.

October 21st

READING: **Jeremiah 17. 1-18**

THE LORD THE SANCTUARY OF HIS PEOPLE

IN THE O.T., the sanctuary usually refers to the temple or tabernacle, "let them make me a sanctuary; that I may dwell among them", Exod. 25. 8. But three times in the major prophets the word refers to the Lord Himself. As a tabernacle or temple, it was a place set apart from ordinary profane use, and it was regarded solely for divine use. How much more when the Lord is set apart by the believer's faith, exercise and practice, when he can find rest, refuge and refreshment in Himself. We shall consider three aspects of our subject: the Lord as sanctuary in heaven, in the church and in the world.

The Lord our sanctuary in heaven, Jer. 17. 12-14. In the earlier verses, we find a contrast: if one trusts in man, this leads to a wilderness experience, vv. 5, 6; but if one trusts in the Lord, there is fruitfulness, vv. 7, 8. Another contrast appears in verses 12-13; either there is a forsaking of the Lord on earth, or there is a recognition of the throne above, the sanctuary, the Lord Himself. Similarly in John 17. 16-21; the Lord was not of this world, but of heaven; He sanctified Himself and was glorified, so that His people are "one *in* us". He is a sanctuary in heaven and His people abide in Him.

The Lord our sanctuary in the church, Isa. 8. 14. Judah was finding a satisfactory association with Samaria and Syria, but for the faithful remnant, they should "Sanctify the Lord of hosts himself", and "he shall be for a sanctuary". "Behold, I and the children whom the Lord hath given me", v. 18, said God dwelling on mount Zion. These words apply to God's earthly people, but we can see an application to God's people today. Zion is the heavenly position to which we are come, and Christ Jesus is made unto us sanctification, 1 Cor. 1. 30, so He is the heavenly sanctuary for His people now, where we can be set apart for Himself.

The Lord our sanctuary in the world. The people of Jerusalem had been taken captive; yet in those far off lands God said, "yet will I be to them as a little sanctuary", Ezek. 11. 16. Today, wherever we may be in the world, He is set apart as our Example and resting place. We are exhorted to "sanctify the Lord God in your hearts", 1 Pet. 3. 15, when we find His presence satisfying in our sojourn on earth.

October 22nd

READING: **1 Corinthians 11. 20-26**

NIGHT AND THE LORD'S SUPPER

THE RECORDS stress the fact that it was evening when the Lord Jesus first instituted what Paul calls the Lord's Supper; it was "even", Matt. 26. 20; "evening", Mark 14. 17; "after supper", Luke 22. 20; "night", John 13. 30; "the same night", 1 Cor. 11. 23. This emphasis is not on the actual time of day when the breaking of bread took place, but rather on the moral conditions that surrounded that upper room on the outside. For the greatest darkness was forming amongst men, as they plotted to put the Lord to death, while there was light, both physical and spiritual, in the upper room when the Lord was in the midst of His apostles. It was amongst men, in their state of darkened hearts and minds, that the Lord moved to His trials at the hands of the Jewish Sanhedrin and then at the hands of the Romans, and finally to the cross for crucifixion. Today, we remember the Lord in the light of the Lord's presence and of our fellow-believers in Christ, but around us are the evil conditions of moral darkness and night in men's lives as we await the Lord's sure and near return. We sometimes sing,

> To look beyond the long dark night,
> And hail the coming day,
> When Thou to all Thy saints in light,
> Thy glories wilt display.

The song of worship in the night. Light in the sanctuary is an important concept. Thus the shepherds were watching over their flock by night, but the Lord's glory manifested light, and there was praise from the angelic host, Luke 2. 9, 13. The psalmist confessed that "in the night his song shall be with me", Psa. 42. 7, for he was cast down in the darkness around, yet he went to the house of God with the voice of joy and praise. In Psalm 134. 1, there were those who blessed the Lord, standing by night in the house of the Lord. See Psa. 77. 6.

Anticipation of the day of light. "Weeping may endure for a night, but joy cometh in the morning", Psa. 30. 5, shows the anticipation of the better day. Also in Song 2. 17. Morally, "Ye are all the children of light . . . not of the night", 1 Thess. 5. 5, for the darkness is without but not within, both in our own hearts and in the local assembly. Truly "The night is far spent, the day is at hand", Rom. 13. 12.

October 23rd

READING: **2 Peter 3. 1-13**

THE LAST DAYS

WORDS SUCH AS "last day", "last days", "latter days", "last time" are scattered throughout the O.T. and N.T.; their several meanings must be determined from the context. Prophetical for Israel, references may be found in Dan. 2. 28; 10. 14; Isa. 2. 2, etc. The Lord Jesus used the words "last day" in John 6. 39; 12. 48. But in the Epistles, we can find a few verses containing "last days, last time", the context referring to the period prior to the rapture, indeed, to the days in which we now live. All state the prevalent evil conditions of darkness, with the Lord's people standing in sharp contrast.

(1) 2 Timothy 3. 1, "in the last days perilous times shall come". The full description of these perilous times is awful to read in detail. Indeed, "evil men and seducers shall wax worse and worse", v. 13, when men will not endure sound doctrine, 4. 3. But for the Lord's people there is the exhortation, "continue thou in the things . . . learned", 3. 14.

(2) 2 Peter 3. 3, "there shall come in the last days scoffers, walking after their own lusts". They mockingly ask, "Where is the promise of his coming?", willingly being ignorant of God's plans for judgment. In such darkness, believers should manifest "all holy conversation and godliness", v. 11.

(3) 1 John 2. 18, "it is the last time . . . even now are there many antichrists; whereby we know that it is the last time". Here are men who teach false doctrines concerning the Son of God, but as far as believers are concerned, "we have an unction (anointing) from the Holy One", and He leads us into truth and keeps us in the truth.

(4) Jude 18, "there should be mockers in the last time, who should walk after their own ungodly lusts". This is similar teaching to that in 2 Peter 3. But believers are building up themselves in their most holy faith, Jude 20, keeping themselves in the love of God. By this means they are immune from the errors around, and assess them for what they are worth.

(5) 1 Timothy 4. 1, "the Spirit speaketh expressly, that in the latter times some shall depart from the faith". Believers are separated from the various heretical sects, and they seek to be good ministers of the Lord Jesus, "nourished up in the words of faith and of good doctrine", v. 6.

October 24th

READING: **Isaiah 52. 13-15**

MY SERVANT

THE TITLES used by God are very important, both when they apply to His Son the Lord Jesus Christ, and when they apply to His people. In Isaiah, God said "my servant" speaking of Isaiah, 20. 3; Eliakim, 22. 20; Israel, 41. 8; Jacob, 44. 1, but on other occasions, the title refers to the Lord Jesus prophetically, 42. 1, 19; 49. 6; 52. 13.

Some of the titles used by God with the adjective "my" are:

My Servant, Isa. 52. 13, etc.

My Son, Psa. 2. 7; Matt. 3. 17; Mark 9. 7.

My King, Psa. 2. 6.

My Anointed (Christ), Psa. 132. 17.

My Servant the Branch, Zech. 3. 8.

It is a blessing and a privilege to know that God has called many of His people by the title "my servant". Thus we have

Moses, Num. 12. 7; Josh. 1. 2; Mal. 4. 4.

Abraham, Gen. 26. 24.

Caleb, Num. 14. 24.

Job, Job 1. 8; 2. 3; 42. 7, 8.

Isaiah, Isa. 20. 3.

Nebuchadnezzar, Jer. 25. 9; 27. 6.

We also read of His servant, Thy servant (Solomon, Simeon), and servant of Christ (Paul, Gal. 1. 10). We cannot supply the contexts of all these references, but the reader may care to examine the ones that particularly interest him; it is remarkable to note that even a man like Nebuchadnezzar is called by the title "my servant", doing the will of God in spite of himself.

The Lord Jesus also used the title "my servants" or "my servant" in a more general way, such as "if my kingdom were of this world, then would my servants fight . . . but now is my kingdom not from hence", John 18. 36; "Jezebel . . . to teach and to seduce my servants", Rev. 2. 20.

By this we know that we are not our own; we belong to the Lord with all authority to control our service. We can find in the Scriptures the following features of a servant of the Lord: faithful in all God's house, called, sent, equipped (by the Spirit, with the Word of God), gifted (with spiritual gifts), guided, and rewarded, "Well done", Matt. 25. 21.

October 25th

READING: **2 Timothy 2. 1-14**

THE APOSTOLIC EXAMPLE TO TIMOTHY

PAUL EXHORTED believers to be an imitator of him as he was an imitator of Christ, 1 Cor. 11. 1. First of all, Paul was a pattern unto salvation, 1 Tim. 1. 16. Then he was a pattern in doctrine, conduct, service and testimony, all according to the Word of God, and particularly suitable for the last days when every kind of religious evil surrounded him. In Paul's second Epistle to Timothy we find many such examples.

(1) *In the doctrine of salvation.* In 1. 13, he wrote, "Hold fast the form of sound words, which thou hast heard of me". In other words, do not deviate from the truth given in verses 9-10, namely that it is the Lord who has saved us and called us, that salvation is not of our works but according to His own purpose given us in Christ before the world began.

(2) *To perpetuate truth.* In 2. 2, Paul wrote, "the things that thou hast heard of me . . . commit thou to faithful men". Timothy must not strive about words to no profit, v. 14; he must shun profane and vain babblings, v. 16; he must avoid foolish and unlearned questions, v. 23. Rather he must rightly divide the word, v. 15, separating the truth of the Word from the evil doctrines of men.

(3) *The godly life.* Paul wrote in 3. 10, "thou hast fully known my doctrine, manner of life, purpose, faith". Paul was so different from those who cannot come to a knowledge of the truth, men who resist the truth with corrupt minds, vv. 7-8. He warned that those who follow him will suffer persecution, from which the Lord can deliver, vv. 11-12.

(4) *Continue when things get worse.* Having stated that evil men will get worse and worse, Paul wrote, "continue thou in the things which thou hast learned . . . knowing of whom thou hast learned them", 3. 14. The truth had come from Paul, who by divine teaching had added to the truth of the O.T. that Timothy had known from his childhood.

(5) *Passing on the example.* Timothy not only followed Paul, but he had to pass this on to others who would in turn pass it on as well, 2. 2. Timothy had to be an example to the believers, in word, manner of life, faith and purity, 1 Tim. 4. 12. His profiting would appear to all, v. 16, thus forming a chain of testimony, of which we stand at its end.

October 26th

READING: **Luke 6. 1-11**

HEALING ON THE SABBATH

THE SABBATH was a cherished tradition held by the Pharisees; it kept men in bondage more than the other commandments. It had been given by God both in creation and in law, yet it was the one commandment that had to be approached with wise discrimination. The Lord Jesus often did important work on the Sabbath day, so He demonstrated divine wisdom, giving many reasons for His necessary work on the Sabbath.

Luke 6. 1, where the disciples were plucking corn and rubbing it in their hands. (1) But David went into the house of God, and did eat the showbread, Matt. 12. 4; Mark 2. 26; Luke 6. 4. *Need.* (2) The priests profaned the Sabbath, referring to regular and special sacrifices that had to be offered on that day, Matt. 12. 5. *Obedience.* (3) "I will have mercy, and not sacrifice", Matt. 12. 7; Hos. 6. 6; ritual means nothing if the heart is not right, and can be bypassed if mercy is needed. *Heart transcends mind.* (4) The Son of man is Lord of the Sabbath, Matt. 12. 8; Mark 2. 28; Luke 6. 5. *Subjection to divine authority.*

Luke 6. 6, the healing of the man with the withered hand. (1) A sheep lifted out of a pit, a man being better than a sheep, Matt. 12. 11-12. *Compassion.* (2) Lawful to do good and to save life, Mark 3. 4; Luke 6. 9. *Preservation of life.*

Luke 13. 11, the woman bowed eighteen years. But an ox or an ass can be loosed, so as to be led to watering, Luke 13. 15. *Necessities of life.*

Luke 14. 1-6, the man with the dropsy. An ass or an ox fallen into a pit can be pulled out. *Salvation.*

Luke 14. 1-6, the infirm man thirty-eight years. (1) "My Father worketh hitherto, and I work", v. 17. God's initial Sabbath had been disturbed by sin, and He has been working for men ever since. *No rest in service.* (2) Circumcision was practised on the Sabbath day, John 7. 22-23; see Leviticus 12. 3. *Obedience to the commands of God.*

John 9. 14, the blind man healed on the Sabbath. No further explanation was given by the Lord; He said to the Pharisees, "your sin remaineth", v. 41.

The Lord referred to the Sabbath when He said, "I do cures . . . to morrow" between death and resurrection, Luke 13. 32.

October 27th

READING: **Psalm 40. 1-17**

"THY" AND "MY" IN PSALM 40

THIS IS a Messianic Psalm, since verses 6-8 are quoted in Hebrews 10. 5-7 relating to the Lord Jesus. This is stated to be a Psalm of David, and he was a prophet, Acts 2. 30, and the Spirit spake by him. He was thus enabled to rehearse the words and thoughts of Christ a millennium before the Lord lived and suffered here below.

There are two little words that are repeated again and again in this psalm, and once this is pointed out, the reader can search through the psalm to see the number of times "thy" and "my (or, mine)" occur. The Lord Jesus is addressing God by the word "thy", and refers to Himself as "my". The "thy" reflects on the divine side, the pure gold of the ark of the covenant; the "my" reflects upon His human character in perfection, the acacia (shittim) wood of the ark of the covenant.

As far as "my" is concerned, in order through the psalm we find "my cry", "my feet", "my goings", "my mouth", "my God", "mine ears", "my God", "my heart", "my lips", "mine iniquities", "mine head", "my heart", "my soul", "my deliverer", "my God".

When we read "mine iniquities", we must interpret this very carefully. He had no iniquities of His own, this goes without saying. But on the cross when He died for our sins, He made them His own so as to bear them that we might be freed. If we do not accept this explanation, then we must exclude verse 12 from the Messianic interpretation, and assert that this was an experience of David the psalmist, and not of Christ.

As far as "thy" is concerned, in order through the psalm we find "thy wonderful works", "thy thoughts", "thy will", "thy law", "thy righteousness", "thy faithfulness", "thy salvation", "thy lovingkindness", "thy truth", "thy tender mercies", "thy lovingkindness", "thy truth", "thy salvation".

Note how these cluster around verses 8-11, where the character of God is so adequately described. In verses 1-4, Christ rehearses what God has done for Him; in the remaining verses He addresses God directly (it is the third person in verses 1-4, but the second person in the remaining verses).

It is a good exercise to link all these features of "my" and "thy" with specific quotations from the N.T.

301

October 28th

READING: **Matthew 14. 22-36**

CONFESSION OF THE SON

IN THIS ARTICLE, we wish to concentrate on confessions that were made directly to the Son. Elsewhere, there were confessions made *about* the Son of God, for example by Paul, "the Son of God, who loved me, and gave himself for me", Gal. 2. 20. There were also the Lord's own words, when He replied "Thou hast said" to the high priest, "I adjure thee by the living God, that thou tell us whether thou be the Christ, the Son of God", Matt. 26. 63. But consider the following direct testimonies spoken to the Lord:

Because of Pre-eminence. "Thou art my beloved Son, in whom I am well pleased", Mark 1. 11, spoken at His baptism. See also Psalm 2. 7. At His transfiguration, the testimony of God was *about* His Son, Matt. 17. 5; Mark 9. 7; Luke 9. 35.

Because of Power. When the wind had ceased, and after Peter had walked on the sea, they said, "Of a truth thou art the Son of God", Matt. 14. 33.

Because of Preaching. Others may leave the Lord, but Peter said, "we believe and are sure that thou art that Christ, the Son of the living God", John 6. 67-69.

Because of Perception. By means of the Lord's words about himself, Nathanael was able to discern by faith who the Lord was, "thou art the Son of God", John 1. 49.

Because of Promise. The Lord promised resurrection, so Martha said, "I believe that thou art the Christ, the Son of God, which should come into the world", John 11. 27.

Because of His Person. Peter's great confession in Matthew 16. 16, "Thou art the Christ, the Son of the living God" did not arise from His miracles and teaching, but by direct revelation from the Father.

Because of Pain. We leave this one to last, since this was the testimony of demons issued because of fear of pain and torment, "What have we to do with thee, Jesus, thou Son of God?", Matt. 8. 29.

Note the occasions when the title "Christ" was also used, showing the unique connection between God's anointed One and the Father's beloved Son. It appears that it is the natural confession of faith to declare the Sonship of Christ, not only to men and to the Father, but directly to the Son Himself.

October 29th

READING: **Hebrews 1. 1-14**

THE CREATOR AND UPHOLDER

IT MATTERS not what men may say about the beginning of the universe. The popular theory at the present time is the so-called "big bang" theory, but Christians are not called upon to place their faith in any of the shifting quicksands of the theories of men, for these tend to change or to be modified with every generation of scientists. In fact, Ecclesiastes 3. 11 tells us that no man can find out the ultimate nature of the work of God in creation.

God's revelation in the Scriptures informs us all that we can know according to the divine will. Moreover, these references to the creation are consistent, and satisfying to the hearts of His people. The great chapter showing the uniqueness of the Son of God, Heb. 1, brings in His creatorial work. "Thou, Lord, in the beginning hast laid the foundation of the earth; and the heavens are the works of thy hands", v. 10, quoted from Psalm 102. 25, showing that He who began all things physically will also end them in His own time. The heavens are the work of God's fingers, Psa. 8. 3, while Isaiah exhorts men to "behold who hath created these things", Isa. 40. 26. Truly, it was in the beginning that God created the heavens and the earth, Gen. 1. 1. In John 1. 1-3, the apostle takes our minds back to the eternal period prior to the creation; then the Word was, and at the appointed time "All things were made by him".

The N.T. is full of references to the creation. Paul had to use the creatorship of God as an argument that sacrifice should not be made to himself and Barnabas, Acts 14. 15. Later, Paul argued that the fact "by whom are all things" is sufficient to show that material idols are but nothing, 1 Cor. 8. 6. The "mystery" hidden since the creation, but revealed to Paul, caused him to confess of God, "who created all things by Jesus Christ", Eph. 3. 9. In Revelation 4. 11; 14. 7 mention is made of the divine act of creation.

But there is not only the creation itself; there is the maintaining of it by "natural laws" ever since. This again is the Lord's doing. Not only did the Son make the worlds, but He upholds all things by the word of his power, Heb. 1. 3. See also Colossians 1. 16-17. But men fail to see the hand of the Lord in the very regularity of nature, 2 Pet. 3. 4.

October 30th

READING: **Isaiah 46. 1-13**

THE PLEASURE OF THE LORD IN ISAIAH

HOW THIS contrasts with the pleasures of men. The Jews had their religion; they sought God daily; they took delight in approaching God; they fasted, afflicting their souls. But in all this, "in the day of your fast ye find pleasure", Isa. 58. 2-3. In other words, here is a feigned religion, men enjoying the world's occupations under the cloke of religious observances, Instead, men should cease "from doing thy pleasure on my holy day" rather than "finding thine own pleasure", v. 13. Today, even some believers profane the Lord's Day by enjoying the pleasures of the world during its hours.

How different are God's pleasures. He delighted in His elect, 42. 1. Yet it pleased the Lord to bruise His Servant, 53. 10, but with redemption accomplished, "the pleasure of the Lord shall prosper" in His Servant's hand, v. 10, for in resurrection "at thy right hand there are pleasures for evermore", Psa. 16. 11.

In Isaiah 46. 10, God said, "My counsel shall stand, and I will do all my pleasure"; the following verse shows that this refers to judgment upon Jerusalem, when after one hundred years the Babylonians would come from a far country and the city would be destroyed. In other words, the nations unwittingly did His counsel and pleasure (such as the Assyrians like an axe in God's hand, 10. 15). Yet after the seventy years captivity, God's pleasure would be concerned with the rebuilding of the temple and the city. He predicted of Cyrus, king of Persia, "He is my shepherd, and shall perform all my pleasure", allowing the Jews to return to build the city and the temple, 44. 28. So there would be Gentile participation in this rebuilding, just as today it is God's pleasure that the Gentiles participate in salvation and in the building of His house spiritually.

The Babylonians had destroyed Jerusalem for their pleasure, not knowing that they were doing God's pleasure. But Babylon was also taken in God's purpose; of the victor, God said, "he will do his pleasure on Babylon", 48. 14, namely, Darius the Mede took the kingdom of Babylon, unwittingly doing God's pleasure, Dan. 5. 31. Wheels within wheels!

May we consciously be doing God's pleasure, without the necessity of His pleasure using us because we may be unwilling.

October 31st

READING: **1 Corinthians 10. 31-33; 11. 16-26**

NAMES OF THE CHURCH

BY A TITLE, we do not mean the popular names ascribed to buildings and denominations. The N.T. knows something quite different. The word "church" is associated with Christ, with God, and with the saints. (The words "church, churches" are usually prefixed with "the, every, a, no, other".)

Church associated with Christ. After Peter's confession of Christ as the Son on the living God, the Lord said, "I will build my church", Matt. 16. 18. This shows the Lord's personal possession of the church, and the divine work of building. The living Head possesses His body, the church. Also individual local churches (in the plural) have this title. The churches round Corinth where Paul was writing to the Romans were called "the churches of Christ", Rom. 16. 16.

Church associated with God. "Church(es) of God" is the usual title of a local church. In his unconverted days, Paul (as Saul) "persecuted the church of God", 1 Cor. 15. 9, a term used here for the totality of the churches at that time. In Galatians 1. 13, the singular also occurs for the totality, as if Paul could view the whole body of Christ at that time. By writing of "the Jews, the Gentiles, the church of God", 1 Cor. 10. 32, he also had in mind all believers on earth.

But when he wrote "the churches of God" are not contentious, 1 Cor. 11. 16, he viewed each church separately. When he wrote of despising "the church of God", v. 22, he had in mind the particular local church in Corinth. He was, of course, writing to "the church of God" in Corinth, 1. 2, obviously the local church in that city. He referred to "the churches of God which in Judaea are in Christ Jesus", 1 Thess. 2. 14, meaning all the persecuted local churches around Jerusalem. To take care of "the church of God", 1 Tim. 3. 5, refers to the local sphere of responsibility of elders; the same may be said of Acts 20. 28. Behaviour in "the house of God, which is the church of the living God" has a local aspect, 1 Tim. 3. 15, though we do not rule out a broader sense.

Church associated with saints. Paul was writing of the conduct of a meeting, 1 Cor. 14. 33, and he used the unique title, "all the churches of the saints", implying that local churches were composed of saints, of separated ones.

November 1st

READING: **John 5. 30-47**

TESTIMONY CONCERNING CHRIST

GOD HAS not left Himself without witness, and He has ensured that there is adequate testimony concerning His Son, so that men are without excuse if they refuse to believe on Him. John chapter 5 is particularly full of different kinds of testimony that show forth the Person of Christ. We may supply a list of those that render testimony to the Son of God.

The Father. "The Father himself, which hath sent me, hath borne witness of me", John 5. 37. For example, at His baptism and transfiguration, Matt. 3. 17; 17. 5. In John 12. 28 the Father spoke to the Son, but the people thought it thundered.

The Lord Himself. In contrast with verse 31, the Lord said in 8. 18, "I am one that bear witness of myself", for example, as the Son and the Good Shepherd, 9. 37; 10. 14, 36.

The Spirit. "The Spirit of truth, which proceedeth from the Father, he shall testify of me", 15. 26. Thus the Spirit enabled Peter and Paul to speak and write about the Son.

Moses. "He wrote of me", 5. 46, meaning that the Jews should have believed Him, since they claimed to trust Moses; for example, he spoke of "a Prophet", Deut. 18. 15, 18.

The Scriptures. "They are they which testify of me", 5. 39. This enabled the Lord to expound "in all the scriptures the things concerning himself", Luke 24. 27, 44-45.

His works. "The same works that I do, bear witness of me", 5. 36. Thus after Peter walked on the sea, and when the wind ceased, they confessed Him as the Son of God, Matt. 14. 33.

John the Baptist. "John, he bear witness unto the truth", 5. 33. Thus in John 1. 7, "The same came for a witness, to bear witness of the Light", for example, of the Lamb of God, v. 36.

The people. For example, those who witnessed the raising of Lazarus "bare record", John 12. 17, causing those who heard them to meet the Lord as He entered Jerusalem.

The apostle John. John saw the death of the Lord on the cross, and the fact that blood and water were shed, writing, "he that saw it bare record, and his record is true", John 19. 35.

The apostles. "Ye also shall bear witness, because ye have been with me from the beginning", John 15. 27.

Truly we are encompassed with "so great a cloud of witnesses", Heb. 12. 1, and all believers should be added to the list.

November 2nd

READING: **Proverbs 12. 1-14**

THE FARMER'S YEAR

SOLOMON SPOKE three thousand proverbs, 1 Kings 4. 32, so we are not surprised that amongst them we find many references to the work of the farmer throughout the year, all of which have a spiritual meaning.

Tilling. "He that tilleth his land shall be satisfied with bread", Prov. 12. 11. Today, we are God's tillage or cultivated plot, 1 Cor. 3. 9. Believers must be prepared, by corrective ministry if necessary, to receive the deep things of the incorruptible Word of God.

Sowing. "To him that soweth righteousness shall be a sure reward", Prov. 11. 18. Thus the sower sows the Word, Mark 4. 14, and Paul planted, 1 Cor. 3. 6, having the end product in view, "the precious fruit", James 5. 7.

Watering. "He that watereth shall be watered also himself", Prov. 11. 25. Thus "Apollos watered", 1 Cor. 3. 6, by his ministry, but the true and living water is given by the Lord, and that springs up into everlasting life, John 4. 14.

Roots. "The root of the righteous shall not be moved", Prov. 12. 3, otherwise the tree that the Father has not planted shall be rooted up, Matt. 15. 13. For growth and stability, we must be rooted and built up in Him, Col. 2. 7.

Fruit. "The root of the righteous yieldeth fruit", Prov. 12. 12. In the parable of the sower, those that produce fruit are those who understand the Word, Matt. 13. 23; those who receive it, Mark 4. 20; and keep it, Luke 8. 15.

Satisfied. "A man shall be satisfied with good by the fruit", Prov. 12. 14. God's order is that the man who labours must also partake of the fruits, 2 Tim. 2. 6. Then he can bring forth abundantly from a satisfied heart, Matt. 12. 34-35.

Feeding others. "Blessing shall be upon the head of him that selleth it (corn)", Prov. 11. 26. Thus elders must feed the church of God, Acts 20. 28; 1 Pet. 5. 2, knowing that they shall receive a crown of unfading glory, v. 4.

The next harvest. "The fruit of the righteous is a tree of life", Prov. 11. 30. The seed of the fruit, if planted, will yield a further tree. Thus the Lord spoke of others who believe through the apostles' word, John 17. 20, while Paul wrote of those who teach others also, 2 Tim. 2. 2.

November 3rd

READING: **Ephesians 3. 13-21**

ROOTS AND ROOTED

THERE ARE many references to men being rooted in evil, and being rooted out for judgment. But it is profitable to trace the idea in a holy and spiritual sense. Roots (1) provide for the rigidity of a tree or plant in the soil, (2) are the means whereby nourishment is extracted from the soil, which is then conducted through trunk, branches and twigs to the growing points, (3) in some trees and plants are the source of fresh saplings which then grow into fullsize trees or plants.

We consider the following points that occur in Scripture.

Israel out of Egypt. Psalm 80. 8-10 shows that Israel was a vine out of Egypt, planted in their land till it covered the hills. Alas, that the vine became burnt with fire; it was cut down and perished, v. 16.

New roots in restoration. Hezekiah saw restoration when he said, "the remnant . . . of the house of Judah shall again take root downward, and bear fruit upward", Isa. 37. 31.

A root out of dry ground. No restoration lasted, but out of that wayward nation the Lord Jesus would come: "as a root out of a dry ground", Isa. 53. 2. This root was divine.

This leads to blessing. In Romans 11. 16-22, the root of the nation of Israel was holy, though in latter times some branches were cut off. The Gentiles were grafted in, but as sustained by the roots the natural branches will be restored.

Righteousness prevails. Spiritual roots of the righteous are important: "the root of the righteous shall not be moved", Prov. 12. 3, and it "yieldeth fruit", v. 12.

Aspects for believers today. Paul knew that believers are "rooted and grounded in love", Eph. 3. 17, and "rooted and built up in him", Col. 2. 7. Here is stability and growth in the Christian faith, but the foundation is Christ.

The future for Israel. Isaiah described the great millennial scene, "He shall cause them that come of Jacob to take root: Israel shall blossom and bud, and fill the face of the world with fruit", Isa. 27. 6. Then they "shall worship the Lord in the holy mount at Jerusalem", v. 13.

The Lord seen in glory. "In that day there shall be a root of Jesse . . . an ensign of the people . . . and his rest shall be glorious", Isa. 11. 10. He will be pre-eminent.

November 4th

READING: **Mark 10. 23-34**

HE WENT BEFORE THEM

THE VERB "to go before" used of the Lord Jesus appears only a very small number of times in the Gospels. It implies, of course, that the disciples were following Him. It appears in John 10. 4, "when he putteth forth his own sheep, he goeth before them, and the sheep follow him". It stands in contrast to Mark 11. 9, where, in the hour of the Lord's triumph, some people went before and others followed, clearly with the Lord in the midst of the multitudes.

We wish to consider (i) Mark 10. 32, where "Jesus went before them", and (ii) Mark 14. 28; 16. 7, both referring to the same event, the Lord going before them into Galilee. There is a series of contrasts between these two events.

In (i), this took place a few days before the death of the Lord Jesus, while (ii) the event took place after His death, perhaps by two weeks. (The first time, the Lord spoke in the night before His death, while the second time it was the angelic visitor who spoke on the resurrection day.)

In (i), the Lord was journeying from Galilee to Jerusalem, via the east side of Jordan and Jericho, Mark 10. 1, 46. In (ii), He would journey from Jerusalem to Galilee, from the place of sacrifice to the region where He had spent so much of the time of His ministry and service here below.

In (i), as the disciples followed Him, they were afraid, knowing that there would be trouble of some kind in Jerusalem, though exactly what they did not know. But in (ii), the angel said "Fear not", and it was with "great joy" that the women heard the words, Matt. 28. 7-8.

In (i), there were twelve apostles following, Judas being still with them, but in (ii) there were only eleven apostles who had to be told.

In (i), the Lord predicted what would happen, namely, His death and rising again. In (ii), all had taken place; "it behoved Christ to suffer . . . and to rise", Luke 24. 46.

Of the prediction in (i), Luke 18. 34 tells us that there was no understanding on the part of the apostles, but in (ii) when the disciples had been told, the Lord opened their understanding, Luke 24. 45.

In (i) they followed Him by sight, in (ii) by faith.

November 5th

READING: 1 Thessalonians 3. 1-13

PAUL'S UNCEASING PRAYER

THE UNCEASING prayer by the apostle for the various churches with which he was associated is found in most of his Epistles. We have considered the matter before generally, but here we shall examine the Epistles to the Thessalonians to see how the subject is developed. These Epistles were written not long after the founding of the Thessalonian church, so this shows how quickly the needs of these believers were impressed on the sincere heart of the apostle.

Paul commenced by stating that he thanked God "always for you all", 1 Thess. 1. 2. This took place in his prayers. The subject matter of his thanksgiving was fourfold: (i) their work of faith, (ii) their labour of love, (iii) their patience of hope, (iv) their election of God. Can we see all these features in our fellowbelievers, and does it call forth thanksgiving from our hearts? Additionally, in 2. 13, he thanked God without ceasing because they had received the Word of God, not as the word of man, but as the Word of God. This is the mark of a true convert listening to a true preacher. Again in 3. 9, Paul thanked God for the joy he had in his heart because of them.

He now prayed specifically. (i) Night and day to be able to see them again; (ii) to be able to perfect what was lacking in their faith; (iii) that God should direct his way to them; (iv) that their love might abound, (v) that their hearts might be stablished unblameable. What subject matter for our prayers!

At the same time, Paul asked them to "Pray without ceasing", and that they might pray for him, 5. 17, 25.

In 2 Thessalonians, the same subject recurs. Paul feels himself bound to thank God always that their faith was growing, and their love was abounding (in answer to the prayer in 1 Thess. 3. 12). He also thanked God always that He had chosen them to salvation through sanctification of the Spirit and belief of the truth, 2. 13.

He was also praying always for them, 1. 11, (i) that God would count them worthy of this calling; (ii) that He would fulfil all the good pleasure of His goodness; (iii) that the Name of the Lord might be glorified. What further subject matter for our prayers! Paul also desired their prayers, that he should have liberty and deliverance from wicked men, 3. 1-2.

November 6th

READING: **2 Samuel 23. 1-7**

DAVID AND THE HOLY SPIRIT

THE SPIRIT is not only a N.T. experience. There believers have been baptized in the Spirit, thereby forming the church; He indwells all believers; He enables them to approach the Father in worship; He fills those empty of self for the service of God. In the O.T. the Spirit came upon the Lord's people to make them useful in many ways in God's service.

In particular, we may consider the example of David (we could also consider men such as Bezaleel, Exod. 31. 3).

Worship. Towards the end of his life, David explained why he, the sweet psalmist of Israel, was enabled to sing so extensively the praises of the Lord: "the Spirit of the Lord spake by me, and his word was in my tongue". We too must realize that true worship from our hearts comes only by the Spirit and not by natural effort, John 4. 24.

The pattern. David produced the design of the temple by the Spirit, by the hand of God upon him, 1 Chron. 28. 12, 19; the reason was that the Spirit of the Lord had been upon David from the time of his anointing, 1 Sam. 16. 13. In our time, the mystery of the spiritual structure of the church was revealed to the apostles "by the Spirit", Eph. 3. 5.

Lordship. Dealing with Psalm 110, the Lord stated that David was "in the Spirit", Matt. 22. 43 R.V. David was "a prophet", and only thus could speak of things to come, Acts 2. 30. Today, believers can say that "Jesus is the Lord" only by the Holy Spirit, 1 Cor. 12. 3.

Ability to teach. David taught a lot in his psalms, as Peter said, "the scripture must needs have been fulfilled, which the Holy Spirit by the mouth of David spake before concerning Judas", Acts 1. 16. Today, the Spirit guides into all truth, John 16. 13, enabling some to be teachers in the local churches, 1 Cor. 12. 7, 29.

Prophecy. David was a prophet, Acts 2. 30, and hence spoke much about the resurrection of Christ, vv. 25-28, 30, 34-35 (from Psalms 16, 132, 110); Peter has told us that "the Spirit of Christ which was in them" testified of the sufferings and glory of Christ, 1 Pet. 1. 11. In our days, we have all the truth concerning the future, because He showed the apostles "things to come", John 16. 13.

311

November 7th

READING: **Romans 3. 19-31**

LETTERS TO THE SEVEN CHURCHES

WE DO NOT REFER to the seven churches in Revelation 2-3, to which John had to write the seven discerning messages from the Lord. After all, God had used the number seven right through the Scriptures, from Genesis 1-2 to the many references in the book of Revelation. The common thought is that of divine completion, whether days in Genesis 2. 2, or the golden lampstands in Revelation 1. 20, the completion of the Lord's discernment of the state of local churches.

It is therefore interesting to note that Paul, in his Epistles, wrote to seven churches, namely to the churches in Rome, Corinth, Galatia, Ephesus, Philippi, Colosse and Thessalonica. This list can be divided into three groups, each showing failure and something positive, each showing something lost, and yet found (thinking of Luke 15).

Group 1. In Romans we have many chapters of doctrine, all centring around the great truth of justification by faith; Paul wanted the church at Rome to have the same basis of doctrine on this important subject as he had. Paul also dealt with the practical responsibilities that follow from holding this doctrine. But in writing to the church at Corinth, Paul had to deal with failure. The doctrine of the resurrection was not grasped, and practical failure on many matters meant that the Corinthians had no intention of abiding by their baptismal professions. Also in the Epistle to the Galatians, doctrinal failure was dealt with. Their desire for the law undermined their understanding of justification by faith.

Group 2. This group consists of the three prison Epistles written to Ephesus, Philippi and Colosse. In Ephesians, the apostle dealt with a subject so dear to his heart, the doctrine of the one body, with all its associated practical truths. But there was failure. In Philippi there was disunity; they were not standing fast in one spirit, and sisters were not of the same mind, Phil. 1. 27; 4. 2. In Colosse, they were not holding the Head, Col. 2. 19.

Group 3. This consists of Thessalonica only. The truth of the Lord's return was explained in 1 Thess. 4. 13-17. Yet failure came in, and false doctrine had entered, which had to be corrected in the second Epistle, 2 Thess. 2. 1-3.

November 8th

READING: **Psalm 110. 1-7**

THE MOST CHRIST-EXALTING PSALM

THE FACT that David was exalted, 2 Sam. 5. 12; 23. 1, did not prevent him from recognizing that there was One exalted far higher than he was, the One whom he called "my Lord" in Psalm 110. 1. In verse 1, he is speaking about Christ; in verses 2-4 he is speaking to Christ about God's dealings with Him; in verses 5-7 he is speaking about Christ to God.

In verse 1, we have the Lord's position at Jehovah's right hand, a position of dignity, majesty, authority and power. It is quoted in Matthew 22. 44 as relating to His *Person*; the Pharisees were silenced. It is quoted in Hebrews 1. 13 as relating to *Power and the Purger* of sins; critical believers were silenced. It is quoted in Acts 2. 34 as to the Lord's *Position* in resurrection; unbelievers were silenced.

Verse 2 shows the Lord's future rule from Zion; the "rod" indicates the method of subjugation of His enemies. He shall rule them with "a rod of iron", Rev. 19. 15, after breaking them with "a rod of iron", Psa. 2. 9. Believers will share in this triumph, also ruling with "a rod of iron", Rev. 2. 27.

In verse 3, the Lord's people are seen with Him in this day of power. For these are the armies that will accompany the Lord when He comes in glory, Rev. 19. 14. They will be clothed "in fine linen, white and clean", this being the implication of "in the beauty of holiness" which refers to garments. This can be seen typically in 2 Chronicles 20. 21, where the singers, clothed in their garments "the beauty of holiness" went before the army to victory, returning to Zion and the house of the Lord, v. 28. "The dew of thy youth" (namely, of Thy youthful ones) suggests the living freshness of the Lord's people who had a beginning but never an end.

Verse 4 contrasts the priestly order of Christ with the order of Aaron. Aaron had a beginning and an end; but the One after the order of Melchizedek had no beginning and will have no end, Heb. 7. 3. The Lord's status is that of King as well as that of Priest; see Zechariah 6. 13.

In verses 5-7, Christ is seen as the Executor of Jehovah's wrath in judgment. For the great day of His wrath is come upon the kings of the earth, Rev. 6. 15-17. Revelation 19. 17-21 describes this scene in all its solemnity.

November 9th

READING: **Matthew 9. 10-38**

FIVE OCCUPATIONS OF THE LORD

THE FIVE aspects of service named by Paul in Ephesians 4. 11 were granted by the Risen Lord to His people, namely, apostles, prophets, evangelists, pastors, teachers. These were granted by One who knew what it was when on earth to be an Apostle, Prophet, Evangelist, Pastor and Teacher. Consider these aspects of the Lord's work when here below.

The divine Apostle. The word "apostle" means "a sent one". The application is a technical one, to the twelve men whom the Lord chose to be His apostles, Matt. 10. 1-6, though the word is used occasionally for men other than these twelve.

In Hebrews 3. 1, readers must consider "the Apostle", namely, Christ Jesus. This corresponds to the truth found in John's Gospel, where the Lord claimed on many occasions that He had been sent by the Father: "My meat is to do the will of him that sent me", 4. 34. All the many other occasions may be found in a concordance, since it is an oft-recurring truth.

The divine Prophet. The Lord was recognized by His disciples as a Prophet: "Jesus of Nazareth, which was a prophet mighty in deed and word before God and all the people", Luke 24. 19. He spoke forth the words of God, and in particular often foretold the future concerning Himself. Thus in Matthew 9. 15 He was a Prophet, explaining that He the Bridegroom would be taken from them.

The divine Evangelist. The Lord is not named by the title Evangelist as such, but many times we find Him preaching the gospel. Thus He came to call sinners to repentance, Matt. 9. 13. In all cities and villages, He preached the gospel of the kingdom, 9. 35, for the kingdom of heaven was at hand, 10. 7. That is also what the apostles did when sent forth by the Lord, "preaching the gospel", Luke 9. 6.

The divine Pastor. Men were as sheep without a shepherd, as far as human leadership was concerned, Matt. 9. 36. To start with, He sent His apostles "to the lost sheep of the house of Israel", 10. 6, but later He presented Himself as the Good Shepherd of all His flock, John 10. 14.

The divine Teacher. Apart from His healing ministry, this work of teaching was His main work. He went about all the cities and villages teaching in their synagogues, Matt. 9. 35.

November 10th

READING: **1 Corinthians 15. 1-11**

FOUR PERSONAL AND PRIVATE INTERVIEWS

THE APOSTLE Paul gave rather a comprehensive list of those chosen to see the Lord in resurrection. There were groups, such as the apostles, and "above five hundred brethren at once". But the Lord also appeared to people as individuals, and we would discuss the four cases briefly.

The case of Mary, the enhancement of faith. Paul has not recorded this event, but we read about it in detail in John 20. 11-18. Mary Magdalene knew the power of her Lord, since He had cast out seven demons; she had witnessed the scene at Calvary, Matt. 27. 56, and had not been alone when she came originally to the sepulchre, 28. 1. But now she was alone weeping, John 20. 11; her faith could not grasp the Lord's promise of resurrection. But as soon as He said "Mary", her faith lept to new heights, and the Lord introduced the great truth that His Father was the Father of all His brethren.

The case of Peter, repentance leading to faith. The other apostles confessed that "The Lord . . . hath appeared to Simon", Luke 24. 34, no doubt the same event as referred to by Paul, "And that he was seen of Cephas", 1 Cor. 15. 5. Clearly this is different from the occasion when the Lord said to Peter three times "lovest thou me?", John 21. 15-17. Peter's failure in denying the Lord Jesus three times led to His looking on Peter, but saying nothing, Luke 22. 61. The Lord had much to say after His resurrection, making Peter a new man.

The case of James, from doubt to faith. During His lifetime, the Lord's brethren according to the flesh did not believe on Him, John 7. 5. But the divine purpose had much work for James to do in the Jerusalem church, and hence the Lord revealed Himself to James, 1 Cor. 15. 7. Both he and his brethren were changed men after that, Acts 1. 14.

The case of Paul, from religious bigotry to the highest apostolic position, 1 Cor. 15. 8-10. This case was exceptional; when Paul (as Saul) was least expecting it, in the midst of his religious crimes, and after the Lord had ascended, He appeared in glory. Saul said hardly anything except "Lord", but the Lord explained the divine purpose to send him to the Gentiles, Acts 26. 16-18. This encounter was with such power, that he was not disobedient to the heavenly vision, v. 19.

315

November 11th

READING: **1 Kings 10. 1-13**

THE CHURCH AND THE HOME

FOR KING Solomon, his home and the house of the Lord were intimately connected. The queen of Sheba saw everything in his home, which was connected by an "ascent" to the house of the Lord, a viaduct that reached over a valley from palace to temple, 1 Kings 10. 5. This was a testimony to others; they could see that Solomon would leave his palace in order to go up to the house of the Lord. There are many examples of this, either in weakness or in strength.

There was weakness in Nehemiah 13. 10-11, for the house of God had been forsaken, and the Levitical servants had fled to their fields. There was weakness in Exodus 33. 8, for men were content to remain in their tent door, while Moses and Joshua went out to the tabernacle. David was glad when they said, "Let us go up to the house of the Lord", Psa. 122. 1, but Michal looked out of a window of her home and despised David in her heart, 1 Chron. 15. 29. Previously, the ark had remained for three months in the home of Obed-edom, and God blessed this house and all that he had, 13. 14. From being before the ark in the tent, David returned to bless his house, 16. 43, where he had the exercise to build a permanent structure for God's dwelling place, 17. 1. Thus there was a balance of activity between man's house and God's house.

In the Lord's case, consider His last week. In the temple courts, he cast out what was unholy, and taught daily in these temple courts, Luke 19. 45-48. But at night He went out to the mount of Olives and abode there, 21. 37. Matthew 21. 17 tells us that this was at Bethany, so we conclude that He abode in the home of Mary, Martha and Lazarus. So the Lord divided His attention between fellowship in a sanctified home and His work in the temple courts.

In Acts 1. 13, the disciples "abode" in the upper room; this was their temporary home. Yet this was used for spiritual work, in prayer and in contemplating the O.T. Scriptures. The church in Jerusalem was formed in that room. Later, in Acts 12. 5, 12, the home of the mother of John Mark was used as a place for the gathering of the church in prayer. In Rome, there was the church that gathered in the home of Priscilla and Aquila, Rom. 16. 5. This is an ascent to the house of the Lord.

November 12th

READING: **1 Corinthians 6. 1-20**

STANDARDS IN THE HOUSE AND TEMPLE

IN THE Epistles, the church is referred to as house or temple, but never as tabernacle. In the O.T., holiness was demanded of God's servants in the house of the Lord. In the N.T., standards are absolutely necessary for fellowship and service relating to members of the church of God.

Standards of personal morality and spirituality of God's people, 1 Cor. 6. 19-20. Chapters 5-6 show acts tolerated by believers in Corinth, but Paul had judged already. For the church was composed of individual members, called "Your body is the temple of the Holy Spirit . . . ye are not your own"; so each individual temple forms a greater one, and the three Persons of the Godhead dwell within each temple.

Standards of fellowship. In 2 Corinthians 6. 13, Paul desired enlargement, yet not going beyond the bounds of what was spiritually acceptable to God. There could be no "fellowship, communion, concord, part, agreement", vv. 14-16, with all opposing forms of evil, for the believers were "the temple of God". Standards must be such that God can dwell in them, so they had to come out of all spiritual opposition.

Standards of behaviour. Paul wrote to Timothy towards the end of his life, so his words came from years of experience in local churches. Thus he wrote of behaviour "in the house of God, which is the church of the living God", 1 Tim. 3. 16. He discussed such topics as prayer, the qualification of elders and servants, and dangers of the latter times.

Paul also discussed *the standards necessary for local building,* 1 Cor. 3. 9-17, where the Corinthians were "the temple of God", and when great care was necessary in what was built on the one foundation. At the same time, Paul looked beyond what was local, and saw the whole church as "an holy temple in the Lord", Eph. 2. 21-22, and saw this as a temple that was growing as a habitation of God.

Peter discussed *the standard of priestly service,* 1 Pet. 2. 5, "a spiritual house, an holy priesthood", for believers offer up spiritual sacrifices, "acceptable to God by Jesus Christ". He also wrote of judgment beginning at the house of God, 4. 17, implying great care on the part of His people.

Note: apostasy has its counter standards, 2 Thess. 2. 4.

317

November 13th

READING: Luke 12. 35-48

MEN THAT WAIT FOR THEIR LORD

WE ALWAYS seem to be waiting for something. We are tired, and we wait for bedtime. Parents wait for their child's first words, their first step. We may wait for summer holidays. Life would be monotonous if there were nothing to wait for! If it is certain that what we wait for will actually occur, then the Bible calls this "hope", quite distinct from an unbeliever's use of this word, when it means something that is uncertain!

What did the Lord wait for? During His lifetime here below, He was waiting for the cross which He knew He had to sustain. On the cross, when made sin for us, He waited for the good things beyond in resurrection: "the joy that was set before him", Heb. 12. 2; "in thy presence is fulness of joy", Psa. 16. 11; "the travail of his soul", Isa. 53. 11.

We wait for blessing and salvation. We do not wait in vain, like the multitude in John 5. 3 who waited for the moving of the water. We do not wait for an angel, but for God Himself and His salvation, Gen. 49. 18; Micah 7. 7. Thus Cornelius waited for Peter with news of salvation, Acts 10. 24; the apostles had to wait for the promise of the Father, 1. 4; Simeon waited for the consolation of Israel, Luke 2. 25.

We wait for the Lord in our lives now. There should be no impatience, no carrying on in our own way. Thus David "waited patiently for the Lord", Psa. 40. 1. "I wait for the Lord, my soul doth wait, and in his word do I hope . . . more than they that watch for the morning", 130. 5-6; "The Lord is good unto them that wait for him", Lam. 3. 25.

We wait for His future coming. This hope should be before all believers. In a miniature parable, the Lord Jesus exhorted His disciples: "ye yourselves like unto men that wait for their lord . . . that when he cometh and knocketh, they may open unto him immediately", Luke 12. 36. The Epistles are quite full of the subject of waiting. "Waiting for the coming of our Lord Jesus Christ", wrote Paul, 1 Cor. 1. 7. How different was the spiritual character of these Corinthians from that of the Thessalonians, to whom Paul wrote, "to serve the living and true God; and to wait for his Son from heaven", 1 Thess. 1. 9-10.

In weakness now, we wait for "the redemption of the body", that is, for its future glorified resurrection state, Rom. 8. 23.

READING: **1 Corinthians 12. 1-14**

THREE FOR THE WELLBEING OF THE ASSEMBLY

BEING A MEMBER of a local church where believers sincerely continue in the service of God is a very solemn privilege. No levity or worldly practices are suitable for the divine presence, otherwise the presence of One divine can hardly be recognized and owned. Moreover, the service of a local church is not based on tradition or the decision of committees, but on the calling and spiritual equipment of all its members.

The Godhead is vitally interested in the service of every local church. Paul lists in three places the various functionings of the members. In 1 Corinthians 12. 11, the Spirit is seen as distributing the gifts; in Ephesians 4. 7, the Lord Jesus is seen, while in Romans 12. 3 it is God who is seen as distributing to every member. This is what we mean by "Three for the wellbeing", since the Godhead works together for the good of local churches and their service. To realize this is the beginning of loyal and faithful service.

We find the three Persons of the Godhead deliberately named by Paul in 1 Corinthians 12 in relation to various aspects of the service of the Lord's people. The chapter commences with a work of the Holy Spirit in every believer; that is, the confession that "Jesus is the Lord". It is possible to say this other than by the Spirit; for example, in Matthew 7. 21, when the will of the Father is not done. This is a spirit of make-believe, to cover up the life of an unbeliever that is empty of Christ. But He cannot be deceived.

The granting of spiritual gift, 1 Cor. 12. 4. Paul is dealing with variety (such as the foot, hand, ear, eye in a human body). There is no such thing as a variety of Spirits, each giving a separate gift. Rather, the variety of gifts form a united local church because one Spirit gives them.

The granting of service taken up, v. 5. Each believer does something different, depending on his gift. But this variety of ministries forms a unified whole, because it is the one Lord who oversees and arranges all true service.

The granting of results in service, v. 6. These operations produce results, else service is in vain. And it is the same God who achieves these ends, which work towards the building up of the believers as a unified body.

November 15th

READING: **2 Chronicles 7. 1-12**

ALL THE PEOPLE

THE HOUSE of God, just completed by Solomon, was to be dedicated. Note how this house was described:

By God. It was chosen to be a "house of sacrifice", 2 Chron. 7. 12. It would be a place of prayer, v. 15; compare this with "my house of prayer", Isa. 56. 7. The house was sanctified, 2 Chron. 7. 16, 20. It was "high", v. 21.

By Solomon. It was dedicated to the Lord, 2 Chron. 2. 4, as an ordinance for ever to Israel. It was "only to burn sacrifice before him", v. 6. It was to be "wonderful great", v. 9. Huram said it was a "house for his kingdom", v. 12.

Note in our reading that the word "all" occurs five times in connection with the people:

"All the children of Israel", v. 3.

"All the people" with the king, v. 4.

"All the people" with the king, v. 5.

"All Israel stood", v. 6.

"All Israel" with Solomon, v. 8.

In other words, the leader, the Levites, and the people were all together in one great act of fellowship and worship. In these five cases, the people saw and worshipped, they offered sacrifices, they dedicated, they stood, and they kept the feast. All this materialistic approach to worship has now passed away, and we have better spiritual means in Christ. We comment on these verbs in order:

(i) The wise men from the east came to Bethlehem, and "saw the young child . . . and worshipped him", Matt. 2. 11. After His resurrection, "they saw him, they worshipped him", 28. 17.

(ii) Today, we offer the sacrifice of praise, Heb. 12. 15; we offer up spiritual sacrifices, 1 Pet. 2. 5.

(iii) To dedicate means to recognize what belongs to the Lord, and to ensure that our service is consistent with this recognition. Thus the church is *His* church, Matt. 16. 18; the church is "the temple *of God*", 1 Cor. 3. 16, and "the house *of God*", 1 Tim. 3. 15. It is not man's posssession.

(iv) To stand means to recognize the divine authority over all that takes place, and our subjection to that authority.

(v) To keep the feast suggests for us the Breaking of Bread or the Lord's Supper, of which we regularly partake.

READING: **Matthew 24. 27-42**

THE LORD'S COMING IN GLORY

THE PROPHETIC programme of God is quite clearly revealed in Scripture. After the rapture of the church, and the resurrection of those who have already passed on from this scene, 1 Thess. 4. 16-17; 1 Cor. 15. 51-54, the judgments described in Revelation chs. 6-19 will take place, followed by the return of the Lord Jesus in power and glory, to be seen by every eye, to be vidicated in the scene where once He was crucified, and to reign victoriously. This great event of His return in glory is amply described in O.T. and N.T. alike, and is the great climax of future prophecy, just as His cross was the climax of all prophecy that spoke of His first advent.

In the O.T., we have verses such as: "The Redeemer shall come to Zion", Isa. 59. 20; "his feet shall stand in that day upon the mount of Olives", Zech. 14. 1-4; "one like the Son of man came with the clouds of heaven . . . and there was given him dominion, and glory, and a kingdom", Dan. 7. 13; "the Lord, whom ye seek, shall suddenly come to his temple", Mal. 3. 1; "the glory of the Lord came into the house by way of the gate whose prospect is toward the east", Ezek. 43. 4.

The transfiguration of the Lord was a foreview of His glory and kingdom, Matt. 16. 27-28. Later, the Lord Jesus said, "all tribes . . . shall see the Son of man coming in the clouds of heaven with power and great glory", Matt. 24. 30; Luke 21. 27. In a parable, He said, "When the Son of man shall come in his glory . . . then shall he sit upon the throne of his glory", Matt. 25. 31, and to the high priest He said, "Hereafter shall ye see the Son of man sitting on the right hand of power, and coming in the clouds of heaven", Mark 14. 62.

The Epistles have the same testimony. Paul wrote of the Lord coming to bring sudden destruction and not peace, 1 Thess. 5. 2-3, and of the man of sin he declared that he would be destroyed "with the brightness of his coming", 2 Thess. 2. 8. Peter also wrote of the "power and coming" of the Lord, 2 Pet. 1. 16.

The book of Revelation shows the beast, seeking world dominion at the battle of Armageddon, 16. 16. In the midst of the battle, the Lord comes in glory. The warring factions will fight against Him, 17. 14, but in the triumph of the Lord's glory, all opposition will be put down so that He can reign.

November 17th

READING: **Jeremiah 44. 1-10**

LACK OF RESPONSE

GOD SPOKE through His servants the prophets so that the people should hear His voice, and that they should respond positively to His commands and exhortations. When they heard His voice directly, they feared, and said, "let not God speak with us, lest we die", Exod. 20. 19; they preferred to hear men's voices since they could the more easily disobey. Consider this lack of response in the three major prophets.

Isaiah. In prison in his own hired house in Rome, Paul received the Jews to whom he expounded the kingdom of God, but some believed and some did not, Acts 28. 23-24. As a result, he quoted from Isaiah 6. 9-10, where God predicted that men had dull ears and closed eyes, so that there would be no response to the message of truth. This lack of response is found several times in Isaiah. "Who hath believed our report?", Isa. 53. 1, interpreted in John 12. 19 as referring to unbelief. Men prefer their own thoughts, and not those of God, Isa. 55. 8; 65. 2.

Jeremiah. God was so concerned about His sinful people, that He *rose up early* to speak to them through His prophets; this idea occurs ten times in Jeremiah and nowhere else in the O.T. For example, "I earnestly protested unto your fathers . . . even unto this day, rising early and protesting, saying, Obey my voice", Jer. 11. 7; "I sent unto you all my servants the prophets, rising early and sending them, saying, Oh, do not this abominable thing that I hate", 44. 4. In all cases they obeyed not, or they hearkened not; there was no positive response. Today, the voice of God is heard through preachers, teachers, in Sunday Schools, by reading the Word, and hearing personal testimonies, and by seeing changed Christian lives. But the majority response is nil, alas.

Ezekiel. We can but quote from 33. 30-33, where men seem to delight in hearing the word from the Lord. "They come unto thee . . . they hear thy words, but they will not do them: for with their mouth they show much love, but their heart goeth after their covetousness. And, lo, thou art unto them as a very lovely song of one that hath a pleasant voice . . . for they hear thy words, but they do them not".

The Lord Jesus said, "and ye would not", Matt. 23. 37.

November 18th

READING: **Revelation 21. 9-27**

THE LAMB THROUGHOUT TIME

JESUS CHRIST "the same yesterday, and to day, and for ever", Heb. 13. 8. This glorious truth applies only to One not-created. Moreover, the truth applies to the Lord Jesus in His character as the Lamb of God; we can trace this from the past to the future.

(1) *In the past eternity*. Peter wrote of the precious blood of Christ "as of a lamb without blemish . . . foreordained before the foundation of the world", 1 Pet. 1. 19-20. This takes our minds back to the eternity past, showing that even then He was the Lamb ready for sacrifice when the time came.

(2) *Types*. In Exodus 12. 3, each house had to have a lamb ready for the Passover. This was no meaningless ritual, but designed by God as a type of the One who was to come.

(3) *Prophecy*. The great chapter on the sufferings of Christ, Isa. 53, would not have been complete had it not been for the reference to the lamb, "he is brought as a lamb to the slaughter . . . and as a sheep", v. 7.

(4) *In His lifetime*. John the Baptist knew that this One was the Fulfiller of the O.T. types: hence he said twice, "Behold the Lamb of God", John 1. 29, 36. This was coupled with his testimony that this was the Son of God, v. 34.

(5) *Teaching*. Philip had to explain what the eunuch was reading in the O.T.: "like as a lamb dumb before his shearer", Acts 8. 32 (note how "lamb" and "sheep" are reversed from Isaiah 53. 7). Paul made no reference to the "Lamb", but this is implied in "Christ our passover is sacrified", 1 Cor. 5. 7.

(6) *Future after rapture*. In heaven in a vision, John was privileged to see "in the midst of the throne . . . stood a Lamb as it had been slain", Rev. 5. 6. The throne is prepared for the judgments that fall in subsequent chapters. This judgment is "the wrath of the Lamb", 6. 16-17.

(7) *Heaven during the millennium*. This will be the end of all false ceremony on earth. In the city above the millennial earth, "the Lamb is the light thereof", Rev. 21. 23.

(8) *Future eternity*. Blessing, honour, glory and power is ascribed "unto the Lamb for ever and ever", 5. 13. Here is no fleeting praise, but that which lasts to eternity.

The Lamb's book of life also spans these eternal periods.

November 19th

READING: **2 Corinthians 5. 14-21**

ASPECTS OF THE WORD

THE SCRIPTURES are often referred to as the Word, usually with another word added following the preposition "of". This shows the wide variety of aspects by which the Holy Scriptures are called. Usually, the description "word of God" is used, but it is important to draw the reader's attention to other descriptions under various groupings.

Creatorial. There are two phases to creation: it was created originally, and now it continues to exist for God's pleasure, Rev. 4. 11. It is by "the word of his power" that creation is upheld, Heb. 1. 3. It was by "the word of God" that the heavens and earth were originally formed, 2 Pet. 3. 5.

Evangelical. In Antioch, Paul stated to the Jews that "the word of this salvation" was sent to them, Acts 13. 26, though they rejected the message. The apostle realized that God had committed to him "the word of reconciliation", 2 Cor. 5. 19, while elsewhere Paul called his preaching "the word of faith", Rom. 10. 8, namely truth to be received by faith. Whatever name may be given to this preaching, Paul knew that what he taught was always "the word of God", and not "the word of men", 1 Thess. 2. 13. It was therefore effectual.

Doctrinal. The basis of doctrine could not be different from the basis of salvation. The truth that must dwell richly in all believers is "the word of Christ", Col. 3. 16. Not that He taught it necessarily when He was here, but that Paul had received it from the Living Lord, and taught it as such. He also called it "the word of wisdom" and "the word of knowledge", 1 Cor. 12. 8, these being what appropriately gifted men passed on to others.

Practical. Both weakness and strength can be displayed; for example, in immaturity, some may be unskilled in "the word of righteousness", Heb. 5. 13. By contrast, there is deliverance, as when Paul commended men to "the word of his grace", Acts 20. 32, and when overcomers are successful by "the word of their testimony", Rev. 12. 11.

Prophetical. What is written is more valuable than what was seen: "a more sure word of prophecy", 2 Pet. 1. 19.

Eternal. Recalling the Lord's life on earth, John used His eternal title "the Word of life", 1 John 1. 1.

November 20th

READING: **Hebrews 12. 25-29**

ACCEPTABLE SACRIFICE

DEGENERATION in service is a dreadful thing; alas that this happened so often in the Scriptural record. When men invent their methods of service, or when they rely on tradition (which consists of inventions of the past), then this is not acceptable to God. However, it is almost impossible to get this across to a mind that had been deceived by bias. Through Jeremiah, God said, "your burnt offerings are not acceptable, nor your sacrifices sweet unto me", Jer. 6. 20, because the people would not hearken to God's words and law.

Rather, because of the operations of God in judgment, we must "have grace, whereby we may serve God acceptably with reverence and godly fear". Certainly the Lord Jesus served acceptably; He was occupied with the Father's will, with the divine counsels and pleasure, with His sufferings even unto death. In the N.T., for sacrifice to be acceptable there is a fourfold measure, relating to service, our bodies, giving and worship.

Paul was a "minister of Jesus Christ to the Gentiles", and he regarded their conversion as a sacrifice; he wrote, "that the offering up (sacrificing) of the Gentiles might be acceptable", Rom. 15. 16. This was acceptable, since the sacrifice was "sanctified by the Holy Spirit". The ministry and its results were in keeping with the divine will; hence the acceptability before God. There are high ideals in gospel work; worldly methods must not deflect from the Spirit's heavenly methods.

Service is effective when the servant's body is presented "a living sacrifice, holy, acceptable unto God", with the servant proving "what is that good, and acceptable, and perfect will of God", Rom. 12. 1-2. The Spirit works through the believer's body, so this must be an unblocked channel of blessing. For example, one's mouth must not go in two directions, James 3. 10.

Gifts sent from the Philippians to Paul were "an odour of a sweet smell, a sacrifice acceptable, wellpleasing to God", Phil. 4. 18. This shows the careful motivation under which gifts are given to God, by being rendered to His people in need.

Believers now, as a holy priesthood, must "offer up spiritual sacrifices, acceptable to God by Jesus Christ", 1 Pet. 2. 5. As Cain's sacrifice was not accepted, believers must ensure that their sacrifice is, like Abel's, acceptable, Heb. 11. 4.

November 21st

READING: **Acts 21. 1-18**

PAUL'S VISITS TO JERUSALEM

PAUL, as Saul, is first recorded as being in Jerusalem at the stoning of Stephen, Acts 7. 58; 8. 1-3, where he had been "brought up in this city at the feet of Gamaliel", 22. 3. It was from Jerusalem that he embarked on his mission to Damascus that led to his conversion. He did not return to Jerusalem immediately to see the apostles, Gal. 1. 17.

His first recorded visit to Jerusalem after his conversion is mentioned in three places, and we assume that all three verses refer to this same visit. After "many days", Acts 9. 23, he escaped from Damascus in a basket, and in Jerusalem tried to join himself to the disciples, to the church, 9. 26. It was only when Barnabas explained the matter that he was received into the church, v. 27. He wrote that he only saw James, not the other apostles, the visit being after "three years", Gal. 1. 18-19. At this visit, Acts 22. 17-21 took place; Paul had a vision that he should go far hence to the Gentiles, since the Jews would not listen to him in Jerusalem.

Several years passed. At the end of his first journey, Paul had to go from Antioch to Jerusalem to discuss the matter of law-keeping being put forward by the Pharisees, Acts 15. 4; Gal. 2. 1. At the end of the second journey, he wanted to visit Jerusalem, Acts 18. 21, but all we read is that he had "gone up, and saluted the church", v. 22.

During the third journey, Paul was asking the various churches to gather a large sum of money especially for the poor saints at Jerusalem, Rom. 15. 25-26. He would take this money personally, "to minister unto the saints". He referred to this in his address to the Ephesian elders, Acts 20. 22, knowing that he would enter into trouble predicted by the Holy Spirit "in every city". The final part of the journey took place in 21. 15, they "went up to Jerusalem". They were received gladly, and explained their service to James and the elders, v. 18. Afterwards, he was taken prisoner by the Roman authorities, and one night had another vision from the Lord, "as thou hast testified of me in Jerusalem, so must thou bear witness also at Rome", 23. 11. He left Jerusalem for the last time in verse 31, bound for Caesarea. Thus Paul's work in Jerusalem was minimal as compared with his Gentile journeys.

READING: **Psalm 22. 1-21**

LIVING THINGS IN PSALM 22

THE EXPERIENCES of the Lord Jesus when He expressed Himself through His sufferings on the cross were too deep and unusual to be formulated through common words of everyday experience. Words are too formal, too cold, to express unique events of a profound character. That is why figurative language is used, seeking thereby to come a little closer to reality. The world of nature is often used in a metaphorical sense in psalm, song, prophecy and parable. In particular, various living creatures are employed in Psalm 22.

Worm, v. 6. The Lord felt that men were treating Him as a worm in verses 7-8, a creature of earth and lowly in the extreme. In Exodus 16. 20, the manna bred worms, speaking of neglect. In Acts 12. 23, Herod was eaten of worms, speaking of death. In Job 25. 5-6, man is like a worm, speaking of impurity. Men would heap such a description upon the Lord.

Bulls, v. 12. "Many bulls have compassed me: strong bulls of Bashan have beset me round". Bulls were clean sacrificial animals in the O.T., so here they would speak of the Jews, thinking themselves ceremonially clean. These would be the priests, high prists, elders, Pharisees, and the whole Sanhedrin, as well as the people generally, Matt. 27. 38-44.

Lion, vv. 13, 21. In 1 Peter 5. 8, the devil is described as a roaring lion, seeking those whom he can devour. Thus in verse 21, the lion speaks of Satan's mouth that would seek to swallow the Lord up in death; see Rev. 12. 4. In verse 13, it is Satanic influence in men, because of the plural "they".

Dogs, vv. 16, 20. Dogs were unclean animals, and here they speak of the Gentile nations. Verse 16 shows their activity against the Lord; it was the Roman soldiers who pierced the Lord's hands and feet when they crucified Him. In several places, the Scriptures show the nature and position of dogs, such as Matt. 7. 6; 15. 27; Phil. 3. 2; Rev. 22. 15.

Unicorns, v. 21. This is the last phrase of the section, and seems to be in contrast with the others. "Thou hast heard me" stands in contrast with "thou hearest not", v. 2. In Psalm 92. 10 there is exaltation like the horn of a unicorn, leading to flourishing in the house of the Lord. So the thought is the power of God in the resurrection of the once-forsaken One.

November 23rd

READING: **Titus 3. 1-15**

GOOD WORKS

THE DOCTRINE of grace taught by Paul insisted that salvation was not of works. "Not of works, lest any man should boast", Eph. 2. 9; "not by works of righteousness which we have done", Titus 3. 5; "who hath saved us . . . not according to our works", 2 Tim. 1. 9. This is very clear to those who have been saved, and who know that they have been saved by the grace of God. But such a doctrine, new at that early period, met with much misrepresentation, as it does today in non-evangelical circles. Some asserted that Paul taught, "Let us do evil, that good may come", Rom. 3. 8; "Shall we continue in sin, that grace may abound?", 6. 1; "shall we sin, because we are not under the law, but under grace?", 6. 15. There were those who would say that a man could have faith but not works, James 2. 14. Paul would correct these false suggestions in one of his last Epistles, that to Titus.

The position of those who are "defiled and unbelieving" is clear, Titus 1. 15-16. Such may profess "that they know God", but their works prove that they really deny Him. They are "unto every good work reprobate", not approved by God. It is important that we have God's mind on the subject of good works that are not really good works, else we can be deceived.

But then Paul writes positively. First he makes a general statement, showing what has resulted from the sacrifice of Christ: "who gave himself for us, that he might . . . purify unto himself a peculiar people, zealous of good works", Titus 2. 14. The earnest desire to do good works has been placed in our hearts as a result of His work.

This leads in chapter 3 to three distinct statements about good works. (i) "That they which have believed in God might be careful to maintain good works", v. 8. We feel that this exhortation relates to works before God. (ii) "Let ours also learn to maintain good works for necessary uses", v. 14. We feel that this refers to honest daily employment before men; see Acts 20. 34; 2 Thess. 3. 10-12; Eccl. 2. 24; 3. 13. (iii) "Put them in mind to be subject to principalities and powers, to obey magistrates, to be ready to every good work", v. 1; this exhortation refers to works before civil leaders. This subject can also be found in Rom. 13. 1-7; 1 Pet. 2. 12-15.

READING: **Isaiah 40. 1-17**

GOOD TIDINGS

THE GOSPEL is something far more than a formal service on a Lord's Day evening; far more, indeed, than a Gospel Campaign. It is something of extreme solemnity, and is unique, as Paul wrote, "which is not another", Gal. 1. 7. We have considered this subject in a N.T. context on page 146. We now consider it in the context of Isaiah, and note that there are four passages referring to "good tidings". These all occur in the second section of this prophecy that deals with a growing crescendo of news about redemption.

A unique Person, 40. 9. In chapter 40, the testimony of John the Baptist is foretold, vv. 3-5, quoted in the N.T. as referring to John. He was but the forerunner. The true "good tidings" comes from Zion and Jerusalem, and the cry is made, "Behold your God", corresponding to John's Gospel.

A unique Servant. Chapter 41. 26 shows that there was no one to show, to declare, to hear. There was no man and no counsellor, v. 28. Except in verse 4, where there is One called "the Lord, the first, and with the last", and in verse 28 "The first" says, "I will give to Jerusalem one that bringeth good tidings", and this One is described as, "Behold my servant, whom I uphold; mine elect, in whom my soul delighteth", 42. 1, corresponding to Mark's Gospel of the Servant.

A unique deliverance. Israel is seen in captivity in Isaiah 52. 1-5. But "the feet of him that bringeth good tidings", v. 7, goes hand in hand with "Thy God reigneth", corresponding to Matthew's Gospel. The results are seen in Jerusalem being redeemed, and the ends of the earth seeing the salvation of God, vv. 9-10.

A unique service. Chapters 60-62 present details of the accomplishment of the glorious restoration promised for God's people in a coming day. This restoration is accomplished by One who said, "I the Lord am thy Saviour and thy Redeemer, the mighty one of Jacob", 60. 16. The city of the Lord will then be called "The Zion of the Holy One of Israel", v. 14. And how is this possible? Because the Lord Jesus says, "the Lord hath anointed me to preach good tidings unto the meek", 61. 1, corresponding to Luke's Gospel. The cry is made, "Behold, thy salvation cometh", 62. 11, referring to the Lord Jesus.

November 25th

READING: **2 Corinthians 8. 1-24**

THE ADMINISTRATION OF FINANCE

WE HAVE discussed this subject already on page 214; we shall now look at the subject again from a different Scripture reading. In chapters 8-9, Paul is discussing the collection being made by many churches for the poor saints in Jerusalem, that he, Paul, was going to take over to them. In 8. 1-6, Paul boasts of the Macedonian collection to the Corinthians; in 8. 7-15, he deals with the fruit of giving: the recipients are blessed. In 8. 16-24, we have the details of the administration of this great collection. In 9. 1-5 Paul boasts of the Corinthian collection to the Macedonians, while in 9. 6-15 he shows again the fruit of giving, but with the donors blessed.

Administration. This must be beyond suspicion, clothed with dignity and confidence. It is performed by those who labour spiritually, not as a cloke to cover up carnality, barrenness and lack of spiritual interest. Paul was going with others to Jerusalem with the proceeds of the collection.

Qualifications. The exercise to this work comes from God, v. 16; at the same time, the worker's own exercise is taken into account, v. 17. The worker's "praise in the gospel" must be known in many churches, v. 18. He must have been proved to be "diligent in many things", v. 22. There is a partnership between workers, v. 23, when they are partakers of the same outlook, zeal, trials, faith and service. Thus in Acts 6, the men were of honest report, full of the Spirit, full of wisdom, full of faith, with power and enablement in spiritual gifts.

Choice. Servants of God occupied with spiritual gifts are chosen by the Lord. But in financial matters, those who serve are "chosen of the churches", 2 Cor. 8. 19. Compare this with "whomsoever ye shall choose", 1 Cor. 16. 3; "look ye out", Acts 6. 3, 5. No doubt this was done by mutual consultation, trustworthiness and honesty being a prime consideration.

Duplication. Financial matters were never left in the hands of *one* man. Men had to see that honest things were provided for, 2 Cor. 8. 21. Thus seven men were chosen in Acts 6; several were involved in 2 Corinthians 8. Note the plural "them" in 1 Corinthians 16. 3. In Acts 4. 37, money was brought to the apostles (in the plural), Acts 4. 37, and to the elders (in the plural) in Jerusalem, 11. 30.

November 26th

READING: Luke 9. 49-62

HE STEDFASTLY SET HIS FACE

THE LORD was passing southwards through Samaria, and His face was set stedfastly to go to Jerusalem; the Samaritans did not therefore receive Him. But the Lord did not deviate from the divinely chosen pathway. This was not like a river, meandering and even reversing in direction. He was a living Example of His later observation, "No man . . . looking back, is fit for the kingdom of God", Luke 9. 62.

In the O.T., we hear His words prophetically, "The Lord God hath opened mine ear, and I was not rebellious, neither turned away back" whatever the consequences brought about by men, Isa. 50. 4-6. "Morning by morning" He was in contact with the will of God, and this meant that He had to sustain cruelty administered to His back, cheeks and face by His enemies.

The temptations through which the Lord passed in the wilderness were designed by Satan to seek to induce Him to deviate from the will of God. "It is written" shows definitely the pathway without deviation.

Through Peter, Satan sought to keep the Lord from going to the cross, Matt. 16. 22, while the people watching at the cross tempted Him to come down, 27. 40. It was impossible to alter the stedfastness of His pathway even unto death. Such a pathway was a lonely pathway; He was effectively alone in Gethsemane, and when nailed to the cross, since He went a little further, and His disciples had fled from Him.

The Lord's people are called to be stedfast today. Any temptation to deviation becomes more intense if it is not resisted in its early stages. *In doctrine*, there are those who depart from the faith, 1 Tim. 4. 1, but after that great doctrinal chapter on the resurrection, Paul exhorts believers to "be stedfast", 1 Cor. 15. 58. *In life*, Solomon would instruct his son Rehoboam not to deviate from the pathway of true morality, "My son, if sinners entice thee, consent thou not . . . walk not in the way with them", Prov. 1. 10-19; "Avoid it, pass not by it, turn from it, and pass away", 4. 15, is the true pathway of stedfastness. *In the local church*, we must continue "stedfastly in the apostles' doctrine and fellowship, and in breaking of bread, and in prayers", Acts 2. 42. Alas, in today's climate, we do not always see this.

November 27th

READING: **2 & 3 John**

THROUGH JOHN THE APOSTLE'S EYES

THE APOSTLE John refers to himself as an "elder", both physically and more importantly spiritually. Hence as we read these two short letters, we can actually see through John's eyes. The second Epistle appears to be written to a local church (there are good reasons for thinking that "the elect lady" refers to a local church, and that "thy elect sister", v. 13, refers to the church from which John was writing). The third Epistle is written to a particular brother, Gaius, in another local church. As John viewed things, there was much to commend, and also much to warn about.

John commended those who walked in truth, II. 4, enabling him to rejoice. Loving one another, v. 6, does not mean that one condones those who bring false doctrine. In III. 3-4, there is not only walking in the truth, but the truth being in Gaius. There is commendation of the faithfulness manifested in offering hospitality to the Lord's servants on their journeys, vv. 5-8. There was a particular man, Demetrius, who had a good report of all, v. 12; John could see him, and he also knew what other believers were thinking about him. Here was truth and reality, not gossip and false assertions.

But John also knew that there were dangers; he had no hesitation in pointing them out. Deceivers and antichrists were gone into the world, to spread their false doctrines which were the opposite of "the doctrine of Christ", II. 9; these deceivers were not to be received into the houses of believers, v. 10, unlike the work of Gaius who received the Lord's true servants willingly. But in the third Epistle, instead of being a deceiver who went out, we have a man who wanted the preeminence and who stayed in. This man Diotrephes spoke evil against John (whose deep spirituality would have lowered his status); he would not receive the brethren (lest their ministry would have put Diotrephes in his place); he cast out of the church those who would offer hospitality (lest other brethren would be doing things while he would not). John sums this man up: "he that doeth evil hath not seen God", v. 11. No believer must follow Diotrephes; rather, he must follow "that which is good". When there are deceivers and preeminent ones today, may we see through John's eyes!

November 28th

READING: **Matthew 13. 36-52**

THE SUN

IN THE SHORT days of late autumn, it is lovely when the sun shines brilliantly and warmly for a day. A day or two later, the weather may be miserable, with fog, mist and snow on the hills. The sun in summer time brings to mind long and warm days, with holidays as a break from normal routine. It is therefore good to read about the sun in the Bible; we have already thought about this subject on page 250. Oftentimes, the sun appears physically, but on other occasions, the sense is metaphorical, and when it is used to describe (i) the Lord, and (ii) believers, the subject is of importance.

(i) *Description of the Lord.* The sun is the most dominant feature of the heavens, so it is not surprising that the sun is used to describe the unique preeminence of the Lord. Thus on the mount of transfiguration, the Lord "was transfigured before them: and his face did shine as the sun, and his raiment was white as the light", Matt. 17. 2. The Lord's body and His raiment could no longer contain the vast expanse of glory within. This scene speaks of the Lord coming in the glory and power of His kingdom. John witnessed this event, and it was John who, many years later on the isle of Patmos, again saw the Lord in glory, this time discerning amongst the seven local churches, "his countenance was as the sun shineth in his strength", Rev. 1. 16. The apostle Paul (as Saul) also saw a light "above the brightness of the sun", Acts 26. 13. This shows that the physical brightness of the sun is far exceeded by the glory of the Lord Jesus Himself. But how this was temporarily eclipsed at Calvary, when there was darkness over the whole land, Mark 15. 33. Yet the resurrection was marked by "the rising of the sun", 16. 2.

(ii) *Description of believers.* The tares in the parable tend to cast a cloud, but when all things that offend are removed, the cloud is also removed. Then "shall the righteous shine forth as the sun in the kingdom of their Father", Matt. 13. 43. In that day we shall be with the Lord; but He gives us glory, and whereas we are the light of the world now, yet then we shall be the light (together with the true Light) in kingdom glory. The bride is described as "clear as the sun", Song 6. 10; that is how God sees us in His grace.

333

November 29th

READING: **Ezekiel 8. 1-18**

BEGIN AT MY SANCTUARY

THE PROPHET Ezekiel was in captivity, hundreds of miles from Jerusalem and the house of God. Both city and house were soon to be destroyed by Nebuchadnezzar, but before this took place, God allowed Ezekiel in vision form to see the evil that was taking place in the temple courts, ch. 8. Then judgment would commence to fall, with the command, "begin at my sanctuary", 9. 6, though God had marked any faithful ones so that they should not be touched. Did not Peter write, "the time is come that judgment must begin at the house of God"?, 1 Pet. 5. 17. In chapter 8. 5-16, four evils are detailed, each attaining to greater abominations; Ezekiel was allowed to see through God's eyes.

(i) Verses 5-6, an image of jealousy in an entrance gate, an idol that provoked God to jealousy, to intervene to maintain the unique honour of His Name. As He had intervened in Shiloh, so He would intervene in His sanctuary, Jer. 7. 12. (ii) Verses 7-12, idols were drawn on the walls of the chambers surrounding the temple. Seventy men claimed that the Lord could not see them as they engaged in their pseudo-priestly activity. (iii) Verses 13-14, women weeping for Tammuz, an idol of the nations, for these women wanted to be like the nations, since all the people "transgressed very much after all the abominations of the heathen", 2 Chron. 36. 14. (iv) Verses 15-16, twenty-five men were worshipping the sun with their backs to the temple.

So men used the house of God, where His glory was, v. 4, to degrade the true ceremony; God saw it all, Ezekiel saw it all. In the Gospels, the religion of the Pharisees was exposed by the Lord to His disciples. In the Revelation, the errors of local churches were exposed by the Lord to John. In Ezekiel, the depths of idolatry in the house were exposed by God to the prophet. Judgment had to begin at the sanctuary when things were beyond restoration, for the subsequent chapters 9-11 show that God's glory forsook the temple and never returned. These tend to be Laodicean conditions, Rev. 3. 16. The Lord intervened in Acts 5. 1-11, in the case of Ananias and Sapphira; He intervened in the case of the Corinthians, 1 Cor. 11. 30. Let us serve God acceptably, Heb. 12. 28, for it is "a fearful thing to fall into the hands of the living God", 10. 31.

November 30th

READING: Acts 27. 6-12, 38-44

LISTENING TO VOICES

WE ARE surrounded by voices, many demanding our attention, and many seeking to form our opinions, for good or for bad. In this story of the voyage and the shipwreck, only the apostle Paul said anything worthwhile. But the centurion who was guarding Paul listened to anyone else. In verse 10, Paul acted as a prophetic spokesman, predicting that the voyage would end in disaster. However, the centurion listened to four other voices, disregarding Paul's prediction.

(i) He listened to the captain of the ship, the voice of the Master, v. 11. Indeed, he believed him rather than Paul, whose message must have appeared strange and improbable.

(ii) He listened to the owner, v. 11, no doubt the same man as the captain. This was the voice of Money; the man would have no delay, since this would cost him a lot in later lost fares.

(iii) He listened to people, "the more part", v. 12, the voices of the Majority. These voices gave advice to depart and not to remain in the harbour; this amounted to expediency.

(iv) He had to listen to the soldiers, the voice of the Military, vv. 42-43. But he did not abide by their counsel which was to kill Paul and the other prisoners.

All the voices were wrong; the centurion would not listen to revelation, and was content with reason. Voices in the world, and speaking of the world, are dangerous; today, they take so many different forms, whether the printed page or the radio. Men with propaganda to disperse take advantage of the mass-methods.

When He was here below, the Lord Jesus was surrounded by voices, most of which were far from pleasant. Thus He heard the voice of Peter saying, "Be it far from thee, Lord", Matt. 16. 22; He heard the voice of the Pharisees stating, "thou art a Samaritan, and hast a devil", John 8. 48; He heard the voices of His brethren according to the flesh, "go into Judaea", 7. 3; He heard the voice of the priests, "He saved others; himself he cannot save", Mark 15. 31. How glad His heart must have been to hear voices of simple faith, such as "Thou art the Christ", and "My Lord and my God".

For ourselves, may we ensure that we listen to voices of profit and truth, and also ensure that when men hear our voice they may hear words of salvation and edification, Col. 4. 6.

December 1st

READING: **2 Corinthians 13. 1-14**

THE GODHEAD AS A UNITY

IT IS solemn to contemplate the unity of the Godhead, a deep mystery that is beyond natural comprehension, yet faith perceives this as a matter revealed in Scripture for faith to appropriate. There are many verses and contexts where the three Persons of the Godhead are viewed; it is helpful to consider a small selection of these verses and contexts. There is, of course, no *explanation* of this Oneness and Unity; the Scriptures present it as a *fact*. Again, there is no explanation as to the *existence* of the Godhead from eternity to eternity; faith goes beyond what is natural, and accepts the revelation as given in the Scriptures.

Matthew 3. 16-17: at His baptism, we note the Spirit descending, the voice of the Father, and the Person of the Son declared; John the Baptist was the sole witness.

Hebrews 9. 14: on the cross, we read of the blood of Christ, the eternal Spirit, and the offering to God.

Matthew 28. 19: baptism of the disciples was to be "in the name of the Father, and of the Son, and of the Holy Spirit".

2 Corinthians 13. 14: this was really a prayer by the apostle, "The grace of the Lord Jesus Christ, and the love of God, and the communion of the Holy Spirit, be with you all".

Galatians 4. 6: here is the means of approach in worship, "God hath sent forth the Spirit of his Son into your hearts, crying, Abba, Father".

John 14. 16, 26; 15. 26; Acts 2. 33: the giving of the Holy Spirit. "The Father . . . he shall give you another Comforter"; "whom the Father will send in my name"; "whom I will send unto you from the Father".

John 14. 17, 23: the Persons of the Godhead dwelling within the believer. "He dwelleth with you, and shall be in you"; "my Father will love him, and we will come unto him, and make our abode with him". See 1 Cor. 6. 19; Eph. 3. 16-17.

1 Corinthians 12. 4-6. We find the Spirit deals with the distribution of gifts, the Lord with the distribution of work, God with the distribution of the results.

Isaiah 61. 1-3: the anointing of the Lord. Here we find the voice of the Son, in Isaiah 42. 1-4 it is the voice of God, while in 11. 1-4 it is the voice of the Spirit of prophecy.

December 2nd

READING: **Malachi 1. 1-14**

MINE ALTAR

FIVE TIMES in the O.T. God speaks of the altar as "mine altar". These appear to answer to various thoughts that are found in 1 Corinthians chs. 8-11. The ceremony associated with the tabernacle and temple did not belong to men, for them to manipulate it according to their own tastes. What belongs to God must be used according to His will. We may make the same remark about the fellowship and service of a local church.

(1) Exodus 21. 14: "thou shalt take him from mine altar, that he may die". There was safety if a man unwittingly slew another, but not if it were done deliberately. For example, Joab had slain innocent blood, and holding the horns of the altar did not save him, 1 Kings 2. 28-29. In 1 Corinthians 8, there is the case of the accidental wounding of the conscience of a weak brother. The remedy is love that edifies, v. 1.

(2) Malachi 1. 10, "neither do ye kindle fire on mine altar for nought", or "that ye might not kindle a fire on mine altar in vain", R.V. In other words, the offering was unacceptable to God, and to men, v. 8. Rather, those who wait at the altar can be partakers of the altar, 1 Cor. 8. 13. Those who give must have the right motives, something the Corinthians did not have, for they were merely boasting opportunists. A sacrifice must be acceptable and wellpleasing to God, Phil. 4. 18.

(3) 1 Samuel 2. 33: a priest "whom I shall not cut off from mine altar". This refers to Zadok replacing Eli. There would be fellowship at the altar with king David. In 1 Corinthians 10. 18 Paul refers to eating and partaking of the altar in the O.T., and draws a parallel with the communion of the body and blood of Christ. This is a lasting fellowship, and we should emulate the faithfulness of Zadok, and not the unfaithfulness of Eli, so as to be in the place of God's choice.

(4) Malachi 1. 7: "Ye offer polluted bread upon mine altar", in other words, bad bread. This answers to 1 Corinthians 11. 20, where they were not partaking of the Lord's Supper, but were engaged in dishonouring practices merely for self.

(5) Isaiah 56. 7: "their sacrifices shall be accepted upon mine altar". What a contrast! Thus Paul reintroduced the holy details of the Lord's Supper, 1 Cor. 11. 23-26. For it is only by Christ that we offer the sacrifice of praise, Heb. 13. 15.

December 3rd

READING: Acts 2. 39-47

CONTINUING STEDFASTLY UNTIL HE COME

IN OUR doctrine, our service, and in our hope for the future, we often tend to keep the various ideas in watertight compartments. We do not readily associate the Lord's return with much of our activity in His Name, and this means that His return is not as prominent in our hearts as it should be. In Acts 2. 42, there are four main phases of activity in a local church; each one should be carried out in the light of the near return of the Lord Jesus. There are texts that support the connection between them.

(1) *The Breaking of Bread*. It is well known how this is connected with the Lord's return: "as often as ye eat this bread, and drink this cup, ye do show the Lord's death till he come", 1 Cor. 11. 26. Thus one looks backwards, forwards and upwards, but not selfwards. There is anticipation of fuller worship on high: "he was . . . carried up to heaven, and they worshipped him", Luke 24. 51-52.

(2) *The apostles' doctrine*. The giving and receiving of ministry is an exercise until He come. Of the servant giving the Lord's household food, He said, "Blessed is that servant, whom his lord when he cometh shall find so doing", Matt. 24. 46. Feeding the Lord's people in ministry is to prepare their souls for the ultimate divine purpose on high; this would save our souls from light unprofitable talk.

(3) *Prayers*. These are needed on earth until He shall come. "The end of all things is at hand . . . watch unto prayer", 1 Pet. 3. 7. For believers, the end will be when the Lord comes (this is not the absolute end, of course); this demands prayer for believers, and also for the unsaved that they may be gathered in prior to His return.

(4) *Fellowship*. This means partnership, not merely in material things, but demonstrating kindred interests as members of the one body. There are several verses that link the present with the future. "Not forsaking the assembling of ourselves together . . . as ye see the day approaching", Heb. 10. 25; "ye became companions . . . he that shall come will come, and will not tarry", vv. 33, 37; "partakers of Christ's sufferings; that, when his glory shall be revealed, ye may be glad also with exceeding joy", 1 Pet. 4. 13.

December 4th

READING: **Hebrews 1. 1-14**

THE SON OF GOD

WE MAY trace the pathway of the Son from the past eternity to the future eternity, noting what happened to Him during the days of His flesh. The record is as follows:

The past eternity. "Glorify thy Son", He said in John 17. 1, 5, "with the glory which I had with thee before the world was".

Creation. "His Son ... by whom also he made the worlds", Heb. 1. 2; "unto the Son he saith . . . Thou, Lord, in the beginning hast laid the foundation of the earth", vv. 8, 10.

Birth. "That holy thing which shall be born of thee shall be called the Son of God", Luke 1. 35; "God sent forth his Son, made of a woman", Gal. 4. 4.

Baptism. "Thou art my beloved Son; in thee I am well pleased", Luke 3. 22.

Sent forth into service. After John the Baptist, God "raised unto Israel a Saviour, Jesus", the O.T. predicting this by the words "Thou art my Son, this day have I begotten thee", Acts 13. 23-24, 33.

Preaching. God "hath in these last days spoken unto us by his Son", Heb. 1. 2.

Profession. After Peter walked on the sea, they said, "Of a truth thou art the Son of God", Matt. 14. 33, while later Peter confessed "Thou art the Christ, the Son of the living God", 16. 16.

Transfiguration. The Father's voice came from the cloud saying, "This is my beloved Son", Luke 9. 35.

His death. "The Son of God, who loved me, and gave himself for me", Gal. 2. 20, wrote Paul, while the centurion claimed, "Truly this was the Son of God", Matt. 27. 54.

Resurrection. "Declared to be the Son of God . . . by the resurrection from the dead", Rom. 1. 4.

Ascension. To the people in Jerusalem, Peter said, "God . . . hath glorified his Son Jesus", Acts 3. 13.

In relation to believers now. We are called "unto the fellowship of his Son Jesus Christ our Lord", 1 Cor. 1. 9.

His coming again. "To wait for his Son", 1 Thess. 1. 10.

The future eternity. "Neither beginning of days, nor end of life . . . like unto the Son of God", Heb. 7. 3.

December 5th

READING: Acts 11. 1-18

INTERRUPTED MEETINGS

THE WRITER recalls a Gospel Meeting in 1944, when he interrupted the preacher to give a simple testimony of faith (admittedly, the preacher indicated that he would like that to happen). Then there was the case when a tramp interrupted a Sunday School session when the writer was present. Again, he recalls an "open" Conference being interrupted by one of the responsible brethren, because the ministry of the speaker was without edification; he was asked to leave the platform. In the N.T. we have examples of interrupted meetings, and it is interesting to note the why and wherefore of such events.

Prayer meeting. Many were gathered together praying in Jerusalem when Peter was in prison awaiting death, Acts 12. 12. In spite of the fact that they were praying to the One who could do exceeding abundantly above all that they could ask, yet when Rhoda interrupted the prayer meeting to state that Peter was present, they said "Thou art mad". How much faith was there in that prayer meeting?

Ministry meeting. When Paul was preaching in Troas until midnight, his discourse was suddenly interrupted; Eutychus had fallen down, and was taken up apparently dead, until a miracle was wrought, Acts 20. 9-10. Physical weariness is not unknown in a meeting; the Lord watched over His own when this happened in the garden of Gethsemane.

Fellowship. We are not told what the apostles were doing in the upper room during the evening after the Lord's rising again. But suddenly their uncertainty was removed by the interruption caused by the Lord suddenly standing in their midst, John 20. 19. This caused gladness when they saw the Lord.

Breaking of Bread. They interrupted the meeting themselves because of their own carnality. Men were eating and drinking their own meal instead of partaking of the Lord's Supper. This kind of interruption must be completely avoided, 1 Cor. 11. 22.

We have followed the activity in Acts 2. 42, but there is one further example to be added:

The gospel meeting. As Peter "began to speak" in the home of Cornelius, the Spirit fell upon the Gentiles, implying that they too had received the gospel by faith. Baptism followed, but we are not told whether Peter concluded his message.

December 6th

READING: **2 Kings 10. 15-29**

ZEAL

BY ITSELF, zeal is no criterion of faithfulness, neither is the doing of the will of the Lord, for sinners can be thus included. It all depends on whether there is a spiritual heart or a fleshly heart, and on the motives that control.

Zeal of a Sinner. In chapters 8-10 of 2 Kings, Israel's kings were Ahab, Joram and Jehu. Jehu was an idolater, as were the kings before him. See 10. 18-31 for a description of Jehu's brand of idolatry, summarized in v. 31. First he slew in Jezreel all that remained of the house of Ahab; then in a spirit of boasting, he let the king of Judah watch him slay what remained in Samaria, saying, "see my zeal for the Lord", v. 16. This was in keeping with the words of Elisha, 9. 7, but it was empty zeal, for although he destroyed the prophets of Baal, yet he retained other forms of idolatry. In other words, the mind and heart of the flesh were really in action; here was no true zeal at all.

Zeal of a Saint. Towards the end of the wilderness wanderings, the children of Israel engaged in idolatry with Moab, Num. 25. 1. While the people were weeping before the tabernacle at the judgment of God, one man brought a woman of Midian into the camp. Phinehas the priest, grandson of Aaron, saved the situation. Of him God said, "he was zealous for my sake among them", or as the margin gives, "zealous with my zeal", v. 11. So God gave him the covenant of an everlasting priesthood, quoted in Psalm 106. 30-31. Here was true zeal that maintained holiness by priestly contact with God.

Zeal of the Saviour. In John 2. 13-22, the Lord Jesus cleansed the temple, for it was rendered impure by the activity of the traders in the temple courts. The disciples associated Psalm 69. 9 with this event, "The zeal of thine house hath eaten me up". The Lord was consumed with divine passion, and He had to act for His Father's honour, when He saw men desecrating what should have been holy.

Our zeal for the house of God, the church of the living God, should be to maintain holiness. We should defend what has been revealed in the N.T. This is spiritual if done from a heart in contact with God, but is carnal if from a mind intent upon acting ungraciously, rather than with the mind of Christ.

December 7th

READING: **2 Timothy 1. 1-18**

THE LORD'S CHOICE OF A SERVANT

ALL OF God's people love to serve Him acceptably, but there are principles of service that make divine service quite distinct from an ordinary employer-employee relationship in everyday life. In his last Epistle, Paul draws Timothy's attention to some of these aspects of true service.

The purpose of God, 2 Tim. 1. 9. "Who hath saved us, and called us with an holy calling, not according to our works, but according to his own purpose and grace". This purpose extends beyond initial conversion, and also involves service afterwards. Of Aaron's service, it is written, "no man taketh this honour unto himself, but he that is called of God, as was Aaron", Heb. 5. 4. Of Paul, the Lord said, "he is a chosen vessel unto me, to bear my name", Acts 9. 15.

The appointment of God, 2 Tim. 1. 11. "I am appointed a preacher, and an apostle, and a teacher of the Gentiles". The appointment of believers to service is not arbitrary or unplanned on God's part. A believer may have a desire after a particular form of service, but this must dovetail with God's purpose. Moreover, God is in no haste to reveal His plan for a young believer. Paul waited many years after his conversion before he was called to his first missionary journey.

The gift of God, 2 Tim. 1. 6. "I put thee in remembrance that thou stir up the gift of God". Any spiritual gift must be exercised, used to greater effectiveness; otherwise it is like the pound hidden in a napkin, Luke 19. 20. Today, God's gift for service is free, but the recipient must hold himself ready, empty and usable by the Holy Spirit.

The will of God, 2 Tim. 1. 1. "Paul, an apostle of Jesus Christ by the will of God". This is an oft-repeated thought at the beginning of many Epistles; this was no formula for Paul, but something to be felt spiritually and always acted upon before God. Thus at the end of his second journey, he promised to return to Ephesus "if God will", Acts 18. 21. Writing to Titus, He observed, "preaching, which is committed unto me according to the commandment of God our Saviour", 1. 3. Today, opportunities are many in the service of the Lord, and it is easy to take up this or that; but to wait for the manifestation of the divine will is a great thing for subsequent success.

December 8th

READING: **Matthew 5. 1-16**

YE ARE THE LIGHT OF THE WORLD

"YE ARE the light of the world", said the Lord Jesus in His teaching, v. 14. Admittedly the apostles hardly acted as lights when the Lord Jesus was here; they must have had a very poor testimony in Matthew 17. 16, when the father said, "they could not cure him". In any case, when the Lord was here, nothing was going to detract from the uniqueness of His Person as the Light of the world.

The Eternal Word is described as, "the life was the light of men. And the light shineth in darkness", John 1. 4, and "the true light", v. 9. As soon as the Lord commenced His public ministry in Galilee, His Person and ministry are described in Matthew 4. 16, "The people which sat in darkness saw great light . . . light is sprung up". But it is in John's Gospel that the Lord as the Light is most prominently seen.

"Light is come into the world, and men loved darkness rather than light, because their deeds were evil", 3. 19. The Light showed men up as sinners and this is what men so disliked. The Light affected the walk of those who came to Him: "I am the light of the world: he that followeth me shall not walk in darkness, but shall have the light of life", 8. 12. This was spoken to the Pharisees in darkness, leading to their contradiction of all that the Lord said in the rest of the chapter. In John 12. 35, the Lord warned that the Light was with them only for "a little while", connecting the fact that He was the Light of the world with belief on Himself, v. 46.

The miracle of the healing of the blind man gave the Lord the opportunity of stating, "As long as I am in the world, I am the light of the world", John 9. 5. In other words, He was the Light of the world only as long as He was present amongst men. For He was a Light to be seen, but now He is in heaven, and exceptionally this Light appeared to Paul at his conversion, but dwells in light that no man can approach, 1 Tim. 6. 16. On earth now, the Lord's people are lights. Thus John the Baptist was "a burning and a shining light", John 5. 35, and for us the Lord would say, "Ye are the light of the world", and men should see this light and glorify the Father, Matt. 5. 14-16. The hymn, "The Light of the world is Jesus" is not quite correct; He was the Light, but now we are the light.

December 9th

READING: **Isaiah 1. 10-28**

WHITER THAN SNOW

WHAT A DIFFERENCE is snow in the Scriptures when used metaphorically, for it is in contrast with an actual snow scene.

Sometimes a heavy fall of snow takes days and weeks to disappear. As freshly fallen, it looks attractive on a photo and if one looks out through a window from a warm room; also for holiday makers it is very desirable at ski resorts. But mostly, heavy snow can be unpleasant, for anyone trapped, for old people who have to go out, for farmers, for householders with burst water pipes, and for city councils who have to spend money in clearing the snow from roads.

But what happens if a hole is dug through the snow? Alas, underneath is dirt, soil, rubbish. And when the snow melts, there is nothing but ugly black slush to contend with. What a difference near the south pole! There the snow has formed into solid pure unsullied ice thousands of feet thick.

But snow used figuratively in the Bible knows nothing of all this unpleasantness, of all this associated filth underneath, for snow is used of absolute purity. That is why snow could adequately describe the character of the Lord Jesus, "His head and his hairs were . . . as white as snow", Rev. 1. 14; "his raiment became shining, exceeding white as snow", Mark 9. 3; "whose garment was white as snow", Dan. 7. 9. Thus He was perfect, and could never be otherwise. His snow-like nature can never be changed and can never disappear.

In Isaiah 1, a terrible description is given of Judah and Jerusalem, but the promise is made, "your sins . . . shall be as white as snow", v. 18. For ourselves, we sometimes sing, "Vile and full of sin I am", knowing that in ourselves dwells no good thing. Paper over it, paint over it, put snow over it, but the sin is still there. What is necessary is for the sin to be removed, and then for pure snow of infinite depth to replace it. And this is what the Lord Jesus has done for us by His sacrifice. Sin is removed, and now we are the righteousness of God in Him. In Psalm 51. 7, David knew that washing was essential first, the removal of sin, and not a mere covering. So he said, "wash me, and I shall be whiter than snow". By this means, sins cannot be remembered against us any more, so we enter into God's presence as gold purified.

December 10th

READING: **Hebrews 12. 18-24**

COMING TO MOUNT ZION

SOMETIMES WE sing "Dwelling on Mount Calvary", but this is not very good theology. No one ever dwelt at Calvary; the Lord Jesus did not, He only suffered there. It was a place of death, but we are called upon to dwell in a place of life. In any case, the word "Calvary" occurs nowhere in the N.T.; in Luke 23. 33, the place of crucifixion is "The skull", R.V., while "Calvary" is merely the Latin equivalent inserted by the translators. Certainly we cannot dwell there.

There are two prominent mountains in the O.T.: (i) Moriah, Gen. 22. 2, a place of sacrifice, where the temple was built, 2 Chron. 3. 1. (ii) Zion, a place of song, 1 Chron. 16. 1. God was jealous of these two hills and their uniqueness. In Deuteronomy 12. 1-14, only in "the place which the Lord your God shall choose" (Moriah) would sacrifice be offered; this was uniquely the place of the altar. But there was no altar on mount Zion and before the tent David erected to receive the ark, although sacrifices were offered there on the first day, 1 Chron. 16. 1. It was given over to song and the sacrifice of praise. Moriah therefore speaks of His sacrifice; Zion speaks of our sacrifice.

Moriah was a place on earth, and ultimately it was attacked and desecrated by men, by Nebuchadnezzar; this is what men have done to the cross of the Lord Jesus: His sacrifice is rejected and denied as efficacious. Zion was never desecrated by men, since its use ended when the temple was built. As a type, Zion is a heavenly position, and is therefore outside the range of the hands of men.

Thus in 1 Peter 1. 11, the sufferings of Christ led to the following glory; Moriah led to Zion. Redemption through His blood led to being seated in the heavenlies in Christ Jesus, Eph. 1. 7; 2. 6. Today, we have come to mount Zion, and there we can dwell by faith. When David said, "I will dwell in the house of the Lord for ever", Psa. 23. 6, he was referring to mount Zion; see Psalm 132. 13-14. There we find the Lord Jesus, since we are come to Him. We view His cross as an act of remembrance; we live in the light of it; this is the subject of our praise, and the grounds of our sanctification; but we do not dwell there. We dwell above by faith.

December 11th

READING: Luke 1. 26-38

THE LORD'S NAMES PRIOR TO HIS BIRTH

IN THESE DAYS, babes are given names *before* there is any indication of their character and abilities. But the Lord was given names from heaven, both prior to, and after, His birth, because His Person and work were completely known by God beforehand; His names were therefore fully consistent with His Person, character and work.

Jesus, Matt. 1. 21; Luke 1. 31. He was given this name by the angel speaking to Joseph in a dream, with the explanation "he shall save his people from their sins". It was the angel Gabriel who announced this name to Mary. Eight days after His birth, the Lord was formally given this name, Luke 2. 21. The shepherds had heard the angel using the name "Saviour", 2. 11, while Simeon called Him "thy salvation", v. 30. The name "Jesus" is used in historical passages in the Gospels; it is a rarity for anyone to address Him as "Jesus", Luke 19. 38, while He used this Name of Himself twice, Acts 9. 5; Rev. 22. 16.

Christ, Luke 2. 11. The angel that appeared to the shepherds announced Him as the "Christ", namely, the anointed One. In the O.T., the priests, kings and prophets were physically anointed with oil; the Lord as the Christ was eternally anointed with the Spirit, evidently for service, Luke 4. 18.

Emmanuel, Matt. 1. 23, "they shall call his name Emmanuel", quoted from Isaiah 7. 14. Its meaning, "God with us", is a vital truth for believers, for it testifies of the Deity of Christ, as does "God was manifest in the flesh", 1 Tim. 3. 16.

Son of the Highest, Luke 1. 32. This is a millennial title demonstrating the outward power of the Lord, and relating to His occupancy of the throne (cf. "Son of the Blessed", Mark 14. 61).

Son of God, "that holy thing which shall be born of thee shall be called the Son of God", Luke 1. 35. This implies Deity, and is eternal, past and future.

The Lord, "a Saviour, which is Christ the Lord", 2. 11; this is One to whom all are subject and obedient, One who is served faithfully. It is a title that shows the complete dependence of His people upon Himself.

The Lord. Simeon said, "Lord, now lettest thou thy servant depart in peace", 2. 29. This title means an Absolute Ruler in righteousness, a divine Despot, as Jude 4; Rev. 6. 10.

346

December 12th

READING: **1 Timothy 1. 1-17**

OBJECTIVES IN SENDING TIMOTHY

THERE WERE at least five occasions when Paul sent Timothy to various places for specific forms of service. Although all believers are subject to the will and calling of God, yet there are properly those times when a believer can be sent on a spiritual errand by another believer who cannot do the work himself at that season.

(1) To *Comfort* the Thessalonians. Paul wrote to this church from Athens, having left the believers suffering much persecution for their faith. At the same time, he sent Timothy "to establish you, and to comfort you concerning your faith", 1 Thess. 3. 2. In verse 6, Timothy returned with good news concerning their faith and love.

(2) To *Cooperate* with the Philippians. Towards the end of his three years in Ephesus, Paul sent Timothy into Macedonia, evidently to cooperate with the church in preparing for Paul's subsequent visit, Acts 19. 22. This visit took place in Acts 20. 1.

(3) To *Communicate* with the Corinthians. Paul wrote the first Epistle to the Corinthians from Ephesus. He stated that he was sending Timothy, who "shall bring you into remembrance of my ways which be in Christ, as I teach every where in every church", 1 Cor. 4. 17. It would appear that this lengthy journey to Corinth was a continuation of the journey (2) into Macedonia. Paul would follow afterwards.

(4) To *Care* for the Philippians. Writing as a prisoner in Rome, the apostle stated that he expected to send Timothy shortly, for only he would "naturally care for your state", Phil. 2. 19-20. Paul could trust Timothy on such an errand, for his character and spiritual abilities led to that end.

(5) To *Charge* some in Ephesus. Having been released from imprisonment, Paul, with Timothy, visited Ephesus. Paul went further into Macedonia, and wrote to Timothy, whom he had left in Ephesus, to "charge some that they teach no other doctrine", 1 Tim. 1. 3. How Paul must have trusted Timothy, to leave him to accomplish such an important task!

John's Gospel is full of the fact that the Father sent the Son. Verses may be quoted that show that the Sent One came into this scene to accomplish the above five spiritual objectives.

347

December 13th

READING: **Psalm 145. 1-21**

UNSEARCHABLE, UNSPEAKABLE

WE ALL admire great things of man's making, particularly when we have no idea as to how they were made in the first place. When we see great bridges, great ships, great aircraft, great buildings, we may well be speechless. But what about spiritual things that are so great that they cannot be searched out or spoken about? Let us consider a few.

(1) *The greatness of the Lord.* David claimed, "Great is the Lord, and greatly to be praised; and his greatness is unsearchable", Psa. 145. 3. Yet throughout the psalm, David stated "I will speak", v. 5; "I will declare", v. 6; "My mouth shall speak", v. 21. And the psalm consists of many aspects of the Lord's greatness searched out by David.

(2) *The greatness of His mercy.* Paul observed that God had placed all men on the same footing in unbelief, so that He can have mercy upon all. Hence, "O the depth of the riches both of the wisdom and knowledge of God! how unsearchable are his judgments, and his ways past finding out!", Rom. 11. 33.

(3) *The greatness of Christ and His love.* Paul claimed to be less than the least of all saints; yet he was chosen to "preach among the Gentiles the unsearchable riches of Christ"; this included "the love of Christ, which passeth knowledge", Eph. 3. 8, 19. There is no poverty in the fulness of riches; Paul's prayer was that the Ephesians could comprehend.

(4) *The greatness of His gift.* In 2 Corinthians chs. 8-9, Paul has been dealing with Christian giving. In the Lord's case, He became poor that we might be enriched, 8. 9. And he concludes, "Thanks be unto God for his unspeakable gift", 9. 15. This is Christ and His salvation, and is "unspeakable" when contrasted with mere financial giving.

(5) *The greatness of Christian joy.* The joy of this world is low in the extreme, and is not exercised when trouble and persecution arise. But Peter held out something better: "ye rejoice with joy unspeakable and full of glory", 1 Pet. 1. 8, in spite of the trial of faith and manifold temptations.

(6) *The greatness of heaven.* Paul alone had a special vision within the third heaven. There he heard "unspeakable words", 2 Cor. 12. 4, which he was not allowed to repeat. But it allowed him to boast in his infirmities.

December 14th

READING: 1 Samuel 2. 27-36

HIGH PRIESTS IN ELI'S LINE

MEN QUICKLY seek to disrupt what God has introduced. Thus the high priests were chosen by God, commencing with Aaron, and proceeding through his son Eleazar. The list is given in 1 Chronicles 6. 4-15. It will be noted that the high priest Eli does not occur in the list, because he was in the line of Ithamar, the other remaining son of Aaron. Thus Ahimelech and Abiathar, descendants of Eli, were not proper high priests. All three of these men were usurping a status that had not been given to them, and so it remained until Zadok was high priest, the proper choice of God. The lesson for today is that, if unsaved men take upon themselves high religious office, then this is not recognized by God.

Eli, who would not recognize the purity necessary. For in 1 Samuel 2. 12-17 we have the sins of Eli's sons; "his sons made themselves vile, and he restrained them not", 3. 31. They stole flesh from the boiling pot so as to roast it to satisfy their own taste. Eli did nothing about it; although he knew God, he would not separate himself from the evil. This is a religion of the flesh, and can operate today when the Word of God is neglected, the carnal appetite substituting what is found more pleasing in tradition and the doctrines of men.

Ahimelech, who would not recognize the presence of God. 1 Samuel 22 makes sad reading, for here was the high priest serving at a tabernacle already forsaken by God, Psa. 78. 60. All the priests were killed except Abiathar, v. 20. So the ways of this system were the ways of death, but Ahimelech failed to own this fact, and so his ways did end in death.

Abiathar, who would not recognize the purpose of God. It was David who realized that God's choice of high priest was Zadok; consequently there were two high priests, Zadok and Abiathar, 1 Chron. 15. 11. Not knowing the purpose of God for Zadok, Abiathar was evidently in competition with the man of God's choice. Zadok did not take the highest position that was his due, for he served at the arkless tabernacle at Gibeon instead of on mount Zion, 16. 39. Only when Solomon was on the throne was Abiathar deposed, 2 Kings 2. 35; then Zadok came out of the shadows and served uniquely as high priest. Do we give the Lord Jesus His unique position, or do men intervene?

December 15th

READING: **Hebrews 8. 1-13**

A MORE EXCELLENT MINISTRY

THIS IS how the present ministry of the Lord Jesus Christ is described. Certainly the Hebrews needed assurance on this matter; they had re-embraced Jewish ceremony together with the activity of the priests in Jerusalem. What had they to offer? Absolutely nothing. Rather, the Lord Jesus has an abundance to offer, and this ministry is called "more excellent". Moreover, the Lord exercises this ministry in heaven for His people still on earth, and this is consequential upon His ascension, "What and if ye shall see the Son of man ascend up where he was before?", John 6. 62.

The Son had said, "I come to thee", John 17. 11, to His eternal native place on high, with the glory that He had had with the Father. There, He is exalted so that every knee shall bow to Him, Phil. 2. 10. It has been given Him to be the Head over all things to the church, Eph. 1. 22. As the Forerunner, He has entered into heaven itself for us, Heb. 6. 20. Such is His position; what does He do in His ministerial activity?

He appears in the presence of God for us, Heb. 9. 24, so all the value of His Person and sacrificial work is available for us. He is the Author and Finisher of our faith, 12. 2, being the One who presents His people to God, 2. 13. He has passed into the heavens as our Great High Priest, being touched with the feelings of our infirmities, 3. 14-15. When we sin, we have Him as an Advocate with the Father (namely, a Paraclete, a Comforter), 1 John 2. 1. Moreover, as ascended, He continues to work with His people, Mark 16. 20, and one way in which He does this is by giving gifts to all believers, Eph. 4. 8.

And His more excellent ministry extends into the future as well, for He that shall come will come, "and will not tarry", Heb. 10. 37. Meanwhile He sits at God's right hand "until I make thine enemies thy footstool", 1. 13. Moreover, as far as His people are concerned, He has gone to prepare a place for us, with many mansions in His Father's house. In the Jerusalem temples there were chambers built around their exteriors, used for the service of the priests and Levites, 1 Kings 6. 6; Neh. 12. 44. So in heaven there will be an abundance of service for the Lord's people; He is actively preparing the Father's house for this eternal occupation.

December 16th

READING: **2 Corinthians 8. 1-15**

GRACE SUPERABOUNDING

IT IS by grace that we are saved, Eph. 2. 5, 8. Grace is a favour from a superior to an inferior, from One infinitely high and lifted up to those who *in themselves* are mere nothingness, meriting nothing. Paul writes about the grace of the Lord Jesus; He had eternal riches, but became temporarily poor so that we may be eternally enriched, 2 Cor. 8. 9. Grace is not niggardly, meagre, but supremely abounding. There are many aspects of grace that apply to the Christian life, and not only to the beginning of that life at conversion. We find many references in the two Epistles to the Corinthians.

Devoted channel. Paul uses "grace" three times in this verse: "By the grace of God I am what I am: and his grace which was bestowed upon me was not in vain; but I laboured more abundantly than they all: yet not I, but the grace of God which was with me", 1 Cor. 15. 10. When we serve as we are gifted, then this is the grace of God, and is not in vain.

Manner of life. "Not with fleshly wisdom, but by the grace of God, we have had our conversation (conduct, manner of life) in the world, and more abundantly to you-ward", 2 Cor. 1. 12, wrote Paul. He was a man who was so different from men in the world, in life and service, and the abundance of this change was due solely to the grace of God.

Manner of service. Again, Paul wrote to the Corinthians, "We then, as workers together (with him), beseech you also that ye receive not the grace of God·in vain", 2 Cor. 6. 1. A list of 28 features is provided in verses 4-10, demonstrating what the grace of God will effect in the lives of believers.

Selflessness. At the beginning of chapters 8-9, dealing with giving and the administration of finance, Paul writes of "the grace of God bestowed on the churches of Macedonia", 2 Cor. 8. 1. Note how this worked out in practice in verse 2, "abundance, abounded". Paul concludes with mention of "the exceeding grace of God in you (the Corinthians)", 9. 14.

Keeping power. Finally, this is a personal reference to Paul, when God said to him, "My grace is sufficient for thee", 2 Cor. 12. 9. In spite of a physical trial, Paul was an overcomer because of the sufficiency of the grace of God; the power of Christ would therefore rest upon him.

December 17th

READING: **Isaiah 37. 1-20**

MEN'S ATTITUDE TO THE HOUSE OF GOD

THERE WERE four kings, in whose reigns Isaiah prophesied, Uzziah, Jotham, Ahaz, Hezekiah, Isa. 1. 1. It is interesting to note their attitude towards the house of God in Jerusalem.

King Uzziah. This king became strong militarily, 2 Chron. 26. 14-15, but "when he was strong, his heart was lifted up", and he usurped the function of the priests, going into the temple to burn incense, v. 16. Thus he became a leper, was ordered out of the sanctuary, and was cut off from the house of the Lord because of his presumption, vv. 18-21. He sought to raise his authority above that of God's authority. No wonder Uzziah had to die before Isaiah could see the Lord's glory high and lifted up, Isa. 6. 1.

King Jotham. How different was this king! He "prepared his ways before the Lord his God", 2 Chron. 27. 6; he would not enter into the house of the Lord, the province of the priests only, v. 2, and he engaged in building work in the courts of the Lord's house, v. 3.

King Ahaz. How different again, no doubt the worst king in Jerusalem so far. He shut up the doors of the house of God, cut in pieces its vessels, and built altars everywhere in the city, 2 Chron. 28. 24. He also had a copy made of a great altar in Damascus, and it was placed in the court of the Lord's house, 2 Kings 16. 10-16. Here is religious falsity at its height, with Ahaz working in direct contradiction to God's will.

King Hezekiah. How different again! He opened the doors of the Lord's house, and repaired them, 2 Chron. 29. 3. Here was a king who appreciated the truth and who practised it. In times of difficulty, he covered himself with sackcloth, and went into the house of the Lord, Isa. 37. 1. He also went up to the house with a letter from the enemy, "and spread it before the Lord", v. 14. Later, in his illness, he asked for a sign to show that he would once again go up to the house of the Lord, 38. 22. He wrought restoration, and maintained it faithfully.

Whether the kings were good or bad, Isaiah remained faithful to his God. Leaders affect people under them, leading them down or up according to their own ideals. But Uzziah and Ahaz could not influence him adversely. May we, too, remain unmoved when religious leaders promulgate doctrines of error and darkness.

352

December 18th

READING: 2 Peter 1. 1-21

THINGS

PETER WAS concerned about the "last days", 3. 3. Broadly speaking, we may see in chapter 1 the true church in the last days; in chapter 2 the apostate nature and conduct of Christendom in the last days; while in chapter 3 we have the world in the last days. Check what any person says about the Lord Jesus, about the church and its service, about future events, and this will show into which chapter he properly fits.

In chapter 1, Peter has a lot to say about "things", a word that embraces much that may or may not be actually expressed in the context. In the first paragraph, vv. 1-4, the word "things" appears once. In the second paragraph, vv. 5-10, the word "things" appears three times, always as "these things". In the third paragraph, vv. 11-21, the word "things" occurs twice, again as "these things". The subject matter of "these things" concerns reception, response and remembrance.

Reception, vv. 1-4. Peter claims that it is the divine power·which "hath given unto us all things that pertain unto life and godliness". To know what these things are, we must not be content with ignorance, but it is "through the knowledge of him". These are "precious faith" and "exceeding great and precious promises".

Response, vv. 5-10. Believers must respond to this, by adding to their faith. A list is given in verses 5-7. If "these things" abound in us, we will not be barren and unfruitful. Alas, some may lack "these things", meaning that they have not added. But those who have added "these things" shall never fall. Diligence is necessary, however, for this blessed progress in the Christian life.

Remembrance, vv. 11-21. The word "remembrance" occurs three times in this paragraph, vv. 12, 13, 15. In the context, "these things" refer to the testimony of Peter concerning the transfiguration of the Lord Jesus. Peter had seen this great event; his readers had not. He stresses that the written word about "these things" is far more important than actually seeing the vision that faded. For the written word is "a more sure word of prophecy". All must take heed to these things, as a light shining in a dark place until the day dawn, and we see the eternal Person of Christ as a non-fading reality.

December 19th

READING: **Galatians 5. 1-26**

LIBERTY IN CHRIST

THE CITIES in Matthew 11. 20-24 thought that they had liberty to do exactly as they liked. But only the ones called "babes", v. 25, had true liberty. After all, His disciples had to become as little children, for of such is the kingdom of heaven, 18. 3; 19. 14. The Lord described this conversion from bondage to liberty in 11. 28-30. Those who were heavy laden were under the law; this was bondage. But those who were under grace had liberty as yoked to Christ. Paul described this transformation: "delivered from the bondage of corruption into the glorious liberty of the children of God", Rom. 8. 21.

For Christ, His yoke was the devotion associated with the burnt offering; His burden was as the sin offering. In the garden of Gethsemane, His yoke was in saying "as thou wilt", and His burden was as being "exceeding sorrowful, even unto death", Matt. 26. 38-39.

Liberty arises from the possession of the Spirit; "where the Spirit of the Lord is, there is liberty", 2 Cor. 3. 17. This is not a pretext to do as we please; rather as children are obedient to parents, so there is obedience to the divine will in all things. The liberty of a believer is freedom under grace to move according to the revealed will of God. To go outside this, is to fall into bondage again.

Paul has some very practical remarks on this subject. "Stand fast therefore in the liberty wherewith Christ hath made us free", Gal. 5. 1. He had just dealt with the child of Hagar as speaking of bondage, and the child of Sarah as speaking of liberty. The Galatians apparently preferred the law again, and this was the yoke of bondage. Rather, when we know the truth, this truth makes us free, John 8. 32.

Again, when believers are called to liberty, they must not use this liberty "for an occasion to the flesh", but by love they must serve one another, Gal. 5. 13. There may be a licence to claim that liberty is the justification for doing everything. That is not love, but a return to preconversion ideals that could never lead to salvation.

Peter was consistent with this truth, though he failed in Galatians 2. 12. He wrote, "not using your liberty for a cloke of maliciousness, but as the servants of God", 1 Pet. 2. 16.

354

December 20th

READING: Luke 24. 44-53

THE LORD ON THE MOUNT OF OLIVES

THE MOUNT of Olives plays a prominent part in the Holy Scriptures, from the time when David ascended the mount weeping, 2 Sam. 15. 30, until the time when the Lord's feet shall stand upon the mount in the future, Zech. 14. 4. It was a place where Solomon introduced idolatry, 1 Kings 11. 7; a place that was cleansed by Josiah, 2 Kings 23. 13; and a place to which the departing glory retired, Ezek. 11. 23. It is a mount associated with prophecy, yet it was a mount that played an important part in the Lord's activity when He was here.

Teaching. Usually the Lord taught publicly, but in Matthew 24. 3, He taught the disciples privately on the mount of Olives. He had departed from the temple to foretell its destruction, and He engaged in His great prophetical discourse about His future coming in glory. Evidently this formed part of the "apostles' doctrine", for Stephen had taught that "Jesus of Nazareth shall destroy this place", Acts 6. 14.

Prayer. The Lord was no stranger to the garden of Gethsemane on the western slopes of the mount of Olives; it was "as he was wont" that He went there, Luke 22. 39. He went a little further, "and kneeled down, and prayed", v. 41. The three apostles with Him were also supposed to pray, v. 40, but the Lord found them asleep on three occasions.

Fellowship. The Lord loved to be with His own, in the quietness of their company which He so much appreciated. Thus at night He abode in the mount of Olives, Luke 21. 37, that is, Bethany on the eastern slopes, Matt. 21. 17; we believe that this was in the home of Mary and Martha, as in John 12. 1. Also the garden was a place of fellowship with His disciples, for He "ofttimes resorted thither", 18. 2.

Worship. On the descent from the mount, "the disciples began to rejoice and praise God with a loud voice for all the mighty works that they had seen", Luke 37. 37. And at His ascension from Bethany (Olivet, Acts 1. 12), when He was carried up to heaven, "they worshipped him", Luke 24. 52.

We have grouped these references in keeping with the activity of the early church, "they continued stedfastly in the apostles' doctrine and fellowship, and in breaking of bread, and prayers", Acts 2. 42. We should do likewise.

December 21st

READING: **2 Kings 20. 1-11**

THE SHORTEST AND THE LONGEST DAY

VERY FEW can love the shortest day and the longest night, though that is, and will be, the experience of the unsaved. On the other hand, believers experience the shortest night and the longest day spiritually. Let us look beyond the natural, and see how God lengthens out time, leading to eternity.

An extra hour. Hezekiah had asked for a sign that he would be healed, and in keeping with the king's request, he asked God to increase the day by one hour, by making the shadow on the sundial go backwards ten degrees; the king thought that ten degrees forward would have been easy, 2 Kings 20. 8-11. God miraculously granted this sign.

An extra day. Josuha was fighting against the Amorites, and needed more time to gain the victory. So Joshua asked by faith, "Sun, stand thou still . . . and thou, Moon". The result was that the sun did not go down for a whole day, a unique day, "for the Lord fought for Israel", Josh. 10. 12-14.

An extra fifteen years. We return to the story of king Hezekiah. He had to set his house in order, for he was about to die, 2 Kings 20. 1. But he prayed and wept before the Lord, and the result was that God said, "I have heard thy prayer, I have seen thy tears . . . I will add unto thy days fifteen years", with the promise that on the third day he would be able to go up unto the house of the Lord, vv. 5-6. It was during these fifteen years that Manasseh was born, 2 Kings 21. 1, the one who proved to be the worst king in Jerusalem.

God's kingdom. This is described in Zechariah 14. 6-7 as one day, without days and nights as now known. There shall be "no night there", Rev. 21. 25, throughout the reign of Christ lasting one thousand years.

Eternal life. No one has this to start with; life is but a shadow, a vapour, as grass. By divine grace, this is granted to believers, "he that believeth in me, though he were dead, yet shall he live", John 11. 25; "whosoever liveth and believeth in me shall never die", v. 26. Such a message of eternal hope is characteristic of John's Gospel. The key verse promises, "that whosoever believeth in him should not perish, but have everlasting life", 3. 16.

So the shortest day leads to the promise of the longest.

READING: **Psalm 39. 1-13**

THE LORD'S SILENCE

MOST OF the psalms are not "Messianic Psalms", since they are not quoted in the N.T. as referring to Christ. Though in many of these psalms we may see something of the Lord's work and character in an odd verse or two. In these circumstances we must not try to see Christ in other verses, since they may deal with the sin and weakness of the authors. And even Messianic psalms may not refer solely to the Lord throughout; great spiritual discernment is necessary. But the Lord drew attention to "the psalms, concerning" Himself, Luke 24. 44.

Psalms 38, 39, 40 are all psalms of David, and evidently speak of his own experiences. But we can perceive verses where something of the Spirit of Christ shines through. These are: "They also that seek after my life lay snares for me . . . But I, as a deaf man, heard not; and I was as a dumb man that openeth not his mouth. Thus I was as a man that heareth not, and in whose mouth are no reproofs", 38. 12-14; "I was dumb, I opened not my mouth; because thou didst it. Remove thy stroke away from me", 39. 9-10. Psalm 40 presents the contrast.

The verses from Psalm 38 refer to what men were doing; the verses from Psalm 39 refer to what God was doing. In Psalm 38, men were laying snares for the Lord; they were criticising Him for what He had said about destroying the temple and building it again in three days; they were tempting Him to come down from the cross, Matt. 27. 40-43, but the Lord remained silent throughout. In Psalm 39. 9-10 (though we *do not* refer to the neighbouring verses) we see the recognition that the Lord was suffering for our sins at the hand of God; He was the sin offering, yet He had no complaint because of His love.

Psalm 40 presents the resurrection side. The Lord looks back and He also shows the results of resurrection. All is now in contrast. Note the verses: "a new song in my mouth, even praise unto our God", v. 3; "if I would declare and speak of them, they are more than can be numbered", v. 5; "Then said I, Lo, I come", v. 7; "I have preached righteousness in the great congregation", v. 9; "I have declared thy faithfulness and thy salvation", v. 10. There is no silence now!

In Isaiah 53. 7, He opened not His mouth, but in 61. 1 He will preach good tidings unto the meek.

READING: **Mark 7. 1-16**

TRADITION

TO THE MIND of the believer, tradition is a most unpleasant word. This is a practice, whose origin is perhaps lost in history, yet that is carelessly and blindly followed without examination, as if it were absolutely right. "There is a way which seemeth right unto a man, but the ends thereof are the ways of death", Prov. 14. 12; 16. 25. Some tradition may be quite harmless, such as relating to food, clothes and houses, but relying on other traditions may lead to death. That is what happened in January 1921 on the railway between Abermule and Newtown in Mid-Wales. The driver of a train accepted a token in a bag that gave permission to proceed. Tradition informed him that it was always correct. Unfortunately through a muddle on the platform, the wrong token was contained in the bag. But the driver did not look at it, and this failure on his part was his death warrant. His train crashed headlong into another train properly on the single line, and many passengers were killed.

When the Lord Jesus was here, the practice of tradition was at its height, and the Pharisees were self-satisfied. In Mark 7. 2-5, they accused the disciples of the Lord of breaking their tradition. The Lord replied that they were rejecting the commandment of God by keeping their own tradition, making the Word of God of no effect through this tradition, vv. 9, 13.

By the time the Lord was here, tradition had made what was the house of God into the house of the Jews, Matt. 23. 38. The feasts of the Lord had become the feasts of the Jews, John 5. 1. The synagogues were "their synagogues", Matt. 4. 23. Their doctrines were but "the commandments of men", Mark 7. 7. As for the law, they boasted in it, but broke it and dishonoured God, Rom. 2. 17-24. The folly of religious tradition!

Each religious man must assess for himself to what extent he follows tradition. For Peter, Christians have been redeemed from the vain manner of life "received by tradition" before conversion, 1 Pet. 1. 18. On the other hand, there are a few occasions in the N.T. when the word "tradition" is used with a spiritual meaning. "Hold the traditions which ye have been taught, whether by word, or our epistle", 2 Thess. 2. 15; "the tradition which he received of us", 3. 6. The apostle Paul's tradition was the true doctrine received through the Spirit.

December 24th

READING: **1 Samuel 16. 1-13**

BETHLEHEM A PLACE TO COME TO

AT THIS time of the year, men think of Bethlehem and the birth of the Lord Jesus. Alas that they do not think of Him again until the next "religious festival". Many carols speak of Bethlehem: "Once in royal David's city". These are sung, and then forgotten, as if Bethlehem were a place to which one can quickly come, and then just as quickly retreat from. An aspect of *change* is often found in the Scriptures.

A place to bury the affections of the world so that another can arise. In Genesis 29. 20, 30, Jacob served fourteen years for Rachel, because he loved her. Yet as he later came to Bethlehem, this loved-one Rachel died, 35. 16-20, and the one who was born, Benjamin, took a place in Jacob's affections.

A place to recognize the emptiness of self so that another can provide fulness. In Ruth 1. 1-2, Naomi, with her husband and two sons, left Bethlehem for Moab. There the three men died, and many years later she returned to Bethlehem empty, vv. 19-22. But this event led to Boaz coming on the scene to provide fulness, this being in the purpose of God.

A place to discard outward appearance, so that another can be chosen. In 1 Samuel 16. 4, Samuel came to Bethlehem so as to anoint a king. Jesse's seven sons passed before Samuel, but he was instructed by God to pass them by, since God does not look on the outward appearance, but on the heart, v. 7. At the end, David the youngest was chosen; he was anointed and the Spirit of the Lord came upon him from that day, v. 13.

A place to recognize thirst, but Another can provide. In 2 Samuel 23. 14-17, three mighty men broke through the lines of the Philistines to obtain water from the well at Bethlehem, for David was thirsty. But he poured it out before the Lord. Rather, in a psalm, he confessed to God that his soul was thirsting after Him, and he was refreshed, Psa. 63. 1.

In the New Testament, we find further examples.

A place to be enrolled. Joseph went up to Bethlehem to be enrolled, Luke 2. 4, at the right time in God's purpose.

A place to see the Saviour. Following their vision, the shepherds said, "Let us now go even unto Bethlehem", v. 15.

A place of worship. The wise men were sent to Bethlehem, and when they were come, they worshipped Him, Matt. 2. 8-11.

December 25th

READING: **Luke 2. 1-20**

POLITICIANS, PRIESTS AND PASTORS

HOLY EVENTS in the Bible always separate men into two distinct camps, as to their relationship and reaction to these events. This applies to the creation, to miracles, and to the Lord's birth, sacrifice, resurrection and coming again. Those who believe are embedded in a world dominated by political and priestly rule, from which they should be spiritually and morally separated. God at least makes this difference, and Luke has shown that the beginning of his Gospel occurred in a world where powerful political and religious forces held sway over the hearts and lives of men.

In Luke 1. 5, we are introduced to Herod the king of Judaea, but he was not in the royal line of David! He was a friend of Rome and had been placed in his position by the emperor of Rome. God passed him by entirely, and the angel appeared to Zacharias, a faithful priest who was "righteous before God".

In Luke 2. 1, we are introduced to the Roman emperor named Caesar Augustus. He held sway, but we may ask, What has he done for the world as contrasted with what Christ has done? He perpetuated the domination of Rome, which crumbled several hundreds of years later; of Christ's kingdom, there will be no end. (Our eighth month, August, is named after this emperor, as a matter of interest.) This emperor introduced the census that caused Joseph to go to Bethlehem. But these great men in Rome were passed by, having no idea that the Saviour had been born in Bethlehem. As Paul wrote, "not many mighty, not many noble, are called", 1 Cor. 1. 26.

Some years later, in Luke 3. 2, we are introduced to the two high priests in Jerusalem, Annas and Caiaphas. God ensured that men of this nature (ready to crucify the Lord when the time came) also had no knowledge of the Saviour born, and who was growing up amongst men.

But in Luke 2. 8, we are introduced to the shepherds watching over their flocks by night. To them God granted the great vision of the angelic host and their words of praise, as well as the opportunity of seeing "the babe lying in a manger". Their simple occupation, following the example of David before them, Psa. 78. 70-72, enabled them to be chosen by God as was David of old.

December 26th

READING: **Daniel 7. 1-14**

THOSE MISSED OUT

WITH EAGER ANTICIPATION, children wait for Father Christmas to come to every child. It is sad if any home is missed out: a home so unpleasant, dirty, evil and cruel, that he just could not come there. No one has ever heard of Father Christmas coming to a ferocious animal in an African forest, and bringing some kind of present appreciated by that animal.

In a sense, the Lord Jesus was a Christmas gift to men. But the wrong men sought to get hold of the gift. "He sent unto them his son . . . come, let us kill him", Matt. 21. 37-38. It is therefore important to see to whom the precious Gift was not sent, and why God would not select such men.

(1) *A horrible beast.* "A fourth beast, dreadful and terrible, and strong exceedingly; and it had great iron teeth: it devoured and brake in pieces", Dan. 7. 7. These four beasts in Daniel 7. 1-7 were the four great Gentile kingdoms in succession, and the empire of Rome is implied, the nation that dominated over men when the Lord Jesus came to earth. As a cruel nameless beast was how God viewed that nation, which had devoured all the world including Jerusalem, which crucified the Lord under Pilate, which later persecuted Christians and killed Paul, and which destroyed Jerusalem with dreadful carnage. God would not trust the Saviour as a Babe to be born in the palace of the emperor in Rome; nor was His birth revealed to them. The greatest man, and the greatest nation, were missed out.

(2) *A wicked king.* Herod the Great had been on the throne for many years when the Lord was born. He had a palace on the coast at Caesarea, and he welcomed any to see his pomp and kingdom; he was rebuilding the temple in Jerusalem to make it the most ornate religious building ever. Thus the Lord Jesus was not born into his house or family. He spent some time in complete ignorance that the Saviour had been born, until he suddenly woke up to the fact that a Rival existed, for the wise men asked after the One "born King of the Jews", Matt. 2. 2.

(3) *Religious leaders and teachers.* There were plenty of them; the high priest, priests, scribes, Pharisees, Sadducees knew their O.T. Scriptures, but failed to see the true Christ therein. The Saviour was not born into any of their families; all were missed out, except the home of Mary and Joseph.

December 27th

READING: **2 Peter 2. 1-17**

FALSE MEN

THE TEACHING of the Lord Jesus, and of the apostles Paul, Peter and John, warns of self-complacency, the danger of submitting to the doctrines and activity of other men without much question. One can thereby fall into a dangerous trap, out of which it may be difficult to extricate oneself. Consider the following brands of false men from which one must be separate; we have considered the subject already on page 90.

False apostles. There were those in Corinth who would not repent, and who sought to teach with authority against the teaching of the apostle. So Paul called them "false apostles", men who sought to transform themselves into the apostles of Christ, 2 Cor. 11. 13. In Ephesus there were men who claimed to be apostles, but were rejected by the church, Rev. 2. 2.

False prophets. The Lord warned, "Beware of false prophets, which come to you in sheep's clothing, but inwardly they are ravening wolves", Matt. 5. 15; 24. 11. In the future, He warned that "false prophets" would arise, 24. 24. Many years later, both Peter and John used the same description of men who brought false doctrine, 2 Pet. 2. 1; 1 John 4. 1.

False evangelists. If men's minds can be gained at the beginning of their spiritual exercises, then their minds may be tarnished for the rest of their lives. Hence false evangelists realize that they have great opportunities with their poison. There were those who presented "another Jesus", 2 Cor. 11. 4, and those who traded in "another gospel (of a different kind): which is not another (of the same kind)", Gal. 1. 6-8; such men were accursed according to Paul.

False teachers. Peter also uses the description "false teachers among you", 2 Pet. 2. 1, with many following their pernicious ways. The whole of chapter 2 is devoted to such men, for as far as Peter described them, lives full of evil deeds went side-by-side with false doctrine.

False pastors. In Ezekiel 34. 2, we find false shepherds who fed themselves. Read vv. 1-10 for a complete description.

False elders. These were the "grievous wolves" who entered the church, and joined themselves to the elders, Acts 20. 30.

False brethren, 2 Cor. 11. 26; Gal. 2. 4. Here were Jews who infiltrated so as to spy out Christian liberty.

362

December 28th

READING: **Isaiah 60. 1-14**

THE HOUSE OF GOD IN ISAIAH

ISAIAH TESTIFIED for God in troublous times; on page 352 we have already considered the attitude of the four kings to the house of God. This house in Jerusalem was such that God's eyes, heart and throne should be amongst His people. In spite of declension around, the prophet remained faithful to his God, and we therefore find many references to this house of God throughout Isaiah. Today, believers are in a similar position, so lessons from the prophecy are not hard to deduce.

The full purpose of God in the house was always before Him even in times of deepest decline. At the beginning of the prophecy, we read, "Come ye, and let us go up . . . to the house of the God of Jacob", 2. 3; at the end we find the faithful remnant in the new world shall bring an offering to Jerusalem to the house of the Lord, 66. 20.

Isaiah saw the house according to God's mind. In 6. 1-4, the prophet appreciated the absolute purity and holiness that were associated with God's presence and His house. This led to the prophet's cleansing, fitting him for God's call to service.

The place of God's people in the house. In times of trouble, king Hezekiah "went into the house of the Lord", 37. 1; later the king spread a letter from the enemy before the Lord in the house, v. 14. Again, he wanted a sign that he would be able to go up to the house of the Lord, 38. 22. In our day, a local church is a place of fellowship with other believers in times of trouble, Acts 4. 23; 12. 12.

Spiritual grief in times of outward declension. Moses, Daniel, Nehemiah, Paul were not men of complacency, but of grief before the Lord. Thus Isaiah was overtaken with grief when he said, "our adversaries have trodden down thy sanctuary", 63. 18; "Our holy and beautiful house . . . is burned up with fire", 64. 11. This should be our grief before the Lord if we see men defiling God's temple, 1 Cor. 3. 17.

The recognition of God's work in the house. He would choose Cyrus to permit the rebuilding of the temple, 44. 28; but God Himself would lay in Zion for a foundation a stone, a tried and precious stone, 28. 16. God will glorify the house of His glory, 60. 7, and He would "beautify the place of my sanctuary", v. 13. Read also Isaiah 56. 5-7.

December 29th

READING: **Acts 1. 1-17**

FROM THE OLD TO THE NEW

ACTS CHAPTER 1 marks a great change in the onward progress of history as recorded in the N.T. The Lord Jesus had risen from the dead, and the disciples were awaiting the promise of the Holy Spirit. It was during this period that we can perceive the changes that took place in Acts 1.

(1) In verse 1, there is the last manifestation of the Lord's activity on earth, a reference to "all that Jesus began to do and teach". His work would continue after His ascent to the throne above, "the Lord working with them", Mark 16. 20.

(2) In verse 4, the disciples were evidently in a position in which the Spirit had not yet been given. This was the cause of so much ignorance, weakness and failure when they had been with the Lord during His three years ministry. But "the promise of the Father" would come, though they did not know the day when this would happen. (Had they known the meaning of the O.T. feasts, they would have understood that the day of Pentecost was to be the chosen day.)

(3) In verse 5, the Lord referred to the baptism of John. He did not refer to the water baptism of believers, but to the baptism with (or, in) the Holy Spirit. John's baptism dealt with repentance and faith in the One then to come, Acts 19. 4, but baptism in the Spirit implied the beginning of the church.

(4) Verses 6-7 show the disciples' minds still fixed on an earthly kingdom there and then freed from Roman domination, but the Lord's reply put that on one side; the times and seasons refer to the future, entirely in the Father's power.

(5) In verse 8, there is expansion of the testimony. When He was here, the gospel went out only in Judaea and Galilee, but now it would go forth to the uttermost part of the earth.

(6) In verses 9-11, sight gave place to faith. In His lifetime, they had watched Him, but now He had disappeared, and all their service would be accomplished on the basis of faith.

(7) In verse 12, the Sabbath would give place to the Lord's Day as characteristic of the Christian era.

(8) In verse 14, they had been used to prayer in His presence, but now prayer had to be in His Name in His absence.

(9) In verse 16, the meaning of the O.T. had been largely unknown, but now Peter understood in depth.

December 30th

READING: **Acts 15. 22-35**

IT SEEMED GOOD

THIS EXPRESSION appears many times in the O.T., but only on a few occasions in the N.T. We draw attention to four occasions in the N.T., and group them into two pairs. Each of the two pairs will contain (i) "seemed good" from the divine point of view, and (ii) "seemed good" from men's point of view. In all four cases, the subject concerns the distribution of truth, all under differing circumstances.

The first pair in Luke's Gospel. Here we have the divine point of view. The Lord said, "I thank thee, O Father, Lord of heaven and earth, that thou hast hid these things from the wise and prudent, and hast revealed them unto babes; for so it seemed good in thy sight", Luke 10. 21. The emptiness of the wise and prudent, and the fulness of babes does not fit in with man's reasoning, but believers seek to appreciate what is good to God. Verses 23-24 contain examples of this: the disciples saw, but the kings have not seen (we except men such as David, who was a prophet and king, and saw a lot!).

Man's side in Luke's Gospel is found in 1. 3. Luke explains why and how he wrote his Gospel. His motive from his heart was "it seemed good to me also, having had perfect understanding of all things from the very first, to write unto thee in order". His exercise came from the Spirit of inspiration, so as to communicate truth to all subsequent readers.

The second pair in The Acts. Paul, Barnabas and the apostles and elders of the Jerusalem church were discussing the penetration by the Pharisees with their false doctrine. In a letter to the churches in Antioch, Syria and Cilicia, they were bold enough to state, "it seemed good to the Holy Spirit", 15. 28, and then detailed necessary things that had to be kept. This was no presumption that the Spirit concurred with the contents of the letter that expressed relevant doctrine for all time; they knew that they were being led by the Spirit.

At the same time, the writers knew that they were correct in their communication of truth. In the letter: "it seemed good unto us, being assembled with one accord", 15. 25, and "it seemed good . . . to us", v. 28. This does not displace the Holy Spirit, but clearly shows how their appreciation was moulded by the Spirit's work in their hearts.

December 31st

READING: Exodus 12. 1-17

THE COMING NEW YEAR

WE CAN ask the question, "What will this year bring forth?", only at the end of an old year. Some may wish to know beforehand, but God had ordained that we can recall the past, but have no certain knowledge of future events. It is therefore interesting to review any past year, and to consider how events worked out, many quite unsuspected at the beginning.

There is one year in the Bible that is full of interest; the book of Exodus chapters 12-40 trace what befell the nation of Israel during a whole year in which they came out of Egypt. The power of God was first seen in delivering His people from a land of bondage, with the blood of the passover lamb and the crossing of the Red Sea. We read of dissatisfied murmurings, of the giving of the manna, of the giving of the ten commandments, and of the details for the construction of the tabernacle, of idolatry and the golden calf, of the building of the tabernacle over the last five months. A great year to look back on, but they could not foresee the future, namely 40 years wandering in the wilderness because of their unfaithfulness.

Similarly, we may have a year that changed our destiny, interests and service for the Lord. We may be able to look back on a year when we were first saved, when we first saw the Lamb of God, when we were brought out of the bondage of sin, when we were fed with the heavenly Manna, being obedient to His will, and seeking the "house of God" as constituted by other Christians likeminded in the faith. On the other hand, for many this experience is unknown, so what does the future hold for them? Perhaps they would like to know, or push the question far from their thoughts.

For believers, the year will open up in many new avenues of service and faithfulness, and when we get to the end in the will of the Lord, we will be able to sing a familiar hymn that only has meaning for the Lord's people.

> All the way the Saviour leads me,
> What have I to ask beside,
> Who through life has been my comfort,
> Who through life has been my Guide?

Alas, for some the end of the year may never come, and then it will be too late to repent and to find life in Christ.

Index

It is not possible to include the Name of the Lord Jesus in this Index, since His Name occurs on almost every page. A few specialized titles are included, however. For the same reason, the name of the apostle Paul is not listed.

368

372